Blender

FOR

DUMMIES®

A Wiley Brand

3rd Edition

Blender
FOR
DUMMIES
A Wiley Brand

3rd Edition

by Jason van Gumster

FOR
DUMMIES
A Wiley Brand

Blender For Dummies®, 3rd Edition

Published by: **John Wiley & Sons, Inc.,** 111 River Street, Hoboken, NJ 07030-54, www.wiley.com

Copyright © 2015 by John Wiley & Sons, Inc., Hoboken, New Jersey

Media and software compilation copyright © 2015 by John Wiley & Sons, Inc. All rights reserved.

Published simultaneously in Canada

For general information on our other products and services, please contact our Customer Care Department within the U.S. at 877-762-2974, outside the U.S. at 317-572-3993, or fax 317-572-4002. For technical support, please visit www.wiley.com/techsupport.

Wiley publishes in a variety of print and electronic formats and by print-on-demand. Some material included with standard print versions of this book may not be included in e-books or in print-on-demand. If this book refers to media such as a CD or DVD that is not included in the version you purchased, you may download this material at http://booksupport.wiley.com. For more information about Wiley products, visit www.wiley.com.

Library of Congress Control Number: 2014957118

ISBN 978-1-119-03953-2 (pbk); ISBN 978-1-119-04713-1 (epub); 978-1-119-04700-1 (epdf)

Manufactured in the United States of America

10 9 8 7 6 5 4 3 2 1

Contents at a Glance

Table of Contents

Introduction

Welcome to *Blender For Dummies,* 3rd Edition, your introduction to one of the most well-known free programs for creating 3D computer graphics. With Blender, you can create characters, props, environments, and nearly anything else your imagination can generate. And it's not just about creating objects. You can set them in motion, too. Tell a story in an animation, entertain people in a video game, or add a special effect to some video footage. It's all possible. They still haven't quite designed a way for Blender to give you a foot massage if you've had a bad day, but in all seriousness, it's difficult to imagine a task in computer animation that you can't do with Blender. And just think: the developers of Blender have included all these features in a package you can download for free and run on nearly any computer. Crazy!

Blender sits at a very unique position in the world of 3D computer graphics. In the past, to get into 3D modeling and animation, you had only a few options, and most of them were too expensive, too limiting, or — *ahem* — too illegal for people just trying to see what this whole 3D thing was all about. Blender circumvents all those issues because it's free. And not just zero-cost free, but freedom Free. Blender is open source. A world full of developers and users regularly contribute code and documentation, adding enhancements and improvements at a mind-boggling pace.

Of course, 3D computer graphics is a complex topic, and all software of this type is dense with buttons, options, settings, and unique ways of working. Perhaps more than any other program like it, Blender carries a pretty heavy reputation for being difficult to understand. Blender isn't typically viewed as software for beginners. But, if I've done my job right, this book will help simplify things. *Blender For Dummies,* 3rd Edition is not just a book on using Blender. Sure, I explain why things in Blender work in their peculiar Blenderish ways, but I also make a point to explain core principles of 3D computer graphics as they are relevant. There's no use in being able to find a button if you're not really sure what it does or how it works. My hope is that with this combined knowledge, you can actually take advantage of Blender's unique traits to create your own high-quality 3D art as quickly and efficiently as possible. Perhaps you can even become as addicted to it as I am!

About This Book

Blender is an extremely complex program used for the even more complex task of producing high-quality 3D models and animations. As such, I can't cover every single feature and button in Blender. For a more comprehensive manual, refer to the excellent online documentation available through Blender's website at `http://www.blender.org/manual`.

Because I want to bring you up to speed on working in 3D space with Blender so that you can start bringing your ideas to life as soon as possible, I focus on introducing you to the fundamental "Blender way" of working. Not only do I show you *how* something is done in Blender, but I also often take the time to explain *why* things are done a certain way. This approach should hopefully put you on the fast track to making awesome work and also allow you to figure out new parts of Blender on your own when you come across them.

Throughout the book, I refer to the Blender community. Blender's user community is probably one of its most valuable assets, and I would be remiss to neglect bringing it up. Not only do many members of the community create great work, but they also write new code for Blender, write and edit documentation, and help each other improve. And understand that when I make reference to the Blender community, I include you in that community as well. As of right now, you are a *Blenderhead* — a fellow Blender user and therefore a member of the Blender community.

Blender is a truly *cross-platform* program, running on Linux, Windows, and Mac OS X. Fortunately, not much in Blender differs from one platform to another. However, for the few things that are different, I'll be sure to point them out for you.

Foolish Assumptions

I've written this book for two sorts of beginners: people who are completely new to the world of 3D, and people who know a thing or two about 3D, but are completely new to Blender.

Because of the various types of beginners this book addresses, I tend to err on the side of explaining too much rather than too little. If you're someone who is already familiar with another 3D computer graphics program, such as 3DS Max, Maya, Lightwave, or even an earlier version of Blender, you can probably skip a number of these explanations. Likewise, if you're a complete newbie, you may notice that I occasionally compare a feature in Blender to one in another package. However, that comparison is mostly for the benefit of these other users. I write so that you can understand a concept without having to know any of these other programs.

I do, however, make the assumption that you have at least a basic understanding of your computer. I assume that you know how to use a mouse, and I *highly* recommend that you use a mouse with at least two buttons and a scroll wheel. You *can* use Blender with a one- or two-button mouse, and I provide workarounds for the unfortunate souls in that grim state (*cough*Mac users*cough*), but it's certainly not ideal.

An exception is if you're using Blender with a drawing tablet like the ones produced by Wacom. Depending on the model, these devices have quite a variety on the number and type of buttons. For that reason, I focus primarily on using Blender with a mouse, although I will occasionally point out where having a tablet is helpful. Because Blender makes use of all your mouse buttons, I stipulate whether you need to left-click, right-click, or middle-click. And in case you didn't already know, pressing down on your mouse's scroll wheel typically accesses the middle mouse button. I also make use of this cool little arrow (⇨) for indicating a sequence of steps. It could be a series of hotkeys to press or menu items to select or places to look in the Blender interface, but the consistent thing is that all these items are used for steps that you need to do sequentially.

I also assume that you're working with Blender's default settings and theme. You can customize the settings for yourself, but if you do, Blender may not behave exactly like I describe. Bearing in mind this point about Blender's themes, you may notice that the screenshots of Blender's interface are lighter in this book than you see on-screen because I created a custom Blender theme that would show up better in print. If I used Blender's default theme colors, all the figures in the book would appear overly dark. I include this custom theme at www.blenderbasics.com if you who want your copy of Blender to match what's shown on these pages.

Icons Used in This Book

As you flip through this book, icons periodically appear next to some paragraphs. These icons notify you of unique or valuable information on the topic at hand. Sometimes that information is a tip, sometimes it's more detail about how something works, and sometimes it's a warning to help you avoid losing data. The following are descriptions of each icon in this book.

This icon calls out suggestions that help you work more effectively and save time.

This icon marks something that I think you should try to keep in mind while working in Blender. Sometimes it's a random tidbit of information, but more often than not, it's something that you'll run into repeatedly and is therefore worth remembering.

Working in 3D can involve some pretty heavy technical information. You can usually work just fine without ever having to know these things, but if you do take the time to understand it, I bet you dollars to donuts that you'll be able to use Blender more effectively.

This icon doesn't show up often, but when it does, I definitely recommend that you pay attention. You won't blow up your computer if you overlook it, but you could lose work.

Blender is a fast-moving target. Quite a bit has changed since the previous edition of this book. These icons point out things that are new or different in Blender so that you can get to be at least as effective (and hopefully *more* effective) with the current version as you were with past versions.

Beyond the Book

Blender For Dummies, 3rd Edition, includes the following goodies online for easy download:

- ✔ **Cheat Sheet:** You can find the Cheat Sheet for this book here:

  `www.dummies.com/cheatsheet/blender`

- ✔ **Extras:** I provide a few extra articles here:

  `www.dummies.com/extras/blender`

I keep and maintain a website at `www.blenderbasics.com` with additional resources. I have a whole bunch of tutorials, both in written and in video format, specifically for readers of this book. Also, Blender's a big, fast-moving program. I do my best on that site to chronical changes in Blender that affect the content of this book (and perhaps share a new tip or two as well).

Occasionally, John Wiley and Sons has updates to its books. If there is an update to this book, it will be posted at `http://dummies.com/go/blenderupdates`.

Where to Go from Here

Wondering where to start? The easy answer here would be to say "Just dive on in!" but that's probably a bit too vague. This book is primarily intended as a reference, so if you already know what you're looking for, flip over to the table of contents or index and start soaking in the Blendery goodness.

If you're just starting out, I suggest that you merely turn a couple of pages, start at Chapter 1, and enjoy the ride. And even if you're the sort of person who knows exactly what you're looking for, take the time to read through other sections of the book. You can find a bunch of valuable little bits of information that may help you work more effectively.

Regardless of how you read this book, though, my one hope is that you find it to be a valuable resource that allows you to flex your creative muscles and, more importantly, have fun doing it.

Part I
Getting Started with Blender

In this part . . .

- ✔ Getting comfortable with Blender.
- ✔ Customizing the interface.
- ✔ Working in 3D.
- ✔ Managing `.blend` files.
- ✔ Visit `www.dummies.com` for great Dummies content online.

Chapter 1

Discovering Blender

In This Chapter

▶ Figuring out what Blender is and what it's used for

▶ Understanding Blender's history

▶ Getting familiar with the Blender interface

*I*n the world of 3D modeling and animation software, programs have traditionally been expensive — like, thousands-of-dollars-and-maybe-an-arm expensive. That's changed a bit in the last few years, with software companies moving to more subscription-based ways of selling their programs. The entry cost is lower, but paying each month can still add up pretty quickly. There are *some* valid reasons for the high prices. Software companies spend millions of dollars and countless hours developing these programs. And the large production companies that buy this kind of software for their staff make enough money to afford the high cost, or they hire programmers and write their own in-house software.

But what about us, you and I: the little guys? We are the ambitious dreamers with big ideas, high motivation . . . and tight budgets. How can we bring our ideas to life and our stories to screen, even if only on our own computer monitors? Granted, we could shell out the cash (and hopefully keep our arms) for the expensive programs that the pros use. But even then, animation is a highly collaborative art and it's difficult to produce anything in a reasonable amount of time without some help.

We need quality software and a strong community to work, grow, and evolve with. Fortunately, Blender can provide us with both of these things. This chapter is an introduction to Blender, its background, its interface, and its community.

Getting to Know Blender

Blender is a free and open source 3D modeling and animation suite. Yikes! What a mouthful, huh? Put simply, Blender is a computer graphics program that allows you to produce high quality still images and animations using three-dimensional geometry. It used to be that you'd only see the results of this work in animated feature films or high-budget television shows. These days, it's way more pervasive. Computer-generated 3D graphics are everywhere. Almost every major film and television show involves some kind of 3D computer graphics and animation. (Even sporting events! Pay close attention to the animations that show the scores or players' names.) And it's not just film and TV; 3D graphics play a major role in video games, industrial design, scientific visualization, and architecture (to name just a few industries). In the right hands, Blender is capable of producing this kind of work. With a little patience and dedication, *your* hands can be the right hands.

One of the things that makes Blender different and special compared to other comparable 3D software is that it is freely available without cost and that it's *Free and Open Source* software.

Being free of cost, as well as free (as in freedom) and open source, means that not only can you go to the Blender website (www.blender.org) and download the entire program right now without paying anything, but you can also freely download the source, or the code that makes up the program. For most programs, the source code is a heavily guarded and highly protected secret that only certain people (mostly programmers hired by the company that distributes the program) can see and modify. But Blender is open source, so anybody can see the program's source code and make changes to it. The benefit is that rather than having the program's guts behind lock and key, Blender can be improved by programmers all over the world!

Because of these strengths, Blender is an ideal program for small animation companies, freelance 3D artists, independent filmmakers, students beginning to learn about 3D computer graphics, and dedicated computer graphics hobbyists.

Blender, like many other 3D computer graphics applications, has had a reputation for being difficult for new users to understand. At the same time, however, Blender is also known for allowing experienced users to bring their ideas to life quickly. Fortunately, with the help of this book and the regular improvements introduced in each new release of Blender, that gap is becoming much easier to bridge.

Discovering Blender's origins and the strength of the Blender community

The Blender you know and love today wasn't always free and open source. Blender is actually quite unique in that it's one of the few (and first!) software applications that was "liberated" from proprietary control with the help of its user community.

Originally, Blender was written as an internal production tool for an award-winning Dutch animation company called NeoGeo, founded by Blender's original (and still lead) developer, Ton Roosendaal. In the late 1990s, NeoGeo started making copies of Blender available for download from its website. Slowly but surely, interest grew in this less-than-2MB program. In 1998, Ton spun off a new company, Not a Number (NaN), to market and sell Blender as a software product. NaN still distributed a free version of Blender, but also offered an advanced version with more features for a small fee. There was strength in this strategy and by the end of 2000, Blender users numbered well over 250,000 worldwide.

Unfortunately, even though Blender was gaining in popularity, NaN was not making enough money to satisfy its investors, especially in the so-called "dot bomb" era that happened around that time. In 2002, NaN shut its doors and stopped working on Blender. Ironically, this point is where the story starts to get exciting.

Even though NaN went under, Blender had developed quite a strong community by this time, and this community was eager to find a way to keep their beloved little program from becoming lost and abandoned. In July of 2002, Ton provided a way. Having established a non-profit organization called the Blender Foundation, he arranged a deal with the original NaN investors to run the "Free Blender" campaign. The terms of the deal were that, for a price of €100,000 (at the time, about $100,000), the investors would agree to release Blender's source code to the Blender Foundation for the purpose of making Blender open source. Initial estimations were that it would take as long as six months to one year to raise the necessary funds. Amazingly, the community was able to raise that money in a mere *seven weeks*.

Because of the Blender community's passion and willingness to put its money where its metaphorical mouth was, Blender was released under the GNU General Public License on October 13, 2002. With the source in the community's hands, Blender had an avalanche of development and new features added to it in a very short time, including somewhat common features like Undo (a functionality that was conspicuously missing and highly desired since the initial releases of Blender by NeoGeo).

Eight years later, the Blender community is larger and stronger than ever. Blender itself is a powerful modern piece of software, competitive in terms of quality with similar software costing thousands of dollars. Not too shabby. Figure 1-1 shows screenshots of Blender from its early days to the Blender of today.

Making open movies and games

One of the cool things about the programmers who write Blender is that many of them also use the program regularly. They're writing code not just because they're told to do it, but because they want to improve Blender for their own purposes. Part of the programmers' motivation has to do with Blender's open-source nature, but quite a bit also has to do with the fact Blender was originally an in-house production tool, built for artists, based on their direct input, and often written by the artists themselves.

Seeking to get even more of this direct artist feedback to developers, the Blender Foundation launched "Project Orange" in 2005. The project's purpose was to create an animated short movie using open source tools,

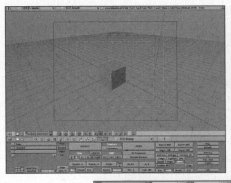
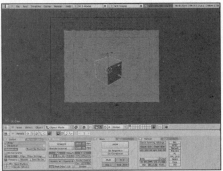
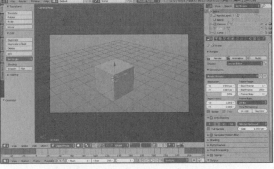

Figure 1-1: Blender through the years: Blender 1.8 (top left), Blender 2.46 (top right), and the major changes apparent in the Blender of today (bottom).

primarily Blender. A team of six members of the community were assembled in Amsterdam, in the Netherlands, to produce the movie. Roughly seven months later, *Elephants Dream* premiered and was released to the public as the first *open movie*. This means that not only was it created using open-source tools, but all the production files — 3D models, scenes, character rigs, and so on — were also released under a permissive and open Creative Commons Attribution license. These files are valuable tools for discovering how an animated film is put together, and anyone can reuse them in their own personal or commercial work. Furthermore, if you don't like *Elephants Dream*, you're free to change it to your liking! How many movies give you that luxury? You can see the film and all of the production files for yourself at the project's website, `www.elephantsdream.org`.

Due to the success of the Orange project, Ton established the Blender Institute in 2007 for the expressed purpose of having a permanent space to create open movie and game projects, as well as provide the service of training people in Blender. Since then, the Blender Institute has churned out open projects (each code-named with a type of fruit) every couple of years. Like with *Elephants Dream*, both the final product *and* the production files for each project are released under a permissive Creative Commons license. Table 1-1 summarizes each of the Blender Institute's open projects.

Table 1-1		Open Projects from the Blender Institute	
Year	*Fruit*	*Title*	*Details*
2005	Orange	*Elephants Dream* (`www.elephantsdream.org`)	Animated Short Film (improved animation, basic hair, node-based compositing)
2008	Peach	*Big Buck Bunny* (`www.bigbuckbunny.org`)	Animated Short Film (enhanced particles, large scene optimization, improved rendering, more animation and rigging tools)
2008	Apricot	*Yo Frankie!* (`www.yofrankie.org`)	Video Game (asset creation pipeline, real-time viewport, updates to the Blender Game Engine)

(continued)

Table 1-1 *(continued)*

Year	Fruit	Title	Details
2010	Durian	*Sintel* (www.sintel.org)	Animated Short Film (battle-test Blender 2.5, detailed sculpting, large environments)
2012	Mango	*Tears of Steel* (www.tearsofsteel.org)	Live Action Short Film (visual effects tools, motion tracking, Cycles rendering)
	TBD	GooseberryCosmos Laundromat (www.gooseberry.blender.org)	Animated Short Film (large scale internationally collaborative productions with Blender Cloud)

Figure 1-2 shows rendered images from each of the open projects.

With the completion of each of these projects, the functionality and stability of Blender significantly increased. Much of the content of this book wouldn't even exist without these projects. For example, Chapter 13 starts with using Blender's particle system to achieve exciting effects along with hair and fur. Half of the content in Chapter 15 is focused on the *node compositor*, a way of combining and enhancing still images and animations. In fact, nearly all of Part III is devoted to features that were enhanced or directly added for one of these open projects.

Figure 1-2: Open projects from the Blender Institute help drive Blender development (Blender Foundation, www.blender.org).

Joining the community

Congratulations! As a Blender user, you're a part of our community. You're joining a diverse group that spans all age ranges, ethnicities, professional backgrounds, and parts of the globe. We are a passionate bunch: proud of this little 3D program and more than willing to help others enjoy using it as much as we do. Have a look at Chapter 18 for a list of community resources that are invaluable, not only for discovering the intricacies of using Blender, but also for improving yourself as an artist.

You can find innumerable opportunities for critique, training, discussion, and even collaboration with other artists, some of whom might also be Blender developers. I've made quite a few good friends and colleagues through the Blender community, both through the various community websites as well as by attending events like the annual Blender Conference. I go by the name "Fweeb" on these sites and I look forward to seeing you around!

All these projects continue to exhibit the strength of the Blender community. Each of them are financed in a large part by DVD pre-sales (and now Blender Cloud subscriptions) from users who understand that regardless of the project's final product, great improvements to Blender are the result, and everyone benefits from that.

Getting to Know the Interface

Probably one of the most daunting aspects of Blender for newcomers and long-time 3D professionals alike has been its unique and somewhat peculiar interface. It's arguably the most controversial feature Blender has. In fact, at one time, merely calling the interface a feature would raise the blood pressure of some of you who tried using Blender in the past, but gave up in frustration when it did not behave as expected.

Although the interface wasn't the primary focus, the interface updates to Blender added in the 2.5 series of release have made great strides toward alleviating that frustration, and the improvements continue through to today. As a small example, when you first launch Blender, the "splash image" provides you with quick links to online documentation, a list of recently opened files, and a choice of interaction presets if you're more familiar with other programs' hotkeys and mouse behavior. Figure 1-3 shows the splash image you're presented with when you start Blender for the first time.

If you click anywhere other than the links provided by the splash image, the splash image goes away, and you're greeted with Blender's default scene, shown in Figure 1-4. If you're looking at the interface for the first time, you

Figure 1-3:
The Blender
splash
image.

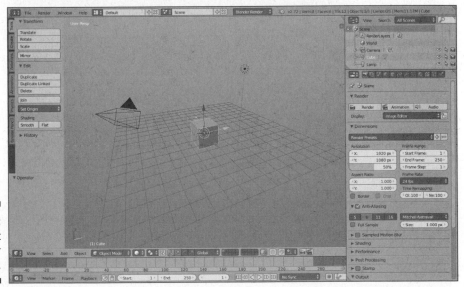

Figure 1-4:
The default
Blender
interface.

Fast to use versus fast to learn

One of the key things to remember is that Blender was originally designed as an in-house tool for commercial production. Working in that industry (especially television production) involves very short turn-around times and extremely tight deadlines. For these reasons, 3D artists have to work very quickly to produce high quality work in a short period of time. Blender has always been designed with facilitating this need as a primary focus. And because artists worked side-by-side with the developers, they could tailor the whole program to match the way they worked.

The upside to this approach is that the program evolved with the artists and enabled them to successfully produce great work at a blazingly fast rate. The downside is that, as with most things that are customized, Blender became somewhat difficult for new people to understand. This trade-off is what I mean when I say "fast to use versus fast to learn." You can be extremely productive with Blender after you understand how it thinks. However, your first few projects with Blender (especially true in earlier versions) might be arduous. Of course, alleviating that potential pain is what this book is all about.

may think it appears pretty daunting. However, the purpose of this book is to help you get the hang of Blender (and its interface) with a minimum of pain.

This book explains some of the design decisions in Blender's interface and ultimately allows you to be productive with it. Who knows, you might even start to like it and wonder why other programs don't work this way!

Working with an interface that stays out of your way

The first thing to understand about Blender's interface is its basic organization. Figure 1-4 displays a single Blender window. Each Blender window can consist of one or more *areas* that you can split, resize, and join at will. In all cases, an area defines the space of an *editor*, such as the 3D View, where you actually make changes and modifications to your 3D scene. Each editor can include one or more *regions* that contain additional features or tools for using that editor. An example of a region that all editors have is a header region at the top or bottom of the editor; the header typically includes menus and buttons to give you access to features in that editor. Figure 1-5 illustrates each of these building blocks of the Blender interface.

Knowing this organizational structure, the next important thing to know is that Blender is designed to be as *non-blocking* and *non-modal* as possible. Areas in Blender never overlap one another (non-blocking) and using one

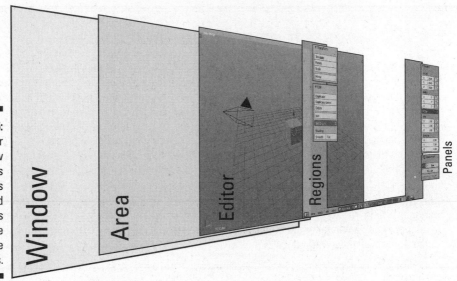

Figure 1-5:
A Blender window contains areas populated by editors that include one or more regions.

feature of Blender typically won't restrict you from using any of the others (non-modal). As an example, in most software, if you want to open a new file or save your project, a file browser dialog pops up. This dialog is an overlapping window that not only blocks things behind it from view, but usually also prevents you from making any changes to your file. This scenario isn't the case with Blender. In Blender, the file browser is an editor just like any other, and it makes perfect sense to be able to make a couple of tweaks to your scene before hitting the Save button. Figure 1-6 shows what it might look like to have a file browser open while you make tweaks.

At first, working in a non-blocking, non-modal interface may seem to be really restrictive. How do you see different types of editors? Can you see them at the same time? Everything looks like it's nailed in place, so is it even possible to change anything? Fortunately, all these things are possible and you get the benefit of never having your view of one area obstructed by another. Having an unobstructed workspace is a great way to be able to see at a glance what's going on in your file. Furthermore, if you absolutely *need* multiple windows that can overlap, you can have them. For example, you might have two computer monitors that are different sizes and you'd like a full-sized Blender window in each. I show you how to do this task in this chapter in the "Duplicating an area to a new window" section.

This non-blocking window philosophy, combined with the fact that Blender's entire interface is written in a standardized programming library for graphics called OpenGL, is the precise reason that Blender looks the same, no matter where you run it. Whether you run it from Linux, Windows, a Mac, or even an

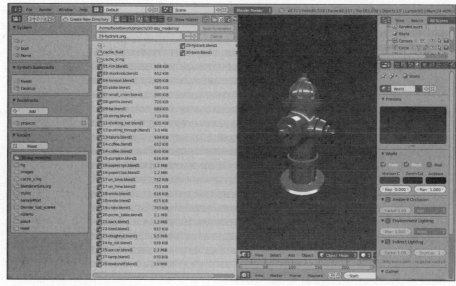

Figure 1-6:
Doing those
last couple
of tweaks
before
finally
saving.

experimental build for Android devices, Blender looks and behaves like Blender. An additional benefit to being written in a 3D library like OpenGL is that many parts of Blender's interface allow you to zoom in on them. Try it! Hover your mouse cursor over the Properties editor (the editor on the right side) and press Numpad Plus (+) or Numpad Minus (-). You can make the panels in this editor much larger or smaller than they are by default. Pretty cool!

Resizing areas

Regardless of the type of editor that's contained in an area, you modify and change all areas in a Blender window the same way. To change the size of an area, left-click the border between two areas and drag it to a new position. This method increases the size of one area while reducing the size of those that adjoin it. If you have only one area in your Blender window, it's exactly the same size as that window. To resize it, you need to either adjust the size of its parent Blender window or split a new area into that space, as covered in the next section.

Splitting and removing areas

While working in Blender, it's pretty common that the default layout isn't quite what you need to work efficiently. Sometimes you may need an additional 3D View or you may want to see the UV/Image Editor in addition to the 3D View.

To create either of these layout changes, you need to *split* an existing area into two. You can split or join areas by right-clicking the border between two areas and choosing either Split Area or Join Area from the menu that pops up. However, there's a faster way. Look at the corners in the bottom left and top right of any area. These *corner widgets* are marked as a triangular region indicated by diagonal lines. To split any area into two, use the following steps:

1. **Left-click one of the corner widgets and drag your mouse cursor away from the area's border.**

2. **Drag your mouse cursor left or right to split the area vertically.**

   Dragging it up or down splits the area horizontally.

As you drag your mouse, the areas update in real time so that you can see the result of the split while you're working.

If you decide that you actually don't want to split the area, you can cancel the operation by right-clicking or pressing Esc.

If you want to remove an area, the process is similar. Rather than splitting an area in two, you're joining two areas together. So instead of left-clicking the corner widget and dragging your mouse cursor away from the area border, drag it *towards* the border of the area you want to join with. This action darkens the area your mouse is in and draws an arrow to indicate which area you want to remove.

Figure 1-7 shows the process of splitting an area and then removing that area. When I work in Blender, I find myself constantly changing the screen layout by splitting and joining new areas as I need them.

Duplicating an area to a new window

In addition to the new way of splitting and joining areas, you can use these corner widgets to duplicate any area into a new Blender window of its own. You can move that window to a separate monitor (if you have one), or it can overlap your original Blender window. And within this new Blender window, you can split the duplicated area into additional ones as you like. This area duplication feature is a slight violation of Blender's non-overlapping principles, but the benefits it provides for users with multiple computer screens make it very worthwhile.

To take advantage of this feature, follow these steps:

1. **Shift+left-click one of the corner widgets in an area and drag your mouse cursor away from it in any direction.**

   This step duplicates the area you clicked in and creates a new Blender window to contain it.

Create a new area

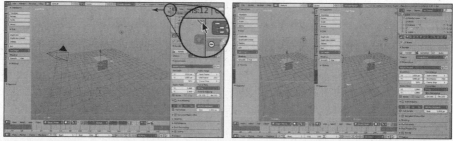

Remove an area

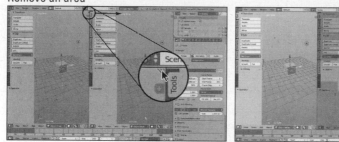

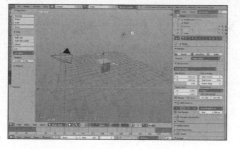

Figure 1-7:
Creating a
new area
and then
removing
that area.

You can also achieve this effect from the header menu of some editors
by choosing View⇨Duplicate Area into New Window.

2. **Close the additional Blender window by clicking the close button that
your operating system adds to the border of the window.**

Maximizing an area

When working in Blender, you also occasionally need to maximize an area.
Maximizing an area is particularly useful when you're working on a model
or scene and you just want to get all the other areas out of your way so you
can use as much screen space as possible to focus your attention on the task
at hand.

Customizing Headers

All editors in Blender have a horizontal region called the *header* running along either the top or bottom of the editor. The header usually features specialized menus or buttons that are specific to the editor you're using. Here are some ways you can customize the header:

✔ **Resize the header.** Like any region, you can resize the header by left-clicking the seam between the header and the main work space of the editor and dragging it up or down.

✔ **Hide the header.** If you drag the seam all the way to the area border, then the header becomes hidden, leaving only a small plus icon (+) in the corner of the editor. If the header is at the bottom of the editor, the plus icon appears at the bottom right. If the header appears at the top, it's at the top left. Left-click this icon and the header reappears.

✔ **Change the location of the header.** You can also change the location of the header to either the top or bottom of the editor it belongs to. To do so, right-click the header and choose Flip to Top (or Bottom, depending on where your header currently is).

To maximize any area, hover your mouse cursor over it and press Shift+Spacebar. You can toggle back to the tiled screen layout by either pressing Shift+Spacebar again or clicking the Back to Previous button at the top of the window. These options are available in the header menus of nearly all editor types by choosing View ➪ Toggle Full Screen. You can also right-click the header and choose Maximize Area from the menu that appears. If the area is already maximized, then the menu item will say Tile Area.

You may notice that the hot keys next to these menu items are Ctrl+Up Arrow for maximizing and Ctrl+Down Arrow for tiling, rather than Shift+Spacebar. Those hotkeys also work, but I find that I don't have to move my left hand as much to hit Shift+Spacebar, so that's much more convenient for me.

The menu that is a pie

There's a recent addition to Blender's user interface that's worth mentioning. That addition is a feature called pie menus. Contrasted with the more conventional linear, list-type menu, a *pie menu* lists your menu options radially around your mouse cursor. This setup has a few advantages:

✔ **Each menu item has a much larger click area.**

With a typical list-type menu, once you find the menu item you want, there's a relatively small area that you need to precisely click. With a pie menu, you only need to have your mouse cursor in the general area around your menu selection (its slice of the pie). Because you don't need to be as precise with your mouse, you can navigate menus faster with less stress on your hand.

✔ **Menu options are easier to remember.**

As humans, we tend to naturally think about things spatially. It's much easier to remember that a thing is up or left or right than to remember that it's the sixth item in a list of things. Because the menu items are arranged in two-dimensional space, pie menus take advantage of our natural way of recalling information. Also helpful for memory is the fact that any given pie menu can only have as many as eight options.

✔ **Selecting menu items is a *gestural* behavior.**

A *gestural interface* relies on using mouse movement to issue a command. Pie menus are not purely gestural, but by arranging the menu items spatially, you get many of the same advantages provided by gestures. Most valuable among these advantages is the reliance on muscle memory. After working with a pie menu for an extended period of time, selecting menu items becomes nearly as fast as using hotkeys, and for essentially the same reasons. You're no longer thinking about the direction you're moving your mouse cursor (or which key you're pressing). You've trained your hands to move in a specific way when you want to perform that task. Once you get to that point (it doesn't take very long), you'll find that you're working very quickly.

Before you get too excited about pie menus, they have a couple of limitations:

✔ Pie menus are basically limited to a maximum of eight menu items. (It's possible to have more items, but if a pie menu has more than eight items, it becomes cluttered and the speed and memory advantages of pie menus are lessened.) Blender has a number of menus that are very long; therefore, they don't translate nicely to the pie menu model. This means that some menus will be pies and others will not. Hopefully, as development continues on Blender, these menus will migrate to being more pie-like.

✔ Pie menus, as of this writing, aren't enabled by default. As Blender development progresses, the plan is that pie menus will eventually be enabled as a default option. For the time being, however, you need to manually enable them. As that's the direction that Blender is currently heading (and Blender development is *fast;* there's a new release nearly every two months), I recommend that you go ahead and enable pie menus so you can get comfortable with them early.

The process of enabling pie menus is easy:

1. **Open User Preferences (File ⇨ User Preferences or Ctrl+Alt+U) and go to the Add-ons section.**

2. **On the category list on the left side of the window, choose the User Interface category (you may need to scroll down to see it).**

   The Pie Menus Official add-on should appear on the list to the right (as of this writing, this add-on is the only one in the User Interface category, so you may need to scroll back up to see it).

3. **Enable the Pie Menus Official add-on by left-clicking its checkbox on the far right.**

4. **Pie menus are now enabled. Left-click the Save User Settings button at the bottom left of the User Preferences window.**

That's it! Pie menus will be automatically enabled each time you start Blender. (Read more about Blender add-ons in Chapter 2.)

To try out pie menus, first close the User Preferences window. With your mouse cursor in the 3D View, press Q to show the View pie menu. You should see a menu like the one in Figure 1-8.

With the menu still visible, move your mouse cursor around the screen. Notice that the highlighted area of the circular slice indicator at the center of the menu points to your mouse cursor. Also notice that as you move your mouse cursor, individual menu items highlight when you enter their slice of the menu. This highlighting is how you know which menu item is currently ready to be picked. Press Esc to close the menu without selecting anything.

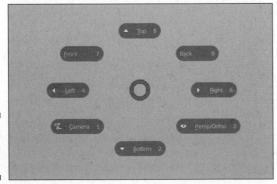

Figure 1-8:
Your first pie
[menu]!

There are two ways to choose menu items in a pie menu:

- ✔ **Press, release, click:** This can be considered the standard method:

  1. *Press and release the hotkey that activates the menu.*

     In this example, press and release Q.

  2. *Move your mouse cursor to your desired menu item's slice.*

  3. *Choose that menu item by clicking anywhere within its slice.*

     The current active slice is indicated by the circular slice indicator at the center of the menu, as well as the highlighting of each menu item as your mouse cursor enters its slice.

- ✔ **Press, hold, release:** I think of this method as the fast way.

  1. *Press **and hold** the hotkey that activates the menu.*

     In this example, press and hold Q.

  2. *Move your mouse cursor to your desired menu item's slice.*

  3. *Release the hotkey to choose that menu item.*

As pie menus are still optional, you can always go back and disable them if you decide that you don't like using them. However, if you decide to keep them enabled, I try to help you throughout the rest of the book. For any given menu or operator, if there's an option for using a pie menu, I make it a point to let you know the hotkey and location of the various pie menu items.

Chapter 2

Understanding How Blender Thinks

In This Chapter

▶ Familiarizing yourself with Blender's windows

▶ Adjusting Blender's interface to fit the way you work

▶ Working in three-dimensional space

▶ Using the regions in the 3D View

*I*t's time to get intimate with Blender. No, I don't mean you need to start placing scented candles around your computer. I mean that this chapter's focus is a detailed introduction to Blender's interface and how you can start finding your way around in it. First of all, it's pretty important to have an understanding of the various types of editors that Blender has and how to access them. These editors are the gateways and tools for creating whatever you want.

With the knowledge of what you can do with these editors, the next thing is actually building those creations. To do so, you need to understand how to work in a virtual three-dimensional space, and specifically, you need to understand how Blender handles that space. I also cover these topics in this chapter.

Looking at Editor Types

In many ways, Blender isn't so much one program as it is a bunch of different programs sharing the same interface and access to the same data. Thinking of it this way, each of Blender's editor types is kind of its own little program in a Blender area.

Menus in Blender

You may have noticed that I refer to the 3D View as the "first" item in the Editor Type menu, even though in Figure 2-1, it's at the bottom of the menu. This is due to a somewhat unique quirk of Blender's menus. They're designed to help you by keeping the distance you need to move your mouse cursor as short as possible. In practice, this means that when you open a menu from an editor's header near the bottom of the Blender window, it flows upward with the first menu item at the bottom, closest to your mouse cursor. When you open a header menu near the top of the Blender window, it flows downward and the first item is at the top.

For floating menus like the Add (Shift+A) menu in the 3D View (covered in Chapter 4), the behavior is a little bit different. Those menus always list the first item at the top; *however*, Blender remembers the last item you picked in any of these floating menus and automatically places that item under your mouse cursor. Again, this is for speedy workflow. The idea is that if you chose one menu item last time, it's likely that you want to pick it again this time. To reduce the distance you have to move the mouse cursor, Blender facilitates this notion by jumping directly to the last menu item you chose.

A Blender area can contain any editor type. You can see what editor types are available by left-clicking the button on the far left of that editor's header. Figure 2-1 shows the menu that appears when you press this button.

Each editor type serves a specific purpose, but you can organize them into four basic categories: animation editors, 2D editors, general editors, and

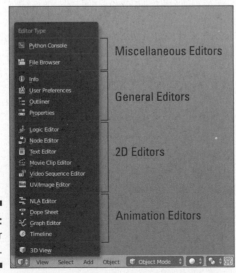

Figure 2-1:
The Editor
Type menu.

miscellaneous editors. The menu shown in Figure 2-1 attempts to organize the editors according to these categories. The exception to this is the 3D View. Technically, it should probably be among the general editors, but since it's used most frequently, it has a distinguished position as the first option in the list.

The following subsections give you an overview of each editor, organized by category.

General editors

The editors covered in this section are usually the most common way of interfacing with objects in your 3D scene, as well as customizing Blender itself.

These editors give you general control over your scene or over Blender itself:

- **3D View (Shift+F5):** Arguably the most-used editor in Blender, the 3D View shows you the three-dimensional view of your model or scene and provides access to many of the tools you can use to modify it.

- **Properties (Shift+F7):** You can manipulate nearly all of the different attributes for your scene and the objects within it via this editor. You can find out more about this topic later in this chapter in the section, "Understanding the Properties editor."

- **Outliner (Shift+F9):** The Outliner gives a hierarchical view of all the objects in your scene along with the ability to see how they're related to one another. It's also a quick way to select objects and do simple manipulations in a complex scene.

- **User Preferences:** Through the User Preferences editor, you can customize how you interact with Blender.

- **Info:** The Info editor contains Blender's main menu and displays basic information about your scene. It also serves as a report space where warnings and errors are logged. This can be used to figure out what happened if a feature doesn't work as expected.

Animation editors

The following editors relate specifically to animation:

- **Timeline:** If you're working on an animation, the Timeline editor offers you a convenient way to quickly jump from one moment in your animation to another as well as play back the animation.

- ✔ **Graph Editor (Shift+F6):** Blender's Graph Editor shows a graphical representation of animatable attributes in your scene as they change over time.

- ✔ **Dope Sheet (Shift+F12):** The Dope Sheet is where you create and adjust your overall animation using actions or keying sets. You can use *actions* to animate all of a character's movement in a scene, or you can mix them together in the NLA Editor. *Keying sets* give you the ability to group together a bunch of different animatable attributes.

- ✔ **NLA Editor:** NLA stands for *nonlinear animation*. This editor allows you to mix pre-animated actions on a single character (such as mixing a waving hand animation with a walking animation to have your character walk and wave her hand at the same time).

2D editors

The following editors manipulate specific kinds of two-dimensional data:

- ✔ **UV/Image Editor (Shift+F10):** With the UV/Image Editor, you can do basic image editing as well as edit the texture coordinates for your models (see Chapter 7).

- ✔ **Video Sequence Editor (Shift+F8):** Blender's Video Sequence Editor (VSE) is a lightweight video editor. The VSE isn't as powerful as some other programs created specifically for editing video, but it's quite effective for stringing a sequence of scenes together and doing basic effects, overlays, and transitions.

- ✔ **Movie Clip Editor:** Currently, the Movie Clip Editor is the primary go-to editor for Blender's motion tracking features. *Motion tracking* is a process where the software analyzes moving parts of a video in an effort to relate them to 3D space. With video that's been successfully motion tracked, you can integrate 3D models into recorded video. Have you ever wondered how they get computer-generated monsters to look like they're in the same room as living actors? Motion tracking!

- ✔ **Text Editor (Shift+F11):** Blender's integrated Text Editor is not only handy for keeping notes about your scenes and models, but once you become a more advanced user, it's also a convenient place to write and test your own Python scripts and material shaders in Blender.

- ✔ **Node Editor (Shift+F3):** Blender has a Node Editor for materials and textures, as well as for compositing. This editor is where you modify these node structures. Cycles, a relatively new rendering engine that's integrated into Blender, makes heavy use of the node editor for its materials and lighting.

Chapters 7–9 cover Cycles extensively.

✔ **Logic Editor (Shift+F2):** Blender has a game engine integrated with it, allowing you to create your own custom video games directly within Blender. The Logic Editor is how you control and design the behavior in your game.

Utility editors

The following two editors aren't easily classified in any of the other categories, so they've found themselves at the end of the list. That doesn't make them any less useful, so it's still worth knowing what they are and what they do:

✔ **File Browser:** This editor allows you to look through the files on your computer. It also allows you to look at the innards of your Blender projects to see how things are structured or for linking to other projects.

✔ **Python Console (Shift+F4):** The Console is a pretty handy editor that's more often utilized by advanced users to help write custom Python scripts. It's a "live" console where you can use the Python language to directly issue commands to Blender.

Understanding the Properties editor

After the 3D View, the Properties editor is probably the second-most used editor type in Blender. You use buttons and values in this editor to modify the attributes of your scene and elements within it. Because this editor can manipulate so many parts of a scene, it's broken down and organized into a series of subsections.

You can access each of the various subsections by using the buttons in the header region of the Properties editor. It's worth noting here that these subsection buttons are ordered logically from large contexts (such as Scene properties) to progressively smaller contexts (such as Object Data properties) as you go from left to right. It's also good to know that the available subsections in the Properties editor can change depending on what your active selection is in the 3D View. For example, if you have a camera object selected, the Modifiers subsection of the Properties editor isn't visible (because modifiers can't be applied to cameras). The following list describes each subsection of the Properties editor:

✔ **Render:** The Render properties determine what the final output of your scene will look like when you decide to render it to an image or video. Chapters 14 and 15 cover these properties in more depth.

- **Render Layers:** You can organize the output of your scene in *render layers*, useful for compositing (see Chapter 15) different render outputs into a final image. The properties in this section give you control over organizing your render layers.

  If you use the Freestyle edge renderer, this section also contains those properties.

- **Scene:** These general properties dictate the nature of your scene, including things like the active camera, units of measurement, and the strength of gravity if you're using simulated physics.

- **World:** The buttons and values in the World properties subsection control the environment that your scene is built in. They have a large influence on the final output of your scene.

- **Object:** Any object in your scene is going to have its own set of properties that you can modify. The Object properties subsection allows you to make changes that affect an object as it relates to the scene.

- **Object Constraints:** When working in 3D — particularly with animation — it's often useful to constrain the properties of one object to that of another. Constraints automate parts of your scene and help make it much more manageable. Chapter 10 goes into constraints more deeply.

- **Modifiers:** A lot of work goes into building 3D models, so it's to your benefit to take advantage of your computer and have it do as much work for you as possible. Let it take care of boring procedural steps like mirroring parts of your object or making it smoother while you focus on the more interesting steps in the process. Modifiers are great tools to facilitate these kinds of healthy shortcuts, and allow for more advanced uses in animation. This subsection is where you manage those modifiers. You can find out more about modifiers in Chapter 5.

- **Object Data:** Like the previous four subsections, buttons and values in Object Data properties change slightly depending on what sort of object you've selected, but their primary purpose is to give you the ability to work with the fundamental structural elements of your object.

"Object Data" is a generic term. Think of this section as properties based on what you've got selected. Even the icon for Object Data Properties changes depending on your selection. For example, if you have a camera object selected, these would be Camera Properties and the icon for this section looks like a camera. If you have a curve object selected, the icon looks like a curve and you'd think of this section as Curve Properties.

- **Bone:** The Bone properties subsection is only available if your active selection is an Armature object. Armatures, sometimes called skeletons in other programs, are used for animation in Blender and they consist of a set of bone sub-objects. Bone properties are where you can adjust attributes of a specific bone that you've selected in the armature.

- ✔ **Bone Constraints:** Similar to the Object Constraints properties, this subsection helps you manage constraints. The difference, however, is that this subsection is only available if your active selection is an Armature in Pose Mode and it's for managing constraints on bones, rather than objects. Chapters 10 and 11 cover constraints and the use of constraints on bones.

- ✔ **Material:** The controls in Material properties allow you to dramatically change the appearance of objects in your scene. Chapter 7 goes into this subsection in much more detail.

- ✔ **Texture:** Textures can have a profound effect on how the surface of your 3D objects appear, making smooth, clean objects look rough, gritty, and believable. You can also use textures as custom brushes when painting and sculpting in Blender. This subsection is where you can edit those textures. You can find out more on texturing in Chapter 8.

- ✔ **Particles:** In computer graphics, particle systems are often used to create special effects or manage the behavior of groups of objects. This subsection of the Properties editor is where you manage particle systems in Blender. Working with particles is a pretty advanced topic. Chapter 13 gives you a brief introduction to the possibilities that they have.

- ✔ **Physics:** In the spirit of making your computer do as much work for you as possible, having the computer simulate physical behavior in your objects is sometimes helpful. It lends realism to animations and can often help you work faster. The Physics properties subsection gives you controls for simulating physics on your objects. See Chapter 13 for more on these topics.

Customizing Blender to Fit You

You can tweak Blender's screen layout to virtually any configuration you can imagine. However, Blender's customization features go much deeper than just readjusting the areas in a Blender window. There are very few parts of Blender that, with a little time and effort, you can't completely overhaul to be as comfortable of a work environment as possible. This ability to customize is especially useful for people who are migrating to Blender from other 3D graphics programs. I won't say that you can make Blender behave exactly like any of these other programs, but sometimes little things like using the same keyboard shortcuts help make the transition smoother.

Although this section gives you the means to completely bend Blender's interface to your will, bear in mind that unless otherwise specified, this book relies on the default settings that ship with Blender. Unless you can remember your customized behaviors, it may be more helpful to use Blender's default settings (File⇨Load Factory Settings).

Using screen layout presets

You can make a variety of layouts depending on the sort of work you're doing. In Blender, these workspace layouts are called *screens*, and, by default, Blender comes with nine presets: 3D View Full, Animation, Compositing, Default, Game Logic, Motion Tracking, Scripting, UV Editing, and Video Editing. When you first load Blender, you're in the Default screen layout. You can cycle through these screens by pressing Ctrl+← and Ctrl+→. If you prefer to use a menu, you can use the datablock (for more on datablocks, see the "Understanding datablocks" sidebar in this chapter) at the top of the window in the Info editor, as shown in Figure 2-2, and left-click the screen icon next to the name of the current screen layout.

You can rename any screen to any name by switching to that screen and left-clicking its name in the Screens datablock. Get used to the idea of naming everything in your projects. Trust me, being in the habit of using a reasonable name makes life infinitely easier. It's especially true when you come back to an old project and you need to figure out what everything is.

The screens, and therefore the order that they're cycled through when you press Ctrl+← or Ctrl+→, are arranged in alphabetical and numerical order, for fast and logical organization. If you want to cheat a bit, you can give a specific order to the list by putting a number in front of each screen's name (such as 1-Default, 2-Animation, and so on).

To create a new screen, left-click the plus icon next to the current screen name in the Info editor's header. Upon clicking this icon, Blender produces a duplicate of your existing screen layout. From here, you can make the

Figure 2-2:
The Screens
menu.

changes to create your own custom layout, such as a materials editing layout or a multi-monitor layout with a separate window for each of your monitors.

You can also delete screens (including the default ones that ship with Blender, so be careful) by clicking the button with the X icon to the right of the Screen datablock. When you're happy with changes you've made and you want to have these screens available (or not available, if you've removed screens) each time you start Blender, save your settings by going to File⇨Save Startup File or using the Ctrl+U hotkey.

If you make an area a Properties editor, Blender defaults to using the same vertical orientation for the editor that's used in the Default screen layout. However, in an area that's wider than it is tall, this can look stretched and weird. You can manually switch between a horizontal and vertical Properties editor by right-clicking a blank spot in the editor and choosing between a horizontal and vertical orientation.

Before creating a new screen that you want to keep around for future use, first return to your default setup by selecting File⇨New or pressing Ctrl+N. When you use the Save Startup File feature, Blender saves your current settings, layout, and even 3D scenes to a special .blend file called startup.blend that gets loaded each time it starts. So any models you have in the 3D View and any changes you make to other layouts are saved, too. Fortunately, if you've made a mistake, you can always return to the default setup by choosing File⇨Load Factory Settings and recreate your custom layouts from there.

This behavior of saving a special startup.blend file is fine for setting up custom screen layouts, but it can be pretty inconvenient if you're just making changes in User Preferences (such as custom hotkeys or themes). For those kinds of changes, it's better to use the Save User Settings button at the bottom of User Preferences (Ctrl+Alt+U). Using this button ensures that your new settings in User Preferences are loaded each time you start Blender, without overwriting your default scene or screen layouts.

When adjusting screen layouts, the menus and buttons in the header can be obscured or hidden if the area is too narrow. This scenario happens particularly often for people who work on computers with small monitors. In this case, you can do three things:

✔ Right-click in the header area and enable Header⇨Collapse Menus.

   The menus are collapsed into a single button with an icon consisting of 3 lines. This frees up a little bit of space, but on smaller monitors, it may not be enough.

Understanding datablocks: Fundamental elements in a Blender file

In Figure 2-2, look at the widget that's used to manage screens. The interface gives you access to something called a datablock. A simple and obvious definition of a datablock is that it's literally a block of data. However, a datablock has more to it. Datablocks are used throughout both Blender's interface and its internal structure, so understanding how they work and how you can take advantage of them goes a long way to understanding Blender itself. Nearly every critical element in Blender is stored in a type of datablock, from screens and scenes to objects and animations.

Not only is a datablock a handy way to store information, but it also allows Blender to treat this information like a database. In particular, you can link datablocks and let them share information. As an example, say that you've created an excellent wood material, and you want to have two objects — a table and a chair — look like they're both made of the same wood. Well, rather than recreate that exact same material for each object, you can simply link both object datablocks to the same material datablock. Your computer uses less memory, and, more importantly, you have less work to do. And because datablocks are used throughout Blender, this same concept works in all kinds of situations: sharing textures between materials, sharing particle systems between objects, and even sharing worlds between scenes. It's an incredibly powerful feature of Blender and I refer to datablocks a lot throughout this book.

✔ Hover your mouse cursor over the header region and scroll your mouse wheel.

  If any parts of the header are obscured, you can scroll them in and out of view.

✔ For a somewhat more direct method, Blender has another trick up its sleeve: Middle-click the header and drag your mouse left and right. The contents of the header move left and right so that you can bring those obscured buttons into view.

Setting user preferences

This section on user preferences is by no means comprehensive. The number of options available in Blender's User Preferences editor is mind-bogglingly large. My intent here is to introduce you to the most helpful and relevant options to get you working effectively. For specific details on every single button, see the online documentation available at www.blender.org/manual.

Of course, the first question is, "Where exactly *are* the buttons for user preferences?" Well, the User Preferences editor is just like any other editor in Blender and can therefore appear in any area you want it to by using the Editor Type menu in the header region of any editor. (For more information, see the section "Looking at Editor Types," earlier in this chapter.) Of course, you can also go to File⇨User Preferences (Ctrl+Alt+U), and Blender creates a new window just for the User Preferences editor. Although creating a separate window is a bit of a violation of Blenders non-overlapping philosophy, it is sometimes nicer because you don't have to replace or split any of your existing areas to get a User Preferences editor.

If you choose File⇨User Preferences, and you don't see a new window with the User Preferences editor, your Blender window may be in a full-screen state and your operating system's window manager may not be allowing the window with User Preferences to sit atop that full-screen window. To get around this issue, toggle off the full-screen view by choosing Window⇨Toggle Fullscreen from the Info editor's header region or by pressing Alt+F11.

When you get the User Preferences to be the way you like, you can save them as your personal defaults by clicking the Save User Settings button at the bottom of the User Preferences editor.

Interface

The first set of available options in Blender's User Preferences (shown in Figure 2-3) relate to how you interact with your scene within the 3D View. Moving from left to right, here are some of the more useful options:

- **Display:** The options in this column toggle the display of various informational elements in the 3D View, such as tooltips, object information, and the small mini axis in the bottom left corner.

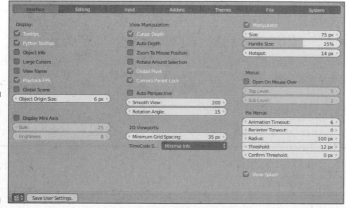

Figure 2-3: The Interface options in User Preferences.

- ✔ **View Manipulation:** The options in this column give you control over how you interact with the environment in the 3D View.

  - **Auto Depth and Zoom To Mouse Position:** If you tend to create large environment scenes, having these two options enabled is often useful so that you can quickly navigate your way through your scene without becoming stuck.

  - **Smooth View:** Smooth View is probably one of the coolest convenience options added to Blender in recent history and as such, it deserves explicit mention here. By default, Smooth View is set to a value of 200. If you go to your 3D View and choose View➪Camera (Numpad 0), the 3D View smoothly animates the change from the default perspective view to the Camera's perspective. Pretty slick, huh? The values in Smooth View are in milliseconds, with a maximum value of 1,000, or 1 second (although that's a bit slow for most tastes). The default value of 200 works nicely, but play with it on your own and see what works best for you.

- ✔ **Manipulator:** The 3D manipulator is the large colored axis at the center of the cube in Blender's default scene. Its main purpose is to move, rotate, or scale your selection in the 3D View. Chapter 3 goes into more detail on how to use the manipulator. The settings here control whether or not the manipulator is enabled by default, as well as its size when visible.

  - **Menus:** Some users prefer to have menus immediately pop open when they run their mouse cursor over them. The options under this heading facilitate that preference. It's disabled by default, but you can enable the Open On Mouse Over check box and then use the values below that to adjust the *delay*, or how long your mouse has to be over a menu's name before it pops up.

  - **Pie Menus:** Pie menus are an optional menu type in Blender that I cover at the end of Chapter 1. The settings here offer a little control over how the pie menus appear, and for how long.

Editing

The next set of options is related to the act of editing objects. As shown in Figure 2-4, the most relevant options are as follows:

- ✔ **Undo:** The options related to undo are pretty important. Here you can adjust how many steps of undo you have when working in Blender (default is 32), as well as toggle Global Undo on and off. Now, you may be wondering why in the world anyone would *ever* want to disable the ability to undo a mistake. The most common answer to this question is performance. Having undo enabled requires more memory from your computer, and each level of undo requires a little bit more. Sometimes, when working with very complex scenes or models, an artist might disable undo to dedicate all the computer's memory to the current scene rather than the steps used to create it. This decision occurs most when artists work with Blender's sculpting tools (see Chapter 5).

✔ **Playback:** When animating, there are times when you need to start animating before the first frame, such as starting the scene with a character, object, or simulation already in motion. By default, however, Blender doesn't allow you to work in the Timeline (or any other editor) on frame numbers less than zero. But if you enable the Allow Negative Frames check box, that limitation is removed.

✔ **Transform:** If you're migrating to Blender from another 3D suite, or if your primary pointing device is a pressure-sensitive drawing tablet, you may find it difficult to use Blender's "click to confirm" default behavior when grabbing, scaling, or rotating your selections. If you enable the Release Confirms check box, you may feel more comfortable.

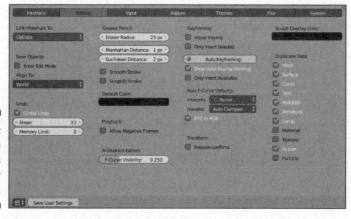

Figure 2-4:
The Editing
options
in User
Preferences.

Input

The settings and controls in the Input options of the User Preferences editor have the greatest influence over how you interact with Blender. As Figure 2-5 shows, this section is extensive.

The largest part of this section — the event editor on the right side — is actually covered later in this chapter in the section "Using custom event maps." However, the left-side column has quite a few useful settings as well:

✔ **Presets:** Blender ships with a small assortment of *application interaction presets* — a fancy way of saying hotkey and mouse configurations. In addition to the default preset, Blender also ships with a few presets that match the interaction styles of other popular 3D programs. You can use this data-block-like menu to choose an existing preset, create a new one, or delete a preset you never want to use.

Figure 2-5:
The Input
options
in User
Preferences.

✔ **Emulate 3 Button Mouse:** Blender was designed to be used with a three-button mouse. However, not all computers have three-button mice, and some artists prefer to work with drawing tablets that don't have an easily accessible middle mouse button. Enabling this option helps these users compensate by using Alt+left-click to do what is normally done with the middle-click.

✔ **Continuous Grab:** Continuous Grab is a cool feature that allows you to continue moving an object even after your mouse cursor has reached the edge of the editor. Continuous Grab is very useful and enabled by default, but it doesn't work as nicely for users working with a tablet interface, so you can disable it here if you need to.

✔ **Select With:** Blender's default behavior is to select objects with the right mouse button. However people migrating to Blender from other programs may be more comfortable selecting with the left mouse button. This control lets you switch between the two. I cover this setting later in this chapter in the section "Selecting objects." A word of warning: Setting this value to Left disables the Emulate 3 Button Mouse feature.

✔ **Emulate Numpad:** This setting is a very handy option for laptop users. As you see in the next section, Blender makes use of the numeric keypad for quick access to top, front, side, and camera views in the 3D View. Unfortunately, most laptop users don't have an easily accessible numeric keypad on their keyboards. As a workaround, the Emulate Numpad option uses the number keys at the top of the keyboard to have the functionality that the corresponding numpad numbers have. This control in User Preferences disables the normal layer-switching functionality that the number keys at the top of the keyboard normally perform, but the ability to quickly change views tends to be more valuable to users than the ability to quickly change layers.

✔ **Orbit Style:** By default, Blender uses the Turntable setting. However, some users have difficulty navigating to a particular part of their scenes or models when using Turntable setting. For them, the Trackball setting may be more comfortable.

The difference between the two settings may seem subtle to a new user, but if you're used to one orbit style, it can be very disorienting to try working in the other.

✔ **Invert Zoom Direction:** Similar to the Orbit Style option, some people are more comfortable scrolling forward to zoom out and back to zoom in. This setting gives users that option.

Add-ons

Blender ships with an assortment of extensions, called add-ons, which provide users with additional capabilities within Blender. For example, if you're a veteran Blenderhead and you're used to the old Spacebar menu from much earlier versions of Blender, there's an add-on that puts that feature back. Other add-ons modify Blender's interface, add new primitive objects, or provide additional tools that can help speed up your work. Another key feature of add-ons is that they are tightly integrated into Blender's interface. Once an add-on is enabled, its functionality looks and works just like native features in Blender, like it was there all along!

You can manage all add-ons from the Add-ons section of User Preferences, as shown in Figure 2-6.

Figure 2-6:
The Add-ons
options
in User
Preferences.

There are three types, or *support levels*, for add-ons:

- ✔ **Official:** These add-ons officially ship with Blender on release. Core development team supports them and ensures that they continue to work with each Blender release.

  Although these add-ons come with Blender, they aren't all enabled by default, because some of them favor very specific workflows.

- ✔ **Community:** These add-ons also officially ship with Blender on release. However, rather than being supported by the core developers, the add-ons at this support level are maintained by community developers (usually the people who first wrote them). None of these add-ons are enabled by default, but many of them are very useful.

  I'm not just saying that because I wrote one of them. I promise!

- ✔ **Testing:** There are two kinds of add-ons at this support level:

  - • Very new add-ons that haven't been thoroughly tested by users.

  - • Veteran add-ons that aren't actively maintained and supported by any developer.

  The Testing add-ons don't ship with Blender's official release, but you can download them individually from the Blender Add-ons Catalog (`http://wiki.blender.org/index.php/Extensions:2.6/ Py/Scripts`).

You can use the buttons on the left side of the Add-ons section in User Preferences to filter the add-ons you see according to support level. By default, all community supported add-ons that ship with Blender are disabled. Most of the officially supported add-ons are for importing and exporting file types to and from other programs. The bulk of these are enabled by default. To enable or disable a specific add-on, use the following steps:

1. **Find the add-on that you're interested in enabling.**

2. **Left-click the check box on the right side of the add-on's box.**

   Left-clicking the triangle on the left of the box expands it so that you can get more details about a specific add-on.

That's it! The add-on is enabled. Depending on what the add-on does, you should be able to find it in the interface and use it immediately.

All of Blender's add-ons are broken down into specific categories, and you can use the buttons on the left to see just the add-ons that are specific to a single category. Alternatively, you can use the search field above the category buttons.

Themes

Blender has quite a bit of flexibility in adjusting how it looks, thanks to the Themes options, shown in Figure 2-7. I took almost all the screenshots for this book using a variation of the Default theme that I created, lightened for readability in black-and-white print. However, when I work in Blender, I use my own theme that's a bit darker and easier on the eyes. Darker themes are particularly helpful if, like me, you're known for sitting behind the computer and working in Blender for 10- to 15-hour stretches (or more). In those situations, the less stress you can put on your eyes, the better.

I include a copy of the theme I use in this book on my website for this book, www.blenderbasics.com. Feel free to use this theme for your Blender sessions or make your own! Everyone has their own tastes. In fact, one of the more popular Blender users, Pablo Vazquez (known as VenomGFX), used to have a theme that's completely purple and pink! He's since moved to something a bit more tame, but pink still is used in it. You can see it by trying out the theme named Amaranth.

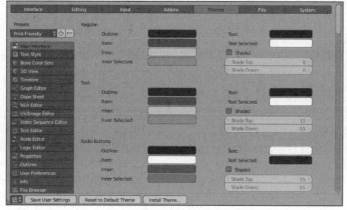

Figure 2-7:
The Themes options in User Preferences.

File

The File options relate to how Blender works with files. Figure 2-8 shows the settings in this section of the User Preferences editor.

The following list describes the important parts of this section:

- **File Paths:** Like most programs, Blender works with files. The values in this column show the default locations where Blender either places files or looks for them. Here you can indicate where your fonts are located, where you want to save your renders by default, and where to look for textures and sounds.

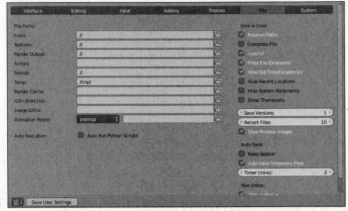

Figure 2-8:
The File
options
in User
Preferences.

Probably the most important path in this section is the one for Temp. This location is where Blender stores auto save files, and it's also where it stores the notorious `quit.blend` file, which is great for recovering your last blender session. The default location for temporary files is `/tmp/` on Linux and Mac OS X. On Windows, it's your user's temporary folder in `C:\Users\<Your Username>\AppData\Local\Temp\`.

Linux users may want to change this location because some Linux distributions like Ubuntu automatically clear the `/tmp` directory on each boot. I can't tell you the number of people who have closed Blender without saving their work and later realized that they couldn't recover any of their work because this path wasn't properly set.

✔ **Auto Execution:** As a security feature, the Auto Run Python Scripts check box is disabled. This provides a bit of a safeguard in the event that you download a `.blend` file from the internet and run it in Blender, preventing potentially dangerous scripts from running right when you open the file. At the same time, this feature can prove to be quite frustrating if you don't download a lot of `.blend` files from untrusted sources and you have animation rigs that rely on Python to work. If that's the case and you trust every `.blend` file that you open, you can enable this check box.

✔ **Save and Load:** These options relate to how Blender opens and saves project files. Of these options, the two most worth knowing about are Compress File and Load UI, both of which you can modify from the File Browser, but these check boxes define the default behavior.

  • **Compress File:** This option is handy because it makes your `.blend` project files smaller when you save.

  • **Load UI:** Load UI is short for Load User Interface, meaning that when you open a `.blend` file, Blender will adjust your screen layout to match the one that was used to create that file.

✔ **Auto Save:** Before Blender had undo functionality, users relied heavily on its auto save features. Even in the age of undo, these options are a life saver. For that reason, the following list goes into these settings in more detail:

- **Save Versions:** Each time you manually save a file in Blender, it takes your last save and stores it as an earlier version. You may have already created work in Blender and noticed some `.blend1` and `.blend2` files in the same place you saved your `.blend` files. Those `.blend1` and `.blend2` files are the earlier versions. This option allows you to determine how many of these earlier versions you'd like Blender to retain for you. Each version has a number appended to the end of it, so if you have `MyFile.blend` and you have Save Versions set at 2, then after a few saves, you should see `MyFile.blend`, `MyFile.blend1`, and `MyFile.blend2` all in the same folder.

- **Recent Files:** The number in this field tells Blender how many of your past files to remember when you go to File⇨Open Recent or press Shift+Ctrl+O. You can also use the File Browser (F1 or Ctrl+O) and look on the sidebar under the Recent heading.

- **Save Preview Images:** When this option is enabled, each time you save, Blender embeds a small preview image of your current screen layout, as well as each texture and material in your project, into your `.blend` file. This way, you can use Blender's Image Browser to see materials and textures when you append or link from other files. Also, with this enabled, `.blend` files will show these previews in your operating system's file manager.

- **Auto Save Temporary Files:** Enabled by default, this option is Blender's auto save functionality. It saves a copy of the current state of your file, or what I call a "hot backup", in your Temp directory (adjustable in the File Paths options) every few minutes, as dictated by the Timer field below this button.

Some file paths begin with two forward slashes (//). These slashes are Blender's notation for a *relative path,* or file path as it relates to the location on your hard drive of your current file. In contrast is an *absolute path,* which is the full path to your file from the root of your file system. For example, if you have a file saved as `/home/user/Documents/project.blend`, then the absolute path to `project.blend` is `/home/user/Documents/`. Now say that you have a folder named `textures` in the same folder as your `project.blend` file, and in that folder is an image named `sandpaper.png`. The absolute path to that image is `/home/user/Documents/textures/`, while its relative path (relative to `project.blend`) is `//textures`.

System

Whereas the Interface options dictate how you interact with Blender, the options in the System section, shown in Figure 2-9, tend to dictate more how Blender interacts with you. Many options here are geared toward optimizing for performance, and generally the defaults work well.

Some of the more interesting options follow:

- ✔ **Compute Device:** If you're using Cycles as your renderer, the settings here are pretty important. If your computer has a sufficiently powerful *graphics processing unit* (GPU) — usually this is your computer's video card — Cycles can take advantage of that additional processing power, dramatically reducing the amount of time required for rendering. Depending on your GPU type, you'll want to set this to either

  - CUDA (for NVIDIA GPUs)

  - OpenCL (for AMD/ATI GPUs)

  You can then choose the specific GPU from the drop-down menu.

  If you don't have the kind of GPU that Cycles can take advantage of, there's no need to worry. The Compute Device defaults to None and Cycles will just use your CPU. You can read more about Cycles in Chapter 14.

  As of this writing, the OpenCL option for Compute Device doesn't work particularly well on AMD GPUs. There's hope that it may be fixed and working in the future, but that depends on AMD changing their drivers. In the meantime, if you have an AMD video card, you're probably best keeping the Compute Device option set to None.

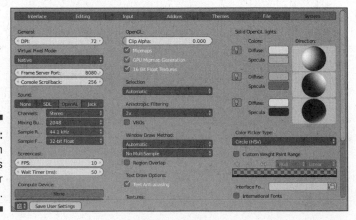

Figure 2-9:
The System options in User Preferences.

✔ **OpenGL:** If Blender is working sluggishly or if the interface looks really odd (noise, strange tears, repeating patterns), these settings are the first place to look to see whether you can get Blender working nicely. In particular, you may want to try enabling *vertex buffer objects* (VBOs). With VBOs enabled, Blender's interface should be snappier on more modern video cards. However, on older hardware, VBOs may cause Blender's screen to behave strangely.

✔ **Window Draw Method:** This drop-down menu is another fine place to look if Blender is displaying bizarrely on you. The default setting of Automatic should give you the best performance on your computer. However, if you're on an older machine, try seeing whether the Overlap or Full methods work better.

✔ **Region Overlap:** If you enable this check box and you have a sufficiently modern video card, the regions in the 3D View (the Properties region and the Tool Shelf) will be semi-transparent, allowing your 3D scene to show through them. Not only is this attractive, but it helps keep as much of your 3D scene visible as possible.

✔ **Solid OpenGL Lights:** With these settings, you can adjust the standard lighting used in your 3D View. Some Blender users set these colors to drastically different settings so that they can have a good sense of each side of their model and more easily see some of the contours. You have the ability to enable up to three lights. On each one, you can adjust the direction of the light by adjusting the X, Y, and Z direction values. You can adjust either of the two colors for the light (main color and highlight or *specularity* color, respectively) by left-clicking them and using the color picker that pops up.

✔ **Color Picker Type:** Speaking of color pickers, Blender gives you the option of a variety of ways to choose colors while working. The default is a circular *hue, saturation, value* (HSV) color picker. It's generally faster to use for choosing colors when painting. However, everyone has different tastes in what color pickers they prefer to use, and some color pickers are better than others for specific purposes. For that reason, a drop-down menu contains a selection of different color pickers that you can use in Blender. Play with the color pickers on the Solid OpenGL Lights and see which one suits you the best.

Using custom event maps

A primary inspiration for the deep structural changes introduced in Blender's code for the 2.5 series was to refactor Blender's *event system*. An event system is required for a complex program to interact with you and me, the users. Each time you press a button or move your mouse, it registers with the program as an *event*. The program then handles the event by performing an action of some sort. As an example, moving your mouse registers as an event, which then triggers your computer to perform the action of updating the location of the mouse cursor on your monitor.

Blender provides you the ability to customize the event system to suit your needs, mapping events to a wide variety of possible Blender operations. Don't like using a particular hotkey in Blender's default configuration? You're free to change it. And that's just the start!

If you refer to Figure 2-5, you should notice that the entire right side of the editor is devoted to modifying how events are handled within Blender. This list of events is particularly daunting to look at, and you can easily get lost among all of those expanding and collapsing categories of events. Fortunately, you can modify how events are handled in a much easier way, and you don't even have use the User Preferences editor if you don't want to. Instead, you can use the following steps:

1. **Find the operation you want to bind in Blender's menu system.**

   Say that you want to change the hotkey for opening a new project from Ctrl+N (the current hotkey) to Ctrl+X, the hotkey used in previous versions of Blender. You can find this operation by going to the Info editor's header and choosing File⇨New. Go to that menu item, but *don't click it* yet. Just hover your mouse cursor over it and proceed to the next step.

2. **Right-click the menu item for the operation you want to add or change hotkeys and choose Change Shortcut from the menu that appears.**

   In this example, go to File⇨New, right-click it, and choose Change Shortcut. Blender prompts you for a new hotkey.

3. **When prompted, use the new hotkey that you want to assign to the operation.**

   In this case, you press Ctrl+X.

   Congratulations! Your new hotkey is assigned!

Figure 2-10 shows this process in action.

As of this writing, Blender doesn't warn you if you attempt to assign a hotkey that has already been bound to another operation. Blender simply double-binds the hotkey, favoring default behaviors over custom ones. Blender's interface will still say your custom hotkey is assigned to the desired action, but it just won't work as expected. Currently, the only way to get around this problem is to make sure that your desired hotkey isn't already assigned.

Figure 2-10:
Customizing
a hotkey
sequence
directly from
Blender's
menus.

Of course, for ultimate control, the Input section of User Preferences is really the way to go. As daunting as this section may appear, it's actually pretty easy to use. The most effective way to make use of the event editor is to use the search feature, a text field with a magnifying glass icon in the upper right corner of the Input section:

1. **In the search filter field, type all or part of the operation you want to customize and press Enter.**

   The listing below updates with Blender's best guesses for the operation you're looking for. Alternatively, you can just drill down through the categories until you find the event you want.

   If you don't know the name of the operator, you can search by the hotkey it uses. Left-click the drop-down menu to the left of the search filter field. You can choose between Name (the default) to search by operator name or Key-Binding to search by hotkey.

2. **Modify the event you want to change.**

   Changing an actual event is much like the process used to add hotkeys to menu items. It works like so:

   1. *Use the Type of Event Mapping drop-down menu displayed to the right or the operation name to stipulate whether the event is coming from a keyboard, mouse, text input, or some other source.* For example, if you're adjusting a hotkey, make sure that you've set it to Keyboard.

2. *Left-click the Type of Event field that comes after the Type of Event Mapping menu.* It will either be blank or already have an event in it. Upon doing so, Blender prompts you for your new custom event (hotkey, mouse click, and so on).

3. *Set the event with the action you want assigned to it.* For example, if you're changing a hotkey, simply enter the key combination you want to use. If you decide that you don't want to change the event, just click anywhere outside of the Event Type field.

While you're editing your events, you might notice that a Restore button appears under the search filter field. At any time, if you decide that you want to revert to the system defaults, click the Restore button. Everything goes back to the way it initially was.

You can also use this interface to activate and deactivate events, delete events, and restore them to their initial values. Furthermore, if you expand the event's details by left-clicking the triangle to the left of the operation name, you have even more advanced controls. Figure 2-11 shows an expanded event.

Figure 2-11: Blender gives you a lot of custom control over its event system.

Customizing the event system can be a pretty involved topic, so if you're really interested in making extensive changes, it's to your benefit to play with the event system editor in the Input section of User Preferences a lot and make heavy use of the Restore buttons so that you can get Blender back to its defaults if something messes up.

After you have your events customized, you can save them to an external file that you can share with other users or simply carry with you on a USB drive so that your customized version of Blender is available wherever you go. To do so, click the Export Key Configuration button at the bottom of the User Preferences editor. A File Browser opens, and you can pick where you want to save your configuration file. The configuration is saved as a Python script. To load your custom configuration, it's possible to load your script in Blender and just run it. However, simply using the Import Key Configuration button at the bottom of the User Preferences editor is much easier.

Navigating in Three Dimensions

The 3D View is probably the most used window type in all of Blender. It also has some of the most unique interface decisions of any 3D software program. The purpose of this section is to guide you to understanding how to wield this part of Blender like a virtual 3D ninja!

All right, so perhaps I am a little over the top with the whole ninja thing, but hopefully this section takes you at least one or two steps closer to that goal.

Orbiting, panning, and zooming the 3D View

When trying to navigate a three-dimensional space through a two-dimensional screen like a computer monitor, you can't interact with that virtual 3D space exactly like you would in the real world, or as I like to call it, *meatspace*. The best way to visualize working in 3D through a program like Blender is to imagine the 3D View as your eyes to this 3D world. But rather than think of yourself as moving through this environment, imagine that you have the ability to move this entire world around in front of you.

The most basic way of navigating this space is called *orbiting*. Orbiting is the rough equivalent of rotating the 3D world around a fixed point in space. In order to orbit in Blender, middle-click anywhere in the 3D View and drag your mouse cursor around.

Occasionally, you have the need to keep your orientation to the world, but you'll want to move it around so that you can see a different part of the scene from the same angle. In Blender, this movement is called *panning*, and you do it by holding Shift while middle-clicking and dragging your mouse cursor in the 3D View. Now when you drag your mouse cursor around, the world shifts around without changing the angle that you're viewing from.

The third way of navigating 3D space is when you want get closer to an object in your scene. Similar to working with a camera, this movement is called *zooming* the view. In Blender, you can zoom in two ways. The easiest method is by using your mouse's scroll wheel. By default, scrolling forward zooms in and scrolling back zooms out. However, this method doesn't always give you fine-grained control, and, even worse, some people don't have a mouse with a scroll wheel. In these cases, you can zoom by holding Ctrl while middle-clicking in the 3D View. Now, when you drag your mouse cursor up, you zoom in, and when you drag your mouse cursor down, you zoom out. If you prefer to move your mouse horizontally instead of vertically for zooming, you can adjust this behavior in the Input section of User Preferences.

Of course, if you happen to be working with a mouse that doesn't have a middle mouse button or you work with a pen and tablet interface, you should go to User Preferences under Input and enable the Emulate 3 Button Mouse check box. With this check box enabled, you can emulate the middle mouse button by pressing Alt+left-click. So orbiting is Alt+left-click, panning is Shift+Alt+left-click, and zooming is done with Ctrl+Alt+left-click. Table 2-1 has a more organized way of showing these hotkeys.

Changing views

Although using the mouse to work your way around the 3D space is the most common way to adjust how you view things, Blender has some menu items and hotkey sequences that help give you specific views much faster and more accurately than you can do alone with your mouse.

The View menu

On occasion, you want to know what a model looks like when it's viewed directly from the front, side, or top. Blender has some convenient shortcuts for quickly switching to these views. The most obvious way is to use the View menu in the 3D View's header, as shown on the left of Figure 2-12. This menu lets you choose a variety of angles, including the top, front, right, and the view from any of the cameras you may have in your scene.

You can also use this menu to switch between orthographic and perspective views. The *orthographic* view of a 3D scene is similar to how technical drawings and blueprints are done. If two objects are the same size, they always appear to be the same size, regardless of how far away from you they are. This view is ideal for getting sizes and proportions correct in your models, especially if they're based on blueprints or technical drawings. The *perspective* view is more akin to how you actually see things. That is, objects in the distance look smaller than objects that are near you.

Table 2-1   Keyboard/Mouse Keys for Navigating 3D Space

Navigation	Three-Button Mouse	Emulated 3-Button Mouse
Orbit	Middle-click	Alt+left-click
Pan	Shift+middle-click	Shift+Alt+left-click
Zoom	Ctrl+middle-click	Ctrl+Alt+left-click

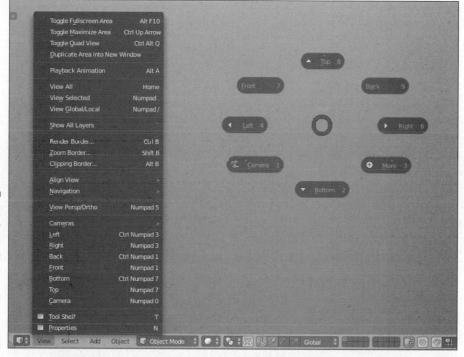

Figure 2-12:
The View
menu in the
3D View
(left) and the
pie menu
version of
the View
menu (right).

If you have the Pie Menus add-on enabled, as described at the end of Chapter 1, there's an even faster menu for changing views. With your mouse cursor hovered over the 3D View, press Q. When you press this hotkey, a pie menu appears under your mouse cursor. The options in this pie menu are conveniently arranged for changing views. Move your mouse cursor up to change to top view, down for bottom view, left and right for their respective views, and so on. It's really incredibly fast. It feels almost like you're flinging the 3D View around in front of you. On the right side of Figure 2-12 is the pie version of the View menu.

Behold the power of the numeric keypad!

The View menu is certainly helpful, even in its pie form, but you can change your view in an even faster way: the numeric keypad. Each button on your keyboard's numeric keypad has an extremely fast way of changing your viewing angle in the 3D View. Figure 2-13 is an image of the numeric keypad with an indication of what each key does.

If the image in Figure 2-13 doesn't quite work for you as a reference, Table 2-2 shows what each key does in a table-based format.

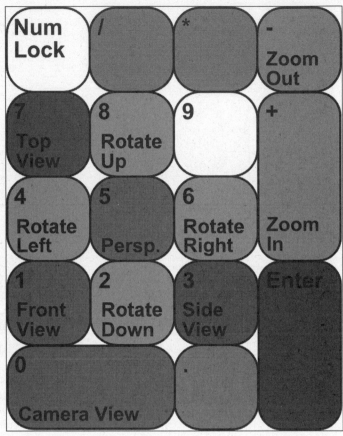

Num Lock

Figure 2-13:
The numeric keypad is your ultimate tool for navigating 3D space.

In Figure 2-13, notice that the hotkeys are arranged in a way that corresponds with how you would expect them to be. Top view is at the top of the keypad at Numpad 7. The front view is accessed at Numpad 1, and if you move to the right on the keypad, you can see the right side view by pressing Numpad 3. Because it's the view you render from, the active camera is the most important and therefore gets the largest key at Numpad 0. Pressing Numpad 5 is a quick way to toggle between orthographic and perspective views. If you have View Name turned on in the Interface section of User Preferences, it actively informs you about which view you're using. And having the very cool Smooth View option enabled definitely helps you keep from getting disoriented while working.

The notions of what is left and right in the 3D View are relative to you, *not* the object or scene you're working in. That is, if you model a character who's facing you from the front view, pressing Numpad 3 (right side view) shows your character's *left* side. This setup can be a bit confusing in writing or conversation, but while you're working, it's really not much of an issue. I actually

Table 2-2		Hotkeys on the Numeric Keypad			
Hotkey	**Result**	**Hotkey**	**Result**	**Hotkey**	**Result**
1	Front	Ctrl+1	Back	+	Zoom in
2	Orbit back	Ctrl+2	Pan down	-	Zoom out
3	Right side	Ctrl+3	Left side	/	Toggle local view
4	Orbit left	Ctrl+4	Pan left	.	View selected
5	Ortho/Persp				
6	Orbit right	Ctrl+6	Pan right		
7	Top	Ctrl+7	Bottom		
8	Orbit forward	Ctrl+8	Pan up		
0	Camera view	Ctrl+0	Set active object as camera	Ctrl+Alt+0	Set user view as camera

tend to think of the right and left side views as *side view* and *other side view* to avoid confusing myself.

Here is where the numeric keypad shows its real power. With the numeric keypad, you can just as easily view the opposite angle (bottom, back, or other side views) as you can the standard views. To see the opposite side of the standard views, press Ctrl while hitting the corresponding Numpad key. For example, if you want to see the bottom view, press Ctrl+Numpad 7.

Now, maybe you got a little bit excited and hit Ctrl+Numpad 0 to see what the opposite of the camera view is and had some unexpected results. Ctrl+Numpad 0 does something entirely different than pressing Ctrl in combination the other Numpad numbers. The Ctrl+Numpad 0 hotkey actually allows you to treat any selectable object in Blender as a camera, with the view looking down the object's local Z-axis. You can also access this functionality from the View menu at View➪Cameras➪Set Active Object as Camera. If you're confused, take a quick look at the beginning of Chapter 3 for more explanation on local and global coordinate systems. The ability to treat any object as a camera may seem like a strange feature to have, but it can be really helpful for doing things like aiming lights and checking the line of sight of an object or a character.

Another cool thing you can do with Numpad 0 is to quickly snap the camera to your user view. For example, say that you've been working on 3D model for a while from a certain angle, and you want to see what the model looks like in a render from that specific angle. Rather than try to grab and rotate your camera to get close to this same angle, you can simply press Ctrl+Alt+Numpad 0 or choose View⇨Align View⇨Align Active Camera to View, and the camera jumps directly to where you're viewing your model. I find myself using this hotkey sequence quite a bit when I'm creating my models. Sometimes it's just easier to change your user view and snap your camera to it than it is to aim the camera how you want it.

The numeric keypad also gives you the ability to navigate your scene like you might normally do with your mouse. You use the 8, 4, 6, and 2 keys on the numeric keypad. Numpad 8 and Numpad 2 orbit the view towards and away, respectively, whereas Numpad 4 and Numpad 6 orbit it left and right. By default, Blender does these rotations in 15-degree increments, but you adjust this amount to be more fine or coarse in User Preferences under Interface with the value labeled Rotation Angle. Orbiting with the Numpad is a nice way to get a quick turntable view of a scene, particularly if you have your View rotation set to Trackball in User Preferences. You can also pan the view by pressing Ctrl in combination with any of these buttons. For example, Ctrl+Numpad 4 and Ctrl+Numpad 6 pan the view left and right. You can even zoom the view by using the Numpad Plus (+) and Numpad Minus (-) keys.

Two more useful hotkeys are on the numeric keypad: Numpad Slash (/) and Numpad Dot (.). These keys are somewhat more esoteric than the other keys, but they definitely come in handy.

Of the two, I tend to use Numpad Slash the most. Pressing Numpad Slash (/) toggles what Blender calls *Local View*. Basically, Local View hides everything in your scene except for the object or objects you've selected. Local View is really helpful for temporarily isolating a single object or set of objects in a complex scene so that you can work on it without anything else getting in your way.

The Numpad Dot (.) hotkey also comes in handy when you want to focus on a specific part of your scene. Pressing Numpad Dot (.) centers the objects you've selected in the 3D View. Centering is particularly useful if you've rotated or panned everything out of sight, and you want to bring your selected objects back into view.

One other key worth mentioning, although it's not exactly on the numeric keypad, is the Home key. Whereas using Numpad Dot (.) brings your selected objects into view, pressing Home zooms your view back until all objects in your scene are visible in the 3D View. Home is a very convenient key for getting an overall idea of what's going on in your scene.

Ways to see your 3D scene

Aside from changing the angle from which you view your 3D world, you may also want to change how the world is shown in the 3D View. In particular, I'm referring to what is called the *viewport shading*. By default, Blender starts in the Solid shading type, which shows your models as solid 3D objects, lit by the OpenGL lights you can set in Blender's User Preferences under System. You can change the viewport shading by going to the 3D View's header and left-clicking the button with a white circular icon, as seen in on the left of Figure 2-14.

Figure 2-14:
Viewport shading types from the 3D View's header (left) and from a pie menu (right).

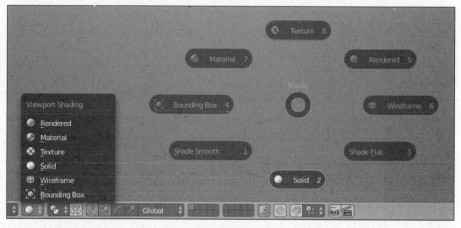

If you have the Pie Menus add-on enabled, you can also change viewport shading type by pressing Z. The options here are the same as the shading types described in the previous paragraph. The only difference is that they're faster to access by using the pie layout. Figure 2-14 has the pie menu of viewport shading types on the right side.

Clicking this button reveals the following possible viewport shading types:

✔ **Rendered:** As you might expect, this renders your scene in the 3D View from whatever arbitrary perspective you want. Depending on the complexity of your scene, this is a great way to get a very accurate preview of your final rendered images.

Fair warning: the Rendered viewport shading type can be extremely slow when using the Blender Internal renderer. It's much more responsive when using Cycles, even more so if you have a powerful GPU. You can toggle this view quickly using Shift+Z.

✔ **Material:** This viewport shading type is only really useful if you're using the Cycles renderer. It gives you a general impression of what the lighting and texturing of your scene will look like when you render it.

✔ **Textured:** The Textured viewport shading type attempts to faithfully show you what your object will look like when textured and lit for the final render. The preview may differ a bit from what the final looks like, but short of rendering, it should give you the best idea to work from. Pressing Alt+Z quickly toggles between this viewport shading type and the Solid one. Note, however, that this viewport shading type works best if you're using the Blender Internal rendering engine. In Cycles, Textured viewport shading shows the currently selected image texture node. See Chapter 8 for more on texturing in Blender.

If you have a modern accelerated video card, you can enable GLSL (OpenGL Shading Language) shaders from the Properties region (View⇨Properties or the N hotkey) under Display⇨Shading. Change this drop-down menu from Multitexture to GLSL; when you use image-based textures, the Textured viewport shading type will be more accurate. More on this topic is in Chapter 8.

✔ **Solid:** Solid is the default viewport shading type that Blender starts with. Press Z to toggle between Solid and Wireframe. For performance reasons, Solid is usually the standard work mode for working in Blender. If you have an older video card, the Textured viewport shading types will perform much slower than this one.

✔ **Wireframe:** This viewport shading type shows the objects in your scene as transparent line-drawings. The wireframe viewport shading type is a good quick way to get an idea of the structure of your models. And because Wireframe is a bunch of lines, Blender doesn't have to worry about shading and therefore doesn't tax your computer's processor as much. On older computers, Blender is a lot more responsive using Wireframe than Solid or Textured.

✔ **Bounding Box:** The Bounding Box draw type replaces your 3D object with a wireframe cube that shows how much space your object takes up in the 3D world. This type isn't as commonly used as the others, but it does come in handy for quickly placing objects in a scene or detecting when two objects might collide. It can also be handy for scenes that feature a lot of complex geometry.

You may also notice that if you have more than one 3D View window, they don't all have to have the same viewport shading type. You can see the wireframe of your model in one editor while adjusting the lighting using the Shaded draw type in another.

Selecting objects

How you select objects is one of the most controversial design decisions in Blender's interface: In nearly every other program, you select things — be they text, 3D objects, files, or whatever — by left-clicking them. This is not the case in Blender. When you left-click in the 3D View, all it seems to do is move around some strange crosshair thing. That "thing" is Blender's 3D cursor. I talk more about the 3D cursor later, but in the meantime, you're probably thinking, "How in the world do I select anything?"

The answer is simple: You select objects in Blender by right-clicking them. Multiple objects are selected and deselected by Shift+right-clicking them.

Although right-clicking to select certainly seems strange, there is actually a reason for doing it this way. This design decision wasn't made at random or just to be different for the sake of being different. There are actually two reasons for doing it this way. One is philosophical, and the other is practical.

- ✔ **Separating selection from action:** In Blender, the left mouse button is intended to be used to perform or confirm an action. You left-click buttons or menus and left-click to confirm the completion of an operation like moving, rotating, or scaling an object, and you use it to place the 3D cursor. Selecting an object doesn't really act upon it or change it. So right-click is used to select objects as well as cancel an operation before it's completed. This setup is a bit abstract, but as you work this way, it does actually begin to make sense. A functional example would be interacting with the 3D manipulator (as covered in Chapter 3). If action and selection are on the same mouse button, it becomes too easy to accidentally move an object using the 3D manipulator when you only meant to select, and vice versa.

- ✔ **Prevention of Repetitive Stress Injury (RSI):** Computer graphics artists like 3D modelers and animators are known for working at a computer for insanely long stretches of time. Repetitive stress injury, or RSI, is a real concern. The more you can spread the work across the hand, the lower the chance of RSI. By making it so that you're not doing every single operation with the left mouse button, Blender helps in this regard.

Bottom line, the right-click-to-select paradigm really is a nice, efficient way of working in 3D space after you get used to it. However, if you try it and still don't like it, Blender offers you the ability to swap left and right mouse button usage in the Input section of User Preferences. Do note, however, that this book is written with the default right-click behavior in mind, so remember that as you read other chapters.

Taking advantage of the 3D cursor

"Okay," you say, "I can handle the right-click-to-select thing. But what's with these crosshairs that move to where ever I left-click? It seems pretty useless."

Those crosshairs are the 3D cursor. It's a unique concept that I've only seen in Blender, and this design is anything but useless. The best way to understand the 3D cursor is to think about a word processor or text editor. When you add text or want to change something in one of those programs, it's usually done with or relative to the blinking cursor on the screen. Blender's 3D cursor serves pretty much the same purpose, but in three dimensions. When you add a new object, it's placed wherever the 3D cursor is located. When you rotate or scale an object, you can do it relative to the 3D cursor's location. And when you want to snap an object to a specific location, you do it with the 3D cursor.

In terms of adjusting your 3D View, you can use the 3D cursor as a quick way to recenter your view. Simply place the 3D cursor anywhere in the 3D View by left-clicking. Now press Alt+Home and watch as the 3D View adjusts to put the cursor at the center of the window. This is similar to pressing Numpad Dot (.), except that you don't have to select any objects. Another convenient hotkey sequence is Shift+C. This combination relocates the 3D cursor to the origin coordinates of the 3D environment and then brings all objects into view. The Shift+C hotkey combination is like pressing Home with the added benefit of moving the cursor to the origin.

In Chapter 3, I cover the topic of grabbing, scaling, and rotating objects. Usually, you want to use Blender's default behavior of doing these operations relative to the median point of the selected objects. However, you can also perform any of these operations relative to the 3D cursor by pressing the Period (.) key on your keyboard or selecting 3D Cursor from the Pivot menu in the 3D View's header, as shown in on the left of Figure 2-15. You can use this menu to switch back to the default behavior or press Comma (,).

If you have the Pie Menus add-on enabled, pressing Period (.) does *not* automatically toggle. Instead, pressing that hotkey brings up a pie menu version of the Pivot menu, as shown on the right of Figure 2-15.

The 3D cursor is also very useful for *snapping*, or moving a selection to a specific point in space. For a better idea of what snapping means, hover your mouse over the 3D View and press Shift+S. A menu like the one in Figure 2-16 appears.

Through this menu, you can snap your selected object to a fixed coordinate on the grid in the 3D View, the location of the 3D cursor, or to the center of

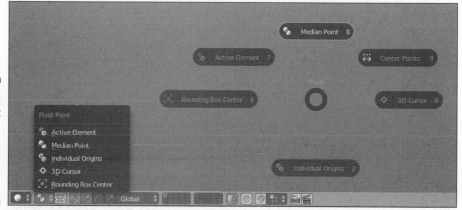

Figure 2-15: The Pivot menu in the 3D View's header (left) and as a pie menu (right).

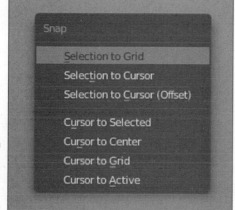

Figure 2-16: The Snap menu.

the grid, also known as the *origin* of the scene. You also have the ability to snap the 3D cursor to the middle of multiple selected objects, a fixed location on the grid, or to the active object in the scene. This method is a very effective way to move an object to a specific point in 3D space, and it's all thanks to the little 3D cursor.

Extra Features in the 3D View

A handful of additional features in Blender's 3D View are worth mentioning before closing this chapter. They can be classified as productivity enhancers, learning aids, or comfort features for users migrating from other programs. This section outlines a few of these features.

Quad View

If you've used other 3D graphics programs, you may be used to something referred to as *Quad View,* where the 3D View is split into four regions: top, front, and right orthographic views, along with a user perspective view. You *can* create a layout similar to this through the somewhat arduous task of manually splitting areas and then setting up each area as a 3D View from each of those perspectives. However, with no way to lock those views in place, you could very easily change one of your orthographic views to user perspective on accident. Fortunately, there's a better way. Go to the 3D View's header and click View➪Toggle Quad View or use the hotkey Ctrl+Alt+Q, and your 3D View will switch to look like the one in Figure 2-17.

When toggling back to Full View from Quad View, Blender chooses the view that your mouse cursor is hovering over when you do the switch. As a result, when you use the View menu (View➪Toggle Quad View), you'll almost always pop back to the top view. However, if you use the Ctrl+Alt+Q hotkey with your mouse cursor over one of the other views, Blender will pick that one as Full View.

Regions

In Chapter 1, I briefly describe regions as areas in an editor that give you additional tools specific to that editor. In fact, you've already had exposure

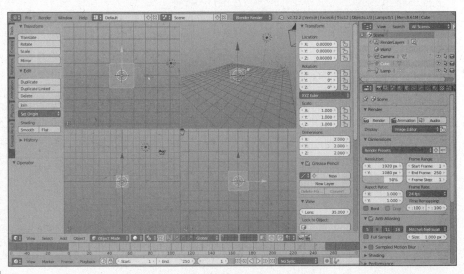

Figure 2-17: Using the Ctrl+Alt+Q hotkey, you can quickly switch between Blender's regular viewport and a Quad View viewport like some other 3D programs have.

to one type of region in this chapter: the header. Figure 2-17 shows the other two regions in Blender's 3D View.

Flanking either side of the 3D View is a Tool Shelf on the left, and on the right is a region for modifying the properties of the 3D View, referred to as the Properties region or the Information region.

The Properties/Information region

You can toggle the visibility of the Properties region by going to View⇨Properties in the header or by pressing N (for iNformation) while your mouse cursor is in the 3D View. In fact, quite a few editors in Blender have a Properties region. And with the exception of the Text Editor, you can consistently open all of them by using the N hotkey.

In the 3D View, the Properties region serves two primary purposes. Most obviously, it allows you to directly modify your selected object by typing in explicit location, rotation, and scale values within the Transform panel. The rest of the region, however, is dedicated to customizing your 3D View. From here, you can control features like the location of the 3D cursor, which axes are displayed, the appearance of the grid floor, and the shading mode used for the Textured Viewport Shading type (Multitexture or GLSL). This region is also where you go if you want to load a background image in the 3D View as a modeling reference. You can find out more about using background images for modeling in Chapter 5.

Because Blender has a Properties editor as well as a Properties region, you may find it useful to think of the Properties region as an Information region instead. It's a game of semantics, but by thinking of it as an Information region, the N hotkey is easier to remember. Throughout the rest of the book, I'll be referring to it as either the Information region or the Properties region for the editor you're working in.

The Tool Shelf

The real gem of a region within the 3D View is the Tool Shelf, shown on the left of the 3D View by default. You can toggle the Tool Shelf's visibility by going to View⇨Tool Shelf in the header or by using the T hotkey.

Think of the Tool Shelf as a place for frequently used tools or operators. Most of these operators also are accessible by hotkey or some other menu, but having shortcuts in the Tool Shelf is extremely helpful for helping you work faster, especially if you haven't memorized all of Blender's various hotkeys. This way, frequently used tools are only a single click away rather than the multiple clicks it might take you to hunt through the menu system. And when it comes to Blender's sculpting and painting tools (covered in Chapter 5 and 8, respectively), the Tool Shelf is indispensable.

The Tool Shelf holds an additional feature that's extremely useful. At the bottom of the Tool Shelf is the Last Operator panel. If you've just opened Blender, this panel should just have the heading of Operator. However, if you perform an action in Blender like moving your selected object or adding a new object, this panel updates to display values relevant to that operation. Using this panel, you can perform a quick, rough operation and then tweak it to be more precise. For example, if you add a UV Sphere to your scene (Shift+A⇨Add Mesh⇨UV Sphere), Blender adds a UV Sphere object to your scene at the location of the 3D cursor with 32 segments and 24 rings. Using the Last Operator panel of the Tool Shelf, you can not only adjust the location of your new sphere, but you can also modify the number of segments and rings it has. You can see more on how the Last Operator panel is used in Chapter 5.

If you happen to have the Tool Shelf hidden, you can still access the last operator panel by pressing F6. Upon doing so, a "floating" Last Operator appears under your mouse cursor. Figure 2-18 shows the floating last operator panel after adding a UV sphere to the scene.

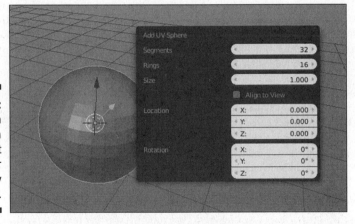

Figure 2-18: You can bring up a floating Last Operator panel by pressing F6.

You should note that the Last Operator panel is only relevant for the last operation you actually performed. It's not a construction history, and it doesn't persistently remain in memory after you perform subsequent operations. For example, if you add a UV Sphere and then immediately rotate that sphere, there's no way for you to adjust the number of segments and rings in it from the Last Operator section. Even if you undo the rotate operation, those Last Operator values won't return (after all, Undo is another operation). The Last Operator section relates to the last thing you did — no more, no less.

Don't know how to do something? Hooray for fully integrated search!

Blender has a search feature that's fully integrated into Blender's interface. If you've been working your way through this chapter, you've probably already used it when adding custom event maps.

The benefit here is that if you know the operation you want to perform, but don't know where to go in Blender's interface to access it, you can simply search for that operator and perform it immediately. How's that for awesome?

The fastest way to access Blender's integrated search feature from any editor is to press Spacebar. A blank menu with a search field at the top appears. From here, simply start typing the name of the operator you want, and Blender updates the menu with search results that match what you've typed. Furthermore, if a hotkey is associated with that operation, it shows up to the right of the operator name in the menu so that you can remember the hotkey in the future. As an example, bring up the search menu (Spacebar) and type **save**. As you type, the menu updates with operations within Blender that relate to saving.

Using the integrated search feature is a great way to familiarize yourself with the way Blender works, even more so if you're migrating from another program. In that case, you know the terminology for what you want to do; you just have to find out how Blender does it. Figure 2-19 shows Blender's integrated search menu.

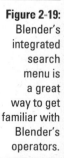

Figure 2-19: Blender's integrated search menu is a great way to get familiar with Blender's operators.

Getting Your Hands Dirty Working in Blender

*B*lender is built for speed, and its design heavily emphasizes working as quickly and efficiently as possible for extended periods of time. On more than one occasion, I've found myself working in Blender for 10 to 15 hours straight (or longer). Although, admittedly, part of this ridiculous scheduling has to do with my own minor lunacy, the fact that I'm able to be that productive for that long is a testament to Blender's design. This chapter gets you started in taking full advantage of that power. I cover the meat and potatoes of interacting with three-dimensional (3D) space in Blender, such as moving objects and editing polygons.

If you've worked in other 3D programs, chances are good that a number of Blender concepts may seem particularly alien to you. Although this divide is reduced with each update, to quote Yoda, "You must unlearn what you have learned" in your journey to become a Blender Jedi. If you've never worked in 3D, you may actually have a slight advantage over a trained professional who's used to a different workflow. Hooray for starting fresh!

Grabbing, Scaling, and Rotating

The three most basic ways of changing an object in a 3D scene are called *transformations* by mathematicians. Blenderese is much more colorful:

✔ Change location using *translation*.

✔ Change size using *scale*.

✔ Change rotation using *orientation*.

Rather than use the mathematical terms of translation, scale, and orientation, people who speak Blenderese use the terms *grab*, *scale*, and *rotate*, respectively. Other programs might use the term *move* in place of grab or *size* in place of scale. Whatever you call them, and whatever program you use, these three operations place any object in 3D space at any arbitrary size and with any arbitrary orientation.

Differentiating Between Coordinate Systems

Before you bound headlong into applying transformations to your objects, you need to understand how coordinate systems work in 3D space. All coordinate systems in Blender are based on a grid consisting of three axes:

- The *X-axis* typically represents side-to-side movement.
- The *Y-axis* represents front-to-back movement.
- The *Z-axis* goes from top to bottom.

This grid system with axes is referred to as the Cartesian grid. The origin, or center, of this grid is at the (0,0,0) coordinate. The difference in the coordinate systems within Blender lies in the way this grid is oriented relative to a selected 3D object. Figure 3-1 shows the Transform Orientation menu in the 3D View header when you left-click it.

If you're coming from another 3D program, you may find the way Blender handles coordinates a bit disorienting. Some programs (such as Cinema 4D and Maya) have the Y-axis representing vertical movement and the Z-axis going from front to back. Currently, you can't change the coordinate system in Blender to match these programs, so this system is one of those things that migrating users just need to get used to.

Figure 3-1:
The Transform Orientation menu.

As Figure 3-1 shows, you can choose from five orientations: *Global, Local, Normal, View,* and *Gimbal.* Working in any of these coordinate systems gives you absolute control of how your object lives in 3D space. Depending on how you'd like to transform your object, one orientation may be more appropriate than the others. Blender also gives you the ability to create custom orientations. That topic is slightly more advanced than I have room to cover in this book, but after you create a custom orientation, it also becomes available on the Transform Orientation menu.

This list describes details of the five possible orientations:

- **Global:** You see this orientation of Blender's base grid in the 3D View. In many ways, the Global orientation is the primary orientation to which everything else relates, and it's the base coordinate system described at the beginning of this section. The Z-axis, marked in blue, runs vertically in the space. The Y-axis is marked in green, moving along the front-to-back line, and the X-axis is in red, along the side-to-side line. The origin is located directly at the center of the grid.

- **Local:** In addition to the Global orientation, each 3D object in Blender has a local coordinate system. The base of this system isn't the same as the Global coordinate system's base. Instead, this coordinate system is relative to the center point, or origin, of your object. The *object origin* is represented by the orange dot that's usually located at the center of your 3D object. By default, when you first add a new object in Blender, its Local coordinate system of the object is aligned to the Global axis, but after you start moving your object around, its Local coordinate system can differ greatly from the Global orientation.

- **Normal:** The Normal orientation is a set of axes that's perpendicular to some arbitrary plane. When working with just objects, this description doesn't really apply, so the Normal orientation is exactly the same as the Local orientation. When you begin editing meshes, though, Normal orientation makes more sense because you have *normals* (imaginary lines that extend perpendicular to the surface of a triangle or plane) to work with. Blender also uses the Normal orientation for the local coordinate system of bones when working with Armatures for animation. A nice way to think about the Normal orientation is the "more local than local" orientation. Chapter 4 covers editing meshes in more detail, and Chapter 11 covers working with Armatures in depth.

- **Gimbal:** When you rotate an object about its X, Y, and Z axes, the angles about those axes are known as Euler (pronounced like *oiler*) angles.

Unfortunately, a side effect of using Euler angles is that you have the possibility of running into *gimbal lock.* You run into this problem when one of your rotation axes matches another one. For example, if you rotate your object 90 degrees about its X-axis, then rotating around its Y-axis is the same as rotating about its Z-axis; mathematically speaking, they're *locked* together, which can be a problem, especially when animating. This orientation mode in Blender helps you visualize where the axes are, so you can avoid gimbal lock.

✔ **View:** The View orientation appears relative to how you're looking at the 3D View. Regardless of how you move around in a scene, you're always looking down the Z-axis of the View coordinate system. The Y-axis is always vertical, and the X-axis is always horizontal in this orientation.

All these coordinate system explanations can be (please forgive the pun) disorienting. An easy way to visualize this concept is to imagine that your body represents the Global coordinate system, and this book is a 3D object oriented in space. If you hold the book out in front of you and straighten your arms, you move the book away from you. It's moving in the positive Y direction, both globally and locally. Now, if you twist the book to the right a few degrees and do the same thing, it still moves in the positive Y direction globally. However, in its local orientation, the book is moving in both a positive Y direction and a negative X direction. To move it in just the positive local Y direction, you move the book in the direction in which its spine is pointing.

To relate this concept to the View orientation, assume that your eyes are the View axis. If you look straight ahead and move the book up and down, you're translating it along the View orientation's Y-axis. Gimbal orientation would be if you rotate the book 90 degrees toward you, rotating about its X-axis. Then it's Y and Z axes are locked together. For a clear reference, the 3D manipulator in Figure 3-2 shows the difference between the coordinate systems.

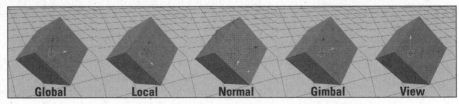

Figure 3-2:
The Global, Local, View, Gimbal, and Normal coordinate orientations.

Global   Local   Normal   Gimbal   View

The last object you select is the *active* object. If you're using the Local, Gimbal, or Normal orientations and select multiple objects, the transform operations happen relative to the active object's orientation.

You can quickly change the coordinate system you're using by using the Alt+Spacebar hotkey.

Transforming an Object by Using the 3D Manipulator

In Blender's default configuration, the 3D *manipulator* is activated and viewable at the center of your selected object. You can use the manipulator to transform any object in a 3D scene. When Blender first starts, the manipulator is in Translate (Grab) mode, which you can determine in two ways:

✔ The manipulator itself looks like a set of colored axes located at the center of the selected object.

✔ In the 3D View's header, the button with the blue arrow icon on it is depressed to indicate that the manipulator is in Translate mode. By default, the manipulator is oriented to align with the Global axis.

In all transform orientations under Blender, red represents the X-axis, green the Y, and blue the Z. If you think about the primary colors for light, a handy way to think of this is XYZ = RGB.

Switching manipulator modes

As you might expect, translation isn't the only transform operation available to you with the manipulator. If you refer to the 3D View's header to the left of where the Transform Orientation menu is located, the button with the blue arc icon on it activates Rotation manipulator mode, and the button with the icon of a line connecting to the corner of a square activates Scale mode. Press the Rotation mode button to see the change in the look of the 3D manipulator. In this mode, the manipulator is a set of semicircles around the object's center, with the proper color representing each axis. Left-clicking the Scale mode button for the manipulator changes it to look much like it does in Translate mode, except that you see a small cube, rather than an arrow, at the end of each axis.

The 3D manipulator should be familiar to you if you've used other programs, where the corresponding tool might be called a *widget* or a *gizmo.* However, the Blender manipulator also does something else: It lets you activate multiple modes at the same time as a *combo manipulator.* Hold down Shift while pressing the appropriate button to activate a manipulator. You can then make any combination of transform modes active simultaneously. Many Blender users find this capability particularly helpful for animation, where some situations require quick access to translation and rotation but not necessarily to adjust the object's scale. Figure 3-3 shows the three separate modes of the manipulator, as well as the combo manipulator.

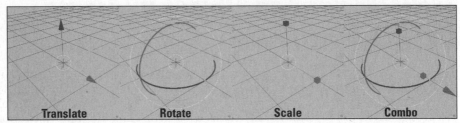

Figure 3-3:
The
Translate,
Rotate,
Scale, and
Combo
manipulator
modes.

Translate   Rotate   Scale   Combo

Using the manipulator

To translate a selected object with the manipulator, follow these steps:

1. **Make sure that Translate mode is active by left-clicking the Translate manipulator mode button in the 3D View's header.**

2. **Left-click the manipulator arrow that points in the direction you want to move the object and drag to the location where you want to place your object.**

   For example, to move an object along the X-axis, left-click the red arrow on the manipulator. To cancel the operation, right-click or press Esc.

Notice also the white circle around the origin of the Translate manipulator in Figure 3-3. To translate a selected object in the X- and Y-axis of the View orientation, left-click and drag this circle. This convenient shortcut prevents you from having to continually switch orientation modes for the manipulator.

You can use the Ctrl and Shift while transforming to have more control. Move in fixed increments with default settings by holding down Ctrl. Hold down Shift while transforming an object to make adjustments on a finer scale. Hold down the Ctrl+Shift key combo while transforming to make adjustments in smaller fixed increments. Interestingly, these same modifier keys work when using any of Blender's value input fields.

This fixed-increment control is similar to (though not exactly the same as) the basic *snapping to the grid*, or *increment* snapping, found in other 2D and 3D applications. Blender also offers the ability to snap your selected object to other objects (or parts of them), called *snap targets,* in your scene. Choices for snap targets are *Increment*, *Vertex*, *Edge, Face*, and *Volume*. Unfortunately, grid snapping is not currently implemented in Blender, so that may be somewhat disorienting if you're migrating from another application. You choose which snap target you want to use by left-clicking the Snap Element menu in the 3D View's header, as shown in Figure 3-4.

Figure 3-4:
The Snap
Target
Mode
button.

Holding Ctrl while transforming is actually a way to temporarily enable snapping behavior based on a chosen snap target. However, you may prefer snapping to be the default behavior (so you don't have to hold down Ctrl). You can enable snapping by left-clicking the magnet icon next to the Snap Element menu in the 3D View's header or by using the Shift+Tab hotkey. This option tells Blender to snap as default and that holding down Ctrl then temporarily disables snapping.

Here are the different available types of snap targets in Blender:

- **Increment:** In Blender's default behavior, your selection is snapped to fixed increments of Blender's base unit.

- **Vertex:** The vertex is the fundamental element of a mesh object in Blender. Using this target, the center of your selection snaps to vertices or points (for curves and armatures) in other objects.

- **Edge:** The line connecting vertices is referred to as an *edge*. Select this target to snap your selection to edges in objects of your scene.

- **Face:** Edges connect to one another to create polygons, referred to as *faces*. Choose this option to snap to them with your selection.

- **Volume:** When faces connect to create a surface, that closed surface is referred to as a *volume*. You can choose this option to snap your selection to an object's volume. This option is particularly useful when creating a rig for animating characters, as described in Chapter 11.

Snapping targets work in both Object mode as well as Edit mode. For more information on Edit mode, vertices, edges, and faces, see Chapter 4.

You can quickly change snap modes by using the Shift+Ctrl+Tab hotkey combination. If you use this hotkey with pie menus enabled, you also have the option of enabling and disabling snapping directly from the menu.

You can observe the changes made to your object in real time by looking in the 3D View's header (remember, it's at the bottom of the 3D View by default) as you transform it. Figure 3-5 shows how the header explicitly indicates how much you're changing the object in each axis.

Figure 3-5:
You can
view
changes
in the 3D
View's
header.

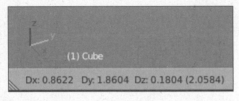

(1) Cube

Dx: 0.8622   Dy: 1.8604   Dz: 0.1804 (2.0584)

Suppose that you don't want to move the object in the direction of just one axis. Instead, you prefer the freedom to move the object in the plane created by two axes, such as the XY, XZ, or YZ planes. Just Shift+left-click on the axis that's perpendicular to the plane in which you want to move. This axis is the one that's normal to the plane. For example, assuming that you want to scale the object in the XY plane, Shift+left-click the Z-axis cube of the Scale manipulator.

I use this technique a lot when modeling furniture and buildings. I can quickly scale a cube with the proper depth along a single plane to create a tabletop or a wall.

Transform operations are consistent across all manipulator modes in Blender, so you can apply any of these methods of interacting with the Translate manipulator in the Rotate and Scale manipulator modes. The only exception is that Shift+left-clicking an axis on the Rotate manipulator operates just like simply left-clicking the axis: It doesn't make sense to try to simultaneously rotate around two axes with any form of control. And don't forget that you aren't limited to working in just the Global coordinate system. You can choose any of the other four orientations from the Transform Orientation menu and the 3D manipulator adjusts to fit that orientation.

Saving Time by Using Hotkeys

Many Blender users find that the manipulator obstructs their view too much when working, so they disable it outright. To disable the manipulator, go to the 3D View's header near the manipulator mode buttons and click the button with the color axis icon. Alternatively, you can press Ctrl+Spacebar.

If you have the Pie Menus add-on enabled, the Ctrl+Spacebar hotkey lets you choose which manipulator you see, in addition to the option of disabling them altogether.

But wait, with the manipulator gone, how do I transform my objects? I'm glad you asked. Enter one of the most powerful features of Blender: hotkeys.

Part of the beauty of Blender's hotkeys are that they take a lot of pressure off of your mouse hand and shorten the distance of mouse-based operations. The accumulation of these little time-saving actions is what makes using hotkeys so powerful.

The default hotkey configuration in Blender is currently in a bit of a state of flux. Blender's user interface team is in the process of rolling out a new set of hotkey defaults. However, since there's a large number of Blender users that are very used to the current hotkeys, the new set is being rolled out slowly. As of this writing, the defaults are the same as they've ever been, though they're likely to change in the months and years to come. Nevertheless, even when Blender gets a new set of default hotkeys, the ones described in this book will still work as a user-configurable option.

Transforming with hotkeys

You can access nearly every piece of major functionality in Blender with hotkeys. Transforms are no exception. *Translating* in Blenderese is called *grabbing*. That naming has specific significance as it pertains to hotkeys. To see what I mean, use the following steps to Grab/Translate your object:

1. **Select the object you want to move by right-clicking it.**

2. **Press G.**

   Congratulations! You're translating your object.

3. **Confirm the translation by left-clicking or pressing Enter.**

   Cancel by right-clicking or pressing Esc.

To rotate your object, press R. Scale it by pressing S. See a pattern here? The majority of Blender's default hotkeys are easy to remember. Most of them just use the first letter from the operation in question. And just like when using the manipulator, the familiar Ctrl, Shift, and Ctrl+Shift keypresses for snapping and fine adjustments still apply.

Also, because Blender tries to maintain consistency throughout its interface, you can use these hotkeys in more than just the 3D View. For example, the same grab and scale operations work when you edit keyframes and motion curves in the Graph Editor. How's that for convenient?

In addition to emphasizing efficiency, Blender is designed to allow you to work for as long as possible while incurring the least amount of repetitive stress. For this reason, relatively few operations in Blender require you to hold down a key. Typically, you press and release a key to begin the operation; you confirm its completion by left-clicking with your mouse or pressing Enter. To cancel the operation instead of confirming, right-click or press Esc. In fact, this keyboard combination even works on some operations that require you to hold down a button. For example, if you try to split an area (left-click and drag a corner widget) and then decide you don't actually want to split it, you can right-click while adjusting the boundary between areas; the operation stops.

Hotkeys and coordinate systems

By default, your transformations all happen in the View coordinate system when you use hotkeys. So no matter how you're viewing the scene, you're working in the XY-plane of the 3D View.

Suppose, however, that you want to grab your object and move it in the global Z-axis. You use a sequence of keypresses to do this action. Use the following steps to grab an object and move it to the global Z-axis:

1. **With your object selected, press G.**

   You're now in Grab/Translate mode.

2. **Without canceling this operation, press Z.**

   A blue line should appear that indicates the global Z-axis. Your object is locked to move only along that line. If you press Y, your object moves only along the global Y-axis and pressing X locks it to the global X-axis.

Pretty neat, huh? This method of using a sequence of hotkeys works with rotating and scaling as well (for example, R⇨Z rotates around the global Z-axis and S⇨X scales along the global X-axis).

What about the Local orientation? That's just one more keypress in the sequence. Follow these steps to grab an object and move it along its local Y-axis:

1. **Act like you are going to translate the object in the global Y-axis by pressing G⇨Y.**

2. **Press Y a second time.**

    You're translating in the local Y-axis. Pressing Y a third time brings you back into moving in the default View coordinate system.

If you want to use the Normal or Gimbal orientations, you can use the same preceding sequence. You just have to make sure that your Transform Orientation is set to either Normal or Gimbal. Even though the 3D manipulator is disabled, Blender still pays attention to your choice here when you press the axis letter for the second time.

Again, this method of using a sequence of keypresses works with scaling and rotation as well. Keying the sequence R⇨X⇨X rotates around the local X-axis and S⇨Z⇨Z scales along the local Z-axis.

One of the more powerful features of the 3D manipulator is the ability to work in a plane rather than just one axis. You can work in a plane with hotkeys as well by using the same logic used in the manipulator. Use Shift plus the letter of the axis that's perpendicular to the plane you want to move in. For example, to scale your object in the global XY-plane, press S⇨Shift+Z. For the local XY plane, press S⇨Shift+Z⇨Shift+Z. This same methodology also works for the Grab operation (though, like with the manipulator, not for the Rotate operation).

Table 3-1 shows most of the useful hotkey sequences for transforming your objects.

An even faster way to constrain to axes involves using the middle mouse button. As an example, select an object and grab (G) it. Now move your mouse in roughly the direction of the X-axis and then middle-click. A red line should appear through your object's origin, and the object should be locked to moving along that line, constraining you to that axis. The same thing works in both the Y- and Z-axes. For an even more interactive way of constraining axes, hold down your middle mouse button while you're grabbing. All three axes appear, and your object locks to one of them as you bring your mouse closer to them. I absolutely *love* this feature.

While you're working with hotkeys to transform your objects in Blender, it's worth noting that Blender has a *tweak mode* that allows for making very fast grab adjustments with your mouse. To activate tweak mode, select (right-click)

Table 3-1	Useful Hotkey Sequences for Transformations		
Grab	*Scale*	*Rotate*	*Orientation*
G	S	R	View
G⇨Z	S⇨Z	R⇨Z	Global Z-axis
G⇨Y	S⇨Y	R⇨Y	Global Y-axis
G⇨X	S⇨X	R⇨X	Global X-axis
G⇨Z⇨Z	S⇨Z⇨Z	R⇨Z⇨Z	Local Z-axis
G⇨Y⇨Y	S⇨Y⇨Y	R⇨Y⇨Y	Local Y-axis
G⇨X⇨X	S⇨X⇨X	R⇨X⇨X	Local X-axis
G⇨Shift+Z	S⇨Shift+Z	N/A	Global XY-plane
G⇨Shift+Y	S⇨Shift+Y	N/A	Global XZ-plane
G⇨Shift+X	S⇨Shift+X	N/A	Global YZ-plane
G⇨Shift+Z⇨Shift+Z	S⇨Shift+Z⇨Shift+Z	N/A	Local XY-plane
G⇨Shift+Y⇨Shift+Y	S⇨Shift+Y⇨Shift+Y	N/A	Local XZ-plane

the object or subobject (vertex, control point, and so on) you want to move and (while still holding down the mouse button) drag your mouse cursor in any direction. This shortcut takes you right into grabbing as if you'd selected the object and then pressed G, only faster! Many beginning users find themselves accidentally popping into tweak mode by moving their mouse while selecting. Now that you know how tweak mode works, you won't be caught by surprise, and you can take full advantage of this time-saving feature.

Numerical input

Not only can you use hotkeys to activate the various transform modes, but you can also use the keyboard to explicitly input exactly how much you would like your object to be transformed. Simply type the number of units you want to change after you activate the transform mode.

As an example, suppose that you want to rotate your object 32 degrees around the global X-axis. To do so, press R⇨X⇨32 and confirm by pressing Enter. Translate your object -26.4 units along its local Y-axis by pressing G⇨Y⇨Y⇨-26.4⇨Enter. These steps can be a very quick and effective means of flipping or mirroring an object because mirroring is just scaling by -1 along a particular axis. For example, to flip an object along the global Z-axis, press S⇨Z⇨-1⇨Enter. For consistency, these numerical input operations are also available when using the 3D manipulator.

A recent addition to Blender is the ability to use simple mathematical equations as part of the numerical input system. To take advantage of this feature, press the Equals (=) key before entering your numerical input. As an example, say you have a model of a car that's 13 Blender units long; you want to move it along the Y-axis by 6 car lengths. Sure, you could do the math in your head (or with a calculator, if necessary), but it's even easier to let Blender handle the math for you by pressing G⇨Y⇨=13*6⇨Enter. This *equation mode* of numerical input even allows for simple math functions and constants, such as sine, cosine, and pi (π). So, if you find that you need to rotate an object about its X-axis by the cosine of 2π (that's 1^, by the way), you could use the following key sequence: R⇨X⇨=cos(2*pi)⇨Enter. If you're coming from an industrial design or architecture background, this is an immensely useful feature.

The Properties region

One other way to explicitly translate, scale, and rotate your object is through the Properties/Information region (see Chapter 2) of the 3D View. To reveal this region, go to View⇨Properties in the 3D View's header or press N while

Blender's layer system

If, as a first-time Blender user, you rush to try to move your object around by attempting to use *M* as a hotkey, you may be surprised when Blender presents you with a funky pop-up panel of 20 unlabeled buttons. Interestingly, the *M* hotkey does activate a move function, but not like you'd expect. It allows you to move your object to one or more layers. Each button in the pop-up panel represents a single Blender layer. Left-click a button, and your selected object moves to that layer.

Blender's layer system is pretty unique among computer graphics software; the layers aren't layers in the traditional sense, where they're arranged in a stack and objects can live in only one layer at a time. Instead, Blender has exactly 20 layers and objects can simultaneously live on multiple layers. As a result, Blender layers tend to be treated as a quick way of grouping objects.

You can control which layers are visible by using the block of layer buttons in the 3D View's header. You can tell if a layer has objects in it at a glance by checking to see if the layer button has an orange circle within it. Shift+left-click a layer button to toggle its visibility. Left-clicking Shift+any layer button makes that layer visible and all others hidden. Pressing the Tilde (~) key makes all layers visible.

A neat feature allows you to arbitrarily enable or disable multiple layers at once, both in the 3D View's header and when moving an object between layers. If you Shift+left-click a layer button to enable or disable it, keep your mouse button pressed; you can drag your mouse cursor around the layer buttons, enabling whichever layers your cursor floats over. This also works in other parts of Blender's interface. Although this feature is most useful in layers, you can use it for check boxes, toggles, and radio buttons, too.

your mouse cursor is in the 3D View. The Properties region sits along the right side of the 3D View and includes a Transform panel that allows you to explicitly enter numerical values (and simple math expressions) for Location, Scale, and Rotation. Close the Properties region the same way that you open it.

When in Object mode, the values in the Properties region don't change depending on which coordinate system you've selected. Location and Rotation are always in the Global orientation, whereas Scale is always in Local.

Chapter 4

Working in Edit Mode and Object Mode

In This Chapter
▶ Making changes to your 3D objects
▶ Adding new objects to a scene
▶ Saving, opening, and appending .blend files

*W*hen working on a scene in Blender, your life revolves around repeatedly selecting objects, transforming them, editing them, and relating them to one another. You regularly shift from dealing with your model in Object mode to doing refinements in Edit mode.

And this process isn't only for modeling, but also for most of the other heavy tasks performed in Blender. Therefore, you can reuse the skills you pick up in this chapter in parts of Blender that have nothing to do with 3D modeling, such as animating, rigging, compositing, and motion tracking. Just as many of the transform operations work in editors other than the 3D View, many of the concepts here transfer nicely to other parts of Blender. Even if you don't know how to do something, chances are good that if you think like Blender thinks, you'll be able to make a successful guess.

Making Changes by Using Edit Mode

Moving primitive objects around is fun and all, but you're interested in getting in there and completely changing the primitive objects that ship with Blender (described in detail in this chapter) to match your vision. You want to do 3D modeling. Well, you're in the right place. This section introduces you to Edit mode, a concept that's deeply embedded throughout Blender for editing objects. Even though this section is focused mostly on polygon modeling, also called *mesh editing,* most of the same principles apply for editing curves, surfaces, armatures, and even text.

When you understand how Blender thinks, figuring out unknown parts of the program is much easier.

Distinguishing between Object mode and Edit mode

In Chapter 3, you do everything in Object mode. As its name indicates, Object mode is where you work with whole objects. However, Object mode isn't very useful for actually changing the internal structure of your object. For example, select (right-click) the cube in the default scene. You know that you can turn it into a more rectangular shape by scaling it along one of the axes. But what if you want to turn the cube into a pyramid? You need to modify the actual components that make up the cube. These changes are made by entering Edit mode.

You can get to Edit mode in one of two ways: with the mouse or with a hotkey (or, if you have the Pie Menus add-on enabled, both!). To use the mouse method, left-click the Object Mode button in the 3D View's header. From the pop-up menu that appears, select Edit Mode (see Figure 4-1). Be aware that if you're working with an object other than a mesh, such as an armature, the contents of this menu may vary slightly to relate more to that object. However, with the exception of Empties (see Chapter 10), Lights, Cameras, and Speakers, all objects have an Edit mode.

Figure 4-1:
On the left, the Mode button allows you to switch between Object mode and Edit mode for a selected object. On the right, the mode selection pie menu (Tab).

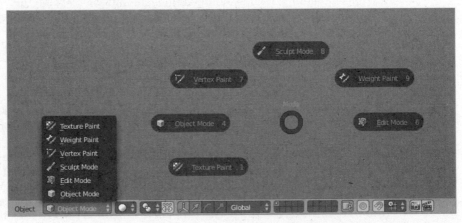

Of course, Blender also has a hotkey to enter Edit mode. Actually, technically speaking, the hotkey toggles you between Object mode and Edit mode. Pressing Tab is the preferred way to switch between modes in Blender, and it's used so frequently that Blender users often use Tab as a verb and say they're *tabbing into* Edit mode or Object mode. This language is something you come across fairly often in Blender user forums and in some of Blender's online documentation.

If you have the Pie Menus add-on enabled, pressing Tab no longer toggles between Object mode and Edit mode. Instead, it brings up a pie menu with the option of many modes. It isn't quite as fast as toggling with Tab, but it can be pretty fast if you use the hold hotkey, drag mouse cursor, release hotkey method of using the pie menu (plus you get the added benefit of easily choosing other modes).

Selecting vertices, edges, and faces

After you tab into Edit mode, the cube changes color and dots form at each of the cube's corners. Each dot is a *vertex*. The line that forms between two vertices is an *edge*. A *face* in Blender is a polygon that has been formed by three or more connecting edges.

In the past, faces in Blender were limited to only three-sided and four-sided polygons, often referred to as *tris* (pronounced like *tries*) and *quads*. Since the last edition of this book, Blender — like many other programs — gained support for something called an *ngon* that can have a virtually limitless number of sides. But don't let Blender's ngon functionality go to your head. There still are some limitations and caveats, as covered in the "A word on ngons" sidebar later in this chapter. Generally, you should think of ngons as a "process" tool. With some exceptions, like architectural models, a *finished* model should only consist of just three- and four-sided faces. In fact, most detailed character models are made almost completely with quads and an occasional triangle, and all 3D geometry is reduced to triangles when it gets to your computer hardware.

For polygon editing, you can use three different types of Edit modes, sometimes called *selection modes:* Vertex Select, Edge Select, and Face Select. By default, the first time you tab into Edit mode, you're in Vertex Select mode.

Two visual cues in the Blender interface clue you in to what selection mode you're using. First, for Vertex Select mode, you can see the individual vertices in the mesh. Second, as Figure 4-2 shows, three new buttons appear in the 3D View's header when you're in Edit mode. The button on the left (it has an icon of a cube with an orange dot over one corner) is enabled, indicating that you're in Vertex Select mode.

Figure 4-2:
The Edit
mode Select
buttons.

To the right of the Vertex Select button is a button displaying an icon of a cube with a highlighted edge. Click this button to activate Edge Select mode. When you do, the vertices are no longer visible on your mesh. Clicking the last button in this block, which has an icon of a cube with one side marked in orange, activates Face Select mode. When Face Select mode is active, vertices aren't visible, and each polygon in your mesh has a square dot in the center of it.

Now, you may notice that these buttons are blocked together, kind of like the 3D manipulator buttons. So, as with the manipulator, can you simultaneously activate multiple modes? Absolutely! Simply Shift+left-click the Select mode buttons to get this function. Some Blender modelers like to have Vertex Select and Edge Select modes active at the same time to speed up their workflow. This combined selection mode gives them immediate control at the vertex and edge level, and you can easily select the faces by using Blender's Lasso select (Ctrl+left-click+drag) across two edges. Figure 4-3 shows the default cube in each of the select modes, as well as a Combo Select mode.

Of course, you can also use a hotkey sequence to access the various select modes. While you're in Edit mode, if you press Ctrl+Tab, you see a menu that lets you switch between modes. This menu doesn't let you set multiple modes; for combo selection, you still have to use the buttons in the 3D View's header.

Figure 4-3:
Vertex
Select, Edge
Select, Face
Select, and
Combo
Select
modes.

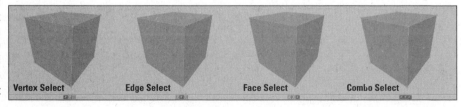

Vertex Select   Edge Select   Face Select   Combo Select

Also, by default, the first time you tab into Edit mode, all vertices/edges/faces are selected. Selecting things in Edit mode works just like selecting anywhere else:

- Right-click any vertex to select it.

- Select and deselect multiple vertices by Shift+right-clicking them.

- Select large groups of vertices by using the Border Select tool (B), Circle Select (C), or Lasso Select (Ctrl+left-click+drag).

  - In Border and Circle Select, left-click and drag your mouse cursor to add to your selection. For Border Select, this action draws a box to define a selection area.

  - Circle Select is sometimes called Brush Select because selection is like painting. Any vertices that you run your mouse cursor over while holding down the left mouse button are selected.

  - Middle-click and drag to subtract from your selection and right-click or press Esc to exit Border or Circle Select.

  - To use Lasso Select functionality, Ctrl+left-click and drag your mouse cursor around the vertices you want to select. Anything within that selection region is added to your selection.

And, of course, all these selection tools work in Edge and Face Select modes, as well as in Object mode. Figure 4-4 shows what the various selection tools look like when in use.

If you want to select everything (in Object mode, all objects; in Edit mode, all vertices in the active object), you can do so by pressing A. The A hotkey is a toggle, so anything previously selected when you press A is deselected. However, if nothing is previously selected, pressing A selects everything. Using this hotkey, you'll find yourself pressing A until you have either everything or nothing selected.

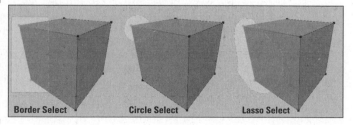

Figure 4-4:
Border
Select,
Circle
Select,
and Lasso
Select.

Border Select   Circle Select   Lasso Select

If you're using Blender's default settings, you can't see through your model. You can't select the vertices, edges, and faces on the back side of the model unless you orbit the 3D View to see those vertices or drop into the wireframe viewport shading setting. (Toggle between wireframe and solid by pressing Z.) On occasion, however, you may find it useful to see (and select) those hidden vertices while in solid viewport shading. To do so, click the Limit Selection to Visible button, sometimes referred to as the Occlude Background Geometry button. Located to the right of the Selection Modes block in the 3D View's header, this button has an icon of a cube with white highlighted vertices on it. (Refer to Figure 4-2.) By default, the Limit Selection to Visible button is enabled, but you can click this button to reveal the vertices, edges, and faces on the back of your model. The hiding of those rear vertices is often referred to as *backface culling,* and it's incredibly useful when you're working with complex models. I recommend that you keep it enabled and just temporarily switch to wireframe viewport shading (Z) if you need to quickly see or select those backface vertices.

If you have the Pie Menus add-on enabled, pressing Z doesn't work as a toggle between solid and wireframe views. Instead, pressing Z presents a pie menu with all of the potential shading options available. Like the mode-switching pie menu bound to Tab, this isn't quite as fast as a straight toggle, but it's still pretty fast while also giving you quick access to other viewport shading styles.

Working with linked vertices

Another handy way to select things in Edit mode is by selecting linked vertices. *Linked vertices* are a set of vertices within a mesh that are connected by edges. In order to understand linked vertices better, go through the following steps:

1. **Select (right-click) your default cube in Blender and tab into Edit mode.**

   All the vertices are selected. If not, press A until they are.

2. **With all the vertices selected, press Shift+D or choose Add ⇨ Duplicate from the Tools tab in the Tool Shelf or Mesh ⇨ Add Duplicate from the 3D View's header to duplicate your selection.**

   Blender creates a copy of your selection and automatically switches to grab mode, allowing you to move the duplicate set of vertices, edges, and faces immediately.

3. **Use your mouse to move your new cube off the original and confirm your placement by left-clicking a second time or pressing Enter.**

   None of the vertices in the original cube are selected. Each cube represents a set of linked vertices. So what if you want to select all the vertices in that cube, too? Sure, you can use the Border, Circle, or Lasso Select tools, but on complex meshes, these tools can get cumbersome. Instead, move to the next step.

4. **Place your mouse cursor near any vertex in the original cube and press L.**

Blam! All the vertices in both of your cubes are selected.

A word on ngons

A longstanding criticism of Blender over the years had been a relative lack of advanced mesh-editing features and tools. Since the release of the last edition of this book, Blender has come a long way, gaining such tools as per-edge beveling, cleaner boolean operations, and the notorious ngon.

Specific to the ngon, there are still some limitations. For instance, an ngon cannot currently have a hole in it. As the figure shows, to get a hole, you need to have two faces. There need to be edges that connect from the inner ring of vertices to the outer ring.

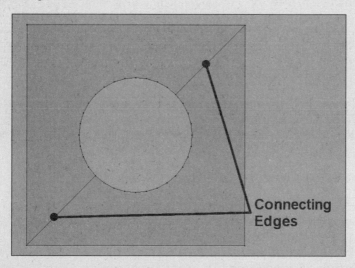

Connecting Edges

As mentioned earlier in the chapter, it's best to think of ngons as a process tool. On any mesh that's likely to be used in animation (like a character model) or included in real-time environment like a video game, the finished mesh should be composed of only tris and quads. An exception to this rule of thumb might be for architectural models or models intended to be rendered as still images. Because those meshes won't be deformed by something like an armature or a lattice and they don't have to work in a game engine, often you can get away with leaving ngons in them.

Of course, the natural next question is, "How do I deselect linked vertices?" That's just as easy. Place your mouse cursor near any vertex on the duplicate cube you created and press Shift+L. All vertices connected to the one near your mouse cursor are deselected. I've found myself using L and Shift+L pretty heavily when trying to place teeth in a mouth I've modeled. These hotkeys are *very* handy.

Quite a few more selection options are available to you when working with meshes. I describe these selection methods in detail in Chapter 5.

While you're in Edit mode, you can work only with the current active object. You can't select and manipulate other objects while you're in Edit mode.

Still Blender's No. 1 modeling tool: Extrude

Besides transform operations (see Chapter 3), the most commonly used modeling tool in Blender is the Extrude function. In meatspace, *extrusion* is a process whereby some material is pushed through a shaped hole of some sort. When you were a kid, did you ever cut out a shape in cardboard and force clay or mud or Play-Doh through it? If so, you were extruding. If not, you certainly missed out on a good solid five to ten minutes of fun (but don't worry, it's never too late to start).

In 3D, extrusion follows a similar concept, except you don't have to create the hole to extrude through. Instead, that shape is determined by your selection and you can extend that selection in any direction. Use the following steps to extrude:

1. **Select the object you want to edit by right-clicking it.**

2. **Tab into Edit mode.**

3. **Select the vertices, edges, or faces you want to extrude.**

   Use any of the selection methods listed in the previous section.

4. **Extrude your selection in one of several ways:**

   1. **Use the E hotkey.**

   2. **Left-click Add⇨Extrude Region in the Tools tab of the Tool Shelf.**

   3. **Choose Mesh⇨Extrude⇨Extrude Region from the menu in the 3D View's header.**

   After you extrude your selection, Blender automatically puts you into grab mode on the newly extruded parts.

Now, if you extrude a polygon, your new extrusion is constrained to move only along its normal. If you don't want this constrained behavior, middle-click your mouse (without moving it) and the constraint is removed, allowing you to freely move your extrusion around.

If you extrude an edge, your extrusion is constrained to a plane perpendicular to your newly extruded edge. If you extrude a single vertex, you're in a *free extrude* mode that's completely unconstrained. In order to use constraints in this case, you need to use the coordinate system constraint hotkeys described in Chapter 3.

The selected orientation in the Transform Orientation menu is active even if you're transforming with hotkeys. So if you set that menu to the Normal orientation, you can press Z⇨Z, and your extruded region is constrained to its face's normal. (Just pressing Z once constrains it to the global Z-axis rather than the face's normal.)

There are advantages and disadvantages to Blender's extrude function leaping directly into grab mode. The advantages are that you have all the transform functionality, such as axis-locking, snapping, and numerical input immediately available to you. The disadvantage is that, because of this autograb behavior, if you cancel the operation by right-clicking or pressing Esc, the newly extruded vertices, edges, or faces are still there, just located in exactly the same place as the vertices, edges, or faces that they originated from.

For this reason, if you cancel an extrude operation, make sure that your duplicate vertices, called *doubles*, are no longer there. A quick way to check is to press G after you cancel your extrusion. If it looks like you're extruding again, you have doubles.

You can get rid of doubles in a variety of ways:

- ✔ **If the canceled extrusion operation was the last thing you did, undo it by pressing Ctrl+Z.** This solution usually is the quickest.

- ✔ **If you still have the doubles selected, delete them.** You can activate the delete operation with hotkeys (X or Del), clicking Remove⇨Delete Vertices in the Tools tab of the Tool Shelf, or by going to Mesh⇨Delete Vertices in the 3D View's header. If you use the delete hotkey, you see a menu where you decide what elements of the mesh you want to delete. In this case, you choose Vertices. The disadvantage of this method is that it also removes the faces created by those vertices.

- ✔ **If you're unsure whether you have doubles from previous canceled extrusions, use Blender's special Remove Doubles function:**

    1. **In Edit Mode, select all by choosing Select⇨(De)select All from the 3D View's header or pressing A until all vertices are selected.**

2. Press W⇨Remove Doubles, and Blender removes all doubles from your mesh.

You can find this option in Mesh⇨Vertices⇨Remove Doubles in the 3D View's header, as well as the Tools tab of the Tool Shelf (Remove⇨Remove Doubles).

If you have Blender's mesh auto-merge feature enabled (it's disabled by default, but can be enabled in the 3D View's header menu in Mesh⇨AutoMerge Editing or by a button in the 3D View's header with an icon of two arrows pointing at each other), you might expect that duplicate vertices automatically are removed/merged if you have a canceled Extrude operation. This isn't the case. Those extruded vertices will remain in place until you move them, so don't assume that you're automatically safe from having doubles when auto-merge is enabled.

If you look in the Mesh menu of the 3D View, you have more than one Extrude option. A second Extrude operation, called Extrude Individual (Shift+E), works, depending on which selection mode you chose. If you're in Face Select mode, then the Extrude Individual operation extrudes each face you selected along its independent normal. Likewise, if you're in Edge Select mode, Extrude Individual extrudes each edge you selected independently of one another. And the same principle works on vertices if you're in Vertex Select mode and choose Extrude Individual.

When you're modeling, the most common type of extrusion you want is related to what you selected. For example, if you want to extrude an edge, you select that edge, or if you select a group of faces, chances are good that you want to extrude that as a region. As expected, Blender has shortcuts for these common modeling tasks.

Blender also has an even faster way to do an extrusion on a mesh. This is a great feature if you're making an organic model that consists of a long series of extrusions, such as a tree or the profile of a wine glass. To perform a quick extrusion:

1. Select your object and tab into Edit mode.

2. Select the vertices, edges, or faces you want to extrude.

3. Ctrl+left-click where you'd like the extrusion to end.

Blender automatically decides what kind of extrusion you want and extrudes your selection right where you'd like. Working this way is particularly useful when you're doing a series of multiple extrusions, one right after the other, such as when you're roughing out a shape by "drawing" with vertices or edges.

For some simple examples of how to make a model using the extrude operator, visit the tutorials I've placed on www.blenderbasics.com.

Proportional editing works in Object mode as well. This capability can be really handy, but it can sometimes yield undesirable results if you want to use this feature only while in Edit mode. For this reason, double-check your 3D View's header before performing a transformation to see whether proportional editing is enabled.

Modeling organically with the Proportional Edit tool

Often, when you're modeling organic objects or objects with smoothly curved surfaces, such as characters, creatures, or sports cars, you may find yourself pushing and pulling a bunch of vertices to obtain that smooth surface. You can simplify this process by using Blender's *Proportional Editing* feature, sometimes referred to as the PET, for Proportional Editing Tool.

If you come from another 3D package, you might recognize proportional editing as being similar to the *soft select* feature. You activate proportional editing by left-clicking the Proportional Editing mode button, which looks like two gray concentric circles in the 3D View's header. The hotkey for this operation is O. Now when you perform a transform operation, a circle appears around your selection. Your transformation influences any vertices that are within this circle with a gradual falloff.

You can adjust the influence circle used by proportional editing by scrolling your mouse wheel or pressing Alt+Numpad Plus (+) and Alt+Numpad Minus (–). Additionally, you can control how gradual the falloff is by left-clicking the button with the curve icon next to the Proportional Editing mode button in the 3D

View's header or by cycling through the options by pressing Shift+O.

The proportional editing feature in Blender has one more useful option. On complex meshes, you may want to use proportional editing on one set of vertices that are connected to each other, but not to other nearby vertices in the same mesh. For example, say that you've modeled a character and her hand is at her side near her leg, and you'd like to smoothly edit her hand and pull it away from the leg without having to gradually adjust the vertices of the arm. Proportional editing is the perfect tool for this job. However, when you try to use proportional editing as described in the previous paragraphs, other leg vertices are within the influence circle, and you end up moving those unintentionally. Wouldn't it be great if proportional editing could understand that you only want to move the hand? Well, I have good news: It can! Click the Proportional Editing mode button in the 3D View header and select Connected or press Alt+O. The Connected option for proportional editing only adjusts vertices that are connected to each other within its influence area. Neat, huh?

Adding to a Scene

There's got to be more to life than that plain default cube, right? Indeed, there is. Blender offers a whole slew of *primitives*, or basic objects, to build from.

Anytime you add a new object in Blender, the origin of that object is located wherever you placed the 3D cursor.

You may notice that for pop-up menus like the Dynamic Spacebar Menu (see sidebar), Blender places the last menu option you choose directly under your mouse cursor. This workflow feature helps increase your speed. The idea is that you often want to do the same task multiple times in a row. Blender makes repetitive tasks easier by shortening the distance you have to move your mouse with each function.

Adding objects

To add a new object to your scene, hover your mouse cursor over the 3D View and use the Shift+A hotkey. From the menu that appears, choose the type of primitive you want to put into the scene. You have the following choices:

Getting to know the toolbox menu

In previous versions of Blender, one of the quickest ways to access any feature in the 3D View is with a toolbox that was activated when pressing spacebar. To access the toolbox, you only had to hover your mouse in the 3D View and press spacebar. Sadly, this feature is no longer a default. Pressing spacebar now only pops up Blender's integrated search menu.

Fortunately, all is not lost! You can still have your good old toolbox back, thanks to Blender's Add-ons system (see Chapter 2). Simply go to the Add-ons section of User Preferences (Ctrl+Alt+U) and enable the Dynamic Spacebar Menu add-on (it's in the 3D View category).

With this add-on enabled, when you go back to the 3D View and press spacebar, a menu pops up with a variety of options beneath your mouse cursor.

The actual content of the menu changes, depending on context like what type of object you have selected or if you're in Edit mode or Object mode, but it's mostly a condensed form of what you find in Blender's Add and Object menus. If you want to use the integrated search feature that is normally bound to spacebar, that option is still there at the top of the Dynamic Spacebar Menu. Click that first option, and the familiar search menu appears.

✔ **Mesh:** Meshes are polygon-based objects made up of vertices, edges, and faces. They're the most common type of modeling object used in Blender. Chapter 5 goes into high detail on modeling with meshes. The other types of primitives listed here are covered in Chapter 6.

✔ **Curve:** Curves are objects made up of curved or straight lines that you manipulate with a set of *control points*. Control points are similar to vertices, but you can edit them in a couple of ways that vertices can't be edited. Blender has two basic forms of curves, Bèzier curves and NURBS (Non-Uniform Relational B-Spline) curves. You can also use curves as paths to control other objects.

✔ **Surface:** A surface is similar to a mesh, but instead of being made up of vertices, edges, and faces, surfaces in Blender are defined by a set of NURBS curves and their control points.

✔ **Metaball:** Metaball objects are unique primitives with the cool ability to melt into one another and create a larger structure. They're handy for a variety of effects that involve blobby masses, such as clouds or water, as well as quick, rough, clay-like models.

✔ **Text:** The text object allows you to bring type into your 3D scene and manipulate it like other 3D objects.

✔ **Armature:** Armature objects are skeleton-like structures that consist of linked bones. You can use the bones in an armature to deform other objects. The bones are particularly useful for creating the puppet-like controls necessary for character animation. There's a lot more detail on armatures in Chapter 11.

✔ **Lattice:** Like armature objects, you can use lattices to deform other objects. They're often used in modeling and animation to squash, stretch, and twist models in a non-permanent way. Lately, lattices are used less and less in Blender because users have gained the ability to deform objects with curves and meshes, but they're still very useful.

✔ **Empty:** The unsung hero of Blender objects, Empties don't show up in finished renders. Their primary purpose is merely to serve as a reference position, size, and orientation in 3D space. This basic purpose, however, allows them to work as very powerful controls.

✔ **Speaker:** If you're using Blender to create a real-time environment such as a video game, you can use a speaker object in your scene to give players an immersive experience with 3D sound.

✔ **Camera:** Like real-world cameras, camera objects define the location and perspective from which you're rendering your scene.

✔ **Lamp:** Lamp objects are necessary for lighting your scene. Just like in the physical world, if you don't have any light, you don't see anything.

✔ **Force Field:** In the simplest terms, a *force field* is an Empty that acts like the source of some physical force such as wind or magnetism. Force fields are used primarily with Blender's integrated physics simulation. I briefly touch upon force fields in Chapter 13.

✔ **Group Instance:** A group is a set of objects you define as being related to each other in some way. The objects in a group don't have to be the same type. Groups are handy for organization as well as appending sets of objects from external files.

When adding new objects, be aware of whether you're in Object mode or Edit mode. If you add while in Edit mode, then your addition options are limited to the type of object you're editing. That is, if you're in Edit mode on a mesh, you can only add new mesh primitives. Also, your new object's data is joined with the object you're editing. If you don't want the object data to join, then make sure that you tab back to Object mode before adding anything new.

Meet Suzanne, the Blender monkey

Many 3D modeling and animation suites have a generic semi-complex primitive that is used for test renders, benchmarks, and examples that necessitate something a little more complex than a cube or sphere. Most of these other programs use the famous Utah teapot as their test model.

Blender has something a little more interesting and unique. Blender has a monkey head that's affectionately referred to as Suzanne, a reference to the ape in two of Kevin Smith's films: *Jay and Silent Bob Strike Back* and *Mallrats* (close to the end). You can add Suzanne to your scene by pressing Shift+A ➪ Mesh ➪ Monkey. If you look through the Blender community's forums and much of Blender's release documentation, you see Suzanne and references to her all over the place. In fact, the annual awards festival at the Blender Conference in Amsterdam is called the Suzanne Awards. Figure 4-5 shows a test render featuring Suzanne.

If you absolutely *must* have a teapot as your test mesh, you can have that, too. It's in the Extra Objects add-on for meshes. Enable this add-on by going to the Add-ons section of User Preferences (Ctrl+Alt+U or File ➪ User Preferences) and looking in the Add Mesh category. Once enabled, you can find the teapot in the Add menu (Shift+A ➪ Mesh ➪ Misc Objects ➪ Teapot+).

Figure 4-5:
Suzanne!

Joining and separating objects

In the course of creating models for your scenes, you may need to treat separate objects as a single one, or break the parts of a single object into their own distinct objects — for example, you may accidentally add a new primitive while you're still in Edit mode. Of course, you can simply undo, tab into Object mode, and re-add your primitive, but why act like you made a mistake and go through all those extra steps?

There's another way. When you add a new primitive while in Edit mode, all the elements of your new primitive are selected, and nothing from your original object is selected. If only there were a command that would let you break this primitive away from this object and into an object of its own. Fortunately, there is. While in Edit mode, press P⇨Selection, and your new primitive is separated into its own object. You can also access this function in the 3D View's header menu (Mesh⇨Vertices⇨Separate⇨Selection).

Tab back into Object mode and select (right-click) your new object. Its origin is located in the same place as its original object's origin. To put the origin of your new object at its actual center, press Shift+Ctrl+Alt+C⇨Origin to Geometry or click Object⇨Transform⇨Origin to Geometry in the 3D View's header. This Origin to Geometry operation checks the size of your object and calculates where its true center is. Then Blender places the object's origin at that location.

You can also specify that the object's origin be placed wherever your 3D cursor is located by pressing Shift+Ctrl+Alt+C⇨Origin to 3D Cursor or clicking Object⇨Transform⇨Origin to 3D Cursor.

A third option is similar to Origin to Geometry, but it moves the object's content rather than the origin itself. Do this operation by clicking Object⇨Transform⇨Geometry to Origin (Shift+Ctrl+Alt+C⇨Geometry to Origin).

As expected, you can also join two objects of the same type into a single object. To do so, select multiple objects. In Object mode, you can use the Border Select or Lasso Select tools, or you can simply Shift+right-click objects to add them to your selection. The last object you select is considered your *active object* and is the object that the others join into. With your objects selected, join them by pressing Ctrl+J or clicking Object⇨Join from the 3D View's header.

You can join objects of the same type only. That is, you can join two mesh objects, but you can't join a mesh object with a curve object. Using parenting or groups (discussed later in this chapter in the section "Discovering parents, children, and groups") may be more appropriate.

Creating duplicates and links

In the section "Working with linked vertices," earlier in this chapter, an example involved duplicating your selected vertices by using Shift+D

Understanding the difference between joins and booleans

This is a bit of a terminology thing. If you've never worked in 3D computer graphics before, you might expect that a join operation on two objects would result in a single, *connected* mesh. That's not quite how it works. Earlier in this chapter, I explain that an object can consist of both linked and unlinked elements. There's no requirement that, for example, all the vertices in a mesh object are linked by faces and edges. When you join two separate objects using Ctrl+J, you're really just bundling them into the same object datablock. You aren't changing any of the mesh data.

To actually merge meshes into a single linked unit, you need to either

✔ Edit the mesh data manually — merging vertices and creating new edges and faces as necessary.

✔ Use a *boolean* — an operation that does a logical (for example, *and, or, intersection*) combination of two meshes.

In Blender, booleans are done with a modifier. Really, I recommend only using the Boolean modifier as a last resort; it can really mess up your *mesh topology* (how vertices and faces are laid out over your mesh). Modifiers are covered in more detail in Chapter 5.

(or Mesh⇨Add Duplicate). As you may expect, this operation also works in Object mode (the hotkey is the same — Shift+D — but the menu item is slightly different at Object⇨Duplicate Objects). This duplication method is great if you intend on taking an existing object and using it as a starting point to model another, more individualized object by tweaking it in Edit mode. However, suppose that you want your duplicated object to be identical to the original in Edit mode. And wouldn't it be nice if, when you do go into Edit mode, your changes happen to the original *as well as* to all the duplicates? For duplicated objects that you have to edit only once, you want to use the power of *linked duplicates*. Linked duplicates are objects that share the same internal datablocks.

Linking objects, in this case, is different from the linked vertices described earlier in this chapter. The fact that the same word is used in a couple different ways can be a bit confusing, but there's a mnemonic that can help you keep things straight:

- ✔ Linked vertices (as described earlier in the chapter) are specific to Edit mode.

- ✔ Linked objects (as described in this section) are specific to Object mode.

Linking data between objects

Linked duplicates are similar to what other programs call instance copies. The process to create a linked duplicate is pretty straightforward:

1. **Select the object you want to duplicate by right-clicking it.**

2. **With the object selected, press Alt+D or Object⇨Duplicate Linked from the 3D View's header.**

   From here, the behavior is just like regular duplication.

   The object is automatically in grab mode.

3. **Place the object with your mouse and confirm its new location by left-clicking or by pressing Enter.**

You can use a few other methods to verify that this duplicated object is, in fact, a linked duplicate. The easiest way is to tab into Edit mode on the original object or on any of the duplicates. When you do, all the linked objects appear to go into Edit mode, and any changes you make here automatically update all the other objects immediately. Figure 4-6 shows three linked duplicates of Suzanne being simultaneously modified in Edit mode.

Figure 4-6:
Editing
duplicated
Suzannes!

A second way to verify the linked status of duplicates is to look in the Object Data section of the Properties editor. At the top of this panel, look at the top datablock field, which is the Datablock Name field. If a number appears to the right of the name, it is the number of objects linked to this datablock. In other words, this number is the count of your linked duplicates. Figure 4-7 shows how this panel looks when one of the Suzannes in the previous figure is selected.

Another way to visualize linked data in Blender is to consider that Blender treats the internal structure of its `.blend` files like a database. As I cover in Chapter 2, all datablocks in your scene — including objects, materials, and mesh data — can be linked and shared between one another. The real power comes in allowing multiple objects to share with each other. For example, you can have objects share materials, mesh data, actions, and even particle systems. And different scenes can even share objects! Taking advantage of this feature not only reduces the size of your `.blend` files, but it can also seriously reduce the amount of redundant work you have to do. Figure 4-8 shows a data schematic for the previous scene involving the three linked duplicates of Suzanne. You can see how the datablocks in that scene relate to one another.

Figure 4-7:
Three
objects are
sharing this
datablock.

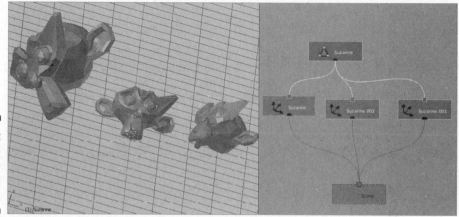

Figure 4-8:
A data
schematic
of linked
Suzannes.

So say that you've been using Blender for a while without knowing about linked duplicates, and your `.blend` file is rife with redundant mesh data. Is there a way to get rid of those regular duplicates and make them linked duplicates? Of course! Follow these steps:

1. **Select all the objects that you want to share the same data.**

   Use any of the selection tools available to you (Border, Circle, Lasso, and Shift+right-click). All the objects must be of the same type, so you can't have a mesh object and a curve object share the same datablock.

2. **With each desired duplicate selected, select (Shift+right-click) the object with the datablock that you want to share with the others.**

   This step makes that last-selected object the active object.

3. **Press Ctrl+L or Object ⇨ Make Links from the 3D View's header menu to bring up the Make Links menu.**

4. **Choose the third option from the top, Object Data.**

   Kerplooie! All the selected objects now link to the same internal data.

Figure 4-9 shows the preceding process, using a bunch of cubes and a Suzanne object.

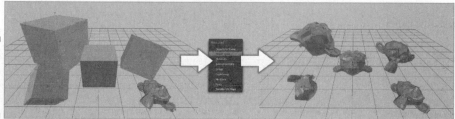

Figure 4-9:
Linking
cubes to
Suzanne.

You probably noticed that the Make Links menu had some other interesting options. Following is a description of what each one does:

- ✔ **Objects to Scene:** If you have multiple scenes in your .blend file, you can make those scenes share the same objects. This option reveals another menu with all the scenes in the file. By choosing a scene, the object or objects that you selected have linked duplicates created in that scene.

- ✔ **Object Data:** This option is the one you used in the preceding example. Object Data links the internal data — be it a mesh, a curve, a lamp, or nearly any other object — of the selected objects to the internal data of the active object. For this option to work, all the selected objects must be of the same type. This is the only option where having objects of the same type is important.

- ✔ **Materials:** Choosing this option causes all the selected objects to share the same material settings. For more information on materials, see Chapter 7.

- ✔ **Animation Data:** This option relates directly to animation. It's the set of keyframes that describe the motion of an animated object, called *actions*. (Chapter 12 has more information on actions.) Choosing this option causes all your selected objects to share the same actions as the active object.

- ✔ **Group:** In the "Discovering parents, children, and groups" section of this chapter, you see how Blender allows you to organize your objects into groups. Choosing this option puts all of the selected objects in the same group.

- ✔ **DupliGroup:** One cool thing about groups is that you can generate them as duplicated instances in a few ways. One of those ways is as a *dupligroup*. Choosing this option allows multiple objects to share the same dupligroup.

- ✔ **Modifiers:** A *modifier* is an operation that Blender performs on your object's data without permanently changing that data (see Chapter 5). Modifiers allow you to have very complex models that are still manageable, while retaining the simple editability of the original data. Unlike the other options in the Make Links menu, this option doesn't link the same modifier to multiple objects. What it really does is copy the modifier and its settings from one object to another. In the future, you may be able to treat modifiers as linkable datablocks, but that is not currently the case.

- ✔ **Fonts:** This option is specific to Text objects. If you want to change the font on a bunch of text objects at the same time, it can be a pretty tedious manual process. However, by choosing this option, you can quickly set the same fonts for all selected Text objects.

✔ **Transfer UV Maps:** UV maps (covered in Chapter 8) are used for mapping a 2D image to the surface of your 3D object. You can share UV coordinate layouts between multiple 3D objects that share the same mesh topology (objects that have the same number and connections between vertices, but not necessarily the same vertex positions).

Like modifiers, this doesn't really link datablocks; it really copies the UV layout from one mesh to the other. If you edit the layout after that, it only has an effect on the active object.

Unlinking datablocks

Of course, if Blender has a way to create links and duplicates, you'd logically (and correctly) think that you can convert a linked duplicate into an object with its own, non-shared datablock. In Blender, this process is called giving that datablock a single user.

The reason for the *single user* terminology goes back to how these datablocks are tied together. From the perspective of the datablock, each object that's connected to it is considered a user. Refer to Figure 4-9: Each Cube object is a user of the Suzanne datablock. By choosing to use the Make Single User operator, you're effectively telling Blender to duplicate that datablock and make sure that it connects to only a single object. To make an object have single user data, select the object you want and then press U or go to Object ⇨ Make Single User in the 3D View's header. You see a menu with the following options:

✔ **Object:** Use this option when you have an object that is linked to multiple scenes and you want to make changes to it that appear only in the specific scene that you're currently working on.

✔ **Object & Data:** For cases like the preceding example with the linked Suzanne meshes where you have a linked duplicate that you'd like to edit independently of the other meshes, choose this option. Doing so effectively converts a linked duplicate into a regular duplicate.

✔ **Object & Data & Materials+Tex:** If you have an object that is not only sharing internal object data with others, but also sharing material settings, choose this option, and both of those datablocks are duplicated and singly linked to your selected object. Using this option is a pretty good way to make sure that your selected object isn't sharing with any other objects at all.

✔ **Materials+Tex:** In cases where you no longer want to share materials between objects, choosing this option makes sure that your selected object has its own material settings independent of all the other objects.

✔ **Object Animation:** This option is the inverse of the Make Links ⇨ Animation Data option. If your selected object is sharing actions with any other objects, choosing this option makes sure that it has actions of its own.

Another way to make object data a single user is to use the datablock buttons in Blender's interface. In Figure 4-7, the number 3 is highlighted, showing that three objects share that particular datablock. If you left-click that number, you make that a single user datablock. This little button shows up in many places throughout the Blender interface. The datablocks that it operates on vary with context (for example, seeing this button in Material Properties means that it's working on a material datablock; seeing it in the Dopesheet means that it's working on actions, and so on), but it always means the same thing: Create a datablock like this one that has only the selected object as its user.

There is one other way to make object data a single user. Use the Outliner. Right-click an object data entry and choose Make Single User from the menu that appears. There are a few datablocks (such as material actions) where this is the only clear way to make them single user.

Discovering parents, children, and groups

Working in 3D, you may encounter many situations where you'll want a set of objects to behave like a single organizational group. Now, if the objects are all the same type, you can join them into a single object, but even with the L and Shift+L linked selection operations in Edit mode, this approach can get unwieldy. And joining them into a single object requires you to tab into Edit mode each time you want to work with an individual item. That's not very efficient, and it doesn't give you the flexibility of working with different kinds of objects as a single unit. The better way to organize your objects is with parent-child relationships or with groups.

Establishing parent-child relationships between objects

Creating parent-child relationships between objects, or *parenting* in Blenderese, organizes the objects hierarchically. An object can have any number of children, but no object can have more than a single parent:

1. **To make an object a parent, first select the objects you want to be children.**

   They don't have to be of the same type.

2. **Make your last selection (the active object) the object that you want to become the parent.**

3. **Press Ctrl+P ➪ Object or click Object ➪ Parent ➪ Object in the 3D View's header menu.**

   After you confirm the operation by left-clicking or pressing Enter, Blender adds a dotted line from the origin of each child object to the origin of the parent. Now when you select just the parent object and perform a transform operation on it, it affects each of its children. However, if you select a child object and transform it, none of the other children or the parent object are influenced.

A good mnemonic device for remembering the correct order for selecting objects when you want to create a parent-child relationship is to think of the order people get off of a boat when they're abandoning ship: "Children first!"

Parenting is a great way to organize a set of objects that have a clear hierarchy. For example, say that you've modeled a dinner table and the chairs to go around it. Now you want to place that table and chairs in a room, but the room is scaled much smaller than the table and chairs. Rather than select, scale, grab, and move each object into place, you can parent each of the chairs to the table. Then you can just select and transform the table. When you do so, all the chairs transform right along with it, as if they were a single object! Woohoo! Figure 4-10 illustrates this example.

To clear a parent relationship, the process is only a click and a hotkey:

1. **Select the child object that you want to remove from the hierarchy.**

2. **Press Alt+P or click Object ⇨ Parent ⇨ Clear Parent in the 3D View's header to clear the parent relationship.**

3. If you use the hotkey, you see a pop-up menu with three options:

   • **Clear Parent:** This option removes the parent-child relationship between your selected object and its parent. If the parent object was transformed after the parenting took place, the cleared child jumps back to the position, scale, and rotation that it was in before it was parented.

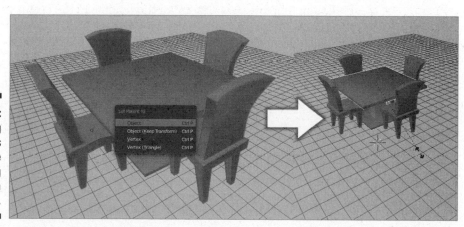

Figure 4-10:
Parenting some chairs to a table and placing them in a room.

- **Clear and Keep Transformation (Clear Track):** This option behaves the same as Clear Parent, except any transformations that were made while the selected object was a child are applied. This means that the cleared child does *not* snap back to its original pre-parented state.

- **Clear Parent Inverse:** This option is a bit tricky to understand. It actually does not remove the link between the selected child object and its parent. Instead, it basically clears the parent's transformation from the child. Clear Parent Inverse is handy for situations where you've transformed an object before parenting it, and you want it to relate to the parent as if it had not been transformed prior to parenting. To be honest, I don't use this option very often, but it's certainly good to have around when you need it.

Another quick way of parenting within Blender is from the Outliner. Within the Outliner, you can left-click the icon of any object and drag it over the name of another object in the Outliner (essentially dropping it in like copying a file into a folder on your computer's file browser). That action automatically creates a parent-child relationship between the two objects. On complex scenes, this is an extremely handy trick.

Creating groups

Of course, under some circumstances, parenting doesn't make sense for organizing a set of objects. A good example is a lighting setup that you want to adjust and reuse. Sure, you can rationalize that perhaps the key light is the most important light and therefore should be the parent, but that logic is a bit of a stretch and doesn't make much sense in more complex setups.

For these cases, Blender's *grouping* feature is ideal. To create a group, select all the objects you want to include in the group and press Ctrl+G or click Object ⇨ Group ⇨ Create New Group. All the objects in the group share a green selection outline rather than the default orange, to indicate that the object is a member of at least one group. The notion of an object being a member of at least one group highlights another example of how grouping and parenting differ. Whereas an object can have only one parent, it can be a member of any number of groups. If you go to the Object ⇨ Group menu, you have a number of options:

- **Create New Group (Ctrl+G):** This option is always available and creates a new group, adding your selected objects to it.

- **Remove from Groups (Ctrl+Alt+G):** This option is always available, and choosing it removes the selected objects from any groups they may be a member of. Removing all objects from all groups doesn't delete those groups while your Blender session is still active.

- ✓ **Remove from All Groups (Shift+Ctrl+Alt+G):** This is a quick shortcut to remove the selected objects from all of the groups they may be a member of.

- ✓ **Add Selected to Active Group (Shift+Ctrl+G):** To use this feature, you need the active object to be the member of a group. Then any objects you have selected become members of all the groups your active object is a member of.

- ✓ **Remove Selected from Active Group (Shift+Alt+G):** Choose this option, and all your selected objects (including the active object) are removed from any groups in the active object.

Furthermore, it's worth knowing that groups have names. Check out the Object section of the Properties editor. This section contains a panel named Groups, listing the groups to which the selected object belongs. Left-click any group name to change it to something more relevant to that group's organization. Clicking the X next to the group name removes the selected object from that group. The set of layer buttons under the group name, labeled Dupli Visibility, have a special application for larger, more complex projects that involve linking groups between .blend files. Basically, if some objects in your group are on a layer that isn't enabled in these buttons, then those objects aren't visible when the group is linked to another file.

Many game engines and other 3D applications have a notion of grouping that's very different from Blender's grouping. They tend to treat all members of a group as a single unit, regardless of which one gets selected. They also tend to treat groups hierarchically; an object can only belong to one group (in turn, that group can be a member of another group, but the basic object is still only a member of one). In fact, this behavior is a lot more like parenting in Blender than grouping. To mimic this behavior more seamlessly, use the following steps:

1. **Create an Empty object near the center of your "grouping" of objects and display it as a cube (Shift+A ➪ Empty ➪ Cube).**

2. **Adjust the size of the Empty (Empty Properties ➪ Size) to roughly include all of the objects in your grouping.**

3. **Name the Empty something clever to indicate the grouping's name (Object Properties).**

4. **Make all objects you're grouping a child of the Empty (select each object, select the Empty, Ctrl+P ➪ Object).**

With this bit of legwork done, you can select the Empty's cube outline to transform your whole grouping. Even better, your grouping will be hierarchically organized in the Outliner. Many game engine export scripts properly recognize and translate this structure to their native means of grouping.

Selecting with parents and groups

When you're using parenting and groups, you gain the ability to rapidly select your objects according to their groupings. Press Shift+G, and you see a pop-up menu with a variety of options:

- **Children:** If you have a parent object selected, choosing this option adds all that object's children to the list of selected objects.

- **Immediate Children:** Similar to selecting all children, except this option traverses down the hierarchy by one step only. Children of children are not added to the selection.

- **Parent:** If the object you've selected has a parent object, that parent is added to the selection.

- **Siblings:** This option is useful for selecting all the children of a single parent. It does not select the parent object, nor does it select any children that these sibling objects may have.

- **Type:** This option is useful for making very broad selections. Use Type when you want to select all lamps or all meshes or armatures in a scene. This option bases its selection on the type of object you currently have selected.

- **Layer:** Use this option to select objects that live on the same layers. If an object is on multiple layers, any objects that share any layer with your selected object are added to the selection.

- **Group:** This option adds to the selection any object that is in the same group as your selected object. If the selected object belongs to more than one group, a secondary pop-up menu displays each of the group names for you to choose from.

- **Hook:** If you've added *hooks,* which are objects that control selected vertices or control points in an object, this option selects them. You can find more information on hooks in Chapter 11.

- **Pass:** Similar to layers, objects may have a Pass Index value that is useful for compositing and post-production work in Blender. Choosing this option selects any objects that share the active object's Pass Index value. You can find more information on passes and the Pass Index in Chapter 15.

- **Color:** This option allows you to select objects that have the same color, regardless of whether or not they link to the same material datablock.

- **Properties:** Blender gives you the ability to add custom properties to objects (like a Health property for characters in a game). Choose this option, and all objects that have the same properties are selected.

✔ **Keying Set:** *Keying sets* (covered more in Chapter 10) are used for organizing a group of objects and properties for animation. They're properties that all have keyframes set at the same time. This option selects all objects that share the current object's keying set.

✔ **Lamp Type:** This option is similar to the Type option, though it's specific to lamps. If you currently have a lamp selected, choosing this option also selects any lamps that are of the same type (such as Spot, Point, Area, and so on).

Saving, opening, and appending

Quite possibly the most important feature in any piece of software is the ability to save and open files. Having quick access to saving and opening files was especially useful for early versions of Blender, which lacked any sort of undo function. Blender users learned very quickly to save early, save often, and save multiple versions of their project files. One benefit is that Blender reads and writes its files *very* quickly, even for complex scenes, so you very rarely ever have to wait more than a second or two to get to work or save your project.

To save to a new file, choose File⇨Save As from the main header or use the Shift+Ctrl+S hotkey. If you're used to older versions of Blender, you can still use the F2 hotkey to do the same thing. One strange thing that you may notice is that Blender doesn't bring up the familiar system save dialog box that Windows, Mac, or Linux uses. This is for three reasons. First and fore-most, such a dialog box violates Blenders non-blocking interface concept (see Chapter 1). Not only that, but by Blender using its own File Browser interface, you can be guaranteed that no matter what kind of computer you use, Blender always looks and behaves the same on each platform. And as a third point, the Blender File Browser has some neat Blender-specific features that aren't available in the default OS save dialog boxes.

Take a look at the File Browser shown in Figure 4-11. The header for this editor features an assortment of buttons for navigating your hard drive's directory structure and filtering the files shown. If you've used the file browser that comes with your operating system, most of these buttons should be familiar to you. The majority of the options in the side region on the left of the File Browser are there to give you shortcuts to various loca-tions on your computer's hard drive. However, at the bottom of the side region is a set of check boxes that change, depending on whether you're loading or saving your project.

The largest portion of the File Browser is devoted to actually showing files and folders. The topmost text field in this region is the current path on your hard drive to the folder/directory you're currently viewing. Below this text field is the text field for the actual name of your file. In this field, type your project's name. Pressing Enter or clicking the Save As Blender File button in the upper right corner saves the file for you. Below this button is a list of the files in the current folder. If you aren't familiar with Linux and Unix, the first item in this list might seem odd to you. This double-dot (..) is a shortcut for going up in the directory structure. Left-clicking it is just like clicking the Up button in the File Browser's header. It takes you to the parent directory of the one you're currently viewing. Figure 4-11 shows the Blender File Browser and labels the various buttons in it.

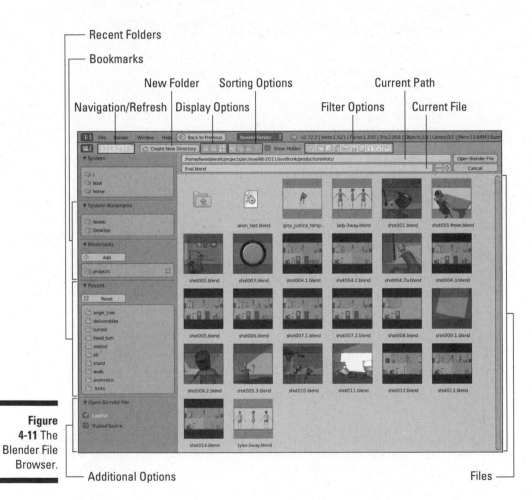

Recent Folders

Bookmarks

New Folder   Sorting Options

Navigation/Refresh   Display Options

Current Path

Filter Options   Current File

Figure 4-11 The Blender File Browser.

Additional Options

Files

Saving after the first time

After you save your .blend file once, saving gets much quicker. To do a fast save while you're working, choose File ⇨ Save from the main header or, even faster, press Ctrl+S and confirm the overwrite by left-clicking or pressing Enter.

On larger projects, however, you may not want to continually overwrite the same file. In those cases, it's often more favorable to save progressive versions of your project as you work on it. You can open the File Browser and type a new name for each version — but it's slow. Often, when people save versions of a project file, they usually append a number to the end of the filename (for example, file1.blend, file2.blend, file3.blend, and so on). Blender knows this habit and aims to help you out.

The ultra-fast way is with the following hotkey sequence: F2 ⇨ Plus (+) ⇨ Enter. Pressing Plus (+) while in the File Browser automatically appends that number to your filename for you. And if the file already has a number, it increments it by one. For logical consistency, pressing Minus (–) decrements that value. How's that for speedy? If you prefer to use your mouse, you can also perform the same function in the File Browser by left-clicking the Plus (+) and Minus (–) buttons after the filename text field.

Opening a file

Opening a .blend file is a straightforward task. Choose File ⇨ Open from the main header or press Ctrl+O. If you've used older versions of Blender, the F1 hotkey still works, too. The File Browser loads again and allows you to choose which file you want to load. To load the file, left-click the filename and click the Open File button in the upper right corner. If you have a large monitor and you don't want to move your mouse that far or you're just interested in speedy shortcuts, you can quickly select and open a file by double-clicking it.

Appending from an external file

Now, what if you have a model of a really excellent character saved in one .blend file, and you'd like to bring it into a scene that you've been working on in another .blend file? Wouldn't it be convenient if you could bring that character in and not have to remodel it from scratch? Of course it would! This capability is precisely what Blender's Append feature is for.

To append an item from an external file, choose File ⇨ Append from the main header or press Shift+F1. The File Browser opens, but now when you click on a .blend file, you can actually drill down into its structure. You can select any datablock in the file and bring it — as well as anything it's linked to — into your project. So if you select an object, you append that object, its object data (mesh, curve, and so on), any materials and textures it may have, and any animation linked to it. If you want to append just a material or texture, you can do that, too!

Appending works very well. However, on large projects it often makes more sense to reference, or *link,* an asset rather than fully copy it in with appending. Blender allows you to make a reference that points to the datablock in the original file. I like to call this reference a *linked appendage*. The advantage of a linked appendage is that any changes you make to the original file are automatically updated in the file that links to it. These updates are really quite handy in large projects where you have a variety of models, materials, and other resources that you'd like to use over and over again.

If you've read through this chapter, you may have noticed that the term "link" is used in three very different ways within Blender. You have linked vertices in Edit mode, linked duplicates in Object mode, and now linked assets between .blend files. It can be a bit confusing. However, if you think about it in terms of scope and context, that can help you keep things organized in your mind. The following mini-table tries to illustrate.

Scope	*Link Type*	*Other Common Term*
File/Asset	Linked appendage	Linked object linked data
Object mode	Linked duplicate	Instance copy
Edit mode	Linked vertices	Connected vertices

One complication of linked appendages, however, is that the linking file can't make any changes to the object that it links to. The only exception to this rule is groups.

When a group is made to a linked appendage, the linking file creates an Empty and binds the group reference to that as kind of a child, known as a dupligroup (I briefly touch on dupligroups earlier in this chapter in the "Creating duplicates and links" section). With this scheme, you can successfully transform and even animate your linked object. If you don't use groups and you want to modify an object appended with a link, your only option is to make that appended object local to the current file by selecting the appended object in Object mode and pressing L⇨Selected Objects. You can also choose Selected Objects and Data or choose All to completely confirm that you're no longer linked to that other file. Of course, making the object local increases the size of your .blend file and removes the collaborative benefit of working with linked appendages.

The moral of this story: If you're appending with links, it's probably in your best interest to create a group in the original file and create a linked appendage to that group from your new file. Using links to groups in external files is the primary way that artists use assets on medium-to-large animation projects.

Part II
Creating Detailed 3D Scenes

In this part . . .

- ✔ Working with vertices, modifiers, and meshes.
- ✔ Modifying curves and surfaces.
- ✔ Manipulating materials.
- ✔ Constructing textures.
- ✔ Employing lighting.
- ✔ Visit www.dummies.com/extras/blender for great Dummies content online.

Chapter 5

Creating Anything You Can Imagine with Meshes

In This Chapter

▶ Working with vertices

▶ Applying modifiers such as Mirror, Subdivision Surface, and Array

▶ Sculpting meshes to have extremely high detail

Polygon-based meshes are at the core of nearly every piece of computer-generated 3D artwork from video games and architectural visualization to television commercials and feature-length films. Computers typically handle meshes more quickly than other types of 3D objects like NURBS or metaballs (see Chapter 6), and meshes are generally a lot easier to control. In fact, when it comes down to it, even NURBS and metaballs are converted to a mesh of triangles — a process called *tesselation* — when the computer hardware processes them.

For these reasons, meshes are the primary foundation for most of Blender's functionality. Whether you're building a small scene, creating a character for animation, or simulating water pouring into a sink, you'll ultimately be working with meshes. Working with meshes can get a bit daunting if you're not careful, because you have to control each vertex that makes up your mesh. The more complex the mesh, the more vertices you have to keep track of. Chapter 4 gives you a lot of the basics for working with meshes in Edit mode, but this chapter exposes handy Blender features that help you work with complex meshes without drowning in a crazy vertex soup.

Pushing Vertices

A *mesh* consists of a set of vertices that are connected by edges. Edges connect to each other to form faces. (Chapter 4 covers this in more detail, along with how to work with each of these mesh building blocks.) When you tab into Edit mode on a mesh, you can manipulate that mesh's vertices (or edges or faces) with the same basic grab (G), rotate (R), and scale (S) tools that work on all objects, as well as the very handy extrude (E) function. These actions form the basis for 3D modeling, so much so that some modelers refer to themselves as *vert pushers* because sometimes it seems that all they do is move little points around on a screen until things look right.

Of course, modeling has more to it. You actually have a choice between three primary methodologies when it comes to modeling:

- ✔ **Box modeling:** As its name indicates, *box modeling* starts with a rough shape — typically a box or cube. By adding edges and moving them around, the artist forms that rough shape into the desired model. Bit by bit, you refine the model, adding more and more detail with each pass.

  This technique tends to appeal to people with a background in traditional sculpture because the processes are similar. They're both primarily subtractive in nature because you start with a rough shape and bring about more detail by cutting into it and reducing that shape's volume. If you need to add more volume to the mesh outside of the initial box shape, you select a set of edges or faces and extrude them out or pull them out. If you need to bring part of the mesh in from the initial box shape, you select those edges or faces and either extrude inward or just pull them in. Box modeling is a great way to get started in modeling, but you run a danger of ending up with really blocky models if you aren't careful about how you move your edges around.

- ✔ **Point-for-point modeling:** Point-for-point modeling consists of deliberately placing each and every vertex that comprises the model and creating the edges and faces that connect these vertices. The process is actually not as bad as it sounds. You can think about point-for-point modeling like drawing in three dimensions. And as you may expect, this technique appeals to people who come from a drawing background (or control freaks like me!). The advantage of this method is that you can control the final look of your model, and you're less inclined to end up with a boxy shape. However, some beginner modelers fall into the trap of getting too detailed too quickly with this technique, so you have to be careful.

- ✔ **3D Sculpting and retopology:** Within the last handful of years, this approach to modeling has taken hold of the 3D computer graphics world to the point that it's now the dominant method. The process works like this: using specialized sculpting tools in 3D software, you start by creating a model with no regard at all for *topology*, or how the vertices, edges, and faces are arranged in your mesh. And then after arriving at a the form you want for your model, you *retopologize* (retopo for short), creating a second mesh with cleaner topology, based on the shape and form of your sculpt. The retopo step uses a combination of specialized retopo tools and the traditional modeling methods described in the preceding bullets. Initially, this technique may sound like you're doing double the work, but it almost always produces better results and is a much more comfortable way to work for artists with a traditional art background. See "Sculpting in Virtual Space" later in this chapter for more detail on this technique.

Figure 5-1 shows the difference between a rough human head started with box modeling techniques, a point-for-point method, and sculpting.

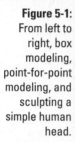

Figure 5-1: From left to right, box modeling, point-for-point modeling, and sculpting a simple human head.

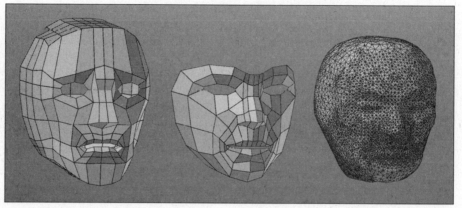

Adding background images in the 3D View

When working with meshes or any other type of 3D object in Blender, reference images are often helpful for getting proper proportions and scale. If you have a separate monitor, you can choose to display your references there. However, you can use a reference more directly by loading an image into the background of the 3D View. To do so, go to the 3D View's Properties region (N) and look for the Background Images panel. Left-click the check box next to this heading and expand the panel by left-clicking the triangle to its left. You see an Add Image button. Left-click the Add Image button, and you get a panel for managing a background image. By default, your image (after you choose it) displays on all orthographic views in the 3D View. You can narrow this scope by using the Axis drop-down menu. For example, if you're modeling a person's face and have a profile photograph, then showing that background image in the front or top views

isn't useful, so you can use the Axis drop-down menu to just display the photo when you're looking from the right or left side view.

To pick an image for displaying in the 3D View, left-click the triangular icon to the left of the text that reads Not Set. Left-clicking that icon reveals an image datablock. Left-click the Open button, and Blender provides you with a File Browser for picking an image on your hard drive. When it's loaded, you can adjust the transparency, size, and positioning of your image. From here, you can continue to work, or you can add more images to display from other orthographic angles in the 3D View. People who model faces like to split the 3D View vertically, showing the front view in one 3D View and the right or left side view on the other. With reference photos of the same size set to display from the proper axis, it makes the process of modeling very speedy.

Working with Loops and Rings

Regardless of whether you're box modeling or point-for-point modeling, understanding the concepts of *loops* and *rings* definitely makes your life as a modeler a lot less crazy.

Understanding edge loops and face loops

Generally speaking, an *edge loop* is a series of edges that connect to form a path where the first and last edges connect to each other — well, that's the ideal case anyway. I like to call this kind of *closed edge loop* a "good" edge loop.

Of course, then you probably want to know what a "bad" edge loop is. Well, you can have a path of edges that don't connect at the beginning and end of the loop, but calling these loops bad isn't really accurate. It's better to refer to edge loops that stop before reconnecting with their beginning as *terminating edge loops*. While you generally want to avoid creating terminating edge loops in your models, you can't always avoid having them, and sometimes you actually need them for controlling how edges flow along the surface of your mesh.

To get a better understanding of the difference between closed edge loops and terminating edge loops, open Blender and add a UV sphere (Shift+A➪Mesh➪UV Sphere). Tab into Edit mode on the sphere and Alt+right-click one of the horizontal edges on the sphere. This step selects an edge loop that goes all the way around the sphere like the latitude lines on a globe, as shown in the left image of Figure 5-2. This loop is a closed edge loop. Press A to deselect all and now Alt+right-click a vertical edge. When you do, you select a path of vertices that terminates at the top and bottom *poles*, or junctions of the sphere, as shown in the right image of Figure 5-2. That's a terminating edge loop.

The vertical loop doesn't go all the way around because, technically speaking, edge loops rely on *four-point poles,* or a vertex that's at the junction of four edges. Imagine that following an edge loop is like driving through a city. The four-point pole is like a four-way stop, where you have the option of going left, right, or straight. Well, to properly follow the loop, you keep traveling straight. However, if you come up to a fork in the road (a three-point pole) or a five-way (or more) intersection, you can't necessarily just go straight and be sure that you're following the loop. Therefore, the loop terminates at that intersection. That's why the horizontal edge loop in Figure 5-2, which is made up entirely of four-point poles, connects to itself, whereas the vertical loop stops at the top and bottom of the sphere, where all the edges converge to a single junction.

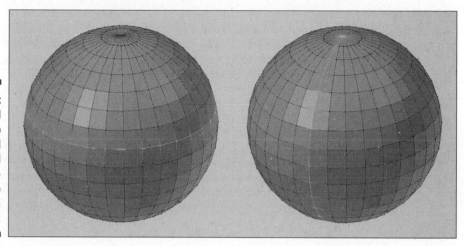

Figure 5-2:
A closed
edge loop
(left) around
a sphere and
a terminat-
ing edge loop
(right) on a
sphere.

In addition to edge loops, you can also have face loops. A *face loop* consists
of the faces between two parallel edge loops. Figure 5-3 shows horizontal and
vertical face loops on a UV sphere. In Blender, you can select face loops when
you're in Face Select mode (in Edit mode, press Ctrl+Tab⇨Faces) the same

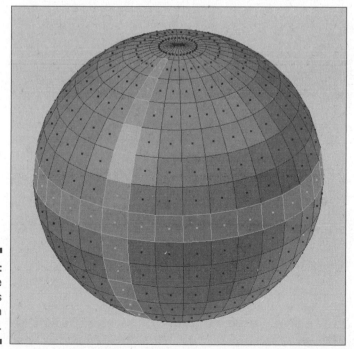

Figure 5-3:
Some
face loops
selected on
a sphere.

way you select edge loops in Vertex Select or Edge Select modes: Alt+right-click a face in the direction of the loop you'd like to select. For example, going back the UV sphere, to select a horizontal face loop, Alt+right-click the left or right side of one of the faces in that loop. To select a vertical face loop, Alt+right-click the top or bottom of the face.

In some Linux window managers, the Alt key manipulates windows, which supersedes Blender's control of it and prevents you from doing a loop select. Most window managers allow you to remap that ability to another key (like the Super or Windows key). However, if you use a window manager that doesn't offer that remapping ability, or you just don't feel like remapping that key, you can still select loops by using Shift+Alt+right-click. This key combination is actually for selecting multiple loops, but if you have no geometry (vertices, edges, or faces) selected, it behaves just like Alt+right-click.

Selecting edge rings

Say that instead of wanting to select an edge loop or a face loop, you'd like to select just the edges that bridge between two parallel edge loops, as shown in Figure 5-4. These edges form an *edge ring*. You can only select edge rings from Edge Select mode (in Edit mode, press Ctrl+Tab⊏>Edges). When you're

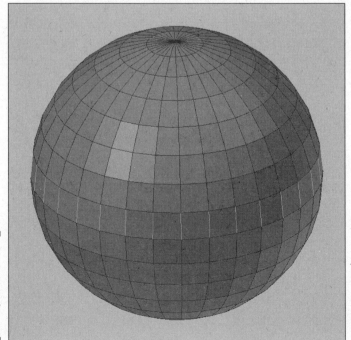

Figure 5-4:
An edge ring selected on a UV sphere.

in Edge Select mode, you can select an edge ring by using Ctrl+Alt+right-click. Trying to use this hotkey sequence in Vertex Select or Face Select mode just selects a face loop.

Being able to use rings and loops for selecting groups of vertices in an orderly fashion can be a huge benefit and timesaver for modeling. More importantly, when creating organic models like humans or faces, using edge loops effectively to control your topology makes the life of a character rigger and animator a lot more pleasant. (You can find out more on this topic in the sidebar "The importance of good topology," later in this chapter.)

Creating new loops

The ability to select loops and rings is nice, but the ability to create new loops is even more helpful when you want to add detail to a model. You can detail with what's called a *loop cut*. When in Edit mode, you can find a button for this operator in the Tool Shelf (Tools⇨Add⇨Loop Cut and Slide). Alternatively, you can simply press Ctrl+R to access the loop cut operation directly. Regardless of how you choose to make a loop cut, when you run your mouse cursor over your model, a pink/purple line is drawn on the mesh, indicating where you might want to add your edge loop. After you decide where you want to cut, left-click to confirm (right-click cancels the whole operation). Doing so creates the edge loop and automatically enables the edge slide function on that loop. With *edge slide*, you can move your mouse around, and your loop travels along the surface of the mesh between its neighboring loops, allowing you to place it precisely where you want it to go when you left-click. If you ever want to use edge slide without creating a new loop, select the edge loop (or portion of an edge loop) that you want to slide and press Ctrl+E⇨Edge Slide, or use the even faster hotkey sequence G⇨G.

If you want your new loop cut to sit at the exact midpoint between its neighboring loops, right-click after the loop cut operator drops you into edge slide.

When doing a loop cut, you can actually do multiple parallel loop cuts at the same time. When you activate the loop cut operator (Ctrl+R), scroll your mouse wheel, and you'll be able to add multiple loops all at the same time. If you don't have a scroll wheel on your mouse or you simply prefer to use your keyboard, you can adjust the number of loops in your cut by pressing Page Up and Page Down.

Cutting edges with the Knife

You can make cuts other than loop cuts. This feature is accessible with the Knife, by pressing K. The Knife is one of Blender's *modal tools*, meaning that once you press K, you're in a Knife mini-mode. With the Knife activated, have a look in the header region of the 3D View and notice the helpful tips. By default it should say the following:

> LMB: define cut lines, Return/Spacebar: confirm, Esc or RMB: cancel, E: new cut, Ctrl: midpoint snap (OFF), Shift: ignore snap (OFF), C: angle constrain (OFF), Z: cut through (OFF)

This handy text in the header region both describes how to use the Knife as well as its current settings. To sum up:

- **LMB:** By left-clicking and dragging your mouse cursor in the 3D View, you can draw across the edges you want to cut. If you just left-click and release without dragging, you can define locations for new vertices in your mesh and the Knife automatically generates the edges between them.

  While you're making cuts, watch the red and green squares that appear along your cut line. These represent the vertices that the Knife will create once you confirm:

  - Red squares are vertices that will definitely be created.

  - Green squares are a pre-visualization of these new vertex locations.

  They only show when you're in the middle of a specific cut. There's more on the green squares in the next set of bullets that cover snapping.

- **Return/Spacebar:** When you finish cutting with the Knife, press Enter or Spacebar to confirm your cuts (the latter is faster because your hand is already closer to Spacebar than Enter).

- **Esc/RMB:** To quit the Knife mini-mode without performing any cuts at all, either right-click or press Esc.

- **E:** You can perform multiple separate cuts while in the Knife mini-mode. Press E and you can start a new cut anywhere else on your current mesh.

- **Ctrl:** If you hold Ctrl while making your cuts, you're telling the Knife that you want new vertices to be placed at the midpoint of any edge your cut line crosses. If you're drawing straight cut lines with the left-click and release method, you can see the planned location of your new midpoint vertices as green squares.

- **Shift:** By default, Blender snaps the Knife to an edge if your mouse cursor is near it. However, there are occasions when you need to precisely place a new vertex near an edge, but not directly on it. In those cases, the default snapping behavior can be particularly frustrating. If you hold Shift while using the Knife, the default snapping behavior is temporarily disabled.

✔ **C:** Occasionally, you need to make a cut that's perfectly horizontal, vertical, or at a 45° angle (relative to the view axis). Press (and release) C to toggle the Knife's ability to constrain your cuts to these axes.

Try to avoid holding down C for the angle constrain feature, otherwise you may notice that your cut line jitters erratically. This is because the angle constrain feature is conflicting with snapping.

✔ **Z:** In some instances, you may want the Knife to cut through both sides of a mesh with the same cut line (for example, if you're modeling a four-post bed and you want to add a cut at the same height on all four posts). If you press Z while in the Knife mini-mode, you toggle the Knife's ability to perform this kind of cut through the mesh.

The Knife's cut through feature works regardless of whether you can actually see the other side of your mesh (such as when in wireframe viewport shading or when you have Limit Selection to Visible enabled). For this reason, it's always a good idea to check the other side of your mesh after doing a cut to make sure you get your intended results.

A nice thing about working with the Knife is that you have full control over navigating within your scene while in the Knife mini-mode. You can pan, orbit, and zoom to your heart's content and place your cuts exactly where you want them.

Simplifying Your Life as a Modeler with Modifiers

Working with meshes can get complicated when you have complex models consisting of lots and lots of vertices. Keeping track of these vertices and making changes to your model can quickly become a daunting and tedious task, even with well-organized topology. You can quickly run into problems if you have a symmetrical model where the left side is supposed to be identical to the right, or if you need more vertices to make your model appear smoother. In these times, you really want the computer to take on some of this tedious additional work so that you can focus on the creative parts.

Fortunately, Blender actually has a feature, called *modifiers,* that helps tackle the monotony. Despite their rather generic-sounding name, modifiers are an extremely powerful way to save you time and frustration by letting the computer assume the responsibility for grunt work, such as adding smoothing vertices or making your model symmetric. Another benefit of modifiers is that they're *nondestructive,* meaning that you can freely add and remove modifiers to and from your object. As long as you don't apply the modifier, it won't actually make any permanent changes to the object itself. You can always return to the original, unmodified mesh.

You can access modifiers for your mesh in the Modifiers section of the Properties editor (its button has an icon of a blue wrench). Left-click the Add Modifier button to see a list of the modifiers that are available. Figure 5-5 shows the Modifiers section with the list of available modifiers for meshes.

Because of space constraints, I can't give an extensive description on every modifier in the list, but I give a brief description of each later in this section. That said, all Blender's modifiers share some of the same controls between them. Figure 5-6 shows the Modifiers section with two modifiers added, Array and Bevel.

The first thing to notice is that the modifiers are stacked one below the other. This stacking is by design. What's more, the order in which the modifiers appear in the stack is important because one modifier feeds into the next one. So the second modifier — Bevel, in this case — doesn't operate on the original mesh data. Bevel actually operates on the new mesh data provided by the first modifier, Array, in this example.

The stacking order for modifiers is a little bit counter-intuitive if you think about it in terms of layers, where one builds on top of another. Blender's modifier stack doesn't work like that. Instead, you're better off thinking of Blender's modifier stack as a snowball rolling down a hill. Each modifier you hit on the way down the hill adds something or changes something about your snowball, modifying it more and more as it comes to the base of the hill.

Figure 5-5:
All the
modifiers
you can use
on mesh
objects.

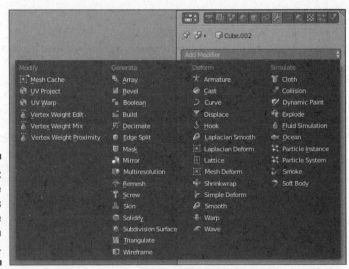

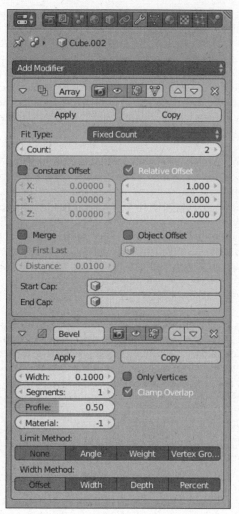

Figure 5-6:
The Array and Bevel modifiers in Modifier Properties.

The topmost modifier is the first modifier and operates on the original mesh data. The modifier immediately below it works on the data that comes from the first modifier, and so on down the line.

In the preceding example, the object is first made into an array. Then the mesh that is created by the Array modifier has its edges beveled so that they're not as sharp-cornered. You can change the stacking order by using the up/down arrow buttons on the right side of each modifier block. Left-clicking the up arrow raises a modifier in the stack (bringing it closer to being first), whereas the down arrow lowers it. You can left-click the X at the top right of any block to remove the modifier altogether. The downward triangle that's to the left of each modifier's name collapses and expands that modifier block when you left-click it. Collapsing the modifier block is useful for hiding a modifier's controls after you've decided upon the settings you want to use.

Between the modifier name field and the stacking order buttons are three or four additional buttons, depending on whether your selected object is in Edit mode. From left to right, the first three buttons control whether the modifier is enabled for rendering (camera icon), viewing in Object mode (eye icon), and viewing in Edit mode (editing cube icon).

You may be wondering why you'd ever want to disable a modifier after you've added it to the stack, instead of just removing it and adding it back in later. The main reason is that many modifiers have an extensive set of options available to them. You may want to see how your object renders with and without the modifier to decide whether you want to use it. You may want to edit your original mesh without seeing any of the changes made by the modifier. If you have a slow computer (or if you want your fast computer to be as responsive as possible), you want to have the modifier enabled only when rendering so that you can still work effectively without your computer choking on all the data coming from Blender.

Some modifiers, like Array, have an additional fourth button with an inverted triangle icon at the end of the button block. Its tooltip says that enabling this button will Adjust Edit Cage to Modifier Result. The edit *cage* is the input mesh, prior to any influence by the modifier. Enabling this button means that not only are the effects of the modifier visible in Edit mode, but you can also select and perform limited changes to the geometry created by the modifier.

Only two more buttons are common among all modifiers: the Apply and Copy buttons. Left-clicking the Apply button takes the changes made by the modifier and directly applies them to the original object. Applying actually creates the additional vertices and edges in the original mesh to make the mesh match the results produced by the modifier and then removes the modifier from the stack. While modifiers are nondestructive, meaning that they don't permanently change the original object, the Apply button is the one exception.

The Apply button works only if the object you're working on is in Object mode.

The Copy button creates a duplicate version of the modifier and adds it to the stack after the modifier you're duplicating. You probably won't be using this function very often, but it's useful when you need to double up a modifier, such as if you want to use one Subdivision Surface modifier with simple subdivisions to get more raw geometry and then use a second Subdivision Surface modifier to smooth or curve that geometry.

Modify modifiers

The first column of modifiers is somewhat of a hodge-podge; it's a bit of a dumping ground for modifiers that don't really fit anywhere else. The main common feature across these modifiers is that they affect vertices or vertex data. With the possible exception of the UV Project modifier, these modifiers are more commonly used in the complex scenes that a more advanced Blenderhead may have, so don't sweat too much if you don't see an immediate use case for them. The six modifiers in this column are

- ✔ **Mesh Cache:** This modifier replaces all of your mesh's geometry with new data from a mesh cache file. In large scale animated productions, it's common practice to take completed character animation (set up with a complex animation rig; see Chapter 11) and "bake" it into the vertex data before moving on to lighting and rendering. This modifier facilitates that workflow.

- ✔ **UV Project:** Think of the UV Project modifier as a video projector or a slide projector. It produces a similar effect to an object-mapped texture (see Chapter 8), though it's more flexible and, unlike object mapping, is usable in Blender's Cycles renderer (Chapters 7, 8, and 9 give a lot more detail on Cycles and how to use it).

- ✔ **UV Warp:** The UV Warp modifier is similar to the UV Project modifier, as it modifies your mesh's UV coordinates (see Chapter 8 for UV coordinates). The difference, however, is that the UV Warp modifier gives you the ability to rig and deform your UV coordinates for animation much like you would rig the vertex data of your mesh.

- ✔ **Vertex Weight Edit/Mix/Proximity:** As their names imply, these three modifiers manipulate vertex weights. Vertices in a mesh can belong to one or more vertex groups (I cover vertex groups in detail in Chapter 11). For each vertex, you can define a *weight* (a numeric value from 0.0 to 1.0) defining how much a vertex belongs to a particular group. These modifiers give you more control over those vertex weights. (They're particularly useful in complex animation rigs.)

Generate modifiers

The Generate category of modifiers contains the most commonly used modifiers in a Blender modeler's arsenal. They're a procedural means of adding — and in some cases removing — geometry in your mesh. And because they're modifiers, they can be stacked to produce pretty complex models from simple base objects . . . and then the parameters in that stack of modifiers can be animated! The list of available modifiers in this category is extensive. The following is a quick run-through of each of them:

- ✔ **Array:** The basic functionality creates one or more copies of your base mesh and places them based on an offset value you define. The Array modifier is one of my favorites; I go into it in more detail later in this chapter.

✔ **Bevel:** Nothing in the real world has perfectly sharp corners or edges. They're always slightly rounded, even if a little bit. The Bevel modifier helps you add that little touch of realism to your object.

✔ **Boolean:** The Boolean modifier allows you to mix two meshes together, adding, subtracting, or intersecting a separate mesh with your current one.

This modifier can generate some pretty ugly topology.

✔ **Build:** With this relatively simple modifier, the individual faces in your mesh appear over time. You can also reverse the effect to have your mesh slowly disappear over time, one face at a time.

✔ **Decimate:** Occasionally you will need to reduce the amount of geometry in your model (for example, your model might need to be used in a video game, a segment of the 3D computer graphics field renowned for having tight geometry budgets for each object). The Decimate modifier can give you a head start in reducing your model's geometry.

✔ **Edge Split:** When modeling, you can define whether a face in your mesh gets rendered as smooth or flat. More often than not, you'll want it to appear smooth. However, in doing this, you lose definition at hard edges in your model. You could add a Bevel modifier to fix this, but if you're trying to keep your vertex count down, that may produce more geometry than you want. The Edge Split modifier lets you keep sharp edges without adding a significant amount of geometry.

✔ **Mask:** The Mask modifier gives you the ability to define some vertices in your mesh as being hidden from view, depending on either their membership in a vertex group or their relation to an armature bone.

✔ **Mirror:** This modifier duplicates the geometry in your base mesh and flips it along one or more of your object's local axes. It's extremely useful when you're modeling anything that's symmetric in nature. I cover the Mirror modifier in more detail later in this chapter.

✔ **Multiresolution:** This modifier subdivides your mesh by the same rules used in the Subdivision Surface modifier (covered later in this section). The difference is that Multiresolution can be applied multiple times and you can use Sculpt mode to freely edit the generated vertices at any of the subdivision levels you generate. I cover the Multiresolution modifier in more detail later in this chapter when discussing sculpting in Blender.

✔ **Remesh:** There are times when the topology of your mesh just is not salvageable (such as when doing heavy sculpting or using booleans). The Remesh modifier can give you a more reasonable starting place for a mesh with cleaner topology (or at least evenly spaced faces for more detailed sculpting).

- **Screw:** The Screw modifier duplicates the geometry of your mesh one or more times and rotates those duplicates about one of its local axes. You can use this to create helix shapes (like springs and, well, screws) as well as a way to generate an object from a simple profile, similar to a "lathe" operator in other software. There's a tutorial that covers this technique on this book's website (www.blenderbasics.com).

- **Skin:** Using the Skin modifier, the vertices and edges in your mesh are given a "skin". That is, new geometry is generated around them, based on a radius you define in Edit mode. In a way, it's similar to increasing the Bevel value on a curve object as described in Chapter 6. This modifier gives you a fantastic way to generate base meshes for sculpting or sprawling organic shapes like vines and other vegetation. As an additional bonus, this modifier can also generate an armature object with properly defined vertex weights so you more easily deform and animate your mesh.

- **Solidify:** Polygon faces in 3D graphics are infinitely thin. So if you try to look at them from certain angles, they simply aren't visible. Of course, that doesn't match the real world. In meatspace, everything has a little bit of thickness. The Solidify modifier is a quick and easy way to add that thickness to any mesh.

- **Subdivision Surface:** This modifier is one of the most useful (and frequently used) in Blender. Simply put, the Subdivision Surface modifier adds vertices to your mesh by subdividing each edge and face. (I cover it in more detail later in this chapter.) This behavior allows for more detail and smoother surfaces on your mesh. It's especially useful for organic models like plants and animals.

- **Triangulate:** Some game engines (the code "under the hood in a video game") require that all meshes consist of only triangular faces. Quads and ngons aren't allowed. Using this modifier, you can get an idea of what your model looks like with all triangular faces, without prematurely committing to that topology.

- **Wireframe:** The Wireframe modifier is somewhat like the Skin modifier in that it creates geometry around each of the edges in your mesh. The controls and purpose of this modifier are different, however. Rather than being used to generate a base mesh as a starting point, the Wireframe modifier is most useful in generating renderable wireframes of your mesh so you can cleanly show its topology to your peers.

Deform modifiers

In computer graphics, the word *deform* doesn't carry any kind of negative connotation. When something is deformed in computer graphics, it means that sub-components of that thing have been moved. In the case of 3D computer graphics, those sub-components are the vertices, edges, and faces that make up your mesh's geometry. Knowing that, it isn't hard to figure out that the modifiers in the Deform category are used to change the position of geometry in your mesh. Unlike the Generate modifiers, none of these modifiers add or remove geometry. They just move that geometry around, based on either a set of rules or external controls. While these modifiers can be used for modeling, they're more frequently employed as tools for creating animation rigs (see Chapter 11). The following is a brief description of each Deform modifier:

- **Armature:** When it comes to animation rigs, the Armature modifier is the tool of choice for starting. This modifier is the mechanism that binds your mesh to an armature object and allows the bones of that armature to control the geometry in that mesh.

- **Cast:** Simply put, this modifier pushes the geometry in your mesh to match one of three primitive forms: a sphere, a cylinder, or a cube.

- **Curve:** The Curve modifier is similar to the Armature modifier, but it uses as curve object instead of the bones of an armature object to define your mesh's deformation. This is useful if you're rigging something that has a naturally curved change in shape, like a cartoon fish.

- **Displace:** Using a grayscale image often referred to as a *height map* (lighter pixels represent high areas, darker pixels represent low areas), the Displace modifier can offset individual vertices from their initial location. This can be a handy way to add bumpy detail or even model some terrain.

- **Hook:** This modifier binds one or more vertices in your mesh to an external object. Hooks are useful for bulging or stretching part of your mesh. They're also useful for controlling curve objects. Chapter 11 has a whole section dedicated to hooks and the Hook modifier.

- **Laplacian Smooth:** Sometimes you have a model with a lot of hard edges and creases, but you need a version that's generally much smoother. The Laplacian Smooth modifier is a great tool for addressing that issue. It can be particularly useful for cleaning up meshes from 3D scanners or the Remesh modifier.

- **Laplacian Deform:** The deformation capabilities of hooks and armatures are very powerful, but they can occasionally "fuzz out" the details in your model or create excessive distortion that doesn't preserve the volume of your base mesh. The Laplacian Deform modifier helps to alleviate that problem computationally (as opposed to the more manual methods using lattices or the Mesh Deform modifier).

- **Lattice:** Lattices are special objects in Blender that consist of a boxy network of interconnected control points. When a mesh has a Lattice modifier, you can use one of these lattice objects to perform broad deformations. In cartoony character animation, lattices can be particularly useful for giving characters convincing squash and stretch effects.

- **Mesh Deform:** In its simplest explanation, the Mesh Deform modifier allows you to use a regular mesh to achieve some of the same deformation effects that a lattice can give you. There are trade-offs, of course, but that gets into a much more advanced discussion on rigging.

- **Shrinkwrap:** Using the Shrinkwrap modifier, you can snap the vertices of your current mesh to the surface of another mesh, as if you wrapped that other mesh in shrinkwrap. As an example, if you're doing a cartoon-style animation that involves the cliché of a bulge of water traveling along a water hose, you can achieve that effect with this modifier. Additionally, some modelers use this modifier to help get a starting point when they retopo a sculpt.

- **Simple Deform:** This modifier gives you the ability to twist, bend, taper, or stretch your mesh relative to its local Z-axis.

- **Smooth:** The Smooth modifier does essentially the same thing as the Laplacian Smooth modifier, but it uses a different algorithm. Generally speaking, it's faster than the Laplacian Smooth modifier, but on complex meshes, the result usually is less appealing. It tends to "melt" the shape of the object a bit, losing volume from all sides, like a lollipop.

- **Warp:** Using the location, orientation, and scale of any two reference objects, you can use the Warp modifier to distort your mesh, stretching its vertices from the origin of one object to the origin of the other.

  If you're familiar with proportional editing, as described in Chapter 4, think of this modifier as a way to give you that capability without directly selecting any vertices.

- **Wave:** If you apply the Wave modifier to a somewhat heavily subdivided plane, it gives an appearance similar to dropping a pebble in a still pond. Of course, you don't have to use a subdivided plane, the Wave modifier works on any mesh. Fair warning: if your mesh only has a few vertices in it, you will not see the wave effect. It will just appear like your whole mesh is moving up and down as a single unit.

Simulate modifiers

The last column of modifiers contains the Simulate modifiers. With a couple of exceptions (Explode and Ocean), you almost never add these modifiers from Modifier Properties. They get automatically added to your mesh when you add a particle system from Particle Properties or add a physics simulation from Physics Properties. It's an advanced topic, but Chapter 13 has a bit more detail on using particles and physics simulations from within Blender.

Doing half the work (and still looking good!) with the Mirror modifier

When I was first learning how to draw the human face, I used to have all sorts of problems because I'd draw half the face and then realize that I still needed to do nearly the exact same thing all over again on the other side of the face. I found it tedious and difficult to try to match the first half of my drawing. Without fail, the first couple of hundred times I did it, something would always be off. An eye would be too large, an ear would be too high, and so on. I'm not embarrassed to say that it actually took me quite a long time to get drawings that didn't look like Sloth from *The Goonies*. (Some of my coworkers might argue that some of my drawings still look that way!)

Fortunately, as a 3D computer artist, you don't have to go through all that trial and error. You can have the computer do the work for you. In Blender, you use the Mirror modifier (Modifiers Properties⇨Add Modifier⇨Mirror). Figure 5-7 shows the buttons and options available for this modifier.

The Mirror modifier basically makes a copy of all the mesh data in your object and flips it along its local X-, Y-, or Z-axis, or any combination of those axes. The Mirror modifier also has the cool feature of merging vertices along the center seam of the object so that it looks like one unified piece. By changing the Merge Limit value, you can adjust how close vertices have to be to this seam in order to be merged.

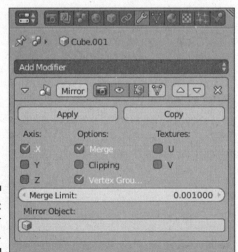

Figure 5-7:
The Mirror modifier.

The X, Y, and Z check boxes dictate which axis or axes your object is mirrored along. For most situations, the default setting of just the local X-axis is all you really need. I nearly always enable the Clipping check box. This option takes the vertices that have been merged — as dictated by the Merge Limit value — and locks them to the plane that your mesh is being mirrored across. That is, if you're mirroring along the X-axis, then any vertices on the YZ plane are constrained to remain on that plane. This feature is great when you're working on vehicles or characters where you don't want to accidentally tear a hole along the center of your model while you're tweaking its shape with the proportional editing (O) enabled. Of course, if you do have to pull a vertex away from the center line, you can temporarily disable this check box.

The next check box is labeled Vertex Groups. As mentioned in the previous section, you can assign vertices in a mesh to arbitrary groups, known as *vertex groups,* which you can designate in Mesh Properties, as shown in Figure 5-8.

Figure 5-8:
Vertex
groups are
created with
the Mesh
Properties.

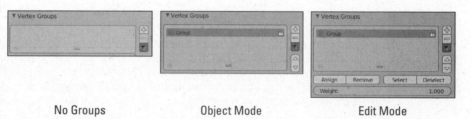

No Groups   Object Mode   Edit Mode

Chapter 11 covers the actual process of creating vertex groups and assigning individual vertices to a group. However, the most basic way uses the following steps:

1. **Left-click the plus (+) icon to the right of the list of vertex groups in Mesh Properties.**

   A new vertex group named Group appears in the list box.

2. **From Edit mode, select some vertices in your mesh and press the Assign button below the vertex group list.**

   You now have a vertex group with a set of vertices assigned to it.

Here's how the Vertex Groups check box in the Mirror modifier works: Say that you've selected some vertices and assigned them to a group named Group.R, indicating that it's the group for some vertices on the right-hand side. And say that you've also created another group called Group.L for the corresponding vertices on the left-hand side, but because you have not yet applied the Mirror modifier, you have no way to assign vertices to this group. Well, if you have the Vertex Groups check box enabled, the generated vertices on the left side that correspond with the `Group.R` vertices are automatically assigned to `Group.L`. You don't even have to apply the modifier to get this result! This effect propagates to other modifiers that are based on vertex group names, such as the Armature modifier.

Referring back to Figure 5-7, the U and V check boxes under the label of Textures in the Mirror modifier do the same kind of thing that the Vertex Groups check box does, but they refer to texture coordinates, or *UV coordinates*. You can find out about UV coordinates in Chapter 8. The simplest explanation, though, is that UV coordinates allow you to take a flat image and map it to a three-dimensional surface. Enable these buttons on the modifier to mirror the texture coordinates in the UV/Image Editor and to possibly cut your texture unwrapping time in half. To see the results of what these buttons do when you have a texture loaded and your model unwrapped, bring up the Properties region in the UV/Image Editor (View➪Properties or N) and left-click the Modified check box. Hooray for nondestructive modifiers!

The last option in the Mirror modifier is the object datablock field at the bottom labeled Mirror Object. By default, the Mirror modifier uses the object's origin as the basis for what to mirror. However, by clicking in this field and choosing the name of any other object in your scene, you can use that object's origin as the point to mirror across. With the Mirror Object feature, you can use an Empty (or any other object) as a kind of dynamic origin. With a dynamic origin, you're able to do fun things like animate a cartoon character splitting in half to get around an obstacle (literally!) and joining back together on the other side.

Blender's text fields have integrated search, which means that you can type the first few letters of an object's name and if the name is unique, Blender displays a list of objects in your scene that match what you've typed.

Smoothing things out with the Subdivision Surface modifier

Another commonly used modifier, especially for organic models, is the *Subdivision Surface* modifier. Old-school Blender users may refer to the Subdivision Surface modifier as the *Subsurf* modifier. If you have a background in another 3D modeling program, you may know subdivision surfaces as *sub-ds* or *subdivs*.

If you're not familiar with subdivision surfaces, the concept goes something like this: Blender takes the faces on a given mesh and subdivides them with a number of cuts that you arbitrarily decide upon (usually one to three cuts, or *levels of subdivision*). Now, when the faces are subdivided, Blender moves the edges of these faces closer together, trying to get a smooth transition from one face to the next. The end effect is that a cube with a Subdivision Surface modifier begins looking more and more like a ball with each additional level of subdivision, as shown in Figure 5-9.

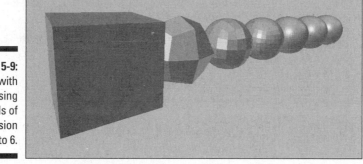

Figure 5-9:
A cube with increasing levels of subdivision from 1 to 6.

Now, the really cool thing about subdivision surfaces is that because they're implemented as a modifier, you get the smooth benefit of additional geometry without the headache of actually having to edit all those extra vertices. In the preceding cube example, even at a subdivision level of 6, if you tab into Edit mode, you control that form with just the eight vertices that make up the original cube. This ability to control a lot of vertices with a relative few is a very powerful way of working, and nearly all high-end 3D animations use subdivision surfaces for just this reason. You have the smooth organic curves of dense geometry with the much more manageable control of a less dense, or *low poly* mesh, referred to as a *cage*.

For a better idea of the kind of results you can get with the Subdivision Surface modifier, break out Suzanne and apply it to her with the following steps:

1. **Add a Monkey mesh (Shift+A⇨Mesh⇨Monkey).**

   Ooh! Ooh! Ooh!

2. **Set smooth rendering on the monkey (Tool Shelf⇨Tools tab⇨Shading⇨Smooth).**

   At this point, Suzanne is pretty standard. She looks smoother than the faceted look she had when first added, but she's still blocky looking.

3. **Add a Subdivision Surface modifier to the monkey (Modifier Properties⟳Add Modifier⟳Subdivision Surface or use the Ctrl+1 hotkey combo).**

   Now *that's* Suzanne! Instantly, she looks a lot more natural and organic, even despite her inherently cartoony proportions. Feel free to increase the View number in the Subdivision Surface modifier to see how much smoother Suzanne can be. I caution you not to go too crazy, though. Setting subdivisions above 3 might choke your computer a bit if it's too slow.

4. **Tab into Edit mode and notice that the original mesh serves as the control cage for the subdivided mesh.**

   Editing the cage with grab (G), rotate (R), scale (S), and extrude (E) directly influences the appearance of the modified mesh within the cage.

Figure 5-10 shows the results of each step.

As powerful as the Subdivision Surface modifier is, only a limited number of options come with it in the modifier stack. Figure 5-11 shows the Subdivision Surface modifier block as it appears in Modifier Properties. The first option is a choice between Catmull-Clark subdivision or Simple subdivision. The former is the default, subdividing and smoothing your mesh as expected. The latter works more like doing W⟳Subdivide multiple times while in Edit mode. It gives you more vertices in your meshes, but not the same kind of organic smoothness that the Catmull-Clark method provides. The simple subdivision method is good for some situations, though, so it's nice that the option is available.

The next set of values, labeled Subdivisions, allow you to set the level of subdivision that you see on your model. The first value, View, dictates the number of subdivisions your mesh uses in the 3D View. You can set View to a whole number from 1 to 6. Because I like to keep my 3D View fast and responsive, I tend to keep this number down at 1. Occasionally, I push it up to 2 or 3 to get a quick idea of what it might look like in the final output, but I always bring it back down to 1 or 0.

Figure 5-10:
Adding the
Subdivision
Surface
modifier to
Suzanne.

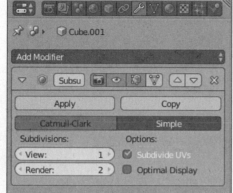

Figure 5-11:
The
Subdivision
Surface
modifier.

Beneath View is a similar value input labeled Render. When you create the final output of your scene or animation, Blender uses this level of subdivision for your model, regardless of which level you set for the 3D View. The Render value has the same range that View does, but typically it's set to a higher value because you usually want smoother, higher-quality models in your final render. Don't go too crazy with setting this value. On most of my work, which can get pretty detailed, I rarely ever use a setting higher than 3.

Use the Subdivide UVs check box for texturing. Like the U and V check boxes in the Mirror modifier, enabling this option adds the additional geometry to your UV map without requiring you to apply the modifier. Again, this timesaver can be quite helpful when you're setting up your model for texturing. It's such a consistently useful feature that this check box is enabled by default. Also, like the U and V options in the Mirror modifier, you can see the results of the Subdivide UVs check box by enabling the Modified check box in the UV/Image Editor.

The Optimal Display check box is something I typically like to leave turned on all the time. Optimal Display hides the extra edges that are created by the modifier when you view the model in wireframe view. On a complex scene, hiding the edges can definitely help you make sense of things when working in wireframe. Figure 5-12 shows the difference Optimal Display makes on a Suzanne model with three levels of subdivision.

When working with the Subdivision Surface modifier, I typically like to have the Optimal Display option enabled, along with the Adjust Edit Cage to Modifier Result button at the top of the Subdivision Surface modifier panel. Everyone's different, though, so play with it on your own and see what works best for you.

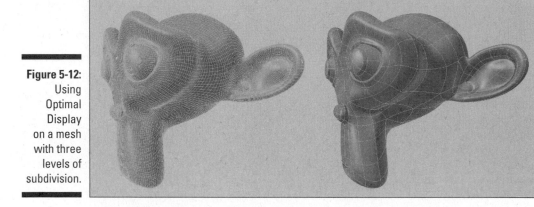

Figure 5-12:
Using
Optimal
Display
on a mesh
with three
levels of
subdivision.

Using the power of Arrays

One of the coolest and most-fun-to-play-with modifiers in Blender is the Array modifier. In its simplest application, this modifier duplicates the mesh a specified number of times and places those duplicates in line, evenly spaced apart. Have a model of a chair and need to put lines of chairs in a room to make it look like a meeting hall? Using a couple of Array modifiers together is a great way to do just that! Figure 5-13 is a screenshot of Blender being used to create that sort of scene.

Figure 5-13:
Filling a
room with
chairs
by using
the Array
modifier.

TIP

You're not limited to using just one Array modifier on your object. I achieved the effect in Figure 5-13 by using two Array modifiers stacked together, one for the first row of chairs going across the room and the second to create multiple copies of that first row. Stacking multiple arrays is an excellent way to build a complex scene with just one object.

Blender's Array modifier is loaded with all kinds of cool functions that you can use in lots of interesting ways. Some ways facilitate a desire to be lazy by making the computer do as much of the repetitive, tedious tasks as possible. (For example, you can use the Array modifier to model a staircase or a chain-link fence or a wall of bricks.) However, you can also use the Array modifier to do some really incredible abstract animations or specialized tentacles or even rows of dancing robots!

The bulk of the power in the Array modifier lies in how it handles *offsets,* or the distances apart that the duplicates are set relative to one another. As shown in Figure 5-14, the Array modifier offers three different sorts of offsets, all of which you can use in combination with one another by enabling their check boxes:

✔ **Constant Offset:** This offset adds a fixed distance to each duplicated object in the array. So setting the X value beneath this check box to –5.0 shifts each of the duplicates five units in the negative X direction. The same behavior happens in the Y- and Z-axes when you set the values for those offsets as well.

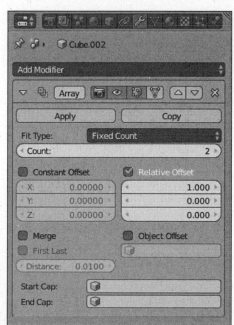

Figure 5-14:
The Array
modifier.

✔ **Relative Offset:** Think of the Relative Offset as a multiplication factor, based on the width, height, and depth of the object. So no matter how large or small your object is, if you set the Z value to 1.0, for example, each duplicated object in the array is stacked directly on top of the one below it. This type of offset is the one that's used by default when you first add the Array modifier.

✔ **Object Offset:** The Object Offset is my personal favorite offset because of its incredible versatility. It takes the position of any object you pick in the Object field — I prefer to use Empties for this purpose — and uses its relative distance from the mesh you added to Array as the offset. But that's just the start of it! Using this offset also takes into account the rotation and scale of the object you choose. So if you have an Empty that's one unit away from your object, scaled to twice its original size, and rotated 15 degrees on the Y-axis, each subsequent duplicate is scaled twice as large as the previous one and rotated an additional 15 degrees. Now you can make a spiral staircase like the one in Figure 5-15. And if you feel inclined to create an animation of a staircase where the stairs can be collapsed into each other and hidden, it's a simple as animating the offset object!

Figure 5-15:
(1) Model the step.
(2) Add an Empty for Object Offset and rotate in Z.
(3) Add the Array modifier.
(4) Make it pretty.

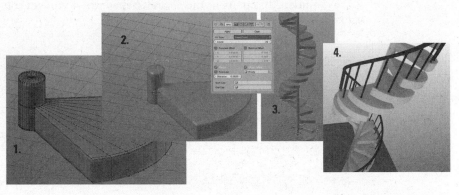

You also have a lot of control over how many duplicates the Array modifier creates, thanks to the Fit Type drop-down menu at the top of the Array modifier block. By default, the Fit Type is set to Fixed Count, and you explicitly enter the number of duplicates in the Count field below it. Fixed Count isn't your only Fit Type option, however. You actually have three:

✔ **Fixed Count:** This option lets you explicitly enter the exact number of duplicates you would like to create, up to 1,000.

The maximum value of 1,000 for the Fixed Count value is what's known as a "soft maximum" in Blender. This means that if you adjust that value using the mouse, it caps out at 1,000. However, if you click in that field, you can manually type numbers much larger than 1,000. Blender will use that manually entered number.

✔ **Fit Length:** This option creates the proper count of duplicate objects to fit in the distance that you define. Bear in mind that this length isn't exactly in whole units. It uses the local coordinate system of the object that you're making an array of, so the length you choose is multiplied by the scale of that original object, as shown in the 3D View's Properties region (N).

✔ **Fit Curve:** If you choose this option, you can choose the name of a curve object in the Object datablock field below it. When you do, Blender calculates the length of that curve and uses that as the length to fill in with duplicated objects. Using this option together with a Curve modifier is a nice quick-'n-dirty way of creating a linked metal chain.

Another cool feature in the Array modifier is the ability to merge the vertices of one duplicate with the vertices that it's near in another duplicate, similar to the Mirror modifier. With the Merge check box enabled and some fine adjustment to the Distance value, you can make your model look like a single unified piece, instead of being composed of individual duplicates. I've used this feature to model rope, train tracks, and stair rails, for example. The First Last check box toggles to determine whether the vertices in the last duplicated instance are allowed to merge with the nearby vertices in the first object of the array. Use merging with Object Offset, and you can create a closed loop out of your duplicates, all merged together.

Say that you're using the Array modifier to create a handrail for your spiral staircase, and you don't want the handrail to simply stop at the beginning and end. Instead, you'd like the end of the handrail to have ornamental caps.

Blender and real-world units

Older versions of Blender didn't have any notion of real-world units. They had only a vague notion of *Blender units*, which you could mentally convert to any unit system available. The typical behavior was to assume that one Blender unit equaled one meter, but that wasn't a hard-and-fast rule.

This oversight has been fixed, giving Blender support for real units. Blender defaults to the old behavior of using Blender units, but Scene Properties has a panel labeled Units. If you need to explicitly use Metric (meters, centimeters, and so on) or Imperial (inches, feet, and so on) units, you can set those values here.

You could model something and try to place it by hand, but that process can get problematic if you have to make changes or animate the handrail in the future. (Hey, this is computer graphics. Handrails that move and are animated make complete sense!) So another way to place ornamental caps on a handrail is to use the Start Cap and End Cap fields in the Array modifier. After you model what you want the cap to look like, you can pick or type the name of that object in these fields, and Blender places it at the beginning and the end of the array, respectively. Pretty slick, huh?

Sculpting in Virtual Space

Over the years, as computers have gotten more powerful and more capable of handling dense models with millions of vertices (sometimes called *high-poly* meshes), computer graphics artists have wanted more and more control over the vertices in their meshes. Using a Subdivison Surface modifier is great for adding geometry to make models look more organic, but what if you're modeling a monster and you want to model a scar in his face? You have to apply the modifier to have access and control over those additional vertices. And even though the computer may be able to handle having them there, a million vertices is a lot for you to try to control and keep track of, even with all the various selection methods and the Proportional Edit Tool. Fortunately, Blender supports *multiresolution meshes* and Sculpt mode that allows for dynamic topology.

Multiresolution (or *multires*) meshes address the problem of having to apply the Subdivision Surface modifier before you can directly control the vertices that it creates. With a multires mesh, you can freely move between a level 1 subdivision and a level 6 subdivision, just like with the Subdivision Surface modifier. However, the difference is that you can directly control the vertices of the level 6 subdivision just as easily as the level 1 subdivision by using Blender's Sculpt mode. And you can see changes made in either level — to varying levels of detail, depending on the level you're looking at. (If you make a very fine detail change in level 6, it may not be readily apparent at level 1.)

Sculpting with the Multiresolution modifier

Creating a multires mesh is just like adding any other modifier to a mesh object. Figure 5-16 shows what the Multiresolution modifier block looks like.

The Multiresolution modifier is similar in appearance to the Subdivision Surface modifier. By default, the Multiresolution modifier starts with zero subdivisions on your mesh. Use the Subdivide button to increase the level of subdivision that you want to add to your mesh. Subdividing increments the values for Preview, Sculpt, and Render. Like the View and Render values in the Subdivision Surface modifier, these values control how many levels of subdivision you see in the 3D View, both while sculpting and when your model is rendered, respectively.

However, unlike with the Subdivision Surface modifier, you don't have exactly six levels of subdivision to switch between. In the Multiresolution modifier, the number can be as low as zero and as high as your computer's processor and memory can handle. And before adding a level, you have the option of choosing Catmull-Clark Subdivision or Simple Subdivision, like you can with the Subdivision Surface modifier.

The only caveat is that you can't freely change between subdivision types on a given level with the Multiresolution modifier. Changing from Catmull-Clark to Simple (or vice versa) has an effect on all multires levels.

If you have a Subdivision Surface modifier on your mesh, I recommend applying it to your mesh or removing it from the modifier stack before adding the Multiresolution modifier. Because the Multiresolution modifier uses the same process to create subdivision levels, you really don't need to have both active at the same time.

After you have a level added, you have some additional options available. Clicking Delete Higher removes all subdivision levels greater than the level you're currently in. So if you have five levels of subdivision and you're at level 3, clicking Delete Higher effectively kills levels 4 and 5.

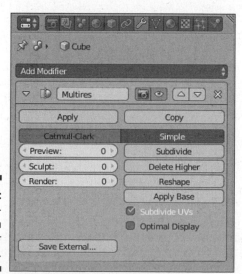

Figure 5-16:
The Multire-
solution
modifier
block.

Enabling the Optimal Draw check box does the same thing that the corresponding check box does in the Subdivision Surface modifier: It prevents Blender from showing subdivided edges in the 3D View. Some 3D modelers who use sculpting tools like to overlay the model's wireframe on the mesh (Object Properties➪Display➪Wire check box) as they work so that they can have an idea of how their topology looks. (See the sidebar "The importance of good topology" in this chapter for more information.) Without Optimal Draw enabled, the 3D View of your model can quickly get cluttered, so enabling this check box simplifies the display for you.

Now, if you try to tab into Edit mode on a multires mesh, you still see only the vertices available to you in the cage provided by the base mesh. So how do you actually edit all those additional vertices created by the Multiresolution modifier? The answer: Sculpt mode. Sculpt mode treats your mesh very much like a solid piece of clay. You have a variety of sculpt brushes that help you shape and form your mesh to look exactly how you want. You can activate Sculpt mode from the Mode menu in the 3D View's header. Alternatively, if you have the Pie Menus add-on enabled, Sculpt mode is a menu item you can choose when you press Tab. When you're in Sculpt mode, the Tools tab of the Tool Shelf (T) updates to show a whole set of options available to you for editing your mesh.

If you have a drawing tablet like the ones manufactured by Wacom, Sculpt mode takes advantage of the pressure sensitivity that a tablet offers.

When working in Sculpt mode and using the Multiresolution modifier, the general workflow is to start at low levels of subdivision to block out the rough shape of your model and then proceed to higher levels of subdivision for more detailed elements of your model. The process is very much like traditional sculpting in meatspace, as well as box modeling in the CG world. The only difference in this case is that the Multiresolution modifier allows you to freely move between high and low levels of subdivision, so you don't have to block out your whole model in a single go.

Nothing says that you're required to use the Multiresolution modifier when sculpting in Blender. In fact, Sculpt mode works just fine without any Multiresolution modifier at all.

Freeform sculpting with dynamic topology (Dyntopo)

One of the most groundbreaking features to hit Blender's modeling community in recent years was the ability to have dynamic topology (dyntopo for short) while in Sculpt mode. Simply put, when you enable dyntopo, your sculpting brush can add or remove geometry from your mesh on the fly.

Need more detail in just one part of your model? There's no need to use the Multiresolution modifier and bump up the vertex count for your whole mesh. Just enable dyntopo and that detail exactly where you need it.

To use dyntopo, you need to be in Sculpt mode. While in Sculpt mode, look at the Tools tab in the Tool Shelf (T). A panel in that tab is named, appropriately, Dyntopo. When you expand that panel, there's a large button at the top labeled Enable Dyntopo. Left-click that button and you're off to the races, sculpting with dynamic topology. Alternatively, you can also enable dyntopo with Ctrl+D while in Sculpt mode. Figure 5-17 shows the Dyntopo panel in the Tool Shelf.

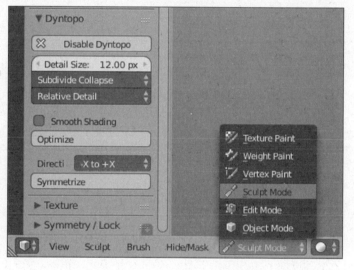

Figure 5-17: The Dyntopo panel in the Tool Shelf allows you to enable dynamic topology while in Sculpt mode.

For such a powerful feature, there are relatively few options that are specific to dyntopo. The following is a quick run-down of the options available in the Dyntopo panel:

✔ **Detail Size:** Dyntopo works by modifying edges within the area of your brush stroke. The Detail Size field defines a value that lets dyntopo decide whether a specific edge gets modified, based on its length. This value can either be in screen pixels or a percentage, depending on the detail type method that you choose (I cover detail types in this list). While sculpting, you can adjust this value with the Shift+D hotkey so you don't have to constantly return to the Tool Shelf.

✔ **Detail Refine Method:** Dyntopo can subdivide edges in your mesh and *collapse* them, removing additional detail. The options in this drop-down menu allow you to control which behavior you want your sculpt brush to use:

- **Subdivide Edges:** The Subdivide Edges option is the default. If an edge within your brush stroke is longer than the detail size, it's subdivided. This refine method is great for fine details, creases, and sharp peaks.

- **Collapse Edges:** When you choose the Collapse Edges option, short edges get collapsed into a single edge. In the case of dyntopo, a *short edge* is defined as being two-fifths ($2/5$) the length of the detail size. This option is great for evening out your topology and removing long skinny triangles that may render weirdly. However, the trade-off is that it also removes any fine details smaller than the detail size.

- **Subdivide Collapse:** Choose this option and edges within the area of your brush stroke are subdivided *and* collapsed, relative to the detail size. This behavior makes the Subdivide Collapse option well-suited for quickly roughing the general forms of your sculpt.

✔ **Detail Type Method:** When sculpting, it's common for artists to arbitrarily navigate around their model as they work, orbiting, panning, and zooming to get the best view of the section that they're sculpting.

Zooming specifically presents an interesting challenge for dyntopo because sometimes you want the detail size to remain the same regardless of how much you zoom in or out from your model; other times, you want to do more detailed work as you zoom closer. The options in this drop-down menu let you choose:

- **Relative Detail:** This is the default setting. Choose this option to define detail size relative to the pixels on your screen. If you zoom out far enough, all of the edges in your mesh become smaller than the detail size. If you zoom in, you only subdivide smaller edges.

- **Constant Detail:** Choose the Constant Detail option if you want the detail size to remain the same, regardless of how much you zoom in or out from your model. With this option, detail size is defined as a percentage of a Blender unit. Additionally, the Detail Size field at the top of the Dyntopo panel gets an eyedropper button. Left-click that button to sample the geometry in your mesh. This means that you can click the eyedropper on a part of your mesh and the Detail Size field is set to match the edge lengths in that region.

✔ **Smooth Shading:** The Smooth Shading check box toggles between smooth shading and flat shading for your entire mesh while sculpting. This is mostly a personal preference, though some sculptors claim to have a more responsive 3D Viewport with Smooth Shading disabled.

✔ **Optimize:** As you sculpt with dyntopo enabled, your brush may become less responsive, with strokes lagging behind your mouse cursor as you work. If you run into that, try left-clicking the Optimize button. When you click, Blender recalculates and rebuilds the underlying data structure that dyntopo uses to speedily edit the edges on your mesh, often alleviating some sculpting performance slowdowns.

✔ **Detail Flood Fill:** The Detail Flood Fill button is only visible if you have your detail type set to Constant Detail. Assuming that you have chosen Constant Detail, you can left-click the Detail Flood Fill button to subdivide (and/or collapse, depending on your chosen detail refine method) every edge in your mesh to match your desired detail size. This is a pretty useful tool for uniformly changing the detail in your mesh (increasing or decreasing it) all at once.

✔ **Symmetrize:** With dyntopo, you can take geometry that you've sculpted on one half of your mesh and mirror it to the opposite side. For example, if you did some sculpting without using the features in the Symmetry/ Lock panel (described in a bit more detail later in this chapter), you may want to mirror that geometry to at least give you a detailed starting point for the other side of your mesh. Left-click the Symmetrize button to do exactly that, based on the direction (such as "from the negative X-axis side of the mesh to the positive X-axis side") defined in the Direction drop-down menu above the Symmetrize button.

As of the writing of this text, the Symmetrize feature of dyntopo does not respect any masking that you've painted on your mesh. (See the next section for more information about the Mask brush.) So if you've painted a mask in the hope that Symmetrize will only have an effect on the unmasked vertices of your mesh, you're a bit out of luck. Symmetrize will happily mirror your mesh regardless of the mask, removing or changing those vertices that you wished to preserve.

Of course, the power that a feature like dyntopo presents also necessarily comes with a few caveats:

✔ You can't have both dyntopo and a multires mesh at the same time. It's kind of difficult to have fixed subdivision levels if the underlying topology is constantly changing.

✔ Because dyntopo dramatically changes your mesh topology, it will not preserve additional mesh data like vertex groups, UV coordinates, or vertex colors. Also, if you have some faces on your mesh set to smooth shading and others to flat shading, that also gets changed so all faces are either one or the other, depending on whether you toggle the Smooth Shading check box in the Dyntopo panel.

✔ Although you can reduce vertices using dyntopo, it's not currently possible to sculpt a hole in your mesh.

✔ Unless your model is being used in a still image and never rigged for animation, it almost always will be necessary to retopo a mesh that's been sculpted with dyntopo enabled. This chapter ends with a primer on doing retopo in Blender.

Caveats and trade-offs aside, dyntopo is an extremely powerful tool for modern 3D modelers. I daresay most of the complex models you see on films, television, and the internet are made with sculpting techniques rather than traditional modeling techniques. In terms of workflow, it goes something like this:

1. **Start with a base mesh.**

   Depending on what you're modeling, the base mesh could be as simple as a cube or a somewhat more complex rough form for the model, such as a 3D stick figure to start a character model. In the ideal case, whatever your base mesh is, it should have evenly distributed faces (that is, all of the faces on your base mesh should be roughly the same size).

2. **Sculpt with dyntopo.**

   With dyntopo enabled, use the various sculpting brushes and options described in the next section to produce your impressive 3D sculpt.

3. **From Object mode, create a new mesh.**

   It doesn't much matter what kind of mesh it is. When you get into Edit mode, you'll need to initially delete all of the geometry in it so you can start the next step.

4. **Retopo the sculpt using the newly created mesh.**

   At this point, you're basically using the sculpt as a 3D reference model to which you can snap your clean topology vertices. The last section in this chapter covers retopo.

5. **Finalize and polish the retopo'd mesh.**

   This is where details are re-added using traditional modeling techniques. In this step, you may also bake some of that additional detail from the high resolution sculpt into a texture that you apply to your retopo'd mesh. Chapter 8 has more on baking textures from your geometry.

Matcaps: A display option for sculpting

When sculpting in Blender, you may find that the material for your object and lighting settings in the 3D View doesn't give you a good enough sense of the detail you're adding to your mesh.

To get around this, you might set up a specific lighting environment and material for sculpting, or you might try adjusting the OpenGL lights from the System section of User Preferences.

However, both of those options can be time-consuming to set up, and they aren't necessarily easy to tweak while in the process of sculpting.

Enter *matcaps*, short for *material captures*. A matcap is an image that encapsulates all the properties of a material, including lighting. By mapping that material to the face normals of a mesh, you can make that mesh appear to have the material and lighting captured by the matcap.

Blender ships with 24 preset matcaps that you can quickly and temporarily map to all visible objects in the 3D View. To use them, go to the Shading panel in the 3D View's Properties region (N) and enable the Matcap check box. Upon enabling matcaps, a large icon appears beneath the check box. This is your currently active matcap. If you left-click that icon, it expands as shown in the figure to let you choose one of the other available matcaps.

Of course, there are a few things to keep in mind if you choose to use matcaps in the 3D View:

✔ The matcap is applied to all objects visible from the 3D View, whether you're sculpting them or not.

Fortunately, this is easy to get around using layers or local view (Numpad-slash {/}).

✔ If you're working in Blender with an older computer or an under-powered video card, you may experience some performance slowdowns if you enable matcaps in the 3D View.

Aside from upgrading your hardware, there's not a clean workaround for this. I've had *some* success splitting my 3D View (or duplicating it to a separate window) and the matcap display visible there while I sculpt in another 3D View with matcaps disabled. If you do that, the matcap view will only update when you finish strokes, so you get the benefit of snappy performance in one 3D View with the matcap visualization after each brush stroke in the other view.

All told, matcaps are a fantastically useful feature for 3D sculptors and modelers. It's worth it to try to take advantage of them as part of your modeling process.

Figure:
Blender's matcaps can be enabled in the Shading panel of the 3D View's Properties region.

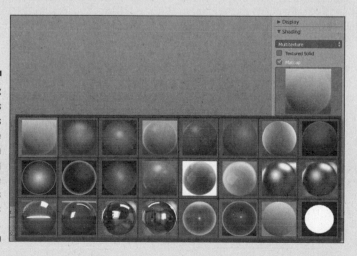

Sculpting options

Figure 5-18 shows the contents of the Tools tab as well as the Options tab in the Tool Shelf when you're in Sculpt mode. The buttons in these panels — Brush, Stroke, Curve, Dyntopo, Texture, and Symmetry/Lock in the Tools tab, and Overlay, Options, and Appearance in the Options tab — are for customizing your sculpt brushes as you work. On the left of Figure 5-18 are the panels in the Tools tab; on the right are the panels in the Options tab.

Figure 5-18:
Panels in the Tool Shelf that are specific to Sculpt mode. On the left are the panels in the Tools tab and on the right are the panels in the Options tab.

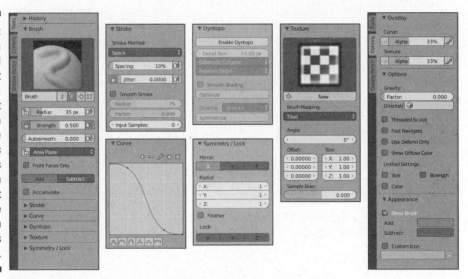

Brush types

As you work your way down the Tool Shelf, you get finer and finer control of your brush. In fact, the first panel, Brush, just contains a list of brush data-blocks, which serve as presets for all the subsequent settings in the Tool Shelf. Switch your brushes by clicking on the brush icon above the datablock and choose the preset brush you're interested in. By default, 18 presets appear in this list, each one modifying your mesh in a very specific way. All brushes work by left-clicking with the brush cursor over the mesh and dragging your mouse cursor around the 3D View. Due to this brush-style of editing, using a drawing tablet can be very beneficial.

Here are brief descriptions of some of the most used sculpt brushes in the list (if the brush has a hotkey, I include it next to the brush name in parentheses):

✔ **Blob:** When you sculpt with the Blob brush, vertices under your brush stroke are pushed outward or inward in a spherical shape.

This brush is good for adding or removing large forms to or from your mesh when creating rough starting sculpts.

✔ **Clay (C):** The Clay brush is pretty unique among Blender's sculpt brushes. Its primary purpose is to make large changes, adding or subtracting volume from your base mesh and dealing with details later.

Unlike the SculptDraw brush, which just moves vertices along their local normals, the Clay brush uses a reference plane that you can customize from this brush's settings. The Clay brush is also useful for merging unlinked meshes within the same object.

✔ **Clay Strips:** This brush behaves similarly to the regular Clay brush, but the technical difference is that it uses a cube to define the brush area instead of a sphere like the Clay brush.

In practice, you should find that the Clay Strips brush feels more like you're building up layers of clay as you work and often yields a textured surface with a bunch of wrinkles and ridges.

✔ **Crease (Shift+C):** In a way, the Crease brush is the opposite of the Blob brush. Rather than pushing vertices away from the center of the brush cursor, the Crease brush pulls vertices closer, sharpening indentations and ridges alike. In contrast to the Pinch/Magnify brush, the Crease brush uses a reference plane, much like the Clay brush does.

✔ **Fill/Deepen:** Using Fill/Deepen brush, you can (depending on the brush settings) raise recessed vertices on your mesh as if filling a ditch or you can deepen that ditch without having an effect on the vertices that are at "sea level."

✔ **Flatten/Contrast (Shift+T):** The Flatten setting of this brush lowers or raises vertices to an average height in an attempt to get them to be as flat, or *planar,* as possible. If you're sculpting a landscape and you decide to remove a hill, this brush is the one to use. The other setting for this brush, Contrast, pushes vertices up and down *away* from that average height, increasing the overall distance between them.

✔ **Grab (G):** When you left-click and drag your mouse cursor on a mesh with the Grab brush activated, the vertices that are within the brush cursor's circle are moved to wherever you drag your mouse to. Grab is like selecting a bunch of vertices in Edit mode and pressing G. In fact, you can also quickly choose this brush in Sculpt mode by pressing G, too.

On a related note, if you're using dyntopo, the Grab brush is one of the few that doesn't add or remove vertices to your mesh. It just moves them around. If you want to add and remove vertices while moving them around, try the Snake Hook brush described a few bullet points after this one.

✔ **Inflate/Deflate (I):** When you run the Inflate/Deflate brush over your mesh, vertices move outward along their own local normals. If the Subtract button in the Brush panel is enabled, the vertices move inward. This brush is good for fattening or shrinking parts of a model. The difference between this brush and the Blob brush is that Blob inflates vertices in a distinctly spherical way, whereas the Inflate/Deflate brush works purely based on vertex normals.

✔ **Layer (L):** The Layer brush is like using the SculptDraw brush with a maximum height that it pulls the vertices, basically creating a raised mesa on the surface of your mesh. For a simple mnemonic, remember that the Layer brush relates to the SculptDraw brush in the same way that the Clay Strips brush relates to the Clay brush.

✔ **Mask (M):** There are occasions in sculpting when you want to preserve a part of your mesh and prevent yourself from accidentally sculpting those vertices. The Mask brush was created specifically for that purpose. Enable the Mask brush and you can paint the vertices on your mesh that you wish to protect.

✔ **Nudge:** Using the Nudge brush, you can push vertices a bit at a time in the direction of your brush stroke. Think of it as a much more nuanced version of the Grab brush.

✔ **Pinch/Magnify (P):** If you enable the Pinch/Magnify brush, vertices are pulled toward the center of your brush cursor as you move it over the surface of the mesh. Pinch is a great way to add ridges and creases to a model, though perhaps with a bit less control than you have with the Crease brush, which more frequently pushes topology inward or outward.

✔ **Scrape/Peaks:** The Scrape/Peaks brush is the logical opposite of the Fill/Deepen brush. Whereas Fill/Deepen raises or lowers only the vertices that are below "sea level," the Scrape/Peaks brush only works on vertices that are above sea level. In practical application, you use this brush to flatten mountains or grow them larger.

✔ **SculptDraw:** The SculptDraw brush is the default brush and it basically pulls the surface of your mesh outward (or inward, if you enable the Subtract button in the Brush panel). By default, the brush works with an even falloff, so the raised areas you draw tend to flow smoothly back into the rest of the mesh.

✔ **Smooth (S):** If you have jagged parts of your mesh or undesirable surface irregularities created while sculpting, using the Smooth brush cleans up those bumpy parts and makes the surface of your mesh, well, smoother.

By pressing and holding Shift while you sculpt, you can have quick access to the Smooth brush at any time, regardless of your current active brush. This quick access feature makes for a very fast sculpting workflow.

✔ **Snake Hook:** The Snake Hook brush is very similar to the Grab brush except it gives you more control over what you can do when you pull the vertices away from the main portion of your mesh. This is especially true if you're sculpting with dyntopo enabled, because the Snake Hook brush generates new geometry and the Grab brush doesn't. With enough geometry, you can actually sketch in 3D with the Snake Hook brush. It's useful for making things like spines, tentacles, and dreadlocks.

✔ **Thumb:** To think about the Thumb brush effectively, imagine you're working with real clay. If you put your thumb on the clay surface and massage it in a particular direction, the area under your thumb also flattens out. That's the basic effect of the Thumb brush. It's like the Nudge brush with the additional feature of flattening the area that you push.

✔ **Twist:** Most of the other Sculpt mode brushes are primarily means of translating or scaling vertices. The Twist brush, in contrast, is a brush for rotating vertices in your mesh. When you left-click and drag your mouse on your mesh, the brush remains stationary and the position of your mouse cursor determines how much the vertices within the area of your brush rotate.

Brush controls

The Radius and Strength sliders below the list of brush datablocks control the size and strength of the brush you're currently using. You can use hotkeys for changing these values while in the 3D View so that you don't have to constantly return to the Tool Shelf:

✔ To change brush radius, press F, move your mouse until the brush cursor is the desired size, and left-click to confirm.

✔ To adjust the brush strength, press Shift+F and move your mouse cursor toward the center of the circle that appears to increase the strength or away from the center to decrease the strength. When you're at the strength you want, left-click to confirm.

Additionally, if you happen to have a drawing tablet, you can bind the Radius and Strength values to the pressure sensitivity of your tablet. Each value slider has a button to its right with an icon of a hand pushing against a blue line with its index finger. Left-click this toggle button on either slider, and Blender recognizes the pressure information from your tablet.

The next set of important controls available while in Sculpt mode are a pair of buttons in the Brush panel. Depending on which brush preset you're using, these labels may be named Add and Subtract, Flatten and Contrast, Inflate and Deflate, or they may not be there (for grabbing brushes like Grab, Snake Hook, and Twist). Regardless of what they're named, if they appear, the first button (Add, Flatten, Inflate) is the default behavior for sculpting brushes.

If you enable the second button (Subtract, Contrast, Deflate), it does the inverse of the default behavior. For example, with Subtract enabled, the Clay brush pushes vertices into the volume of your mesh instead of pulling them out.

Also, note that regardless of whether you enabled the first or second button in this block, pressing Ctrl while using the brush does the opposite behavior. For example, if you're using the SculptDraw brush with Add enabled, the normal behavior creates a small hill wherever you move your mouse cursor. If you Ctrl+left-click and drag, you sculpt a small valley instead.

When working with brushes like SculptDraw, Inflate, or Layer, an additional check box, labeled Accumulate, appears under the Add/Subtract buttons. By default, when you use these brushes, they move the faces on your mesh relative to the normals that they have when you start making your stroke, regardless of how many times you paint over them in a single stroke. This default behavior is helpful because it prevents your mesh from quickly expanding uncontrollably. However, if you want to use a face's immediate normal when you run your brush over it, then you should enable this check box.

Other settings in the Sculpt mode Tool Shelf

The next few panels in the Tool Shelf while in Sculpt mode — Texture, Stroke, Curve, and Symmetry/Lock in the Tools tab, and Overlay, Options, and Appearance in the Options tab — are devoted to creating custom brushes. The next section gets into custom brushes in more detail. The following describes each panel in the Tools tab:

- ✓ **Texture:** Any texture you can create in Blender can be used in a brush. The Texture panel is where you assign a texture to your current brush. See Chapter 8 for more information on creating textures. If you already have textures created in your file, left-clicking the texture icon gives you the ability to choose which one you want to use on your active brush.

- ✓ **Stroke:** The Stroke panel holds settings that dictate what happens when you're dragging the brush over your mesh. The most valuable setting in this panel is Stroke Method. The options in this menu dictate how your brush movement influences your mesh. For fun, choose the Layer brush and set the Stroke Method to Anchor. When you left-click and drag your brush over your model, you get a neat mesh tsunami that originates from the location you clicked.

- ✓ **Curve:** Within this panel are settings for adjusting how the influence of your brush changes from its center to its extremities.

- ✓ **Dyntopo:** If you choose to enable dyntopo for dynamic topology sculpting, your controls for dyntopo behavior are in this panel, as covered in detail earlier in this chapter.

✔ **Symmetry/Lock:** This panel controls how the sculpt brushes modify your mesh relative to the object's local axes. For example, if you left-click the X check box, anything you do on the left side of the mesh automatically also happens on the right side of the mesh. Symmetry is an excellent timesaver for doing involved tasks like sculpting faces. The X, Y, and Z lock buttons in this panel prevent your sculpted vertices from moving along any of those axes if they're enabled.

There are also additional panels specific to sculpting in the Options tab of the Tool Shelf:

✔ **Overlay:** Overlays give you more detail about the nature of your brush. They can show the fall-off curve of the brush as well as the texture you're using. However, they can have a significant impact on the responsiveness of the 3D View when you're sculpting. Use the settings in this panel to enable overlays and control how much they're visible as well as when (that is, you can make it so overlays only appear when you're not drawing a stroke).

✔ **Options:** The settings in this panel are commonly used to speed up your performance while sculpting. In particular, the Threaded Sculpt and Fast Navigate check boxes are very helpful. Threaded Sculpt (enabled by default) toggles Blender's ability to take advantage of all the cores of your CPU if your computer has more than one; Fast Navigate (disabled by default) drops the subdivision level of your mesh while orbiting in the 3D View. The Fast Navigate option is only relevant if you're sculpting with the Multiresolution modifier on your mesh.

✔ **Appearance:** From the Appearance panel, you can stipulate whether your brush is visible and what color to use for your brush's outline if it is. Also, if you have an image that you'd like to use as a custom icon for your custom brush, you can enable the Custom Icon check box and point Blender to the location of that image on your hard drive. Then that image will appear as the representation of your custom brush in the brushes menu at the top of the Tool Shelf. This is particularly useful if you start creating your own custom brushes, as described in the next section.

Creating custom brushes

Using the controls in the Tool Shelf while in Sculpt Mode, you can create your own custom brush datablock. Use the following steps:

1. **Create a new brush datablock by clicking the Plus (+) button in the datablock beneath the list of brushes in the Brush panel at the top of the Tool Shelf.**

   Adding a new brush datablock in this manner duplicates the current active brush. So for efficiency, select the brush most similar to the custom one you want to create before adding.

2. **Name your new brush by typing in the datablock field.**

   Now you can go about customizing your brush.

The importance of good topology

If you listen to modelers talk or if you visit some of the Web forums where 3D modelers hang out, you'll hear the words *topology* and *edge flow* pretty often. These concepts are very important for a modeler, particularly if your model is destined to be animated. These terms refer to how the vertices and edges of your mesh lay out across its surface. Even when sculpting, 3D modelers will often use a base mesh that has good topology as their starting point. Or, when they're done sculpting, they'll take the model through a process known as *retopology* to give it a clean edge flow that's usable in animation. To that end, whether you're sculpting or just straight modeling, keep a few key guidelines in mind:

✔ **Use quads.** Try to avoid triangles and ngons in your final mesh whenever possible. They're fine to use as stand-ins while your work, but four-sided polygons look better when subdivided, and they also tend to deform more cleanly when an armature is used to animate them.

✔ **Minimize the use of poles that don't have four edges.** Remember that a pole is where multiple edges join at a single vertex. The UV Sphere mesh has two large poles at its top and bottom. Poles are harder to avoid than triangles, but you should do what you can to minimize their use because they can terminate edge loops, and they don't deform as nicely as four-edged poles. If you're forced to use a pole, try to put it in a place on the mesh that won't deform a lot when it's animated.

✔ **Holes such as mouths and eye sockets should be encircled by concentric edge loops.** This guideline is particularly important for character models that may be animated. Having concentric edge loops makes it easier to deform and animate these highly expressive parts of the face.

✔ **Edges should follow anatomy (at least on the face).** Following the flow of anatomy — particularly musculature — is important on face models because doing so yields cleaner, more natural deformations. For instance, the crease from the side of the nose flows around the mouth. For limbs, following musculature is less imperative; tube-type topology usually should be fine. But if you're aiming for anatomical realism in your models, following these little rules really makes the lives of riggers and animators much easier (and it helps make the final animation look better).

Using Blender's texture system to tweak brushes

In the Texture panel, you can pick a texture to influence the behavior of your brush. Any texture made in Texture Properties can be used as a brush when you sculpt. Textured brushes are an excellent way to get more details added to your mesh while sculpting. Choose an existing texture by left-clicking the texture square in this panel and picking from the thumbnail images that appear. (See Chapter 8 for more information on creating and loading textures in Blender.) Refer to Figure 5-18 to see the Texture panel in Sculpt mode's Tool Shelf.

You may want to choose the Rake option from the Texture Angle Source drop-down menu when you've loaded a texture. With this option chosen, the texture is rotated as you sculpt to match the motion of the brush. Using Rake helps you avoid creating unnatural patterns from your textures when you sculpt.

If you're sculpting with the Multiresolution modifier and you have a high level of subdivisions, it can be taxing on your computer, using a *lot* of memory to store all those additional vertices. If you use too many levels of subdivision, your computer may run out of memory, and Blender may lock up or crash. This can also happen if you're sculpting with dyntopo and add a lot of fine details to your sculpt. In an effort to prevent a crash and give themselves more vertices to play with, many 3D sculptors in Blender often go to the User Preferences under Editing to disable Global Undo and change the number of undo steps from the default value of 32 down to 0. This modification removes the safety net of undo, but it can often significantly improve Blender's performance while sculpting.

Understanding the basics of retopology

When it comes to doing retopo, Blender doesn't really have much in the way of dedicated tools built into it. A few very useful add-ons, such as Contours and Polystrips (or their bundled combination, RetopoFlow), have been created by third-party developers to help with the retopo process, but they don't ship with Blender by default. That said, if you find that sculpting and modeling are your favorite aspects of 3D computer graphics, you'll be going through the retopo process a lot. In that situation, I recommend that you investigate and ultimately purchase those add-ons. But it's still worthwhile to know what Blender can do on its own as well. Retopo add-ons can get you part of the way there, but most of the time, you still need to finish with Blender's native tools.

So if there aren't any dedicated retopo tools in Blender, exactly how do you retopologize your mesh? The answer is deceptively simple. You combine Blender's native modeling tools with clever use of snapping (see Chapter 3 for a more thorough overview of snapping). There are some shortcuts, such as trying to use the Shrinkwrap modifier to snap the vertices of a clean topology mesh to the surface of your sculpt. However, when it comes down to it, you're really going to need to do point-for-point modeling.

Once you finish your 3D sculpt, use the following steps as the basic process for retopologizing:

1. **From Object mode, create a new mesh (Shift+A⇨Mesh⇨Plane).**

   In this example, I'm using a plane, but it could be any mesh, as you'll see in the next step. In fact, some modelers use an add-on that creates a zero-vertex mesh object for exactly this kind of thing.

2. **Rename your new mesh object to something that makes sense.**

   It could be something like `Character.retopo`, for example, as long as it's anything other than the primitive mesh's name.

3. **Tab into Edit mode on your new mesh.**

4. **Select all of the vertices in this new mesh and delete them.**

   Now you have a mesh object with no data inside.

5. **Enable snapping (Shift+Tab or left-click the button with the magnet icon in the 3D View's header).**

   Also, make sure that the Snap Element drop-down menu is set to use face snapping. This step is important; it's what makes the rest of the retopo process possible.

6. **Ctrl+left-click on the surface of your 3D sculpt.**

   This creates the first vertex of your retopo mesh. By enabling face snapping, your new vertex should be located right on the surface of your sculpt mesh.

7. **Extruding from that first vertex (Ctrl+left-click or E), use point-to-point modeling techniques to lay out the vertices of your retopo'd mesh.**

   As you work, keep in mind the basic guidelines outlined in the sidebar in this chapter, "The importance of good topology". This step comprises the somewhat tedious and time-consuming process of retopologizing your mesh. However, when you've already made your sculpt, you have a clear plan that shows what your final mesh should look like. At this point, you're basically playing "connect the dots" on the surface of your 3D sculpt. Once you get up to speed, this is a much more effective way of modeling than traditional box modeling or point-to-point modeling methods.

Figure 5-19 shows a mesh sculpted using dyntopo and that same model after it's been retopo'd.

Figure 5-19: On the left, a model sculpted with dyntopo; on the right is the same model after being retopologized.

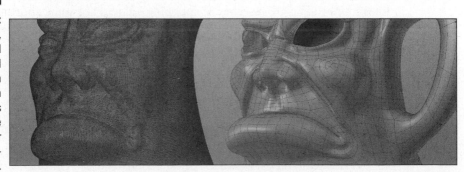

Chapter 6

Using Blender's Non-mesh Primitives

In This Chapter

▶ Working with curve objects and NURBS surfaces

▶ Understanding the benefits of metaball objects

▶ Using text in Blender

Although polygon-based meshes tend to be the bread and butter of modelers in Blender, they aren't the only types of objects that are available to you for creating things in 3D space. Blender also has curves, surfaces, metaball objects, and text objects. These objects tend to have somewhat more specialized purposes than meshes, but when you need what they provide, they're extremely useful.

Curves and surfaces are nearly as general purpose as meshes; they're particularly handy for anything that needs to have a smooth, non-faceted look. They're also important for models that require mathematical precision and accuracy in their appearance. Metaball objects are great at creating organic shapes that merge into one another, such as simple fluids. You can also use them to make a roughly sculpted model from basic elements that you can detail further in Sculpt mode. Text objects are exactly what they sound like: You use them to add text to a scene and manipulate that text in all three dimensions. This chapter tells you more about working with all these types of objects.

Using Curves and Surfaces

So, what's the biggest difference between curves and surfaces when compared to meshes? *Math!* Okay, I'm sorry. That was mean of me; I know that math can be a four-letter word for many artists, but don't worry; you won't have to do any math here. What I mean to say is that you can describe curves and surfaces to the computer as a mathematical function. You describe meshes, on the other hand, using the positions of all the individual vertices that they're composed of. In terms of the computer, curves and surfaces have two advantages:

- ✔ **Curves and surfaces are very precise.** When you get down to it, the best that a mesh can be is an approximation of a real object. A mesh can look really, really good, but it's not exact. Because curves are defined by math, they're exactly the correct shape, which is why designers and engineers like them.

- ✔ **Curves and surfaces take up less memory.** Because the shape is mathematically defined, the computer can save that shape by saving the math, rather than saving all the individual points. Complicated curves and surfaces can often take up quite a bit less hard drive space than the same shape made with meshes.

Of course, these advantages come with some caveats, too. For one, curves and surfaces can sometimes be more difficult to control. Because curves and surfaces don't really have vertices for you to directly manipulate, you have to use *control points*. Depending on the type of curve, control points can sit directly on the shape or float somewhere off of the surface as part of a control *cage*.

Even though curves and surfaces are perfect mathematical descriptions of a shape, the computer is actually an imperfect way of displaying those perfect shapes. All 3D geometry is eventually tessellated when the computer processes it (see Chapter 5). So even though curves and surfaces can take less memory on a computer, displaying them smoothly may actually take more time for the computer to process. To speed up things, you can tell the computer to use a rougher tessellation with fewer triangles. As a result, what you see in Blender is an approximation of that perfect curve or surface shape. Do you find yourself thinking, "But hey, I thought curves were supposed to be perfect mathematical descriptions of a shape. What gives with these facets?" Well, the curve *is* perfect. It's just hard for the computer to show it to you directly.

But despite these minor disadvantages, using curves and surfaces is a really smart move in quite a few cases. For example, most designers like to use curves for company logos because curves can scale in print to any size without looking jagged or *aliased* around its edges. As a 3D artist, you can easily import the curves of a logo design and give the logo some depth, dimension, and perhaps even some animation.

And speaking of animation, curves have quite a few handy uses there as well. For example, you can use a curve to define a path for an object to move along. You can also use curves in Blender's Graph Editor to display and control the changes to an object's properties over time. For modeling purposes, curves are great for pipes, wires, and ornate organic shapes. Figure 6-1 shows a park bench. Only curves were used to model its sides.

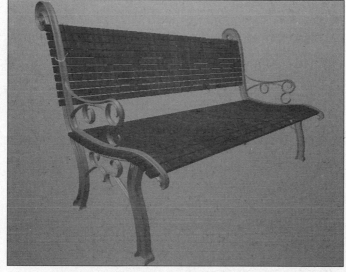

Figure 6-1:
With the exception of the slats for the seat and back, this entire park bench was modeled with curves.

Model credit: Bob Holcomb

A set of curves used to define a shape in three dimensions is a *surface*. In some ways, curve surfaces are very similar to meshes that have the Subdivision Surface modifier applied because they both have a control cage defining the final shape that's created. The difference is that the curve surface has space and precision benefits that meshes don't have. Also, surfaces are a little bit easier to add textures to because you don't have to go through the additional step of *unwrapping,* or flattening the surface, so you can apply a two-dimensional texture to it. When you use a surface, you get that unwrapping for free because it's already done for you.

For these reasons — especially the precision — architects, industrial designers, and engineers prefer to work with surfaces. Someone designed just about everything in your house, including your water faucet, your coffee maker, your television, your car, and even the house itself. If an item was manufactured within the last 20 years, chances are good that it was designed on a computer and visualized with surfaces. Also, before the advent of subdivision surfaces, early characters for computer animations were modeled using curve surfaces because they were better at achieving organic shapes. Of course, if you're seen using curves to build a character these days, you may be viewed as a bit of masochist . . . especially if you try to do it in Blender.

Understanding the different types of curves

In Blender, you can add curves by using Shift+A➪Curve and choosing the type of curve you'd like to use from the menu that appears. As shown in Figure 6-2, you can use two main kinds of curves: *Bézier curves* and *NURBS curves.* (The Path curve is a specific type of NURBS curve.)

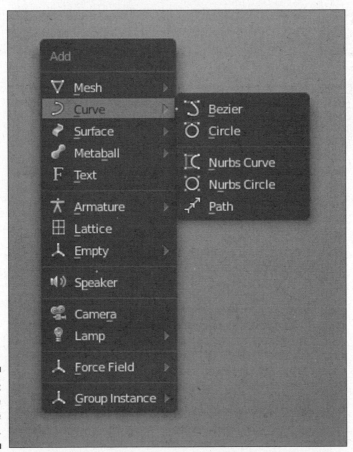

Figure 6-2:
The
Add➪Curve
menu.

You generally use Bézier curves more for text and logos. Bézier curves work in three dimensions by default, but you can get them to lock to a single 2D plane if you need to. You can tell that you're using a Bézier curve because if you tab into Edit mode to look at it, each control point has a pair of handles that you can use to give additional control over the curve's shape.

NURBS stands for *Non-Uniform Relational B-Spline*. The control points in NURBS curves don't have handles like Bézier curves do. By default, NURBS control points don't normally even touch the curve shape itself. Instead, the control points are *weighted* to influence the shape of the curve. Control points with higher weights attract the curve closer to them. Figure 6-3 shows the same curve shape made with Bézier curves and with NURBS curves.

Figure 6-3:
An arbitrary shape created with Bézier curves (left) and NURBS curves (right).

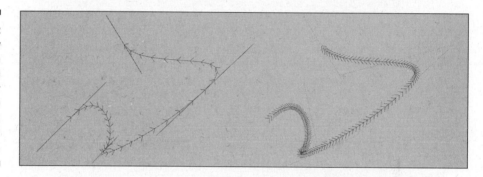

Although curves can work in three dimensions and can even create three-dimensional shapes like the park bench in Figure 6-1, you can't arbitrarily join them to create a surface. If you want to create a surface, you need to actually navigate to the Surfaces menu (Shift+A➪Surface), as shown in Figure 6-4. Notice that NURBS Curve and NURBS Circle are also options on this menu. Be aware, however, that Blender treats these types of NURBS differently than the NURBS curves available in the Curve menu. In fact, Blender doesn't even allow you to perform a Join (Ctrl+J) between NURBS curves and NURBS surface curves. This limitation is a bit inconvenient, I know, but the situations where you'd actually want to do something like that are rare enough that you don't need to worry about it that much.

Working with curves

Surprisingly few specialized controls are specific to curves. Grab (G), rotate (R), and scale (S) work as expected, and, like with meshes, you can extrude a selected control point in Edit mode by either pressing E or Ctrl+left-clicking where you would like to extrude to. You can join separate curves in Edit mode by selecting the end control points on each curve and pressing F, like making a face with meshes.

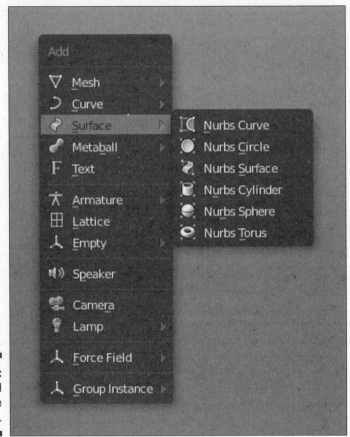

Figure 6-4:
The Add
⇨Surface
menu.

When working with curves, the extrude operation (E) only works on the *end points* (the first and last control points of the curve). If you try to extrude a control point that isn't an end point, Blender just does the grab operation.

If the two control points you select are at the start and end of the same curve, pressing F closes the curve, or, in Blenderese, you're making the curve *cyclic*. You can also make a curve cyclic with any control point selected (not just the start or end) by pressing Alt+C while in Edit mode or going to Curve⇨Toggle Cyclic in the 3D View's header. Figure 6-5 shows a cyclic (closed) and non-cyclic (open) Bézier curve.

If you make a 2D curve cyclic, it creates a flat plane in the shape of your curve. And putting one cyclic curve within the borders of another curve actually creates a hole in that plane. However, this trick doesn't work with 3D curves because they aren't planar. In those situations, you want to use a surface.

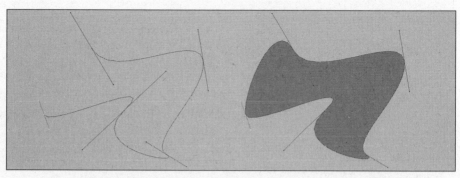

Figure 6-5:
The same
Bézier
curve,
cyclic
(left) and
non-cyclic
(right).

Changing 3D curves into 2D curves

Curves are initially set to work in three dimensions by default. Working in three dimensions gives you the ability to move curve control points freely in the X-, Y-, or Z-axes. You can optionally lock curve objects to work in any arbitrary two-dimensional plane you want. In this case, the control points on the 2D curve are constrained to its local XY plane.

To lock the curve to working only in two dimensions, go to Curve Properties (see Figure 6-6) and left-click the 2D button.

When you tab to Edit mode on a 3D curve, you may notice that the curve has little arrows spaced along it. These arrows are *curve normals* and indicate the direction of the curve. To adjust the size of these curve normals, change the Normal Size value in the Properties region of the 3D View (N) in the Curve Display panel. You can hide curve normals altogether by deactivating the Normals check box that is also in the Curve Display panel. In 2D curves, curve normals aren't displayed.

That said, all curves have direction, even cyclic ones. The direction of a curve isn't normally all that important unless you're using the curve as a path. In that situation, the direction of the curve is the direction that the animated object is traveling along the curve. You can switch the direction of the curve by choosing Curve⇨Segments⇨Switch Direction from the 3D View's header, clicking the Curve⇨Switch Direction button in the Tools tab of the Tool Shelf, or pressing W⇨Switch Direction.

Figure 6-6 shows Curve Properties when a curve is selected.

The controls in Curve Properties are relevant to all curves, regardless of type. Some of the most important ones are in the Shape panel. You've already seen what the 2D and 3D buttons do. Below them are the Preview U and Render U values. These values define the resolution of the curve. Remember

Figure 6-6:
The controls
for editing
curves.

that Blender shows you only an approximation of the real curve. Increasing the resolution here makes the curve look more like the curve defined by the math, at the cost of more processor time. That's why you see two resolution values:

- ✔ **Preview U:** The default resolution. It's also what you see in the 3D View.

- ✔ **Render U:** The resolution that Blender uses when you render. By default, this resolution is set to 0, which means Blender uses whatever value that is in Preview U.

Extruding, beveling, and tapering curves

The controls in the Geometry panel pertain primarily to extruding and beveling your curve objects. The Offset value is the exception to this rule. It's pretty interesting because it allows you to offset the curve from the control points. The effect of the Offset value is most apparent (and helpful) on cyclic curves. Values less than 1 are inset from the control points, whereas values greater than 1 are outset.

The ability to inset or outset your curve with the Offset value is a quick way to put an outline on a logo or text because Blender doesn't have a stroke function for curves like what's available in Inkscape or Adobe Illustrator.

The Extrude value is probably the quickest way to give some depth to a curve, especially a 2D curve. However, you don't want to confuse the curve Extrude value with the extrude capability you get by pressing E. The Extrude value affects the entire curve in Object mode, rather than just the selected control points in Edit mode. On a cyclic 2D curve, the flat planar shape that gets created extends out in both directions of the local Z direction of the curve object, with the caps drawn on it. And you can even control whether Blender draws the front or back cap by using the Fill drop-down menu in the Shape panel. If you extrude a non-cyclic curve, you end up with something that looks more like a ribbon going along the shape of the curve. The ribbon look is also what happens when you increase the extrude value on a 3D curve. Figure 6-7 shows some of the different effects that you can get with an extruded curve.

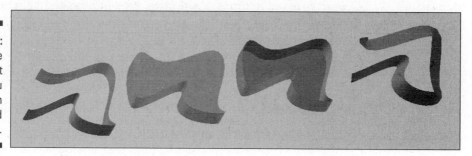

Of course, one drawback to extruding a curve is that you get a really sharp edge at the corners of the extrusion. Depending on what you're creating, harsh edges tend to look "too perfect" and unnatural. Fortunately, Bevel can take care of that for you. To give an extruded curve more natural corners, simply increase the Depth value under the Bevel label. When you do, the bevel is really kind of simple: just a cut across the corner. You can make the bevel smoother by increasing the Resolution value. Like the Preview U and Render U values, this value increases the resolution of part of the curve. In this case, it's the resolution of the bevel. Increasing the Resolution value makes a smoother, more curved bevel. Beveling works on both cyclic and non-cyclic curves.

But say that you want something more ornate, kind of like the moulding or trim you'd find around the doorway on a house. In that case, you want to use a *bevel object*. Using a bevel object on your curve basically means that you're going to use the shape of one curve to define the bevel on another.

To get a better idea of how you can use bevel objects, use the following steps:

1. **Create a Bézier circle (Shift+A⇨Curve⇨Circle).**

   In Curve Properties, make sure that the circle is a 2D shape. Scale (S) up the circle nice and large so that you can see what's going on.

2. **Extrude the circle by increasing the Extrude value in the Geometry panel of Curve Properties.**

   The circle doesn't have to be excessively thick, just thick enough to give it some form of depth.

3. **Create a Bézier curve (Shift+A⇨Curve⇨Bézier Curve).**

4. **Tab into Edit mode and edit this curve a bit to get the bevel shape that you want.**

   Keep the curve non-cyclic for now.

5. **When you're done editing, tab back out to Object mode.**

6. **Select your Bézier circle and, in the Bevel Object field of the Geometry panel in Curve Properties, type or click the name of your Bézier curve.**

   If you didn't rename it (although you should have!), it's probably called something like Curve or Curve.001. After you select your bevel object, the corners of your Bézier circle are beveled with the shape defined by your Bézier curve. Now for fun, follow the next step.

7. **Go back and make the bevel object curve cyclic (Alt+C in Edit mode).**

   Doing so actually removes the front and back planes from the extrusion. You're left with a curve shape that follows the main Bézier circle's path.

8. **For extra kicks, select the Bézier circle and tab into Edit mode; select any control point and press Alt+S to shrink or fatten the beveled shape around that control point.**

   Slick, huh?

When you use a bevel object, you're essentially handing control of the curve's shape over to the bevel object. That being the case, after you use it, changing the values for Extrude, Bevel Depth, and Bevel Resolution has no effect on the curve for as long as you have the bevel object there.

Figure 6-8 shows the results of these steps.

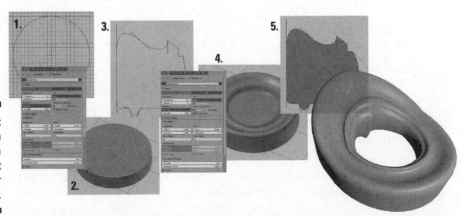

Figure 6-8:
Having fun by adding a bevel object to a Bézier circle.

TIP

If you're using a curve to model anything roughly cylindrical in shape such as a pipe or a tube, you actually don't need to use a bevel object curve at all. It's a bit of a hidden function, but you can get the same effect by just beveling the curve. I know that sounds odd (how do you bevel something that doesn't have any corners?), but trust me, it works. Use the following steps:

1. **From Curve Properties, set the Fill drop-down menu in the Shape panel to None if you have a 2D curve. Set it to Full if you have a 3D curve.**

2. **Increase the Bevel Depth in the Geometry panel.**

3. **Increase the Bevel Resolution value to make the cross-section more circular.**

   I usually get good results with a value around 3 or 4. Hooray! One less bevel object to hide!

4. **Thicken or make thinner your new tube-y pipe at different points along its length by selecting individual control points in Edit mode and using the Alt+S hotkey.**

   You can also adjust this value from the Properties region of the 3D View (N). It's the Mean Radius value in the Transform panel.

In the preceding examples, I show that you can use Alt+S on individual control points to shrink or fatten the thickness of the extrusion (or bevel). However, perhaps you'd like to have more control along the length of the curve. This situation is where you'd use the *Taper Object* field. Like bevel objects, the taper objects use one curve to define the shape of another. In this case, you're controlling the thickness along the length of the curve, and it works in very much the same way: Create a separate curve that dictates the taper shape and then type the name of that curve in the Taper Object field of the curve you'd like to control. Figure 6-9 shows how a taper object can give you complete control of a curve's shape along its length.

TIP

I prefer to create my bevel object and taper object curves in the top view (Numpad 7) along the X-axis. This way, I have a good frame of reference for the curve's center line. That's important because bevel objects use the center line to define the front and back of a curve's extrusion. You can think of taper objects as a kind of profile that revolves around its local X-axis. Bringing your control points to the center line makes the tapered curve come to a point, whereas moving them away from the center line increases the thickness.

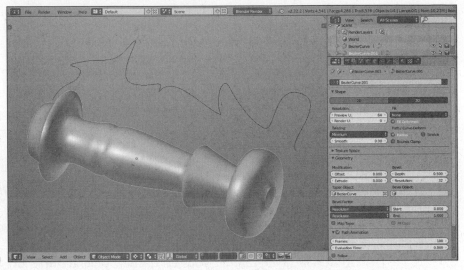

Figure 6-9:
Using a
taper object
to control
a curve's
lengthwise
shape.

The datablock drop-down menus for Taper Object and Bevel Object can get really crowded in a complex scene. Scrolling through all of the curve objects can be tedious; even if you did a good job of using sensible naming, it can be annoying or time-consuming to type in that name or search for it. Fortunately, Blender offers two shortcuts that makes filling these fields (and any other fields like them) very convenient:

✔ **Drag and drop:** If you're using the Default screen layout, then you have an Outliner in the area above your Properties editor. If you navigate to your object in the Outliner, you can left-click its icon in the Outliner and drag it to the Taper Object or Bevel Object field in Curve Properties.

✔ **Object eyedropper:** If you hover your mouse cursor over the Taper Object or Bevel Object fields and press E, the cursor should change to appear like an eyedropper. You can then left-click on any object in the 3D View. If you left-click a curve object, its name automatically populates this field. This is a fantastic tool for complex scenes or if you (ahem) didn't give your objects good, clear names.

Adjusting curve tilt

One other thing that you can control on curves is the *tilt* of the control points. In other programs, the tilt may be called the *twist* property. To get a good idea of what you can do with tilt, try the following steps:

1. **Create a Bézier Curve (Shift+A➪Curve➪Bézier) and tab into Edit mode.**

2. **Make the curve cyclic (Alt+C).**

   You may also want to select (right-click) the handles and rotate (R) them so there's a cleaner arc.

3. **Select one of the handles and press Ctrl+T or click the Tilt button in the Tools tab of the Tool Shelf.**

   Move your mouse cursor around the selection in a clockwise fashion and watch how the Tilt value in the 3D View's header changes.

4. **Confirm completion (left-click or Enter).**

   If you increase the Extrude and Bevel Depth values, you should now have something that looks a bit like Figure 6-10.

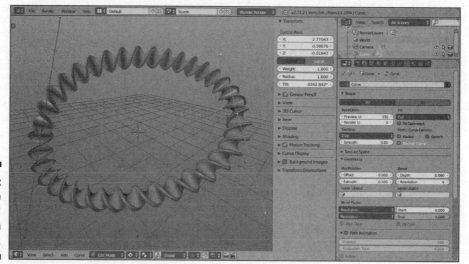

Figure 6-10: Fun with the tilt function! Mmmmmm . . . twisty.

Editing Bézier curves

The most defining aspect of Bézier curves are the handles on their control points. You can switch between the different types of handles by pressing V in the 3D View or choosing Curve⇨Control Points⇨Set Handle Type. Handles on Bézier curves are always tangential to the curve and come in one of four varieties in Blender:

- **Automatic:** These handles are set by Blender to give you the smoothest possible result in the shape of your curve. They appear in yellow and generally form a straight line with equal lengths on either side. If you try to edit an Auto handle, it immediately reverts to an aligned handle.

- **Vector:** Vector handles are not aligned with each other. They point directly to the next control point. The shape of the curve is an exactly straight line from one control point to the next. Editing a handle on a vector control point turns it into a free handle.

✔ **Aligned:** Aligned handles are locked to one another, always forming a straight line that's tangential to the curve. By default, they display in a pinkish color. If you grab (G) and move one handle on a control point, the other moves in the opposite direction to balance it out. You can, however, have aligned handles of differing lengths.

✔ **Free:** Free handles are sometimes referred to as *broken* handles. They display in black and don't necessarily have to be aligned with one another. Free handles are best suited for giving you sharp points that smoothly flow to the next control point.

✔ **Toggle Free/Align:** This is an additional option for quickly toggling a control point between being free and aligned.

Figure 6-11 shows four curves with the same exact control points, but each with different types of handles. And, yes, you can mix handle types in a single curve. It's actually quite handy when you need a figure to be smooth in some parts and pointy in others.

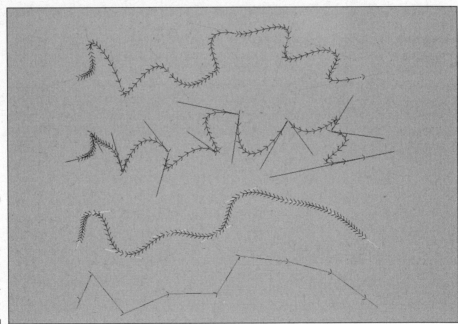

Figure 6-11:
The same curve with aligned, free, auto, and vector handles.

Editing NURBS curves and surfaces

NURBS are a different kind of beast in terms of controls. They also have control points, but NURBS curves are conspicuously without handles.

Blender treats a NURBS curve differently than a NURBS surface curve. With that caution in mind, though, whether you're dealing with a curve or a surface curve, the following things generally apply to all NURBS:

- **Each control point has a weight.** The weight, which is a value between 0 and 1, influences how much that control point influences the curve. In Blender, you set the weight in the Transform panel of the 3D View's Properties region (N). There, for any selected control point, you have the ability to directly modify the X, Y, or Z location of the control point as well as its weight, indicated by the W value. The value in the W field is averaged across all selected control points. (Note that the W field weight value affects the curve differently from the value in the Weight field below it. The latter refers to actual weight for purposes of simulating physics. Chapter 13 touches briefly on physics simulation in Blender.)

- **NURBS have knots.** In math terms, *knots* are vectors that describe how the resulting curve is influenced by the control points. In Blender, you have three settings that you can assign to knots from the Active Spline panel in Curve Properties: Uniform, Bézier, and Endpoint. By default, with the Bézier and Endpoint check boxes disabled, NURBS are assigned uniform knots. You can tell they're uniform because the curve doesn't go all the way to the end control points. Those control points' weights are factored in with all the other control points. Endpoint knots, in contrast, bring the curve all the way to the last control points, regardless of weight. Bézier knots treat the control points like they're free handles on a Bézier curve. Every three control points act like the center and two handles on a Bézier curve's control points.

- **NURBS have an order.** An *order* is another math thing. What it really means, though, is that the lower the order, the more the curve directly follows the lines between control points. And the higher the order, the smoother and more fluid the curve is as it passes the control points. You can also change the values for order in the Active Spline panel below the Bézier and Endpoint check boxes.

Figure 6-12 shows the influences that curve weights, knot types, and order can have on a NURBS curve.

If you're using a NURBS surface, you might notice in the Active Spline panel that you can independently set the knot, order, and resolution controls for a U or a V value. If you're dealing with just a curve, the U direction is all you need to worry about and, therefore, all that Blender shows you. However, a NURBS surface works in two directions: U and V. If you add a NURBS Surface (Shift+A⇨Surface⇨NURBS Surface), you can visually tell the difference between the U segments, which are reddish, and the V segments, which are yellow.

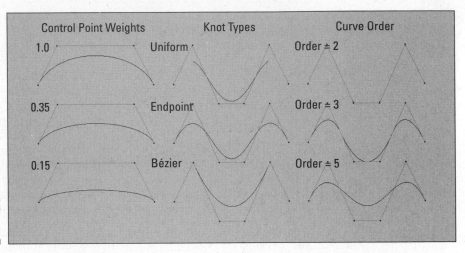

Figure 6-12:
Decreasing
curve
weights
on a con-
trol point,
differences
between the
three knot
types, and
increasing
the order of
a curve.

One really cool thing you can do easily with NURBS surfaces that's difficult to do with other types of surfaces is a process called *lofting*. (Other programs may call it *skinning*, but because that term actually means something else for rigging, I use lofting here.) Basically, lofting is the process of using a series of NURBS surface curves with the *same number of control points* as a series of profiles to define a shape. The cool thing about lofting in Blender is that after you have the profiles in place, the process is as simple as selecting all control points (A) and pressing (F). The classic use for lofting is modeling the hull of a boat, as you see in the following steps and in Figure 6-13:

1. **Add a NURBS surface curve (Shift+A⇨Surface⇨NURBS Curve) and tab into Edit mode.**

2. **Select All and Rotate –90 degrees around the X-axis (A⇨R⇨X⇨–90).**

   The bottom of your boat forms.

3. **Model a cross-section of the boat's hull.**

   You can add more control points using extrude (E or Ctrl+left-click) and move them around with grab (G). When modeling your cross-section, it would be a good idea to press Alt+C and make the curve cyclic.

   Try to keep the cross-section as planar as possible. I like to work from an orthographic (Numpad 5) front view (Numpad 1).

4. **Select all control points in your cross-section and duplicate it along the Y-axis (A⇨Shift+D⇨Y).**

5. **Make adjustments to the new cross-section to suit your tastes, but *do not add or remove any control points*.**

   Lofting requires that each cross-section has the exact same number of control points. If you add or remove control points from a cross-section, it doesn't work.

6. **Repeat Steps 4 and 5 until you're satisfied.**

7. **Select All and press F.**

   You've made a canoe!

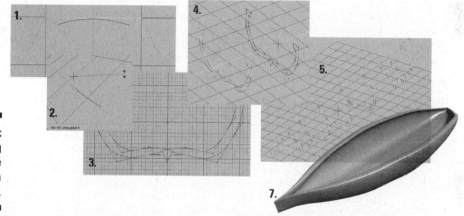

Figure 6-13:
Using lofting to create the hull of a boat.

A quick note on paths

You might be begrudging the fact that I glazed over adding a Path curve (Shift+A⇨Curve⇨Path). The reason is that you can turn just any curve into a path. By default, when you add a path, it's really a shortcut for adding a straight NURBS curve with one check box enabled in Curve Properties: Path Animation. By enabling this check box, Blender understands that this curve is a path that you can use to control the movement of an animated object. To make any NURBS or Bézier curve into a path, all you have to do is left-click this check box. I get more into the use of paths as animation controls in Chapter 10.

Understanding the strengths and limitations of Blender's surfaces

When compared to other tools that work with NURBS surfaces, Blender admittedly falls short in some functions. You can extrude surface endpoints, do lofting, and even *spin* surface curves (sometimes called *lathing* in other programs) to create bowl or cup shapes. However, that's about it. Blender currently doesn't have the functionality to do a ton of other cool things with NURBS surfaces, such as using one curve to trim the length of another or project the shape of one curve onto the surface of another.

However, there's hope. It's been slow coming, but Blender gets a little progress on the integration of better NURBS tools from time to time. However, that progress ultimately is excruciatingly slow. If you want to work exclusively with NURBS, your only real choices are to wait or use a different program.

Using Metaball Objects

Metaball objects are cool little 3D surfaces that have been part of computer graphics for a long time. Sometimes metaball objects are referred to as *blobbies*. The principle behind metaball objects is pretty simple: Imagine that you have two droplets of water, and you begin moving these two droplets closer and closer to each other. Eventually, the two droplets are going to merge and become a single, larger droplet. That process is basically how metaball objects work, except you have complete control over when the droplets merge, how much they merge, and you can re-separate them again if you'd like.

You can also do something that's more difficult in the real world: You can subtract one droplet from the other, rather than add them together into a merged object. They're a ton of fun to play with, and there are some pretty neat applications for them. Figure 6-14 shows two metaballs being merged.

Meta-wha?

Metaball objects are a bit like curves and NURBS in that their entire existence is defined by math. However, unlike NURBS or even meshes, you can't control the surface of a metaball object directly with control points or vertices. Instead, the shape of their surface is defined by a combination of the object's underlying structure (a point, a line, a plane, a sphere, or a cube) and its proximity to other metaball objects.

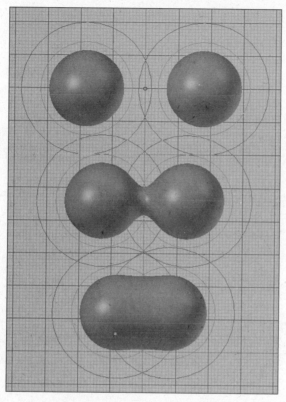

Figure 6-14:
Merging
two
metaballs.

There are five metaball object primitives:

- **Ball:** The surface in this primitive is based on the points that are all the same distance from a single origin. You can move and scale a metaball ball uniformly, but you can't scale it in just one direction.

- **Capsule:** Whereas the basis for a metaball ball is a single point, the basis for a metaball capsule is the line between two points. You can scale the surface uniformly, like a metaball ball, but you can also scale it in its local X-axis.

- **Plane:** The metaball plane's underlying structure is, as you may have guessed, a plane. You have both the local X- and the local Y-axis for scaling, as well as scaling uniformly.

- **Cube:** The metaball cube is based on a three-dimensional structure — specifically, a cube. You have the ability to scale this primitive independently in the X, Y, or Z directions.

✔ **Ellipsoid:** At first glance, you might mistake this metaball object for a metaball ball. However, instead of being based on a single point, this object is based on a sphere. So if you keep the local X, Y, and Z dimensions equal, a metaball ellipsoid behaves just like a metaball ball. However, like the metaball cube, you can also scale in any of the three individual axes.

A cool thing about metaball objects is that while you're in Edit mode, you can change from one primitive to another on the fly. To do so, use the Active Element panel in Metaball Properties. Figure 6-15 shows each of the primitives along with the default settings for them in the Active Element panel.

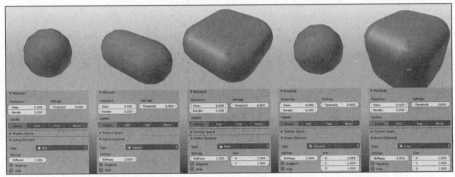

Figure 6-15: The five metaball object primitives.

The Active Element panel always displays the Stiffness value for the selected metaball object. This value controls the influence that the selected metaball object has on other metaball objects. The Stiffness value is indicated visually in the 3D View with a green ring around the metaball object's origin. You can adjust the Stiffness value here in the panel, or if you select the green ring (right-click), you can Scale (S) to adjust the Stiffness visually. By right-clicking the reddish, pinkish ring outside of that green ring, you can select the actual individual metaball object.

And depending on the type of metaball object primitive you're using, other values of X, Y, and Z may appear in the Active Element panel while you're in Edit mode. You can adjust these values here or in 3D View by using the S⇨X, S⇨Y, and S⇨Z hotkey sequences. At the bottom of the panel are buttons to either hide the selected metaball object or give it a negative influence, subtracting it from the positive, and therefore visible, metaball objects.

When you tab back out to Object mode, you can move your combined metaball object (a meta-metaball object?) as a single unit. Note, however, that even though you've grouped these metaball objects into a single Blender object, they don't live in a vacuum. If you have two complex Blender objects made up of metaballs, bringing the two of them together actually causes them to merge. Just keep that as something you may want to bear in mind and take advantage of in the future.

As a single Blender object, though, you can control a few more things using the Metaball panel, as shown in Figure 6-16. This panel is always available to metaball objects, whether in Object mode or Edit mode, and it sits at the top of Metaball Properties.

Figure 6-16:
The
Metaball
panel.

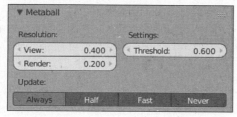

The first two values in the Metaball panel are resolution values:

- **View:** Controls how dense the generated mesh is for the metaball object in the 3D View. Lower values are a finer mesh, whereas higher values result in much more of an approximation.

- **Render:** Does the same thing as the View value, except it has an effect only at render time. The reason is that metaball objects can get really complex quickly, and because they're generated entirely by math, these complex combinations of metaball objects tend to use a lot of computer-processing power.

TIP

Working at a larger View size in the 3D View helps keep your computer responsive while you work, whereas a finer Render value keeps things pretty on output.

The Threshold value is an overall control for how much influence the metaballs in a single Blender object have over each other. This value has a range from 0 to 5, but in order for a metaball object to be visible, its individual Stiffness value must be greater than the Threshold value.

At the bottom of the Metaball panel are four buttons that control how the metaball objects get updated and displayed in the 3D View:

- **Always:** The slowest and most accurate, this setting is the default. Every change you make in the 3D View happens instantly (or as fast as your computer can handle it).

✔ **Half:** This option reduces the resolution of the metaball object as you move or edit it, increasing the responsiveness of the 3D View. When you finish transforming the metaball object, it displays in full resolution again.

✔ **Fast:** As the name implies, this setting is nearly the fastest. When you enable this button, Blender hides the metaball objects when you perform a transform and then re-evaluates the surface when you finish. Fast works very nicely, but the downside is that you don't get the nice visual feedback that Always and Half give you.

✔ **Never:** This method is certainly the fastest update. Basically, if you try to edit a metaball object, it hides everything and never updates in the 3D View. Although Never may not seem useful at first, if you decide to bind your metaball object to a particle system as a way of faking fluids, turning this setting on definitely increases performance in the 3D View.

What metaball objects are useful for

So what in the world can you actually use metaball objects to make? I actually have two answers to this question: all sorts of things, and not much. The reason for this seemingly paradoxical answer is that you *can* use metaball objects to do quick, rough prototype models, and you *can* also use them with a particle system to generate simple fluid simulations. However, with the advent of advanced modeling tools like sculpting and subdivision surfaces, metaball objects don't get used as often for prototyping. And with more advanced fluid simulation and rendering technology, metaball objects are also used less for those applications as well. They have a tendency to use a lot of computer-processing power and don't often give good topology by themselves.

That said, even though metaball objects are used *less* for these purposes, that doesn't mean that they're never used. In fact, not too long ago, I used a set of metaballs with a glowing halo material to animate the life force being forcefully pulled out of a guy in a scene for a local filmmaker. I could probably have used a particle system or fluid simulator to do this effect, but using metaballs was actually faster to set up, and I had more direct control over where everything was placed on the screen. So don't count metaball objects out just yet. These little suckers still have some life left. Besides, they're still fun to play with!

Adding Text

Over the years, working with text in Blender has come a long, long way. The way you work with text in Blender has quite a few differences from what you might expect of word-processing software like LibreOffice or Microsoft Word. What you may not expect is that Blender's text objects share a few features in common with desktop publishing programs like Adobe InDesign or QuarkXPress.

Blender's text objects are really a specialized type of curve object. Nearly all the options I describe for curves also apply to text. (See the section "Using Curves and Surfaces," earlier in this chapter.) For example, you can quickly bring text objects into the third dimension using the Extrude, Bevel, and even the Bevel Object and Taper Object fields. Figure 6-17 shows an example of the interesting things you can do with a single text object in Blender.

Figure 6-17:
Taking
advantage
of the
curve-based
nature of
Blender text
objects.

Adding and editing text

You add a text object in Blender the same way you add any other object. Press Shift+A⇨Text, and a text object appears at the location of your 3D cursor with the word "Text" as its default content.

To edit the text, you tab into Edit mode. After you're in Edit mode, the controls begin to feel a bit more like a word processor, although not exactly. For example, you can't use your mouse cursor to highlight text, but if you press Shift+← and Shift+→, depending on where the text cursor is located, you can highlight text this way.

Shift+Ctrl+←/→ highlights whole words at a time. Backspace deletes text and pressing Enter gives you a new line.

In addition to the curve-like controls, formatting controls also are available in Text Properties, as shown in Figure 6-18.

  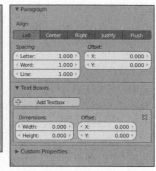

Figure 6-18:
Text
Properties.

In the Paragraph panel is a block of alignment buttons to help you align your text relative to the origin of the text object. You have the following options:

- **Left:** Aligns text to the left. The text object's origin serves as the left-hand guide for the text.

- **Center:** All text is centered around the text object's origin.

- **Right:** Aligns text to the right. The text object's origin serves as the right-hand guide for the text.

- **Justify:** Aligns text both on the left and on the right. If the line is not long enough, Blender adds spacing, or *kerning,* between individual characters to fill the space. This option requires the use of text boxes. (See the next section, "Working with text boxes," for more details.)

- **Flush:** This option works similar to the way Justify does, but with one exception: If the line is the end of a paragraph, it forces the text to align both sides. Like Justify, this option requires the use of text frames.

Working with text boxes

Both the Flush and the Justify options require the use of something called *text boxes.* The Left, Center, and Right align options all work relative to the location of the text object's origin. However, if you want to align your text on both the left and the right side, you need more than one reference point. Text boxes are a way of providing those reference points, but with a couple of additional benefits as well. Basically, text boxes are a rectangular shape that defines where the text in your text object lives. Text boxes are similar to the *frames* you might use in desktop publishing programs. They're also one of those things that you normally don't see in 3D software.

To work with text boxes, you use the block of values in the panel labeled Text Boxes. The X and Y fields under the Offset label determine where the top-left corner of the text box is located, whereas the Width and Height fields define its size. As you adjust these values while in Edit mode, you should see a dashed rectangle in the 3D View.

Now, the cool thing about text boxes is that you can actually define more than one and place them arbitrarily in your scene. Add a text box by left-clicking the Add Textbox button in the Text Boxes panel. If you have more than one text box defined, the text can overflow from one box into another. Using multiple text boxes is an excellent way to get very fine control over the placement of your text. You can even do newspaper-style multi-column text this way, as shown in Figure 6-19.

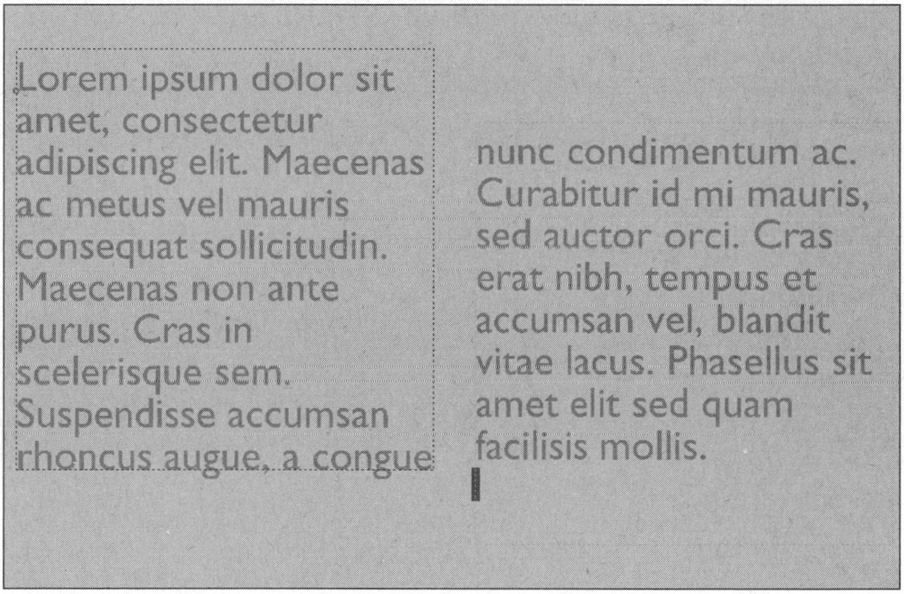

Figure 6-19:
Using text
boxes to
get multi-
column text
layouts.

Lorem ipsum dolor sit amet, consectetur adipiscing elit. Maecenas ac metus vel mauris consequat sollicitudin. Maecenas non ante purus. Cras in scelerisque sem. Suspendisse accumsan rhoncus augue, a congue

nunc condimentum ac. Curabitur id mi mauris, sed auctor orci. Cras erat nibh, tempus et accumsan vel, blandit vitae lacus. Phasellus sit amet elit sed quam facilisis mollis.

A particularly cool feature for text objects is Paste File (from Edit mode, Text⇨Paste File). If you already have a bunch of text created and don't feel like retyping it in Blender, choose Paste File and use the File Browser to find the text file you want to load. After you do, the content of whatever is in that text file is added from the location of the text cursor. This is also a bit of a cheat you can use to get special characters (like π) in a text object; many of them are difficult to type on a standard US-layout keyboard.

If you're working with a lot of text, you may find that Blender doesn't perform as speedily as you'd like while editing. If you left-click the Fast Editing check box in the Shape panel, Blender uses just the outline to the text in the 3D View while in Edit mode. This adjustment gives Blender a bit of a performance boost so that you're not waiting for characters to show up seconds after you finish typing them.

Controlling text appearance

The block of buttons in the Font panel control how the text appears in the selected text object:

- ✓ **Size:** This field allows you to adjust the font size on a scale from 0.010 to 10. Changing the font size value is generally a better way to change the size of your text rather than simply scaling the text object.

- ✓ **Shear:** Shearing is a quick-and-dirty way to fake italic on a font. Values between 0 and 1 tilt characters to the right, whereas values between –1 and 0 tilt them all to the left.

- ✓ **Object Font:** Using this field, you can actually define Blender objects as characters in a font. I cover this later in the "Changing fonts" section.

- ✓ **Text on Curve:** If you need your text to flow along the length of a curve object, use this datablock field to choose that particular curve object.

   To use an eyedropper for picking an object from the 3D View, press E with your mouse cursor hovered over this field (as I described earlier in this chapter for Taper Objects and Bevel Objects).

- ✓ **Underline Position:** Adjust this value to control the position of the underline, if enabled (Ctrl+U on highlighted text). This value has a range from –0.2 to 0.8.

- ✓ **Underline Thickness:** From this field, you can control the thickness of the actual underline, if enabled (Ctrl+U on highlighted text). You can set this value between 0.01 and 0.5.

- ✓ **Character:** The three check boxes under the Character label — Bold, Italic, and Underline — add those attributes to the selected text in your 3D View, if you've defined fonts for those font variations (see the "Changing fonts" section).

You can adjust the appearance of your text using still more controls in the Paragraph panel:

- ✓ **Spacing:** You can customize the amount of spacing between characters and lines in your text. To do so, you have the following three values available to adjust:

  - • **Character:** The global distance between all characters in your text object, also known as *tracking*. This value has a range from 0 to 10.

- **Word:** Globally defines the space between words in your text object. This field also has a range from 0 to 10.

- **Line:** Line distance, also referred to as *leading* (pronounced "leding"). This value defines the distance between lines of text in your text object and it also has a range from 0 to 10.

✔ **Offset:** These values offset the text object from its default position. X values less than zero shift it left and Y values less than zero shift down, whereas values greater than zero shift it right (X) or up (Y).

If you're familiar with typography, you may notice two things right off the bat. First, the terms used here are not the standard typography terminology, and second, the values are not in your typical percentage, point, pica, or pixel sizes. These differences exist for two primary reasons. First, Blender is a 3D program intended for 3D artists, many of whom may not be familiar with typography terms and sizes. The second reason dovetails with the first one, but it's a bit more on the practical side. Blender text objects are 3D objects that can be just about any size in virtual 3D space. Sizes like points, pixels, and picas don't really mean anything in 3D because there's not a frame of reference, like the physical size of a printed piece of paper.

Changing fonts

Another thing that's different about Blender's text objects is the way they handle fonts. If you're used to other programs, you may expect to see a drop-down menu that lists all the fonts installed on your computer with a nice preview of each. Unfortunately, Blender doesn't currently have that ability. Instead, what you need to do is left-click the Load button to the right of the Regular Font datablock in the Font panel of Text Properties. Blender then shows you a File Browser where you can track down the actual font file for the typeface that you want to use.

Here are the standard places you can find fonts on Windows, Mac, and Linux machines:

✔ **Windows:** `C:\Windows\Fonts`

✔ **Mac OS:** `/System/Library/Fonts` or `/Library/Fonts`

✔ **Linux:** `/usr/share/fonts`

After you load a font, it's available for you to use in that specific `.blend` file whenever you want it from the font drop-down list. You always have Blender's built-in font available as well.

Now you would think that after you have a font loaded, you should be good to go, right? Well, not quite. See, Blender's method of handling bold and italic in text is *also* kind of unique. You actually load a separate font file for each one (hence the four separate Font datablocks: Regular, Bold, Italic, and Bold & Italic). Typically, you use these datablocks to load the bold and italic versions of the font file you choose in the Regular datablock. However, that's not a hard-and-fast requirement. You can actually use an entirely different font altogether. While the ability to choose different fonts in the Bold and Italic datablocks is perhaps a mild abuse of the terms, that ability does provide a pretty handy workaround. Technically speaking, Blender doesn't allow you to arbitrarily change fonts in the middle of a text object. However, using the different font datablocks, you can get around that problem by making your Bold or Italic font the other fonts you want to use. To choose a font file for any style of font is pretty straightforward:

1. **In the Font panel of your text object's Object Data Properties, left-click the Load button on the font datablock you want to change.**

   By default, the built-in font, Bfont, is chosen for all four datablocks.

2. **Navigate your hard drive using the File Browser and choose the font you want to use.**

3. **Use your chosen font in your text object.**

   As an example, say that you chose a new font for the Bold datablock. You can assign that font to characters in your text object with the following steps:

   a. **From Edit mode (Tab), highlight the text you want to change (Shift+← or Shift+→).**

   b. **Enable the Bold check box under the Character label in the Font panel of Text Properties (or press Ctrl+B in the 3D View).**

Figure 6-20 shows the results of using multiple fonts in a single text object

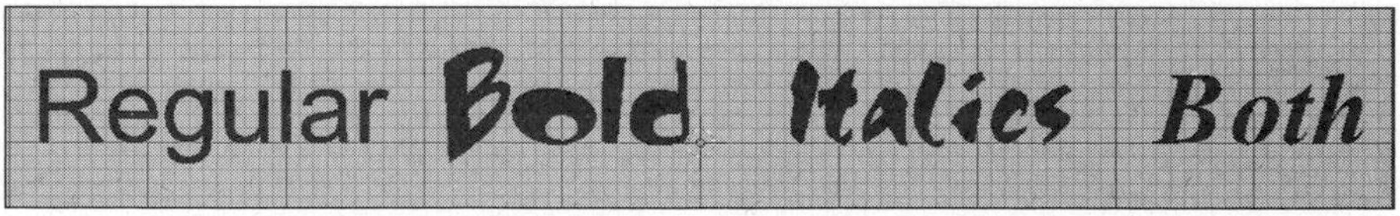

Figure 6-20:
Using the
Bold and
Italics
fonts to
use widely
different
fonts in a
single text
object.

Regular **Bold** *Italics* *Both*

You may find that while you're typing, you need certain special characters like the copyright symbol or the upside-down question mark for sentences written in Spanish. For these situations, you have three options:

- ✔ If the special character is common, you may find it in Text⇨Special Characters.

- ✔ You can memorize the hotkey combination for various commonly used special characters as listed in Blender's online documentation.

- ✔ If the character is rare or just not in the menu, but you have it in a text file outside of Blender, you can use the Text⇨Paste File to get that character into your text object.

Another unique feature that Blender's text objects have is the ability to use any other Blender object as a font character. So if you want to use Suzanne the monkey every time the uppercase S character is used, you can actually do that. If you want to model letters with metaball objects and spell something with them, like in Figure 6-21, you can do that, using the Object Font field in the Font panel. Just use the following steps:

1. **Type the name of your font "family" in Object Font.**

   You can choose any name you like. I like to end my name with a dot (.) so I can differentiate my characters later. For example, you may use `MetaLetter.` (ending in the period) in this case.

2. **Model a character you want to use.**

   In this example, I'm using metaball objects, so I use Shift+A⇨Metaball⇨Ball as my starting point and work from there.

3. **Name this object with the family name plus the character it will represent.**

   In this case, if you modeled an uppercase W, you'd call it `MetaLetter.W`. A lowercase W would be `MetaLetter.w`.

   Now you see why I use the dot (.) at the end of the family name in Step 1. It helps keep things organized.

4. **Repeat Steps 2 and 3 for each character you need.**

5. **Select (right-click) your text object and turn on Dupliverts (from Object Properties, Duplication⇨Verts).**

6. **Adjust size and spacing to fit.**

   And *poof*! You've got metaletters!

7. **To finish, move the original font text to another layer so that it's out of the way of your metaletters.**

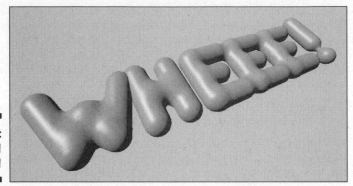

Figure 6-21:
Wheeeee!
Metaletters!

One detail to note here is that your metaletters don't merge into each other like you might expect them to. This is a shortcoming within Blender. To my knowledge, a good workaround currently doesn't exist.

Deforming text with a curve

Another really powerful thing you can do with Blender's text objects is have the text flow along the length of a curve. This way, you can get text that arcs over a doorway or wraps around a bowl or just looks all kinds of funky. The key to this feature is the Text on Curve field in the Font panel. To see how this feature works, use the steps in the following example:

1. **Create a text object (Shift+A⇨Text).**

   Feel free to populate it with whatever content you would like.

2. **Create a curve to dictate the text shape (Shift+A⇨Curve⇨Bézier).**

   This curve is your control. You're using a Bézier curve here, but a NURBS curve works fine as well. Also, I like to make my curve with the same origin location as my text object. Granted, that's just my preference, but it works nicely for keeping everything easily manageable.

3. **Select the text object and type or click the name of your control curve in the Text on Curve field (or use the E hotkey eyedropper trick described earlier in this chapter).**

   Blam! The text should now follow the arc of the curve. If you select (right-click) the curve and tab into Edit mode, any change you make to it updates your text object live.

Figure 6-22 shows 3D text along a curve.

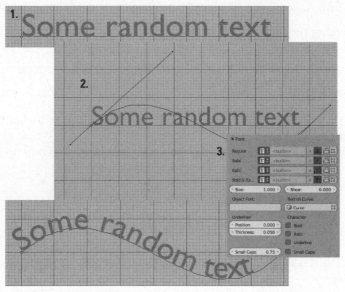

Figure 6-22: Text on a curve.

You should keep your curve as a 2D curve. Because the text is technically a special type of 2D curve, trying to get it to deform along a 3D curve won't work. For text to follow a 3D curve, you're going to need to convert the text into a mesh. You can do that conversion explicitly, as described in the next section, or you can do it implicitly by giving the text object a Curve deform modifier. Modifiers work on curve objects, but internally those curves are converted to meshes. In simple cases, this may work just fine. More often than not, you'll want the control of explicitly doing the conversion yourself.

Converting to curves and meshes

Of course, while Blender's text objects are pretty powerful, curves and meshes just do some things better. Fortunately, you don't have to model your text by using meshes and curves unless you really, really want to. Instead, you can convert your text object into a curve or a mesh by pressing Alt+C in Object mode and choosing Curve from Mesh/Text or Mesh from Curve/Meta/Surf/Mesh. If you're curious as to some specific cases why you'd want to do make this conversion, here are a few:

✔ Custom editing the characters for a logo or a specific shape (convert to a curve)

✔ Needing to share your .blend file, but the license of your font prevents you from legally packing it into the .blend (convert to a curve)

✔ Getting extruded text to follow a 3D curve (convert to a mesh)

✔ Rigging the letters to be animated with an armature (convert to a mesh or curve)

✔ Using the letters as obstacles in a fluid simulation (convert to a mesh)

✔ Using the letters to generate a particle system (convert to a mesh)

Using Alt+C also works on curve objects, surfaces, and metaball objects to convert them to meshes. Just be aware that most of these conversions are permanent. You can't go back on them without using the undo operator.

Chapter 7

Changing That Boring Gray Default Material

In This Chapter

▶ Understanding how Blender handles materials

▶ Taking advantage of Vertex painting

▶ Trying your hand at a practical example

As you work on your models in Blender, you're eventually going to get tired of that plastic gray material that all Blender objects have by default. Nothing against neutral colors — or plastic, for that matter — but the world is a vibrantly colorful place, and you may occasionally want to use these colors in your 3D scenes. To add colors to your scenes and models, you use materials and textures. Think of a *material* as a collection of instructions that you give Blender to describe the appearance of your 3D object. What color is it? Is it see-through? Is it shiny enough to show a reflection? In some ways, Blender's way of adding materials and textures to an object is one of the most confusing parts of the program. It can be a pretty big challenge to wrap your brain around the full functionality of it.

This chapter is intended to give you the skills to know enough to be dangerous with Blender's materials. Hopefully, with a little practice, you can become lethal. Well, *lethal* might be the wrong word: I don't think I've ever heard of anyone killed by excessively sharp specular highlights. (Don't worry if you don't get the joke right now. After you finish this chapter, you'll realize how horrible a pun this is.)

Understanding Materials and Render Engines

Before you throw yourself down the rabbit hole of working with materials, it's worth it to stop and consider the type of image you're trying to produce.

Are you trying to achieve photorealism? Do you want a more cartoony look? Is your image (or animation) meant to have the appearance of a technical illustration? It's important to ask the questions before you start working on your materials, because the answers will dictate the render engine that you choose. A *render engine*, or renderer, is what you use to convert the 3D data in your scene to a 2D image (or series of images, for animation). As you can imagine, there are all kinds of ways to convert 3D data into an image. Each has its own strengths and weaknesses. More importantly, every render engine has a different way of going through this conversion, so each has its own preferred way to work with materials and textures. So it's best to know the final look you're trying to attain and by extension, the most suitable renderer to get there — before you start to seriously add materials to your objects.

Blender supports a wide array of render engines, but three are built in:

✔ **OpenGL:** This one is a bit of a technicality, but if you're working in Blender, you're already using the OpenGL render engine. Blender's entire interface, including the 3D View, is generated by using OpenGL.

The benefit of this renderer is that it's very fast. You can orbit around your scene in the 3D View without lag because the OpenGL renderer is producing a full frame in fractions of a second. The trade-off for that speed is that the materials are pretty simplistic and not particularly real-looking. Generally, the OpenGL renderer does the best it can to give an approximation of what your scene looks like using the other two render engines.

✔ **Blender Internal:** Blender Internal (BI) is the old man of rendering in Blender. The core of this renderer is essentially the same as when Blender was first released over 20 years ago. It's simply had additional features bolted onto it over the years, like the Junk Lady in the 1980s film, *Labyrinth*. Despite its age, BI still is a very capable render engine. It can be very fast, especially if you're aiming for a stylized or cartoony look. BI's material system is more straight-forward for simple materials, but it can quickly become a slow, tangled mess of kludges and fakery as you create more complex or realistic materials.

✔ **Cycles:** This render engine is the newest. It's been added to Blender since the last edition of this book. For images that need to appear real-istic, it's the best Blender renderer for the job. Sure, you *can* achieve a level of realism using Blender Internal (or even OpenGL, to a degree), but that's at the expense of a lot of time and confusion. The material system that Cycles uses can be a bit intimidating for first-timers, but Cycles materials also have a stronger relationship to materials in the physical world. Numerical values and properties are a lot less arbitrary and generally correlate very well with their meatspace counterparts.

This increase in realism does come at the expense of rendering speed, but that cost is mitigated by two facts:

- **Artist time vs. computer time:** If a realistic look will take more time, it's less costly (both financially and mentally) to have that time absorbed by a computer churning through rendering than by an artist sweating over hacky tweaks in every shot.

- **GPU acceleration:** Unlike BI, Cycles can take advantage of additional processing power on the graphics processing unit (GPU) of some video cards. Using GPU acceleration, a Cycles render process can often be ten times faster than rendering on the CPU alone.

You can find more detailed information on the differences between Blender Internal and Cycles in Chapter 14. Currently, Blender's default renderer is BI, but Cycles likely will be enabled as the default in future releases. In general, I recommend that if you still don't know what final look you're trying to achieve, you should render with Cycles. Realistically behaving materials are easier to set up; if you decide that you want a more stylized look, it's not too difficult to either cheat that stylized look in Cycles or start over in BI.

To change the current render engine in a given scene, left-click the Render Engine drop-down menu in the Info editor's header (usually at the top of the Blender window).

It *is* actually possible to take advantage of features in both render engines, but the process is a bit advanced. The short version goes something like this (this assumes all of your modeling and animation is done and you just need to do materials, lighting, and rendering):

1. **From the Scene datablock, name your current scene according to its current renderer (for example, `Scene.BI`).**

2. **Make a full copy of your current scene (left-click the Plus[+] button next to the Scene datablock in the Info editor's header and choose Full Copy).**

3. **Name your new scene according to the other render engine (for example, `Scene.Cycles`).**

4. **In your new scene, change the render engine to the other render engine (for example Cycles, if the original scene used BI).**

5. **Create a new empty scene (Scene datablock Plus[+]⇨New) and name it `Composite`.**

6. **In the `Composite` scene, combine render layers from your BI scene with those from your Cycles scene using the Compositing nodes in the Node Editor.**

   This is the advanced part. See Chapter 15 for more on render layers and compositing.

Quick n' Dirty Coloring

By default, all newly added objects in Blender share a gray, plastic-like material, whether you're using BI or Cycles. Unless your model is a rhinoceros or a stretch of sidewalk, you may be wondering how you change the material's color. There are quite a few ways to make that change, and they vary a bit depending on what your final goal is in your image. This chapter starts with the simple methods and builds up to some of the more advanced ones.

Setting diffuse colors

The simplest way to set an object's color is from Material Properties. If your object doesn't have a material, Material Properties looks the same regardless of whether you're using BI or Cycles. Use the following steps to add a new material to your object:

1. **Left-click the Plus(+) button next to the list box at the top of Material Properties.**

2. **Left-click the New button in the materials datablock that appears.**

Once you do those steps, Material Properties can look very different depending on which renderer you're using. Figure 7-1 shows the different Material Properties settings available based on the render engine you've chosen.

Although Material Properties looks quite a bit different depending on whether you're using BI or Cycles, the basic steps for defining a base color are the same. You need to set the diffuse color for the material. A *diffuse color* is the color that a material reflects when light hits it. Referring back to Figure 7-1, you should notice that in the BI Material Properties, there's a color swatch in the Diffuse panel just beneath the preview. In the Cycles Material Properties, the Diffuse Color swatch is in the Surface panel. Left-click on the color swatch and Blender's color picker pops up. Figure 7-2 shows what the color picker looks like.

The default color picker is a bit different from what you might find in other graphics applications. Left-click anywhere in the large color wheel to choose the color you want to use. Scroll your mouse wheel or use the vertical slider to the right of the color wheel to adjust brightness.

Picking absolute white with your mouse in this color picker is difficult. You can use the value sliders at the bottom of the picker, but the fastest way is to press Backspace on your keyboard and scroll your mouse wheel all the way up.

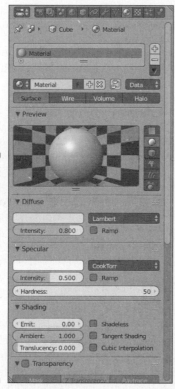
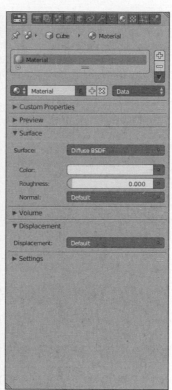

Figure 7-1:
Material
Properties
with a single
material
added. On
the left is
how it looks
when using
BI and on
the right is
how it looks
when using
Cycles.

Figure 7-2:
Blender's
color picker.

Another cool feature is that the color picker gives you a sampler. Left-click the Sample button below the value slider (it has an icon of an eye dropper), and your mouse pointer changes to a color dropper. The next place you left-click is sampled for color, making it your selected color. The cool thing is that you can sample any color in Blender's interface, including the buttons and icons, if you want to.

In fact, when working in design, it's often best to work with a limited and consistent color palette. So some artists will paint an image (or set up objects in the 3D View) with blobs of the exact colors they want to limit themselves to. Then whenever they need that color, it's readily available to be sampled with the eyedropper.

If you find Blender's current color picker to be a bit disorienting, you have the ability to choose other color pickers in the User Preferences editor under System.

Assigning multiple materials to different parts of a mesh

Using the same material across an entire object is great for objects that are the same uniform material, but what if you want to use multiple different materials on the same object? For that situation, you want to use material slots. Basically, you create a *material slot,* sometimes referred to as a *material index,* by defining a set of object subcomponents — faces in meshes, individual characters in text, and control points in curves and surfaces — and assigning them to a material.

Whether you've chosen to render with BI or Cycles, you create material slots directly from the top of Material Properties. In fact, if you added a diffuse color (as described in the previous section), you've already added one material slot. You add more material slots the same way: left-click the Plus(+) button next to the material slots list box and then left-click the New button in the materials datablock that appears. However, in order to actually use those new materials in each material slot, you have to be in Edit mode.

For an idea of how this process works, say that you want to model a beach ball and give it the classic primary-colored panels. Use the following steps:

1. **Add a UV sphere mesh (Shift+A⇨Mesh⇨UV Sphere).**

   Using the Last Operator panel of the Tool Shelf or the F6 pop-up panel, edit the UV sphere to have 12 segments, 12 rings, and a radius of 1.00. You may also add a Subdivision Surface modifier (Ctrl+1) and set the faces to render as smooth (Tools tab of the Tool Shelf⇨Shading⇨Smooth).

2. **Tab into Edit mode and switch to Face Select mode (Tab, Ctrl+Tab⇨Face).**

3. **Add a new material using the material datablock.**

   Left-click the New button to add a new material or choose an existing material from the datablock drop-down menu.

4. **Use the datablock text field to name your material.**

   For this example, name it White.

5. **Change the diffuse color to white as described in the previous section.**

   The entire ball turns white. All the faces are currently assigned to this material slot.

6. **Use face loop select to select two adjacent vertical face loops (Alt+right-click, Shift+Alt+right-click).**

7. **Add another new material slot.**

   Left-click the button with the Plus (+) icon in the upper left of the materials list box. An empty material slot appears at the bottom of the materials list box.

8. **Left-click the New button in the material datablock.**

   You should get a material named something like Material.001.

9. **Change the material name to Blue.**

10. **Change the diffuse color to blue like in Step 5.**

    After you change the color of this swatch, you might expect the faces that you have selected to automatically change to match this color. That's not quite how it works: Even though you have these faces selected, they're still assigned to the White material slot. Use the next step to remedy that situation.

11. **Assign the selected faces to the current material slot, Blue, by clicking the Assign button beneath the material list box.**

    The moment you left-click the Assign button, the selected faces all change to the blue color you picked in Step 10.

12. **Using the process in Steps 6 through 11, work your way around the sphere, creating and assigning colors for the other panels.**

    If you create a beach ball like the one in Figure 7-3, you should end up with four material slots, one for each color on the ball.

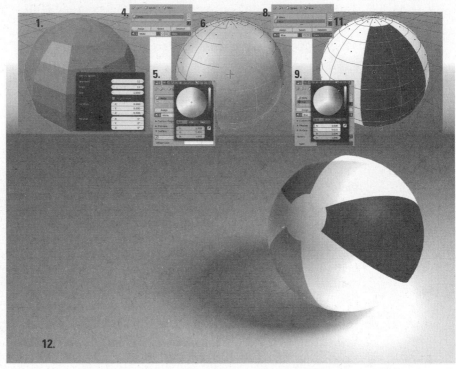

Figure 7-3:
Creating a
beach ball
with a UV
sphere and
four mate-
rial slots.

Material slots aren't limited to be used only by meshes. You can also use them on curves, surfaces, and text objects. The process is similar to meshes, with one main exception. Meshes, as shown in the preceding example, allow you to assign individual faces to different material slots. This exception isn't the case with curves, surfaces, and text objects, which assign material slots to discrete closed entities. So you can assign individual text characters and curves to a material slot. However, you can't set the material slot of an individual control point or a portion of a text character. Figure 7-4 shows material slots working on a curve, surface, and text object.

Using vertex colors

One downside to material slots is the fact that, although they make defining multiple colors and materials on a single mesh easy, there's a very distinct line between materials. The color of one material doesn't smoothly transition into the next. For example, if you want to create a car with a paint job that's light blue near the ground and smoothly transitions to a bright yellow on its roof and hood, you can't effectively do this color graduation with material slots. You could use a texture, as described in Chapter 8, but that might be overkill for a simple object. There is another technique that gives you an effective way of quickly coloring a mesh without the hard-edged lines that material slots give you: vertex colors.

Figure 7-4:
Material
slots on
curves, sur-
faces, and
text objects.

The way vertex colors works is pretty simple. You assign each vertex in your mesh a specific color. If the vertices that form a face have different colors, a gradient goes from each vertex to the others; the color is most intense at the vertex and more blended with other colors the farther away it gets.

Although vertex colors are a very flexible way of adding smoothly transitioning colors to your object, they only work on mesh objects. You can't use vertex colors on other objects like curves, text, or metaballs.

Of course, trying to explicitly set the color for each and every vertex in a mesh can get really tedious on complex meshes. To alleviate this problem, Blender has a Vertex Paint mode. You activate Vertex Paint mode by selecting (right-click) the mesh object that you want to paint in the 3D View and then pressing V. You can also use the mode drop-down menu in the 3D View's header. If you're using the Pie Menus add-on, you can choose Vertex paint from the pie that appears when you press Tab.

When you enter Vertex Paint mode, your mouse cursor changes to include a paint brush circle similar to the one you see when in Sculpt mode and the Tools tab of the Tool Shelf updates with paint options. The Tool Shelf panels for vertex painting are shown in Figure 7-5.

The most options for vertex painting in the Tool Shelf are in the Brush panel. Here you set the color you want to use and control how that color is applied to the selected object. You can choose the color you want by adjusting the embedded color picker.

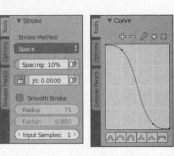

Figure 7-5:
The paint options in the Tool Shelf while in Vertex Paint mode.

Below the Radius and Strength sliders in the Brush panel of the Tool Shelf is a drop-down menu labeled Blend. Typically, the option chosen in this menu is pre-set, depending on the specific brush you've chosen. However, by adjusting it manually, you can have direct control over how the paint color is applied to your vertices. The following are your choices:

- **Mix:** Mix simply blends the defined color with the color that the vertex already has assigned, according to whatever value is set by the Strength slider.

- **Add, Subtract, Multiply:** Choose one of these options to take the current color and respectively add, subtract, or multiply that with the current vertex color under the brush in the 3D View.

- **Blur:** This option is the only paint setting that doesn't use the selected color. It uses the vertices that are within the radius defined by the Radius slider and mixes their colors, effectively blurring them.

- **Lighten, Darken:** These options take the value of the color you choose and use that to control how much influence it has on the already existing colors. So if you have your color set to full white, painting with Darken enabled won't change the vertex colors at all. But using that color to paint with Lighten enabled makes it appear everywhere you work.

After you pick the color you want to use, left-click and drag your mouse over vertices in the 3D View. Those vertices take on the color you defined. To get an idea of where the vertices that you're painting actually exist on your mesh, you may want to have Blender overlay the object's wireframe in the 3D View. To do so, navigate to Object Properties and left-click the Wire check box in the Display panel. Blender adds the wireframe over the surface of the object, making it much clearer where each of the vertices of the mesh lie.

By default, the base vertex color for an object is a flat white. If you would rather start with a different base color, choose Paint⇨Set Vertex Colors (Shift+K) from the 3D View's header. Doing that sets all the vertices in your mesh to have the color you defined in the Vertex Paint color swatch.

If you're familiar with Sculpt mode (see Chapter 5) or Texture Paint mode (see Chapter 8), you may be tempted to try to adjust the radius of your brush by using the F hotkey. Go ahead, try it; it works! The same goes for using Shift+F to adjust the strength of your brush. If you have a drawing tablet with pressure sensitivity, you can take advantage of that by enabling the pressure sensitivity buttons to the right of the Radius and Strength sliders in the Brush panel on the Tool Shelf.

You can have multiple sets, called *layers,* of vertex colors. Over in Mesh Properties, there's a Vertex Colors panel near the bottom with a list box in it. When you enter Vertex Paint mode for the first time, this list box automatically gets a vertex color layer, named Col, added to it. You can rename the layer by double-clicking it. New vertex color layers can be added by left-clicking the Plus (+) button next to the list box. Figure 7-6 shows the Vertex Colors panel in Mesh Properties with a few vertex color layers.

Figure 7-6: You can add multiple layers of vertex colors to a single mesh object from the Vertex Colors panel of Mesh Properties.

While you can have multiple layers of vertex colors, you can only set one as active for rendering. To make a vertex color layer active for rendering, left-click the camera icon to the right of the vertex color layer's name. You should notice that only one vertex color layer can have that camera icon active.

Defining color palettes

In the preceding section, labeled "Setting diffuse colors", I mentioned that it's a common practice for artists and designers to work with a palette of very specific colors. If you're painting the walls of your house blue and green, you usually want to make sure that if you run out of paint, you get the exact same blue and green. Otherwise your walls are going to look all kinds of hideous. Likewise when vertex painting, if you choose a particular color, it's good to have a way to come back to that color later if you need to. Fortunately, in Blender's painting system, you have this capability built-in. Conveniently, they're called palettes.

Look at the bottom of the Brush panel (if you need to, refer back to Figure 7-5). Notice a datablock menu there with a New button next to it? That's the palette datablock. You can create, transfer, and reuse palettes in Blender, the same as any other datablock.

To create a new palette, left-click the New button in the palette datablock. A new palette is created, named `Palette`. You should also notice that below the color picker, there are now two new buttons: Plus (+) and Minus (-). Left-click the Plus(+) button and the current color gets added to the current active palette. You can tell because a square color swatch with your chosen color appears beneath the Plus (+) and Minus (-) buttons. You can add as many colors as you want to your palette. As you work, if you want to go back to a color in your palette, just left-click its square swatch.

When a color in your palette is picked, a little dark triangle appears in the upper left corner of the palette square. If you ever want to remove a color from the palette, simply choose the color and then left-click the Minus (-) button.

Creating painting masks

Occasionally when vertex painting, your mesh may have some faces on it that you don't want to receive any of the color you're currently painting. In this case, you define face selection masking by left-clicking the Painting Mask button in the 3D View's header. It has an icon of a cube with one face showing a checkerboard pattern, as shown in Figure 7-7.

When you enable the painting mask, you can select faces of your mesh by right-clicking. After you do, these faces are the only ones that are affected by your painting. This is an excellent method of isolating a portion of your mesh for custom painting without changing the color of the faces around that area. By using a painting mask, you can actually get the hard-edged color changes that you get with material slots, should you want such a thing.

Figure 7-7:
Enabling
the Painting
Mask
button.

Making vertex paint renderable

One of the things that really highlights the difference between BI and Cycles becomes evident when trying to get vertex colors to show up when you render. In BI, it's pretty simple:

1. **Find the Options panel in Material Properties.**

2. **Enable the Vertex Color Paint check box.**

That's it! Now when you render using BI (press F12 or toggle Rendered viewport shading by pressing Shift+Z), your vertex colors appear on your mesh object.

For Cycles, the situation is a bit more complex. Go to Material Properties and use the following steps:

1. **In the Surface panel, left-click the Use Nodes button.**

   Clicking Use Nodes should expand the Surface panel. Instead of a simple diffuse color swatch, you should see a drop-down menu labeled Surface and it should already have Diffuse BSDF as the chosen option. Cycles' material system is node-based. For all but the most simple of materials, you should use the Node Editor to tweak and customize your materials. There's more on that later in this chapter. Fortunately, for this example, it can stay pretty simple. You just need to enable the functionality of nodes at this point. You don't actually need to work in the Node Editor right now.

2. **Left-click the connector button (its icon is a small circular dot) to the right of the color swatch and choose Attribute from the menu that appears.**

   This act tells Blender that, rather than use the color defined by the swatch, you want to connect some attribute (in this case, the vertex colors you've painted) to control the color. After you choose Attribute (it's in the far left column of the menu that appears), the color swatch is replaced with a drop-down menu that has Attribute | Color as the chosen option. Below that menu is a text field, labeled Name.

3. **In the Name field, type in the name of the vertex color layer you want to use.**

If you're going with defaults, you'd type `Col` here. Otherwise, take a quick glance at the Vertex Colors panel in Mesh Properties to check the name of your vertex color layer.

That should do the trick. Now when you render (F12) or use Rendered viewport shading, your vertex colors should be visible on your object. Figure 7-8 shows what your Surface panel in Material Properties should look like. The figure also shows the corresponding node configuration that Blender automatically creates for you.

Figure 7-8: On the left, the Surface panel of Material Properties when you use vertex colors on your mesh. On the right is the node graph that Blender automatically creates as a result.

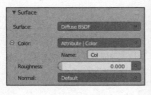
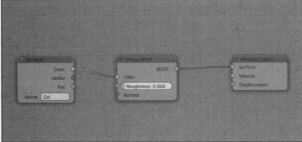

Setting Up Node Materials in Cycles

As covered earlier in this chapter in the section titled "Making vertex paint renderable", it's entirely possible to work with Cycles materials from Material Properties. However, working that way can be a bit clunky and it doesn't take full advantage of the power afforded by Cycles. When Cycles was first integrated into Blender, the developers decided that they would take full advantage of Blender's Node Editor. While this section details parts of the Node Editor that are specific to Cycles materials, see Chapter 15 for a broader overview of the Node Editor in general. That chapter covers the Node Editor in the context of compositing, but the interaction and navigation work the same for materials as well.

Blender Internal's materials can be customized with the Node Editor as well, but it's a bit "bolted on." The node integration with Cycles was part of its design from the beginning.

Adjusting your layout to work with node materials

Blender doesn't ship with a screen layout that's specific to working with materials. Fortunately, for Cycles materials, you can make a few quick adjustments to the default layout and you should be good to go. Starting with the Default layout, follow these steps:

1. **Left-click and drag upward the seam between the 3D View and the Timeline.**

   The Timeline should take up a third to a half of the Blender window.

2. **Change the area containing the Timeline to instead contain a Node Editor (Shift+F3).**

   Your screen layout should now look a bit like Figure 7-9.

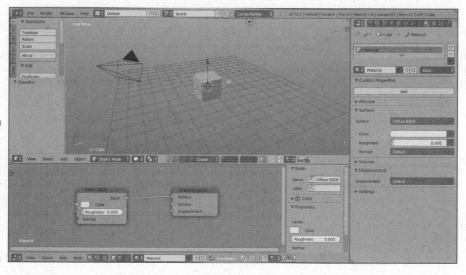

Figure 7-9: A screen layout that's ideal for working with node materials in Cycles.

Working with nodes

Earlier in this chapter (see the section titled "Quick n' Dirty Coloring"), I cover how to add a material to your object. Now, if the material is added with Cycles as your chosen renderer, you should have something that looks like Figure 7-9. However, if the material was added when you still had Blender Internal as your renderer, there are a couple of steps you need to do. You need to either

- ✔ Remove the existing material and add a new one
- ✔ From Material Properties, left-click the Use Nodes button in the Surface panel.
- ✔ Enabling nodes gives you full access and control of the Cycles material system using the Node Editor.

When the use of nodes is enabled on your Cycles material, the default node network you have is very simple; a Diffuse BSDF shader node connected to a Material Output node. All materials need to have a Material Output node. The Material Output node is how material properties get mapped to your object; if your material node network doesn't have this node, then Cycles doesn't know anything about your material.

If you've already worked with the Node Editor for compositing, you should notice that material nodes have another socket color in addition to the standard yellow, blue, and gray sockets. Material nodes may also have a green socket that indicates a shader input or output. Cycles shaders are similar to shaders in BI, but you have much more fine-grained control over them and how they work. See the next section for more detail on the shaders available to you in Cycles.

Understanding shaders

The workhorses of Cycles' materials are the shaders. By intelligently mixing them with each other (often using textures — see Chapter 8), you can create some very striking and convincing materials in your 3D scene. To see the shaders available to you, press Shift+A⇨Shaders in the Node Editor or click the Surface drop-down menu in Material Properties. Figure 7-10 shows the list of shaders.

Many of the shaders, like the Diffuse BSDF, have "BSDF" at the end of their names. BSDF is an abbreviation for *bidirectional scattering distribution function.* That's a fancy way of saying "mathy description of how light interacts with a surface." The Diffuse BSDF is Cycles' rough equivalent to the Diffuse panel when working with BI materials. Due to length limitations, I can't give a thorough description of all the things that can be done with node-based shaders and materials. Complete books can be (and have been!) written on that topic. My website for this book, www.blenderbasics.com, gives a practical example that should give you a clear idea of how to proceed.

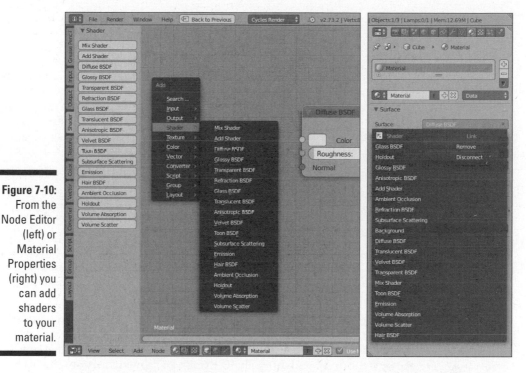

Figure 7-10:
From the
Node Editor
(left) or
Material
Properties
(right) you
can add
shaders
to your
material.

Figure 7-11 shows each of the available shader nodes so you can see their configuration settings.

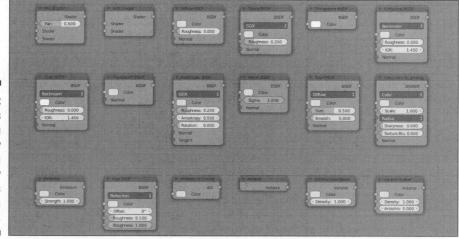

Figure 7-11:
Cycles
gives you
the ability
to assign a
wide variety
of shaders
materials in
your scene.

The following is a brief description of each of the shaders available in Cycles:

- ✔ **Mix Shader:** This shader, along with the Add shader (covered next), is a powerful way of layering multiple shaders in a single material. The key to its strength is the Fac (short for *factor*) socket. You can uniformly control how shaders are mixed by adjusting this slider, or you can connect a grayscale texture to make one part of your object have the properties of one shader and another part of your object have properties of another (for example, a partially tarnished spoon will only be glossy where there isn't any tarnish).

- ✔ **Add Shader:** When creating materials, there are times when you want your material to have the properties of multiple shaders. For instance, glass is glossy, transparent, and refracts light. Car paint has a diffuse color, but it's also glossy. The Add shader allows you to account for these multifaceted materials.

- ✔ **Diffuse BSDF:** The Diffuse BSDF shader is the foundation that most materials are based upon. Nearly all materials have a base color of some sort. This shader is the primary way you define those colors. As mentioned previously, it's similar to the Diffuse panel in BI.

- ✔ **Glossy BSDF:** Some materials have a mirror-like reflectivity. In BI, that's controlled from the Mirror panel in Material Properties. In Cycles, the Glossy BSDF shader wields that control. The Glossy BSDF is also how you get a little specular highlight (in fact, BI's specularity settings are really a way to fake the reflection of a light source on a glossy material).

A good starting point for a glossy material is to have a Diffuse BSDF and a Glossy BSDF, mixed with a Mix shader. As a starting point, let the Diffuse BSDF and the Glossy BSDF have the same color (remember that you can copy and paste color swatches by hovering your mouse over the swatch and using Ctrl+C and Ctrl+V, respectively).

- ✔ **Transparent BSDF:** The closest parallel to this in BI is z-transparency. You can achieve similar effects using a Refraction BSDF with a white color and an IOR of 1.00. However, if that effect is what you're trying to achieve, the Transparent BSDF is a less resource-hungry way of getting it.

- ✔ **Refraction BSDF:** Most naturally occurring transparent materials like glass and water bend, or *refract*, light as it goes through them. The Refraction BSDF shader adds this property to your material.

- ✔ **Glass BSDF:** When covering the Mix shader, I mentioned that some materials, like glass, share the attributes of multiple shaders. Well, glass is a bit of a special case. It (and materials like it) shows up so frequently in 3D renders that it makes sense to have a convenience node that has all of the attributes pre-mixed so you don't have to re-make it every time you need glass in your scene. The Glass BSDF is that convenience node in Cycles.

✔ **Translucent BSDF:** Some materials, like sandblasted glass or thin linens, aren't transparent, but things do show somewhat through them, like shadowy silhouettes. This is translucent behavior, and you can use the Translucent BSDF lend it to materials in your object.

✔ **Anisotropic BSDF:** Not all glossy materials reflect light evenly. For example, the brushed aluminum used in many industrial designs has a highlight that's stretched along the grain of the brushing. In computer graphics, this effect is called an *anisotropic highlight*. In Cycles, the Anisotropic BSDF shader node is what you use to replicate it.

✔ **Velvet BSDF:** The Velvet BSDF behaves similarly to the Diffuse BSDF with the key difference being that light bounces off it less evenly. Where the Diffuse BSDF gives an even hue to a material, the Velvet BSDF yields a more mottled, uneven tone. Used smartly, you can use this shader to give a natural feel to cloth-like materials.

✔ **Toon BSDF:** Cycles is typically thought of and used as a physically correct renderer that can produce photorealistic results. However, Cycles isn't limited to just photorealism. Using the Toon BSDF, you can produce a cel shaded look in Cycles, too.

✔ **Subsurface Scattering:** I mentioned the subsurface scattering effect earlier in this chapter when covering BI. It's basically what you see on the back of your hand when you hold a flashlight against your palm. You can try to achieve this by combining a bunch of the other BSDF shaders, but the result won't be very accurate. This is because the subsurface scattering algorithm can't be generalized as a BSDF. It's a bidirectional surface-scattering reflectance distribution function (BSSRDF). That's a lot of words to basically say, "light can bounce around beneath the surface of a material, too." What you need to know is that the Subsurface Scattering shader is used in realistic shaders for materials like skin, candle wax, and milk.

✔ **Emission:** When using BI, you illuminate your scenes using lamps. In Cycles, it's often more desirable to have meshes behave as light sources. And even if you're using lamp objects, the Emission shader is still what you use to add light to your scene. See Chapter 9 for more on lighting in Blender using Cycles and BI as your render engines.

 If you're rendering fire, consider connecting the Emission shader to the Volume socket on the Material Output node rather than the Surface socket.

✔ **Hair BSDF:** I don't care what you do in computer graphics, any part of it that involves hair always is complex. And materials for hair are no exception. However, the Hair BSDF node in Cycles goes a long way toward giving you refined control over how hair on your objects appears when rendered.

✔ **Ambient Occlusion:** I cover the concept of ambient occlusion (AO) in more detail in Chapter 9. However, the most basic explanation of AO is that it's a way of emphasizing recesses and crevices in a model. In order to use AO in Cycles or BI, you need to enable it from World Properties. Once enabled for Cycles, you can use the AO shader node to control how much the global AO effect has an influence on your material.

✔ **Holdout:** The Holdout shader is pretty unique among the shaders, as it has absolutely no basis in physical reality. With a Holdout shader, you're basically saying, "there's nothing here, not even background." When Cycles renders a material with a Holdout shader, it makes that section of rendered image completely transparent, with an alpha of zero. This can be useful in compositing, as the effect can give you a 3D mask (much like setting the Alpha value to zero without actually enabling transparency in the Transparency panel of Material Properties when using BI).

✔ **Volume Absorption:** This shader, along with the Volume Scatter shader (covered next), should be connected to the Volume socket on the Material Output node. You can use this shader alone for materials like black smoke or colored glass. For fire or materials with more of a sub-surface scattering look, you'll want to mix it with Volume Scatter, and possibly the Emission shader.

✔ **Volume Scatter:** It's pretty rare that you'll want to use this shader on its own. Typically, the Volume Scatter shader gets mixed with the Volume Absorption shader for volumetric effects like smoke and dust.

Of the three shaders that it makes sense to connect to the Volume socket of the Material Output node (Volume Absorption, Volume Scatter, and Emission), it's helpful to think of them this way:

- The Volume Absorption shader controls how much light gets trapped by the volume (black smoke).

- The Volume Scatter shader controls how much light the volume reflects (a bright cloud).

- The Emission shader controls how much light the volume generates (fire).

As you work with your material in the Node Editor, it can sometimes feel like you're "flying blind" because it's not immediately obvious what some changes to your node network do to your final material. You *could* use Rendered viewport shading in the 3D View (Shift+Z), but that could be slow on a large scene, especially if you're not rendering with GPU acceleration. So another solution would be to expand the Preview panel in Material Properties. It works just like the Preview panel that's there when working in BI; it's just collapsed by default when you use Cycles. You just need to left-click the panel title to expand it and make it visible.

Playing with Materials in Blender Internal

As I mentioned earlier in this chapter, the way you configure materials is different in BI and Cycles. This section covers the parts that are specific to BI.

In BI, the place to change the look of an object is Material Properties. Twelve panels are visible in Material Properties:

- **Context:** Like other sections of the Properties editor, Material Properties starts with a context panel. This panel provides a list of material data-blocks associated with your selected object and the means to define some basic attributes of those materials. It's always the first panel and it's the only one that can't be moved or collapsed.

- **Preview:** The Preview panel displays an image of the material on a variety of preset objects: a plane, a sphere, a cube, Suzanne's head, hair strands, and a sphere on a sky background.

- **Diffuse:** As covered earlier in this chapter, the *diffuse color* is the main color of the object, or the primary hue that the material reflects to the camera. The controls in this panel allow you to set that color, as well as how it reflects light.

- **Specular:** One cool thing about working in computer graphics — and especially when using BI — is that you have a say over things that you don't normally control in the real world. The *specular color,* or *spec,* is the color of highlights on your object. From the Specular panel you can adjust the specular color object, its intensity, and how it reflects light.

- **Shading:** The Shading panel gives you a set of broad controls to dictate how your object reflects light, regardless of the settings chosen in the Diffuse and Specular panels.

- **Transparency:** As advertised, this panel controls how transparency is handled on your material, if you choose to enable it by clicking the check box at the heading.

- **Mirror:** If you want your material to be reflective, you enable and configure that feature here. I go into reflection and transparency more in depth later in this chapter in the section named "Reflection and transparency."

- **Subsurface Scattering:** Have you ever put your hand in front of a flashlight and seen the light shine through your hand with a slightly reddish glow? In computer graphics, that effect is called *subsurface scattering,* or *SSS* for short. The light is scattered beneath the surface of your skin. The settings in this panel give you control over SSS in your material, should you need it.

✔ **Strand:** If your material is destined to be used for hair particles (see Chapter 13), this panel gives you control over settings for that specific purpose.

✔ **Options:** The Options panel is a bit of a grab bag of check boxes for material controls that don't really fit in other panels. However, most of these check boxes have a big influence over how your final render looks (and more important, how long that render takes to process). If you worked through the previous section on vertex colors, you've already worked with this panel a little bit.

✔ **Shadow:** The settings in this panel control how your material treats shadows. In particular, you can dictate if (and how) the material receives shadows cast by other objects and if (and how) the material casts shadows itself.

✔ **Custom Properties:** All sections of the Properties editor allow you to create custom properties. They're used primarily by people who do more advanced work with Blender that involves scripting in Python. This panel is where you add those properties.

Figure 7-12 shows the panels in Material Properties when using BI.

Figure 7-12:
Material Properties for Blender Internal.

Understanding how light reflects

To understand materials, it helps if you have an idea of how human sight works. Most render engines use eyesight as the basic model for how they work. In order to see, you need to have light. The light comes from one or more sources and bounces off of any object within its range. When the light hits these objects, they influence the direction that the light bounces and how much of the incoming light is absorbed versus reflected. When you look around, you're seeing light that is bounced off of these objects and into your eyes.

Most render engines, BI and Cycles included, use a simplified version of this scenario. The following sentence sums up the biggest difference as it pertains to BI: *Unless otherwise stipulated, light bounces only once.* Professional photographers often have their flash aimed away from their subject and into an umbrella-shaped reflector that bounces light back to whatever they're shooting. The light from the flash has at least two bounces to get to the camera's lens; once off of the umbrella and once off of the subject. Because this fairly common meatspace scenario uses more than one light bounce, it's a bit difficult to set up something similar in BI and expect it to work accurately (although it's gotten easier in recent releases of Blender). Instead, you're better off directly lighting your scenes, so then your materials themselves control that one bounce of the light into the 3D camera.

Exceptions to this rule do, of course, exist, as do ways to cheat around them. You can use techniques (particularly those including ray tracing) covered throughout this chapter and in Chapter 8, to implement those cheats. Or you could render using Cycles.

Of these panels, the Context panel gives you the most high-level control over the material, defining which material gets assigned to the selected object and how BI recognizes the material. The first control element is a list box. This list box shows all the material slots associated with your object.

Below the list box is a datablock field. From this datablock field, you can tie a material to the current active material slot in the list box. This datablock functions the same as any other datablock field, as explained in Chapter 4.

From left to right, here is a description of what each button in the datablock does.

- ✔ The Material button on the left gives you the ability to load an existing material that you've already created.

- ✔ The text field allows you to give your material a custom name. Simply left-click in the field and type the name you want to use. The name is automatically updated in the list box of material slots.

- ✔ If your material is linked to more than one object, it has a numbered button next to it, representing the number of objects using this material. Left-clicking this button ensures that the datablock has only a single user — it creates a copy of the material that is used only by the current active object.

✔ Enable the button with an F on it to give your material a *fake user*. Without a fake user, if you unlink a material from all objects, it has no users and won't be saved in your `.blend` file. Giving the material a fake user ensures that your material sticks around when you save. Fake users are great if you want to create a `.blend` file as a material library.

✔ Clicking the Plus (+) button adds a new material datablock and assigns it to your active material slot.

✔ The X button disconnects the material datablock from the active material slot in the list. It's important to remember that clicking the X button doesn't necessarily delete the material from your `.blend` file. That only happens if your material has no users and you reload your `.blend` file after saving.

To the right of the datablock control buttons is a Nodes button. This button activates the advanced node-based material editor. It's similar to how nodes are used in Cycles (covered later in this chapter), but not quite as powerful. Because that's a more advanced topic, look to Blender's online documentation for more information.

The Link drop-down menu after the node button is a pretty unique control. Using these menu options requires recalling information about how `.blend` files are structured. Chapters 2 and 4 detail how `.blend` files are structured, but basically Blender objects are just containers for the low-level data (mesh, curve, and so on). Now, here's how this information relates to materials. By default, Blender's materials link to the low-level data, as indicated by the Link drop-down menu in the Context panel being set to Data. However, you also have the option of linking the material to the object as well, as shown in the schematics of Figure 7-13.

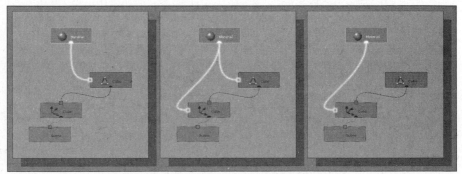

Figure 7-13:
A schematic showing a material linked to a mesh and to an object.

Why is having the ability to link a material to either the mesh or the object a useful option? Well, say that you have a bunch of objects that are linked duplicates (Alt+D), sharing the same mesh information. If the material is linked to the mesh, all your linked duplicates have the exact same material. If you want to have a different material for each duplicate, you can link the material to the object datablock rather than the mesh datablock. Figure 7-14 shows a set of linked duplicate Suzanne heads, each with a different material. This control over linking is available to you in both BI and Cycles.

Figure 7-14:
Linked
duplicates
of Suzanne,
except they
don't share
the same
material.

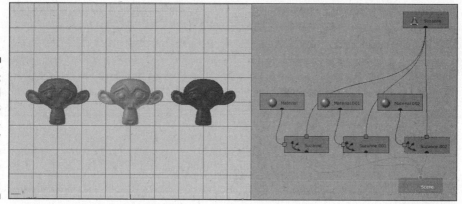

Adjusting shader values

Ah, computer graphics: You have nearly complete control over how your materials look. Part of this control is how the diffuse and specular colors are dispersed across the surface of the object. You control both of these attributes independently in BI with shader types. A *shader type* is a computer algorithm that defines how the color reacts in the material, and it's usually named after the computer scientist or mathematician who came up with it. So although the names may seem weird or arbitrary, the good news is that their names are pretty universal from one piece of 3D software to another.

Your shaders are set and controlled in the panel tied to the type of color you're adjusting. Both the Diffuse and Specular panels have a drop-down menu to the right of the color swatch where you can pick the shader you want to use. To change your diffuse shader type, left-click the drop-down menu at the upper right of the Diffuse panel. By default, its value is set to the Lambert shader, but you have the following options:

✓ **Lambert:** The only adjustable setting for this good, general-purpose shader is the Intensity slider. This slider controls how much light the material reflects. The default setting of 0.8 means that the material reflects 80 percent of the light and absorbs 20 percent.

✔ **Oren-Nayar:** The Oren-Nayar shader is similar to the Lambert shader, although it is slightly more realistic due to an additional Roughness slider that takes into account the imperfections on an object's surface.

✔ **Toon:** In sharp contrast to the previous two shaders, the Toon shader doesn't aim to be realistic. Instead, it tries to reproduce the hard-edged *cel shading* that's often seen in traditional hand-drawn animation.

✔ **Minnaert:** This shader is pretty slick. By default, it's set up to behave just like the standard Lambert shader. However, if you adjust its Darkness value to a number less than 1, the edges of an object with this material get lighter. Darkness values greater than 1 darken the parts of the object that point to the viewer. The Minnaert shader is a great way to fake a backlight on an object or give it a somewhat velvety look.

✔ **Fresnel:** Pronounced "FRAY-nel," this shader is also a nice one to use for metals and glassy materials. It's like the Minnaert shader, except instead of working relative to the viewer, the Fresnel shader works relative to the light source. Higher Fresnel values darken parts that point toward the light source and this multiplies by the Factor value.

Figure 7-15 shows Suzanne shaded with each of the different diffuse shaders. For simplicity, the specular intensity has been reduced to 0 in this figure.

Figure 7-15:
Suzanne with Lambert, Oren-Nayar, Toon, Minnaert, and Fresnel shaders.

You also have control over the way the specular highlight appears on your materials. You change this in the Specular panel the same way you change the diffuse shader: Left-click the drop-down menu next to the color swatch. All specular shaders share an Intensity value that controls the strength of the specular highlights. Higher values make the highlights brighter; lower values make them dimmer and can reduce the specularity altogether. As with the diffuse shaders, you have a choice of algorithms that control how the specular highlight appears:

✔ **CookTorr (Cook-Torrance):** The Cook-Torrance shader is Blender's default specular shader. In addition to the Intensity slider, this shader also has a setting to control Hardness. Higher Hardness values make the highlight smaller and more compact, whereas lower values spread the highlight over more of the object's surface. This shader is good for shiny plastic materials.

✔ **Phong:** This shader is nearly identical to the Cook-Torrance shader, although not quite as optimized. The edge of the specular highlight is softer, making it a bit nicer for less shiny plastics and organic materials.

✔ **Blinn:** The Blinn shader is a more refined shader that is generally more accurate than the Cook-Torrance or Phong shaders. In addition to the Intensity and Hardness values, this shader also has a IOR, or Index of Refraction, setting. This refraction isn't quite like you might expect. The IOR value, in this case, controls the softness of the highlight. This shader works well for getting materials that behave more like materials in the real world.

✔ **Toon:** Like the Toon diffuse shader, the Toon specular shader breaks the specular highlight into discrete bands of lightness to re-create the look of traditional cartoon coloring.

✔ **WardIso:** I like to use the WardIso, short for Ward Isotropic, shader along with the Minnaert and Fresnel diffuse shaders for metallic or shiny plastic materials. The Slope value is a mathematical variable in the shader algorithm, which controls the sharpness of the highlight's edge. Lower values are sharper and higher values are more dispersed.

Figure 7-16 shows Suzanne with the default Lambert diffuse shader and each of the different specular shaders.

Figure 7-16:
Suzanne with Cook-Torrance, Phong, Blinn, Toon, and Ward Isotropic specular shaders.

TIP

When it comes to setting colors for materials, more often than not, I keep my specular color set to white. The only exception is that, on occasion, it makes more sense to set the specular color to a value that is slightly lighter than the diffuse color. This technique is sometimes used when faking a metallic look on materials. Of course, no hard-and-fast rule tells you when to go one way and when to go another in terms of the specular color. It's really a matter of experience and changing to what looks right in your final render.

Reflection and transparency

A common challenge of 3D computer graphics is making your materials reflective and transparent. Fortunately, adding those properties to your materials in Blender isn't too difficult when using BI. The bulk of the work is done in two panels of Material Properties (see Figure 7-1): Mirror and Transparency.

Adding reflectivity to your material

Enable mirroring by left-clicking the Mirror check box and increasing the Reflectivity slider within the Mirror panel of Material Properties. An important thing to know about doing reflections this way is that it uses *ray tracing*. To create accurate reflections, BI follows, or traces, a ray of light as it bounces off of objects and into the camera. This is the exact same technique used in Cycles, but the implementation in BI is quite a bit less efficient. To ensure its accuracy, BI follows thousands of these rays. This accuracy comes at the expense of using more processing power from your computer and has a high likelihood of lengthening the rendering process. Figure 7-17 shows an example image with high reflectivity.

Figure 7-17:
An example image with high levels of ray traced reflectivity.

In order to properly see any ray traced results in your render when using BI, make sure that the Ray Tracing check box is enabled in the Shading panel of Render Properties.

Ray traced reflectivity is also one of those exceptions to the "light only bounces once" rule. In order to get a reflection, you have to have at least two bounces. The light comes from the light source, bounces off of one object, and then off of your reflective object before it reaches the camera. You can actually define how many bounces BI recognizes by adjusting the Depth value in the Mirror panel. Of course, the higher the Depth value, the more bounces that Blender has to trace and therefore the longer your renders are likely to take.

Making your material transparent

In addition to reflectivity, you can also control an object's transparency. The main control for a 3D material's transparency is its *alpha* value. The alpha value in BI materials runs on a scale from 0, for completely transparent, to 1, for completely opaque. You adjust this value with the slider labeled Alpha in the Transparency panel of Material Properties.

You can adjust the alpha value even if you have the Transparency check box disabled. If you keep Transparency disabled, however, the preview panel shows a white-to-blue gradient over the preview object instead of the checkerboard pattern in the background. This gradient shows that as you reduce the alpha value, the more your object's material is replaced with your scene's sky color. The sky color is set in World Properties. Chapter 9 covers setting the sky color and other World Properties in greater detail.

Getting the object's material to show the sky color rather than what's actually behind it doesn't initially seem useful, but it's actually a really quick way to create a material that can make an object behave as a three-dimensional mask. Of course, you may not want a mask and instead you want to see the actual 3D environment through your object. Enable the Transparency check box to make the checkerboard background show up through the preview object.

By default, Blender uses *Z transparency* to get the rest of your scene's environment to show up through your object. However, if you're trying to re-create glass, you might realize that things don't look quite right. With real glass, you have refraction. The transparent material actually bends the light, warping what you see through it, like a magnifying glass. Regular Z transparency can't easily re-create this effect. In order to get that effect, you should use ray traced transparency instead.

You can activate ray traced transparency by left-clicking the Raytrace button in the Transparency panel. When you enable this button, it automatically disables the Z Transparency button. You can't have both of these settings active at the same time. In addition, initially, it doesn't look like much changed by enabling Raytrace. This is because the IOR value for ray traced transparency is set to 1.00. A value of 1.00 means that the material has the same IOR as the air around it and therefore doesn't bend light as it passes through it. However, increasing the IOR warps the checkerboard pattern seen through the object. Now, the cool thing about the IOR value is that it actually matches the physical IOR values of real-world materials. You could look up the IOR value of a specific material, like glass or jade, on a table online or in a physics book and use it to get an accurately transparent material.

Figure 7-18 shows the difference in results that you get with straight alpha transparency, Z transparency, and ray traced transparency.

Figure 7-18:
From left to right, alpha transparency, Z transparency, and ray traced transparency with an alpha value of 0.5.

Common values for reflectivity and transparency

When it comes to the ray tracing settings, both the Mirror and Transparency panels have a few values in common. The first ones you might notice are the Fresnel and Blend sliders. The Fresnel setting adjusts an effect that's similar to the Fresnel diffuse shader, but with a specific influence on reflectivity and transparency. For reflectivity, rather than decreasing the material's color value in the direction of the light source like the Fresnel diffuse shader, increasing this value reduces the reflectivity relative to the camera. The Blend slider acts like a multiplication factor for the Fresnel effect, with higher values intensifying the effect.

For transparency, it's a bit different. It's also relative to the camera view, but instead of clouding out the transparency in that direction, it actually increases the transparency, reducing the color in the direction of the camera. Another interesting thing about the Fresnel setting for ray traced transparency is that it also works on Z transparency, so you can take advantage of the Fresnel effect without having to fake it.

TIP

If you want Fresnel or Blend (or any other value for that matter) values to be consistent in both the Transparency and Mirror panels, you can use Blender's copy-and-paste feature. Hover your mouse cursor over the value you want to copy (*don't click!*) and press Ctrl+C. Then hover your mouse cursor over the value you paste into (again, without clicking) and press Ctrl+V. Alternatively, you can copy and paste using the menu that appears when you right-click a value.

Another common setting between these ray traced effects are the Gloss settings. The default value of 1.00 makes the material perfectly reflective and transparent. Reducing this value in either panel blurs the reflection or makes the material more translucent than transparent. When changing the glossiness, the blurry reflection may look dirty or pixelated. This blurriness is because of how Blender Internal handles glossiness. The glossiness is approximated based on the Samples value, which is located beneath the Gloss slider for both ray traced reflection and ray traced transparency. Increasing the number of samples makes the glossiness appear more accurate, but at the expense of longer render times. Figure 7-19 shows some of the cool effects that you can get by varying the Gloss value.

Controlling how materials handle shadows

In the "Adjusting shader values" section earlier in this chapter, I cover how BI gives you control over the way your materials reflect diffuse color and deal with specular highlights. You can also control how your BI material works with shadows. Most important, you can dictate the type of shadows the material can receive, as well as whether the material itself casts a shadow.

Figure 7-19:
Playing with the gloss value on an object with ray traced reflections and ray traced transparency.

All these controls live in the Shadow panel of Material Properties. The following list describes the most important controls in this panel:

- **Receive:** Enabled by default, the Receive check box controls whether your material receives shadows cast by other objects.

- **Receive Transparent:** If your scene has other objects with transparent materials, you may want to enable the Receive Transparent check box. If you don't, the shadows cast from the transparent object appear as if they're cast from an opaque material. It's disabled by default for performance reasons; if your scene doesn't have transparent materials, there's no reason to waste computer resources trying to account for them.

- **Shadows Only:** I mention many times throughout this book that the beauty of computer graphics is that you can do things that are impossible in the real world. The Shadows Only check box is another example of that fact. Enable this check box, and your material is transparent *except* for where shadows are cast upon it.

- **Cast:** This check box (enabled by default) controls whether your material casts a shadow, regardless of whether it's a ray traced shadow or a buffer shadow. If you don't want your object to cast any shadows at all from any kind of light, disable this check box.

- **Cast Only:** Occasionally, you run into a situation where you only need the shadow cast from your object, and you don't need to see the object at all. This situation — impossible in meatspace — is easy to make happen by enabling the Cast Only check box.

- **Cast Buffer Shadow:** The Cast Buffer Shadow — enabled by default — controls whether your material casts a shadow from a lamp that generates buffer shadows (like a buffer spot lamp). However, if the lamp generates ray traced shadows, this check box has no effect. If you run into a situation where you don't want your object casting a buffer shadow, disable this check box.

Chapter 8

Giving Models Texture

· ·

· ·

*I*f you want a more controlled way of adjusting the look of your object than what's described in Chapter 7, then using material settings alone won't get you there. You can use Vertex Paint (V), but if you're working on a model that you intend to animate, Vertex Paint can cause you to have many extraneous vertices just for color. Those vertices end up slowing down the processes of rigging, animating, and even rendering. Also, you may want to have material changes that are independent of the topology and edge flow of your mesh.

For those sorts of scenarios, you're going to want to use textures, which is the focus of this chapter. One thing to note is that, like working with materials (see Chapter 7), there are differences in how you add textures, depending on whether you're rendering with the Blender Internal (BI) or Cycles render engine. As you work through this chapter, I point out where the differences are.

Adding Textures

Generally speaking, a *texture* is a kind of image that you stretch or tile over the surface of your object to give it more detail without adding more geometry. Not only can textures influence the color of your object, but they can also allow you to make additional adjustments, such as stipulating the shininess of some specific parts of the model. For example, on a human face, skin tends to be shinier across the nose and forehead, and somewhat duller around the eyes. With textures, you can control these sorts of things.

Working with textures in Blender Internal

If you're working with BI, you add and edit textures to a material in Texture Properties, as shown in Figure 8-1.

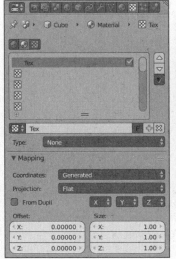

Figure 8-1:
Texture
Properties.

Like Material Properties, Texture Properties has a Preview panel that displays the texture as you work on it. If you're working from the material and texture in Blender's default scene with the cube, the Preview panel is hidden because the texture type is None. You can change this type in the Context panel with the Type drop-down menu. The texture slots list box at the top of the Context panel is similar to the material slots list box in Material Properties. With these texture slots, you can control the textures applied to your material (which, in turn, is applied to your object). However, unlike material slots, you can't arbitrarily add and remove texture slots. You have exactly 18 texture slots to work with. Left-click any texture slot in the list to choose that slot as the one you want to work on. The texture slots that are populated with a texture display the name of that texture next to its icon. You can customize the name of the texture by double-clicking its texture slot or by editing the texture datablock name field below the texture slot list box. This field is part of a set of datablock controls just like the ones used in Material Properties or Object Properties (see Chapter 7).

When you pick a specific texture type (other than None) by clicking the Type drop-down menu, a Preview panel appears in Texture Properties. By default, the Preview panel has a window that displays your current texture. However, if you left-click the Material button beneath the preview window, it's updated with the same preview panel you see in Material Properties. With this preview type, you can actively see how your texture is mapped to an object without the hassle of bouncing between Material Properties and Texture Properties. If you left-click the Both button, the preview splits to display the texture preview on the left and the material preview on the right. Figure 8-2 shows the three different views of the Preview panel.

Including textures on a Cycles material

If you're rendering with Cycles, Texture Properties doesn't give you very much that's useful. That's because, in Cycles, textures are just other nodes that you add to your node network. It's possible to add a texture from Material Properties from the connector button to the right of any property (it's the button with a small dot in its center). However, you have a lot more control if you do it from the Node Editor by pressing Shift+A ⇨ Texture and choosing your desired texture node from the menu. If you compare the list of textures available in Cycles (as shown in Figure 8-3) to those that are available in BI (see Figure 8-4 in the next section), you should notice that they aren't the same. Fortunately, the next section should help demystify some of that for you.

Figure 8-2:
From left to right, the Preview panel in Texture Properties allows you to preview your texture, see how your texture is applied in your material, and see a split view of both.

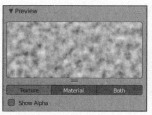 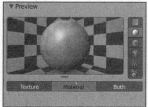 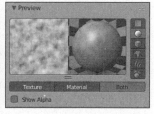

Figure 8-3:
If you render with Cycles, you add textures directly in your material node network.

Using Procedural Textures

Blender offers basically two kinds of textures: image-based textures and *procedural textures*. Unlike image-based textures, where you explicitly create and load an image (or sequence of images) as a texture, procedural textures are created in software with a specific pattern algorithm.

The advantage of procedural textures is that you can quickly add a level of detail to your objects without worrying about the unwrapping described later in this chapter in the section "Unwrapping a Mesh." The software handles mapping the texture to the mesh for you. Another advantage of procedurals is that they're *resolution independent*; they don't get blurry or pixelated when you zoom in very close.

Of course, procedurals can be a bit more difficult to control than image-based textures. For example, if you have a character with dark circles under his eyes, getting those circles to show up only where you want can be pretty tough, maybe even impossible if you're only using procedurals. So the ideal use for procedural textures is as broad strokes where you don't need fine control. Procedural textures are great for creating a foundation or a base to start with, such as providing the rough texture of an orange rind's surface.

Understanding Blender Internal's procedurals

Besides the None texture type, Blender Internal has 14 procedural texture types that you can work with, accessible through the Type drop-down menu in Texture Properties. In addition to these procedurals, you can also choose Image as a texture type. Figure 8-4 shows all available texture types.

The following are brief descriptions of each type of procedural texture:

✔ **Blend texture:** The Blend texture is one of the unsung heroes in Blender's procedural texture arsenal. This texture may seem like a simple gradient, but with the right mapping, it's really quite versatile. I use Blend textures for mixing two other textures together, creating simple toonlike outlines for meshes, and adjusting the color along the length of hair strands. You can see the real power of the Blend texture when you use it with a ramp that you define in the Colors panel.

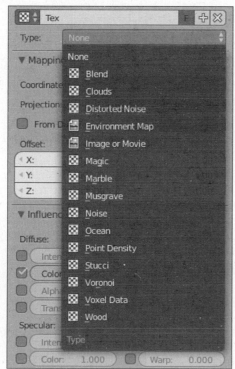

Figure 8-4:
The available textures you can use that are built into Blender Internal.

Noise basis option

Roughly half of all the procedural textures share an option labeled Basis, short for *noise basis*. The noise basis is a specific type of pseudorandom pattern that influences the appearance of a procedural texture. Noise basis has two controls:

- **Basis:** The Basis menu allows you to choose one of several algorithms for generating noise.

- **Nabla value:** The Nabla value offers more advanced control of the sharpness or smoothness of the texture when it's applied to the material.

The types of noise basis fall roughly into three different kinds of noise:

- **Cell noise:** A blocky, pixelated type of noise, cell noise stands apart from the other noise basis types because it's the least organic-looking. If you're interested in a very digital-looking texture, this type is the one to choose.

- **Voronoi family:** These noise types include Crackle, F2-F1, F4, F3, F2, and F1 and are all roughly based on the same algorithm. A primary attribute of Voronoi noise is a somewhat distinct partitioning throughout the texture with generally straight lines. This partitioning is most apparent in the Voronoi Crackle noise basis. These noise types are good for hammered metal, scales, veins, and that dry desert floor look.

- **Cloudy noise:** *Cloudy* is my own terminology, but it includes the Improved Perlin, Original Perlin, and Blender Original noise basis types. These types of noise tend to have a more organic feel to them and work well for generic bump textures and clouds or mist.

- **Clouds texture:** The Clouds texture is a good general-purpose texture. You can treat the Clouds texture as a go-to texture for general bumps, smoke, and (of course) clouds.

- **Distorted Noise texture:** The Distorted Noise texture is pretty slick. Actually, strike that; this type of texture is best suited to very rough, complex surfaces. The way the Distorted Noise texture works is pretty cool, though. You use one procedural noise texture, specified by the Noise Distortion menu, to distort and influence the texture of your noise basis. With this combination, you can get some really unique textures.

- **Environment Map texture:** An *environment map* is a way of using a texture to fake reflections on your object. It works by taking the position of a given object and rendering an image in six directions around that object: up, down, left, right, forward, and back. These images are then mapped to the surface of your object. So, an environment map isn't exactly a procedural texture in the traditional sense, but because the environment images are taken automatically, I say it's part procedural and part image-based. Environment maps aren't as accurate as using ray traced reflection (see Chapter 7), but they can be quite a bit faster. So if you need a generically reflective surface that doesn't need to be accurate, environment maps are a handy tool that keeps your render times short. In the Environment Map panel, the Viewpoint Object field is set, by default, to be the object that you intend on mapping the texture to. However, sometimes you can get a better reflective effect by using the location of a different object, such as an Empty. Using an Empty as a Viewpoint Object is particularly useful when applying an environment map to an irregular surface.

When using environment maps, make sure that you do two things. First, choose the Reflection option from the Coordinates drop-down menu in the Mapping panel of Texture Properties. Second, make sure the Environment Map check box in the Shading panel of Render Properties is enabled. Unless you do both of these things, your environment map won't work properly.

- **Magic texture:** At first glance, the Magic texture may seem to be completely useless — or at the very least, too weird to be useful. However, I've found quite a few cool uses for this eccentric little texture. If you treat the Magic texture as a bump map or a normal map, it works well for creating a knit texture for blankets and other types of cloth. If you stretch the texture with your mapping controls, you can use it to re-create the thin filmy look that occurs when oil mixes with water. And, of course, you can use it to make a wacky wild-colored shirt.

- **Marble texture:** This texture has a lot of similarities with the Wood texture covered later in this section. However, the Marble texture is a lot more turbulent. You can use the Marble texture to create the look of polished marble, but the turbulent nature of the texture also lends itself nicely to be used as a fire texture and, to a lesser extent, the small ripples you get in ponds, lakes, and smaller pools of water.

- **Musgrave texture:** This procedural texture is extremely flexible and well suited for organic materials. You can use the Musgrave texture for rock cracks, generic noise, clouds, and even as a mask for rust patterns. As a matter of fact, with enough tweaking, you can probably get a Musgrave texture to look like nearly any other procedural texture. Of course, the trade-off is that this texture takes a bit longer to render than most of the other textures.

- **Noise texture:** Noise is the simplest procedural texture in Blender. (Well, the None texture type is probably simpler, but it's not very useful.) This texture has no custom controls of its own; it's simply raw noise, which means that you'll never get the same results twice using this texture. Each time you render, the noise pattern is different. This lack of predictability may be annoying if you're looking to do a bump map. However, if you're looking to have white noise on a TV screen, this texture is perfect.

- **Ocean:** This texture is for the specific (and somewhat advanced) case where you have a scene that has an object that's using the Ocean modifier. (I briefly cover the Ocean modifier in Chapter 5; it's basically a modifier that you use to make a mesh look like the surface of a large body of water.) The Ocean texture is a procedural texture based on the geometry that the modifier generates.

- ✓ **Point Density texture:** The Point Density texture is used primarily with Blender's particle system to generate volumetric textures. These kinds of materials are well suited for creating smoke and clouds. (See Chapter 13 for more on Blender's particle system.)

- ✓ **Stucci texture:** Stucci is a nice organic texture that's most useful for creating bump maps. The Stucci texture is great for industrial and architectural materials like stucco, concrete, and asphalt. This texture is also handy if you just want to give your object's surface a little variety and roughen it up a bit.

- ✓ **Voronoi texture:** The Voronoi procedural texture doesn't have a noise basis because it's the same algorithm that is used for the Voronoi noise basis options, but with more detailed controls. It may be helpful to think of those basis options as presets, whereas this texture gives you full control over what you can do with the Voronoi algorithm. The Voronoi texture is pretty versatile, too. You can use it to create scales, veins, stained glass, textured metals, or colorful mosaics.

- ✓ **Voxel Data texture:** A *voxel*, short for *volumetric pixel*, is the three-dimensional equivalent to a pixel. The Voxel Data texture type is primarily used in Blender for smoke simulations, but you can also use it for other forms of volumetric data, such as the image slices provided by medical CT scans.

- ✓ **Wood texture:** The Wood texture is a bit of a misnomer. Sure, you *can* use it to create textures that are pretty close to what you see on cut planks of wood. However, the Wood texture has a lot more versatile uses. You can use the Wood texture to create nearly any sort of striped texture. I've actually even used it to fake the look of mini-blinds in a window.

Discovering procedurals in Cycles

Like in BI, you also have a set of procedural textures available in Cycles. Many of them are the same as their BI counterparts, though there are a few different ones. The following is a list of procedural textures available in Cycles:

- ✓ **Environment texture:** It's tempting to confuse Cycles' Environment texture with the Environment Map texture in BI, but don't make that mistake. Because everything in Cycles is ray traced, there's very little performance benefit to having the fake reflections that BI's Environment Map texture provides. In fact, in Cycles there's nothing procedural about the Environment texture. I'm including it in this list solely because some people confuse the two and may come to this section of the book. The Environment texture in Cycles is an image-based texture that's typically connected to the Color socket of the Background node for the World shader network. See Chapter 9 for more setting up your World in both Cycles and BI.

Behold the power of the ramp!

A powerful and under-recognized tool in Blender is the *ramp*. A ramp is basically a gradient, and its editor interface is used in procedural textures, ramp materials, the material node editor, and even the node compositor. For BI materials, you can enable ramps by clicking the Ramp check box tab in the Diffuse and Specular panels of Material Properties. For procedural textures, the Ramp check box appears in the Colors panel. In the Node Editor, you can add ColorRamp node by using Shift+A ⇨ Converter ⇨ ColorRamp. Ramps are a great way, for example, to adjust the color of the stripes in the Wood texture or determine which colors you want to use for your Blend texture. You can even use ramps to have a more controlled custom toon coloring than you can get with the diffuse or specular Toon shaders. The ramp editor works much like gradient editors in other programs. By default, it starts with a color positioned at either end of a *colorband* bar, and the color smoothly transitions from one side to the other. The color can be any value in the RGB spectrum, and, using the color picker, you also can control its transparency with the alpha value.

To change a color, first select it by either left-clicking its position in the colorband or adjusting the position value in the number field above the colorband. Color positions count up from left to right, starting at 0. So with the default arrangement, the transparent black color on the left is 0, and the white color on the right is 1. After you select the color, you can change its value by left-clicking the color swatch and using the color picker. To move the color position, you can left-click and drag it along the colorband, or you can adjust the Pos, or Position, value after you've selected it.

To add a new color position, left-click the Add button. A color position appears at the halfway point in the colorband. You can delete any position by selecting it and left-clicking the Delete button.

It may not seem like much, but mastering ramps and knowing when to use them makes your workflow for adding materials and textures much faster.

- ✔ **Sky texture:** The Sky texture is similar to Cycles' Environment texture in that it's typically used in the node network for the World shaders. The difference is that the Sky texture is not image-based. It's procedural and can be tweaked to give your scene the feeling of a wide array of external environments. See Chapter 9 for more on how to use this node.

- ✔ **Noise texture:** The Noise texture in Cycles produces results that are similar to the Clouds texture in BI. Do note that Cycles does *not* have an equivalent to BI's Noise texture, so the naming can be a bit confusing here.

- ✔ **Wave texture:** If you've worked with BI, you may notice that the Marble and Wood textures are nearly the same texture; the only difference being that Marble looks more turbulent than Wood. Well, in Cycles, those two procedural textures are consolidated into the Wave texture node.

- ✓ **Voronoi texture:** This texture node produces the same results as its doppelganger in BI.

- ✓ **Musgrave texture:** Much like the same-named texture in BI, the Musgrave texture in Cycles is a great organic noise-type texture. Although it has the same performance overhead as its BI counterpart, it seems to be less noticeable in Cycles.

- ✓ **Gradient texture:** The Gradient texture is Cycles' equivalent of the Blend texture in BI.

- ✓ **Magic texture:** The quirky Magic texture from BI also has a counterpart in Cycles. Happily, it shares the same quirky name, too.

- ✓ **Checker texture:** As its name implies, this procedural texture node creates a simple checkerboard texture. Many times, it gets used as a placeholder or test pattern, but it's also useful for quickly making textures for race flags, plaid, picnic blankets, and — yes — checker boards. There is no equivalent of this texture in BI.

- ✓ **Brick texture:** Similar to the Checker texture, this procedural texture's name explains exactly what it does. This may seem like an awfully specific texture to generate procedurally, but I've also used it to create grid patterns and stripes.

Understanding Texture Mapping

After you create your texture, be it procedural or image-based, you're going to have to relate that texture to your material and, by extension, the surface of your object. This process is called *mapping*. Mapping basically consists of relating a location on a texture to a location on the surface of an object. This section walks you through the process of texture mapping, both in BI and in Cycles. Regardless of which render engine you're using, texture mapping is conceptually the same; the main differences are in user interface. That being the case, I strongly recommend that you read through both sections. I make sure to point out when something only applies to one of the renderers and not the other.

Applying textures when using Blender Internal

If you're using BI, the mapping controls are located in Texture Properties in the Mapping and Influence panels, as shown in Figure 8-5. The next two sub-sections explain how to use the properties in these panels to wield full control over how your textures are applied to your objects.

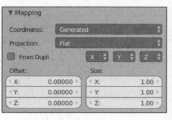

Figure 8-5:
The
Mapping
and
Influence
panels in
Texture
Properties
when you're
rendering
with BI.

The Mapping panel

The Mapping panel controls how the texture is mapped to the object, defining how the texture coordinates are projected on it. The most important button is the drop-down menu labeled Coordinates. The following list explains the types of coordinate mapping available:

- **Global:** Choosing this option uses the scene's coordinates to define the texture space. So if you have an animated object with a texture mapped this way, the texture will seem to be locked in place as the object moves across it. Global coordinates produce kind of a strange effect, but it's helpful in a few situations, such as faking shadows on a moving character.

- **Object:** This neat option allows you to use a different object's location as a means of placing a texture on your object. To tell Blender which object you want to use, pick or type its name in the Object field. For example, you can load an image texture of a logo and place that logo on a model of a car by using the location, size, and orientation of an Empty. Though Object coordinates are available in Cycles, usually they aren't used for this effect. In Cycles, Object coordinates refer only to *that* object's coordinates and not those of another object.

- **Generated:** This option is the default for procedural textures, and it generates texture coordinates based on the object's local coordinates. The Generated option works fine for most situations, especially when you're using procedural coordinates on a deforming animated object.

- **UV:** UV coordinates are probably the most precise way of mapping a texture to an object. NURBS surfaces have UV coordinates by default. For meshes, however, getting UV coordinates requires you to go through a process called unwrapping, covered later in this chapter in the "Unwrapping a Mesh" section.

✔ **Strand:** This option is useful only when your object has a particle system with the Strand render option enabled. As the name indicates, the Strand option is intended specifically for particle strands. When activated, the texture is mapped along the length of the strand.

✔ **Camera:** Camera coordinates are only available in Cycles. They are a way of getting a somewhat precise mapping based on the location and orientation of the camera.

✔ **Window:** This option is similar to the Global coordinates option, but instead of using the scene's global coordinates, it uses the coordinates from the finished render window. In other words, it uses the camera's coordinates. But unlike Camera coordinates, which keeps the texture undistorted, this option always stretches the texture to fit the window's dimensions.

✔ **Normal:** Choosing this option causes the texture to be mapped according to the normal vectors along the surface of the object. This option is helpful for effects that require textures to react to the viewing angle of the camera.

✔ **Reflection:** The Reflection option uses the direction of a reflection vector to map your texture to the object. Basically, you want to use this option with an environment map texture to get fake reflections when you don't need the accuracy of ray tracing.

✔ **Stress:** Stress maps are a pretty cool option that's intended for use with dynamic or simulated geometry. The *stress value* is the difference between the location of an original texture coordinate and location of the coordinate when rendered. As an example, say that you have a character with stretchy arms. You can use stress mapping as a mask to make the arms more translucent the more they stretch. Stress coordinates are not available in Cycles.

✔ **Tangent:** In some ways, this option is similar to Normal coordinates. However, instead of using the surface normal, it uses an optional tangent vector to map the texture coordinates. Notice that I wrote *optional* tangent vector. In BI, by default, no tangent vector is on the material, so choosing this option by itself doesn't do much to it. However, if you left-click the Tangent Shading check box in the Shading panel of Material Properties, you have a tangent vector for your texture to work with.

In addition to these map inputs, you can also control what's called the *texture projection*. Texture projection, along with the map input, controls how the texture is applied to the mesh for everything except UV textures. Because UV textures explicitly map a texture coordinate to a coordinate on the surface of your object, changes to projection don't have an effect.

Blender has four different types of projection:

- **Flat:** This type of projection is the easiest to visualize. Imagine that you have your texture loaded in a slide projector. When you point the projector at a wall, you get the best results. However, if you point the slide projector at a curved or uneven surface, you get a little bit of distortion. This behavior is basically what happens with Flat projection.

- **Cube:** Cube projection uses the same idea as Flat projection, but instead of having just one projector, imagine that you have one pointing at the front, left, and top of your object (and shining through to the other side). The texture appears on all six sides of the cube. Of course, when you try to project on a more curved surface, you still get some seams and distortion.

- **Tube:** Tube projection is where the slide projector metaphor kind of stops making sense. Imagine that you have the unique ability to project on a curved surface without the distortion — of course, such projection is pretty close to impossible in the real world, but it's pretty trivial in computer graphics. Using Tube projection is ideal for putting labels on bottles or applying other sorts of textures to tubular objects.

- **Sphere:** Spherical projection is best suited for spherical objects, such as planets and balls, and it's also the cleanest way to apply a texture to an arbitrary three-dimensional surface because it usually doesn't leave any noticeable seams like Cube projection does.

Figure 8-6 shows a set of primitive objects with Flat, Cube, Tube, and Sphere projection.

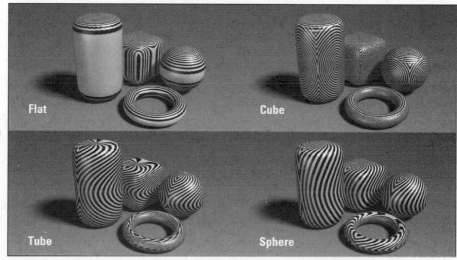

Figure 8-6: Projecting textures in different ways on the same set of 3D objects.

At the bottom of the Mapping panel are fields that give you finer control over how your texture is positioned on your object. The Offset values define an offset in the X, Y, and Z directions. And the Size values scale the texture in each of those directions.

The Offset and Size values aren't relative to the global or local coordinates in the 3D View. They're actually relative to the texture image itself. The X and Y values are horizontal and vertical, whereas the Z value is a depth value into the texture. The Z values don't have a lot of influence unless the texture is a procedural texture with a noise basis because many of those textures actually have 3D depth information.

The Influence panel

Not only do you control how a texture is mapped to an object, but you also control how that texture affects the material in BI, thanks to the controls in the Influence panel.

Each Influence value is enabled using a check box to the left of each slider. After you enable a check box, you can adjust its slider to dictate the level of influence. Most sliders span both positive and negative values, typically from –1 to 1. Using this range, values greater than 0 enable the option and increase its effect, but negative values indicate that the texture's effect on the material is inverted.

You can use any combination of the following options:

- **Diffuse controls:** Use these values to dictate how your texture influences various attributes of your material's diffuse shader. You have four options:

  - **Intensity:** Influences the intensity value in the material's diffuse shader, controlling how much light the material reflects.

  - **Color:** Affects the material's diffuse color.

  - **Alpha:** Controls the transparency and opacity of the material.

  - **Translucency:** Affects the amount of translucency in the material.

- **Specular controls:** These controls are like the Diffuse values, but they relate specifically to the material's specularity. You have three options:

  - **Intensity:** Influences the strength in the material's specular shader.

  - **Color:** Affects the material's specular color.

  - **Hardness:** Affects the specular hardness values for the specular shaders that support it.

✔ **Shading controls:** The values here dictate how your textures influence corresponding values in the Shading panel of the Material Properties. You have four options:

- **Ambient:** Affects the amount of ambient light the material gets.

- **Emit:** Affects the material's emit value.

- **Mirror Color:** Affects the material's mirror color.

- **Ray Mirror:** Influences the amount of ray traced reflection that the material has.

✔ **Geometry controls:** With the values in this section, your textures can actually deform geometric elements of your object, be they the face normals or the location of faces themselves. You have three options:

- **Normal:** Influences the direction of the surface normals on the material. Enabling this check box enables bump mapping. This option can give your object the appearance of much more detail without the computational slowdown of additional geometry.

- **Warp:** This value actually controls how one texture in the list of textures affects the next one in the stack. Higher Warp values cause this texture to influence the coordinates of the next texture in the stack.

- **Displace:** This option is similar to the Normal option, except that it actually moves the geometry of the object based on the texture map. Whereas bump mapping only makes it *look* like geometry is added and moved around by tricking out the surface normal, displacement actually moves the geometry around. The downside to Blender's displacement is that you have to have the vertices already in place to move around. Blender won't create the vertices for you on the fly. You can use the Subdivision Surface modifier to get around this a bit, but creating your additional vertices with that tool definitely increases your render times.

  Another thing to note is that you can't see the results of texture displacement in the 3D View unless you use Rendered viewport shading. If you want to see the shifted geometry in a different viewport shading (such as Solid or Wireframe), I recommend that instead of using this texture control, you use the Displace modifier. You can read more on modifiers in Chapter 5.

Mapping textures when using Cycles

If you're using Cycles, there's a Mapping panel in Texture Properties that's similar to the corresponding panel when rendering with BI. However, you have far more control using the Texture Coordinates node in concert with a Mapping node, as shown in Figure 8-7.

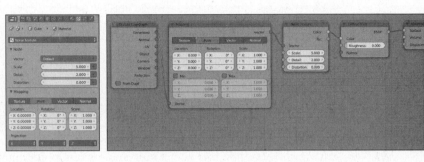

Conceptually, there are a lot of similarities between mapping textures on your object in BI and doing the same thing in Cycles. If you skipped over the previous section on applying textures using BI, I strongly recommend that you go back and read it. The content of that section is very relevant to this one. Most of the differences are in terms of user interface. Rather than making your adjustments from a handful of panels in Texture Properties, you're connecting a series of nodes together.

Using texture coordinates

In Cycles, texture mapping is handled in the nodes (particularly the Texture Coordinates node and the Mapping node), while the Cycles equivalent to BI's Influence panel is implicit, based on how you wire the nodes together.

As shown in Figure 8-7, the basics of it work like this:

1. **Add a Texture Coordinate node (Shift+A ⇨ Input ⇨ Texture Coordinate) to your material in the Node Editor.**

   Most of the texture coordinates listed in the preceding section are available: Generated, Normal, UV, Object, Camera, Window, and Reflection. There are a few differences, but they aren't exceedingly significant. I cover the differences later in this section.

2. **Connect the socket of your desired texture coordinate to the Vector input socket on your chosen Texture node in your material.**

   The Texture node could be any of the ones available in the Node Editor when you press Shift+A ⇨ Texture. All of them have a Vector input socket.

3. **Optionally, add a Mapping node (Shift+A ⇨ Vector ⇨ Mapping) and wire it on the noodle between your Texture Coordinate node and your Texture node.**

   The Mapping node (look back to Figure 8-7 to see it) is what gives you more control over the texture coordinates on your object. It's akin to the Offset and Size values in BI's Mapping panel, but with even more controls (such as giving the texture coordinates an arbitrary rotation).

4. **Connect the Color output socket on your Texture node to the Color input socket on your desired shader node.**

   This is Cycles' equivalent to BI's Influence panel. If you want your texture to influence the color of your diffuse shader, you explicitly connect it to the Diffuse BSDF node's Color socket. Want your grayscale texture to influence the roughness of your glossy shader? Connect it to the Roughness socket on a Glossy BSDF. In a way, using nodes is a much more direct way of mapping and applying textures to a material, because you can zoom out on the node network and get a really complete understanding of the material all at once.

You may be reading all of this and find yourself saying, "Great, but how do I fake having more detail with a bump map or a normal map? In BI, I just need to work with the Geometry properties, like Normal and Displace in the Influence panel." Fortunately, that's also easy in Cycles. If you have a grayscale texture that you want to use as a bump map, all you need to do is wire it to the Displacement socket of the Material Output node, as shown in Figure 8-8. Easy!

Figure 8-8:
Bump mapping is easy in Cycles. Just connect your texture to the Displacement socket of your Material Output node.

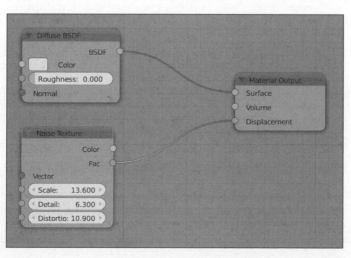

TIP

If you want to have different bumps on different shaders in the same material, that's also possible, though a bit more complex. Rather than wire your grayscale texture to the Displacement socket on the Material Output node, add a Bump node (Shift+A⇨Vector⇨Bump) and wire your texture to its Height socket. Then wire the Normal output socket of your Bump node to the Normal input socket of any shader node. And voilà! Custom bumpiness on any shader!

Looking back at the Texture Coordinates node, you may notice that quite a few of the coordinate systems listed in the previous section appear to be missing. Fortunately, a few of them — including Global coordinates and Tangent coordinates — are available (along with a few bonus coordinate systems); you just need to use a different node. Specifically, you need to use the Geometry node. This is for organizational reasons. Basically, global coordinates and tangent coordinates have more to do with object geometry than they do with the texture. They're really independent of the texture. For that reason, Blender's developers felt it made more sense to organize them in the Geometry node. In fact, the Geometry node gives more than just those options. If you add it by pressing Shift+A⇨Input⇨Geometry, you have the following sockets available:

- ✔ **Position:** The Position vector is the equivalent to using BI's Global texture coordinates.

- ✔ **Normal:** At first, this may appear to be the same as the Normal socket in the Texture Coordinates node. However, the difference here is that this vector doesn't change if the object is deformed by an armature or lattice in an animation rig. So if you're texturing an object that's meant to be animated, you're best off using the socket in the Texture Coordinates node.

- ✔ **Tangent:** This socket is the equivalent of using the Tangent coordinate system in BI.

- ✔ **True Normal:** If your object is using smooth shading (most organic objects are) or bump mapping, that effect is achieved by manipulating the normals of a mesh. However, there are occasions where you want the "true" normal — the geometry's normal *before* those additional manipulations. The vector from this socket gives you that normal.

- ✔ **Incoming:** The vector from this socket points back toward the camera. You can use this kind of like a Fresnel value to influence the effect of a texture based on whether the underlying geometry points to the camera.

- ✔ **Parametric:** This socket is typically for much more advanced use. It gives the actual world space coordinates of the *shading points*, or the places on the surface of your object where a ray tracer's rays intersect it.

- ✔ **Backfacing:** This is the only non-vector socket on the Geometry node. It's an array of 1s and 0s; 1s for faces of the object that point to the camera, and 0s for the faces that point away.

Object coordinates in Cycles and the UV Project modifier

Aside from Stress coordinates, the only other coordinate system that Cycles doesn't seem to have — or at least doesn't have as fully-featured as BI — are Object coordinates. There *is* the Object socket on the Texture Coordinates node, but unfortunately, there's no way to explicitly tell Cycles to use another object's coordinates for projecting a texture on your object. This means that the use for Object coordinates is a bit more limited. In Cycles, they're primarily useful for getting undistorted procedural textures applied to your object.

There are two main differences between Generated coordinates and Object coordinates:

- ✔ Generated coordinates "stick" to your object and Object coordinates do not. If your object is deformed by an animation rig, such as with an armature or lattice, and you're using Generated coordinates, the texture will move with your object. If you're using Object coordinates, those deforming parts of the object will appear to slide under the texture — not usually the desired effect.

- ✔ Generated coordinates stretch a texture to the bounding box of your object, while Object coordinates impart no such distortion. This point is especially important if you're creating a procedural material that needs to look nice and unstretched, regardless of your object's size.

So there's a bit of a trade-off here. Fortunately, this trade-off isn't a frequent problem. If an object uses deforming animation (see Chapters 11 and 12), you typically don't use procedural textures, so it's less common to use Object mapping on them.

But what if you really want to place a texture on your object in Cycles with the same decal-like effect that Object coordinates give you in BI? For that, you need to use a workaround. Namely, you should make use of the UV Project modifier. The UV Project modifier treats one or more objects as external "projectors" that project a texture on your object much like a movie projector shows a movie on a screen. The only limitation is that your object must already be UV unwrapped. If you're working with a NURBS surface, the unwrapping already is done automatically. However, for mesh objects — the more common case — you need to unwrap manually (see the next section).

Assuming that your object already is unwrapped, use the following steps to project a texture on your mesh with the UV Project modifier:

1. **Add an Empty object to your scene (from the 3D View, Shift+A ⇨ Empty ⇨ Plain Axes).**

   This Empty object is what you'll use as your "projector". The image texture will appear to project along the Empty's local Z-axis. I recommend giving this Empty a custom name like Projector, but you can leave it with its default name. Just remember that name.

2. **With your object selected, add a UV Project modifier from Modifier Properties (Modifier Properties ⇨ Add Modifier ⇨ UV Project).**

   I know I'm drilling the point, but again, make sure that your object is already unwrapped.

3. **Fill in fields on the UV Project modifier.**

   a. *(Optional) If your mesh has more than one UV unwrapping, use the UV Map field to choose the UV layer on which you want the UV Project modifier to work.*

   b. *Enable the Override Image check box.*

   c. *In the Object field below the Projectors property, type or pick the name of the Empty you're using as a projector.*

4. **Set up your material to use UV textures in the Node Editor (Shift+F3).**

   a. *Add an Image Texture node (Shift+A ⇨ Texture ⇨ Image Texture) and load an image texture from your hard drive.*

   b. *Add a Texture Coordinates node (Shift+A ⇨ Input ⇨ Texture Coordinates).*

   c. *Connect the UV socket in the Texture Coordinates node to the Vector input socket on the Image Texture node.*

   d. *(Optional) Add a Mapping node and place it inline on the noodle between the Texture Coordinates node and the Image Texture node. Enable the Min and Max check boxes in this node.*

   By default, UV mapped image textures *tile*, or repeat, when they reach the end of the image. If you don't want this repeating behavior, enabling these check boxes in the Mapping node prevents it.

5. ***Connect the Color output socket of the Image Texture node to the Color input socket of the Diffuse BSDF node.***

With those steps complete, you should be able to move the Empty around and see the texture slide around the surface of your object in the 3D View.

To properly position the texture, split the 3D View into two and display one of the 3D Views in Rendered viewport shading (Shift+Z). This way, you can both see your projector Empty and see the results of moving it around.

Figure 8-9 shows what your Blender screen layout might look like.

When your texture (in this kind of usage, it's sometimes called a *decal*) is applied how you like it, you may want to consider vertex parenting your projector Empty to some nearby vertices on your mesh (see Chapter 4 for more on vertex parenting). I especially recommend vertex parenting if your

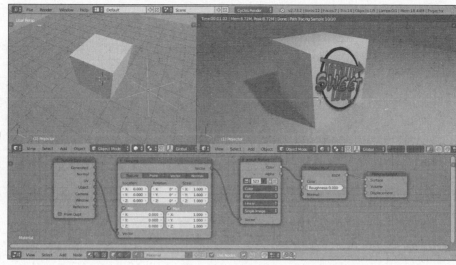

Figure 8-9:
Positioning
a texture on
an object
using the
UV Project
modifier.

object is going to be animated. This way, when you animate your object, the projector Empty goes along with it and the decal doesn't get distorted.

Alternatively, if you create a separate UV layer in the UV Maps panel of Mesh Properties, you can apply the UV Project modifier on that layer. Then, using those modified UV coordinates (covered in the last section of this chapter, "Using UV Textures"), your decal texture is mapped without any need for that projector Empty to remain in the scene.

Unwrapping a Mesh

The most precise type of mapping you can use is UV mapping. UV mapping also allows you to take advantage of other Blender features, such as Texture Paint mode, the UV Project modifier (see the preceding section), and texture baking. With NURBS surfaces, you get UV coordinates for free as part of their structure. However, Blender is predominantly a mesh editor, and in order to get proper UV coordinates on your mesh objects, you must put those meshes through a process known as unwrapping.

To understand this process, think about a globe and a map of the world. The map of the world uses the latitude and longitude lines to relate a point on the three-dimensional surface of the globe to the two-dimensional surface of the map. In essence, the world map is an unwrapped texture on the globe, whereas the latitude and longitude lines are the UVs. Figure 8-10 shows a visualization of this process.

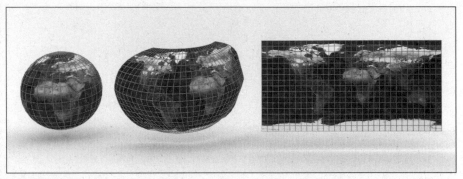

Figure 8-10:
UV unwrapping a 3D mesh is like making a map of the Earth (image texture credit: NASA).

Marking seams on a mesh

You unwrap a mesh in Blender by selecting all vertices (A) and, while in Edit mode (Tab), either pressing U or choosing UV Mapping⇨Unwrap in the Tool Shelf. You then see a menu with a handful of options.

However, despite the menu's variety of options, unless your mesh is simple or a special case, you should use the first menu item, Unwrap. Blender has very powerful unwrapping tools, but to take full advantage of them, you need to first define some seams. Remember that you're basically trying to flatten a 3D surface to a 2D plane. In order to do so, you need to tell Blender where it can start pulling the mesh apart. This location on your mesh is a *seam*. If you were unwrapping a globe, you might choose the prime meridian as your seam. I like to think about seams for unwrapping in terms of stuffed animals, such as a teddy bear. The seam is where the bear is stitched together from flat pieces of cloth.

To add a seam to your mesh, use the following steps:

1. **Tab into Edit mode and switch to Edge Select mode (Tab ⇨ Ctrl+Tab ⇨ Edges).**

   You can also add seams from Vertex Select mode, but I find that it's easier in Edge Select.

2. **Select the series of edges you want to make into a seam (right-click ⇨ Shift+right-click).**

   Using edge loop selection (Alt+right-click) can really be helpful here. Everyone has their own tastes when it comes to defining seams, but a good general rule is to put the seams on parts of the mesh that are easier to hide (for example, behind the hairline on a character, the under-carriage of a car, and so on).

Though edge loop selection can be helpful, it sometimes selects more edges than you want. So a handy feature in Blender is Select ⇨ Shortest Path in the 3D View's header menu (you can also get to this operator by searching for it using Blender's integrated search when pressing Spacebar). With this feature, if you select two vertices or edges, Blender will select the shortest path of edges from one to the other. That path often works very well as a seam for unwrapping.

3. **Use the Edge Specials menu to make the seam (Ctrl+E ⇨ Mark Seam or, in the Shading/UVs tab of the Tool Shelf, UV Mapping ⇨ Mark Seam).**

Seams on your mesh are highlighted in red. If you mistakenly make a seam with the wrong edges, you can remove the seam by selecting those edges (right-click) and pressing Ctrl+E ⇨ Clear Seam or choosing UV Mapping ⇨ Clear Seam in the Shading/UVs tab of the Tool Shelf.

With your seams defined, you're ready to unwrap your mesh. In order to see what you're doing, though, you should make a couple changes to your screen layout:

1. **Change the viewport shading of your 3D View to textured (Alt+Z).**

2. **Split off a new area and change it to be a UV/Image Editor (Shift+F10).**

Alternatively, you can switch to the default UV Editing screen that ships with Blender by clicking the screen datablock at the top of your Blender window.

Your layout should look something like what is shown in Figure 8-11.

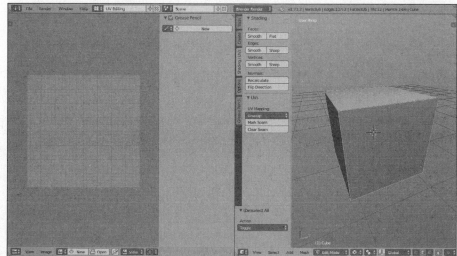

Figure 8-11:
A typical screen layout for UV unwrapping and editing.

Adding a test grid

The next thing you need is an image for mapping to your mesh. Using a *test grid* — basically an image with a colored checkerboard pattern — is common practice when unwrapping. A test grid is helpful for trying to figure out where the texture is *stretched*, or unevenly mapped, on your mesh. To add a test grid, go to the UV/Image Editor and choose Image⇨New or press Alt+N. A floating panel like the one in Figure 8-12 appears. Name the image something sensible, such as Test Grid, and choose either Color Grid or UV Grid from the Generated Type drop-down menu. Leave the other settings at their defaults for now. The UV/Image Editor updates interactively.

Figure 8-12:
The New Image floating panel for adding a test grid image.

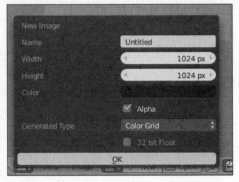

You can unwrap your mesh without adding a test grid, but a test grid gives you a good frame of reference to work from when unwrapping.

Also, note the height and width of the test grid image. The most obvious thing is that it's square; the height and width are equal. When you create the image, you can make it nonsquare, but UV texturing is often optimized for square images (particularly in some game engines), so consider where your 3D model will be used; if it makes sense, keep its image textures square.

Another tip that helps performance when working with UV textures (especially for video games) is to make your texture size a *power of two* — a number that you get by continually multiplying 2 by itself. The default size is 1,024 pixels square, or 2^{10}. The next larger size is 2,048 (2^{11}) pixels, and the next size down would be 512 (2^9) pixels. This strange sizing is because computer memory is measured and accessed in values that are powers of two. So even if you're not using your 3D model in a video game, it's still a good idea to stick to the power of two guideline. It's an easy guide to stick to, and every, every little bit of performance optimization helps, especially when you start rendering (see Chapter 14).

Generating and editing UV coordinates

Alrighty, after marking seams on your mesh and adding a test grid for reference, *now* you're ready to unwrap your mesh. From Edit mode, unwrapping is pretty simple:

1. **Select all vertices (A).**

   Remember that the A key is a toggle, so you may have to hit it twice to get everything selected.

2. **Unwrap the mesh (U ⇨ Unwrap).**

   Poof! Your mesh is now unwrapped! If you used a Suzanne to practice unwrapping, you may have something that looks like Figure 8-13.

From this point, you can edit your UV layout to arrange the pieces in a logical fashion and minimize stretching. You can tell a texture is stretched with your test grid. If any of the squares on the checkerboard look distorted or grotesquely nonsquare-shaped, stretching has taken place. If you don't see the test grid texture on your monkey, make sure that you're using Textured Viewport Shading (Alt+Z). The controls in the UV/Image Editor are very similar to working in the 3D View. The Grab (G), Rotate (R), and Scale (S) hotkeys all work as expected, as well as the various selection tools like Border select (B), Circle select (C), and Edge Loop Selection (Alt+right-click). There's even a 2D cursor like the 3D cursor in the 3D View to help with snapping and providing a frame of reference for rotation and scaling.

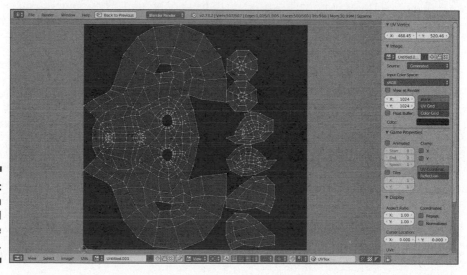

Figure 8-13:
An unwrapped Suzanne head.

If you're trying to fix stretching, you may notice that moving some vertices in your UV layout to fix stretching in one place distorts and causes stretching in another part. To help with this problem, Blender offers you two features: vertex pinning (P) and Live Unwrap (UVs⇨Live Unwrap). They actually work together. The workflow goes something like these steps:

1. **In the UV/Image Editor, select the vertices that you want to define as** *control vertices* **(right-click⇨Shift+right-click).**

   The control vertices are usually the vertices at the top and bottom of the center line and some corner vertices. I tend to prefer using vertices that are on the seam, but sometimes using internal vertices is also helpful.

2. **Pin these selected vertices (P).**

   The vertices now appear larger and are a bright red color. If you want to unpin a vertex, select it (right-click) and press Alt+P.

3. **Turn on Live Unwrap (UVs⇨Live Unwrap).**

   If a check mark appears to the left of this menu item, you know it's currently enabled.

4. **Select one or more pinned vertices and move them around (right-click⇨G).**

   As you edit these pinned vertices, all the other vertices in the UV layout automatically shift and adjust to compensate for this movement and help reduce stretching.

When using pinned vertices and Live Unwrap, selecting and moving unpinned vertices isn't normally going to be very helpful. The moment you select and move a pinned vertex, any manual changes you made to unpinned vertices are obliterated.

The UV/Image Editor also offers you the ability to edit your UVs, like sculpting in the 3D View (see Chapter 5). To toggle UV sculpting, choose UVs⇨UV Sculpt from the UV/Image Editor's header menu or press Q. Options for UV sculpting are in the Tools tab of the UV/Image Editor's Tool Shelf (T). If you try to sculpt and you don't see your UV vertices moving, try disabling the Lock Borders check box Tool Shelf⇨Tools⇨UV Sculpt.

You can actually see the changes you make in the UV/Image Editor in real time if you left-click the Lock button in the header of the UV/Image Editor (it's the last button, with an icon of a lock). The Lock button is enabled by default. Of course, if your computer seems to be performing slowly with this option on, you can always disable it by left-clicking it.

Figure 8-14 shows the unwrapped Suzanne head from before, after a bit of editing and adjustment.

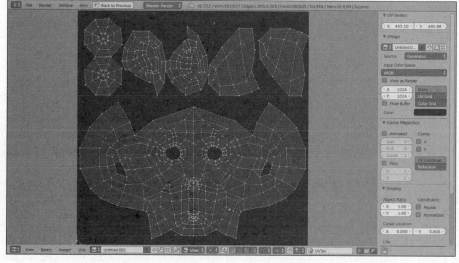

Figure 8-14:
An unwrapped and [mostly] stretchless Suzanne head.

Painting Textures Directly on a Mesh

If you followed the earlier sections in this chapter, you have an unwrapped mesh and a texture on it that doesn't stretch. Woohoo! But say that, for some crazy reason, you don't want your object to have a checkerboard as a texture, and you want to actually use this UV layout to paint a texture for your mesh. You can either paint directly on the mesh from within Blender or export the UV layout to paint in an external program like Krita or Photoshop. I actually prefer to use a combination of these methods. I normally paint directly on the mesh in Blender to rough out the color scheme and perhaps create some bump and specularity maps. Then I export that image along with an image of the UV layout to get more detailed painting done in an external program.

Preparing to paint

After you have an unwrapped mesh, the starting point for painting textures on it is Blender's Texture Paint mode. Activate Texture Paint mode by left-clicking the mode button in the 3D View's header. Alternatively, if you have the Pie Menus add-on enabled, Texture Paint mode is available from the pie that appears when you press Tab. When you activate Texture Paint mode and look to the 3D View's Tool Shelf, you may see some errors at the top of the Tools tab. There will be a warning that says "Missing Data." If you haven't unwrapped your mesh, there will be a message that says "Missing UVs". In that case, Blender offers a button, Add Simple UVs, that quickly unwraps your mesh for you without seams.

Although it's tempting to use this means of unwrapping, rather than the steps covered in the preceding section, I don't recommend it (especially if you intend on finalizing your image texture in a 2D painting program like Krita or Photoshop). That said, Blender's texture painting tools have gotten a lot more powerful over the years. So if you plan on painting your textures *only* within Blender, the simple UV unwrap you get from clicking this button may be sufficient for your needs. As always, it's about knowing what you want and accepting certain trade-offs based on that knowledge.

The other missing data warning that you may get is one that states you're "Missing Texture Slots." This warning is because you need an image texture (even a blank one) so Blender knows what you're painting on. You can add an image texture to your material as described in the first section of this chapter, but there's also a convenience button labeled Add Paint Slot directly below the warning in the Tool Shelf. Left-clicking this button reveals a list of texture types to apply to your material. After you pick one (such as Diffuse Color), Blender shows a floating panel like the one for adding a new image in the UV/Image Editor. Decide on the size and type (Blank, UV Grid, or Color Grid) of your image texture and left-click the OK button at the bottom of the panel. Blender then automatically generates your image texture and applies it to your material. (Blender automatically connects sockets if you're using Cycles or enables the correct check boxes in the Influence panel of Texture Properties if you're using BI.) Figure 8-15 shows the Tools tab of the Tool Shelf in Texture Paint mode before and after these warnings are resolved.

After you add your first paint slot, you can add additional ones from the Slots tab of the 3D View's Tool Shelf. Many Blender artists like to use these slots like layers in a 2D painting program like Krita or Photoshop.

Working in Texture Paint mode

From here, things are pretty similar to Vertex Paint mode (see Chapter 7), with a few exceptions. The Tools tab of the Tool Shelf updates with an array of paint options, but the specific content of the Tool Shelf has some differences from Vertex Paint. The Brush panel is largely the same, though with a few more preset brushes.

There's also a Texture panel in the Tool Shelf where you can actually define a texture for your brush, so you're not just painting flat colors. Regardless of whether you're rendering with BI or Cycles, you define brush textures in Texture Properties. In fact, editing brush textures is the only thing you can do in Texture Properties if you're using Cycles. If you're rendering with BI, there are three buttons at the top of Texture Properties where you can choose the type of texture you want to edit: world textures, material textures, or brush textures. Using Blender textures to paint UV textures gives your painting quite a bit more flexibility.

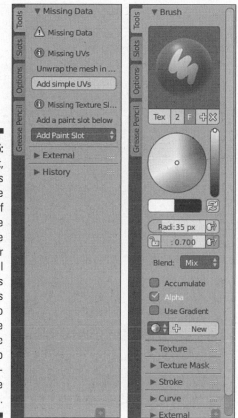

Figure 8-15: On the left, the Tools tab of the Tool Shelf in Texture Paint mode if your material has no UVs or textures applied to it. On the right is the same tab after resolving those issues.

When you're in Texture Paint mode, start painting directly on your mesh by left-clicking and dragging your mouse cursor on it. If you have a test grid image already loaded as your image, your paint strokes appear directly on this image. In fact, if you still have the UV/Image Editor open, you can watch your image get updated as you paint your mesh. And actually, you can paint directly on the UV image itself by enabling painting in the UV/Image Editor. Enable painting in the UV/Image Editor from the editing context drop-down menu in the header. It defaults to View; by left-clicking that context drop-down menu, you can also choose the Paint or Mask contexts. With Image Painting enabled in the UV/Image Editor, the Tools tab of the Tool Shelf in that editor has the same painting controls that are available in the corresponding Tool Shelf tab of the 3D View.

Because of this cool ability to paint in both the 3D View and the UV/Image Editor, when I paint textures in Blender, I like to have my screen laid out like Figure 8-16. I have the 3D View and UV/Image Editor both in Texture Paint mode. If I need to tweak a texture for my brush, I temporarily switch one of the areas

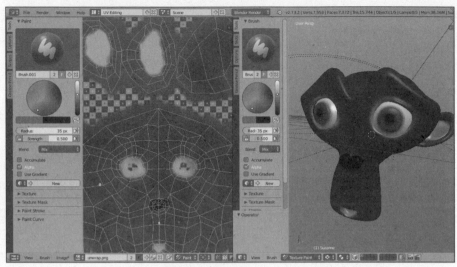

Figure 8-16:
A good
screen
layout for
texture
painting
directly on
your mesh.

to a Properties editor (Shift+F7) and make adjustments from Texture Properties, then switch back (Shift+F5 for the 3D View, Shift+F10 for the UV/Image Editor). This layout and workflow is a pretty effective way to get work done.

Saving painted textures and exporting UV layouts

Of course, despite the cool things that you can do with Blender's Texture Paint mode, there are some things that are easier in a full-blown 2D graphics program like Krita or Photoshop. To work on your image in another program, you need to save the texture you already painted as an external image. You should also export your UV layout as an image so that you have a frame of reference to work from while painting.

To save your painted texture, go to the UV/Image Editor and choose Image ⇨ Save As. A File Browser appears, allowing you to save the image to your hard drive in any format you like. I prefer to use PNG because it has small file sizes and lossless compression.

Regardless of whether you're continuing to paint on your texture in an external program, I *strongly* recommend that you save your image file externally. Not only does doing so reduce the size of your .blend file, but it also serves as a completion milestone that you can always come back to, like a save point in a video game. And from the perspective of a person who's paranoid about data safety (like me), external saving ensures that your texture is preserved in the event that your `.blend` file become corrupt or unreadable. It's a credo I have whenever I do anything with a computer: Save early, save often, save multiple multiple copies.

If you don't explicitly save your image texture, it *will not* be saved with your `.blend` file. If you close Blender and then re-open the file, all of your painting will be lost. There are only two workarounds for this:

✔ **Save your image externally.** As described in the preceding paragraphs, choose Image⇨Save As from the UV/Image Editor.

✔ **Pack your image in your `.blend` file.** Also from the UV/Image Editor, choose Image⇨Pack As PNG. This bundles the image in your `.blend` file so it will be there when you re-open the file.

In either case, if you continue to paint on your texture in Blender, you will need to continue to either save it externally or repack it to avoid losing your changes.

With your image saved, the next thing you probably want out of Blender for your 2D image editor is the UV layout of your object. To export the UV layout, you need to be in the UV/Image Editor while in Edit mode (Tab). Navigate to UVs⇨Export UV Layout. This brings up a File Browser where you can choose where to save your UV layout on your hard drive.

This UV export feature gives you the option (in the last panel of the left sidebar in the File Browser) to save in the familiar PNG image format as well as two other formats: SVG and EPS. Both SVG (Scalable Vector Graphics) and EPS (Encapsulated PostScript) are vector image formats. If your UV layout is in a vector format, you can scale it to fit any image size you need without losing any resolution. So you can use the same UV layout file to paint both low-resolution and high-resolution textures.

Most graphics applications should be able to read SVG files just fine. If you run into a problem, though, I recommend opening the SVG in GIMP (`www.gimp.org`) or Inkscape (`www.inkscape.org`). Both applications are powerful open-source graphics programs, and freely available to download from their websites. You can edit your UV texture directly in these programs, or you can use them to convert the SVG file to a raster format that your graphics application of choice recognizes, such as PNG or TIFF.

Baking Texture Maps from Your Mesh

Another benefit of unwrapping your mesh is *render baking*. Render baking is the process of creating a flat texture for your mesh that's based on what your mesh looks like when you render it. What good is that? Well, for one example, render baking is really useful to people who want to create models for use in video games. Because everything in a game has to run in real time, models can't usually have a lot of complicated lighting or highly detailed meshes with millions of vertices. To get around this limitation, you can fake some of these effects by using a texture. And rather than paint on shadows and detail by hand, you can let the computer do the work and use a high-resolution render instead.

Although this technique is used a lot in video games, render baking is also helpful when creating animated models for film or television. If you can create a model that looks really detailed but still has a relatively low vertex count, your rendering and animating process goes faster.

Another use of render baking is for texture painters. Sometimes it's helpful to have an ambient occlusion or shadow texture as a frame of reference to start painting a more detailed texture. A technique that I like to use is to first rough in colors with vertex painting (see Chapter 7). Then you can bake out those vertex colors to a texture, which can serve as a great starting point for a hand-painted texture.

So how do you create these baked textures? Well, the magic all happens in the Bake panel at the bottom of Render Properties. Depending on whether you're baking with Cycles or BI (you choose which engine you're baking with the same way you choose your renderer: use the Render Engine drop-down menu in the Info editor's header), there are slight differences in what you see in the Bake panel, as shown in Figure 8-17.

Figure 8-17:
The Bake panel in Render Properties. On the left is the Bake panel when you use Cycles and on the right is the same panel when using BI.

Discovering texture bake options in BI

You have 14 different kinds of images that you can bake out, accessible from the Bake Type drop-down menu in the Bake panel. However, the first six are the most common:

- ✔ **Full Render:** This is the whole mess — textures, vertex colors, shadows, ambient occlusion, specular highlights — the works.

- ✔ **Ambient Occlusion:** *Ambient occlusion,* or AO, is an approximated form of *global illumination,* or the effect that happens from light bouncing off of everything. If you have AO enabled in World Properties, you can bake its results by choosing this option. See Chapter 9 for more on AO.

- ✔ **Shadow:** Any shadows that fall on this object are baked out as a texture.

- ✔ **Normals:** A normal map is similar to a bump map, but instead of just using a grayscale image to define height, normal maps can get even more detailed by using a full-color image to define height as well as direction. A common workflow is to bake the normals from a mesh detailed in Sculpt mode to a low-resolution version of the mesh. This way, you can get details on the model without the additional geometry.

- ✔ **Textures:** This option takes all the textures you applied to the mesh, both image-based and procedural, and flattens them out to a single texture.

- ✔ **Displacement:** Baking displacement is similar to baking normals. The difference is that normal maps just redirect surface normals to provide the illusion of more geometry, whereas a displacement map can actually be used to move geometry around and create real depth on the surface of the object. Using displacement maps in Blender can be computationally expensive. However, a few third-party rendering engines have a nice way of handling displacement maps without the need to heavily subdivide your mesh.

As mentioned in the introduction to this section, another bake mode that that I like to use is Vertex Colors. It's not in the more frequently used first six modes, but it is available from the Bake Type drop-down. See my website for this book, www.blenderbasics.com, for more on how I paint textures by first starting with vertex colors.

Discovering texture bake options in Cycles

If you're baking with Cycles, the choices in the Bake Type drop-down menu are quite a bit more numerous: 19 available types. Fortunately, quite a few of them are the same. The following are the most commonly used bake types when working with Cycles (for any that are listed as being the same as their BI counterparts, please read the preceding section for more detail):

- ✔ **Combined:** This is the same as choosing the Full Render option if baking with BI.

- ✔ **Ambient Occlusion:** The AO bake option in Cycles is the same as its corresponding option when using BI.

- ✔ **Shadow:** Like its BI counterpart, the Shadow bake type makes a grayscale image texture of the shadows that fall upon your mesh.

- ✔ **Normal:** The Normal bake type in Cycles generates a normal map like one created in BI. It should be noted, however, that there are more controls when baking normal maps from Cycles that give you the ability to generate better results.

- ✔ **Environment:** Earlier in this section, I mentioned that Cycles materials have no native support for automatically generating environment maps, so there's no Environment Map texture type that's available when you're using Cycles. However, an environment map *can* be generated manually from Cycles if you use this bake type.

- ✔ **Diffuse Direct:** Using this option you can bake any colors connected to the Color socket of a Diffuse BSDF shader in your material node network. If you want to bake vertex colors, this is how you do it.

Baking textures

After you have an unwrapped mesh, the steps to bake a new texture are pretty straightforward. The key is in telling Blender where the baked image data should go. If you're baking with BI, it uses the active image texture in the UV/Image Editor. The process looks something like this:

1. **Create a new image in the UV/Image Editor (Alt+N) at the size you want the texture to be (see "Adding a test grid" earlier in this chapter).**

2. **Choose the type of texture that you'd like to bake from the Bake panel of Render Properties.**

3. **Adjust any additional settings in the Bake panel to taste.**

4. **Left-click the Bake button and wait for the texture to be generated.**

   Texture baking uses render settings, so baking a texture should take roughly as long as rendering the object in your scene.

If you're baking with Cycles, the preceding sequence is slightly different. Rather than use the UV/Image editor, Cycles uses the Node Editor, treating the last selected Image Texture node in the Node Editor as the active texture. The Image Texture node does not need to be connected to the sockets of any other shader, it just needs to exist in the Editor. So the process for baking in Cycles goes something like the following:

1. **Create a new image in the UV/Image Editor (Alt+N) at the size you want the texture to be (see "Adding a test grid" earlier in this chapter).**

   Make a mental note of your new texture's name. Even better, name it something that makes sense, like `Diffuse Bake`.

2. **In the Node Editor, add a new Image Texture node (Shift+A ⇨ Texture ⇨ Image Texture) to your object's material.**

3. **From the image datablock in your new Image Texture node, choose the image you created in Step 1.**

   Don't select any other nodes after this. Your last selected Image Texture node is your active image texture; this is the texture that Blender bakes to.

4. **Choose the type of texture that you'd like to bake from the Bake panel of Render Properties.**

5. **Adjust any additional settings in the Bake panel to taste.**

6. **Left-click the Bake button and wait for the texture to be generated.**

   Texture baking uses render settings, so baking a texture should take roughly as long as rendering the object in your scene.

Regardless of whether you're baking with Cycles or BI, your mesh *must* be visible in your scene. Baking relies on rendering; if the render engine can't see your mesh for rendering, it also can't see it for baking. If your object is hidden (or on a hidden layer), you'll end up with a baked image that's completely blank.

After you bake an image texture, be sure to save it (press F3 with your mouse cursor in the UV/Image Editor or choose File ⇨ Save as Image from the UV/Image Editor's header menu). Saving your `.blend` file is *not* enough. You need to explicitly save your bake as a separate image. If you don't, your baked image texture could be blank the next time you open your `.blend` file.

You may notice that the second-to-last step in either baking scenario is "Adjust any additional settings in the Bake panel to taste." The following describes the other options in the Bake panel:

✔ **Generic options:** These properties are available whether you're baking in BI or Cycles.

• **Margin:** You can tell Blender to extend the baked colors beyond the outer edges of *islands,* or patches of linked vertices, in your UV layout. You want to have a bit of a margin to make the seams in your texture less visible. The default value of 16 pixels is usually fine, but if the islands in your UV layout are close together or the image edge, you may want to reduce this value.

• **Clear:** Enable this check box to blank out an image prior to baking. If you're baking multiple objects to the same image texture, you may need to bake multiple times. If that's the case, you'll want to disabled the Clear check box so you previous bakes don't get obliterated.

• **Selected to Active:** This check box is most useful when baking normal maps and displacement maps. The idea is to bake details from one mesh (the selected object) to another one that has a much lower vertex count (the active object). Enable this check box to get that effect. See my website for this book, www.blenderbasics.com, for a quick tutorial on baking normal maps.

When you select multiple objects, the last object you select is the active object.

✔ **Cycles-only options:** These settings can only be accessed if you're baking with Cycles.

• **Ray Distance:** This option is only available if the Selected to Active check box is enabled and the Cage check box is disabled. When baking textures from one object to the other, it's ideal to have the target object fully enclosed by the source. However, this isn't always a possibility, so you can adjust the Ray Distance value to massage the final output to look more favorable.

• **Cage:** This option is only available if the Selected to Active check box is enabled. It's not uncommon that tweak Ray Distance is insufficient for producing a completely clean baked texture. There may occasionally still be *artifacts* (unexpected glitches in the baked image). It's often useful to duplicate your target mesh and push its vertices around (do not add or delete vertices) so they cleanly fit within the geometry of the source mesh. This duplicated mesh is called a cage object. Enabling the Cage check box gives you the ability to reference the cage object when baking and get that refined control.

- **Cage Extrusion:** When using a cage object to bake (see the next option), you still may need to have control similar to what Ray Distance gives you. That control is what you get with the Cage Extrusion property.

- **Cage Object:** Use this field to type or pick the name (you named it something meaningful, right?) of your cage object.

✔ **BI-only options:** These configuration options are only available if you bake with BI.

- **Bake to Vertex Color:** It may seem backwards, but in BI it's possible to bake material data to vertex colors rather than to an image. While it's true that vertex colors can't have as much detail as an image texture, sometimes you don't need that detail and instead you need faster render speed. Or (in the case of some game engines for mobile devices) you have a limited number of materials or textures on an object. Using vertex colors can get you a more detailed look, but with only one material and no textures at all.

- **Split:** The way BI bakes textures, it must split non-triangular geometry (quads and ngons) into triangles. The options in this drop-down menu give you refined control over how that splitting happens. Usually, the default value of Automatic works fine, but the other options are available if you need more explicit control.

- **Distance/Bias:** These values are available only if you have the Selected to Active check box enabled. Together, they're BI's equivalent to Cycles' Ray Distance value. Use them to try to rid your baked texture of ugly artifacts.

Using UV Textures

If you've painted your UV textures in Blender (as described earlier in this chapter), they're already part of your object's material, regardless of whether you're using Cycles or BI. However, you may want to use a baked UV texture or some image texture from another source. Like with procedural textures, there are differences based on the rendering engine you plan on using. In the case of BI, you're using Image textures in Texture Properties. Figure 8-18 shows Texture Properties with image textures on two different texture slots, one for a color map and another for a bump map.

The process for adding an Image Texture in BI is pretty similar to adding any of the procedural textures:

1. **Choose Image or Movie from the Type drop-down menu in Texture Properties.**

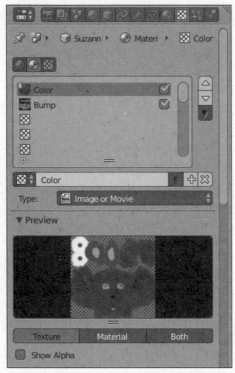

Figure 8-18:
Texture
Properties
with two
Image
textures
loaded.

2. In the Image panel, left-click the Open button.

A File Browser opens, and it's where you can find the image you want to load as a texture. Alternatively, if you already have an image loaded, such as your baked image, you can use this datablock to select that image by clicking the image datablock button on the left of the datablock field.

3. Choose your image from the File Browser.

4. With the image loaded, choose Clip from the Extension drop-down menu in the Image Mapping panel.

This step isn't critical, but it's something I like to do. Basically, it prevents the image from tiling. Because I'm loading a UV texture, I don't typically need it to tile.

5. Choose UV as the type of Coordinates in the Mapping panel.

This step tells the material to use your UV layout for texture coordinates to properly place the texture. Even if the image isn't the original one you painted in Texture Paint mode, as long as you painted the texture using the UV layout as your reference, it should perfectly match your mesh.

6. **In the Influence panel, choose the material attributes you want the texture to influence.**

   If the texture is just a color map, left-click the Color check box. If it's a bump map, left-click the Normal check box, and so on.

If you're rendering with Cycles, you don't do any texture work from Texture Properties. Instead, you need to use the Material context of the Node Editor. The steps for adding a UV mapped image texture in Cycles are as follows:

1. **In the Node Editor, add an Image Texture node (Shift+A ⇨ Texture ⇨ Image Texture).**

2. **In the Image Texture node, left-click the Open button.**

   A File Browser opens where you can choose your image. Alternatively, if you already have an image loaded in Blender, you can use the image datablock in the node to pick the image datablock.

3. **Add a Texture Coordinates node (Shift+A ⇨ Input ⇨ Texture Coordinates) and wire its UV socket to the Vector input socket on your Image Texture node.**

   This step isn't necessary (because image texture default to using UV coordinates), but I like to do this explicit step to keep things unambiguous. Also, if I want to use the Mapping node (Shift+A ⇨ Vector ⇨ Mapping) to tweak my mapping, it's useful to have these connections already setup.

4. **Wire the Color socket of your Image Texture node to the Color input socket of the node you want your texture to influence.**

   If you want the texture to be control your diffuse color, connect it to a Diffuse BSDF's Color socket. For a bump map, connect it to the Displacement socket of your Material Output node.

Figure 8-19 shows an example node network with a UV mapped image texture.

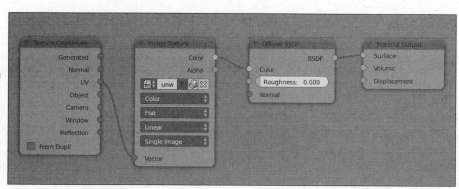

Figure 8-19: Using a UV mapped image texture in Cycles.

Chapter 9

Lighting and Environment

In This Chapter

▶ Taking advantage of different types of lights in Blender

▶ Setting up effective lighting

▶ Changing the look of your scene with background images, colors, and ambient occlusion

In terms of getting the work you create in Blender out to a finalized still image or animation, having your scene's environment and lighting set up properly is incredibly important. It goes along hand in hand with setting up materials on your object (see Chapter 7) as well as the rendering process (see Chapter 14). Without light, the camera — and by extension, the renderer — can't see a thing. You could create the most awesome 3D model or animation in the world, but if it's poorly lit, it won't be turning any heads.

This chapter covers the types of lights available to you in Blender and details some of the best practices to use them in your scenes. In addition to lighting details, I go into setting up the environment in your scene with the settings in World Properties. In many ways, the topics covered in this chapter are what give your scenes that final polish, making them look really good.

Lighting a Scene

Lighting has an incredible amount of power to convey your scene to the viewer. Harsh, stark lighting can give you a dramatic film noir look. Low-angle lights with long shadows can give you a creepy horror movie feeling, and brighter high-angle lights can make things look like they are taking place during a beautiful summer day. Or, you can use a bluish light that projects a hard noise cloud texture and makes your scene feel like it's happening under water.

Equally important is setting up your environment. Depending on how you set it up, you can achieve a variety of looks. You can set your scene in an infinitely large white space, commonly known as *the white void* in film and television.

Or, you can adjust your environment such that your scene takes place outside during the day or somewhere on the moon. When you combine good lighting and a few additional tricks, you can make your scene take place just about anywhere. Figure 9-1 shows a pretty simple scene with a few different environment and lighting schemes to illustrate this point.

Understanding a basic three-point lighting setup

Before I get too deep into how you light a scene in Blender, you should understand some standard lighting setups and terminology. The cool thing is that most of this information isn't limited to use in 3D computer graphics. It's actually pretty standard in professional film, video, and still photography. In fact, quite a few photographers and directors like to use 3D graphics as a form of previsualization to test out lighting setups before arriving on set for the actual shoot. (And you thought you were just making pretty pictures on a computer screen! Ha!)

One of the most common ways to arrange lights is called *three-point lighting*. As the name implies, it involves the use of three different sets of lights. It's a common studio setup for interviews, and it's the starting point for nearly all other lighting arrangements. Figure 9-2 shows a top-down illustration of a typical three-point lighting setup.

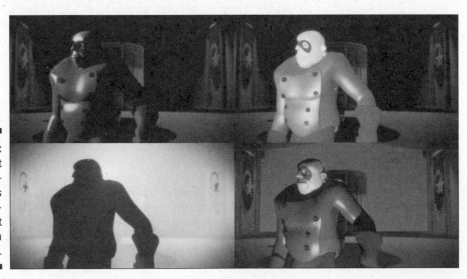

Figure 9-1: Different lighting configurations can drastically affect the look of a scene.

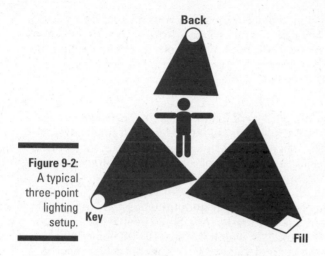

Figure 9-2:
A typical
three-point
lighting
setup.

The key light

Setting up a three-point lighting scheme starts with placing your subject at the center of the scene and aiming your camera at that subject. Then you set up your main light, the *key light*. The key light is usually the most powerful light in the scene. It's where your main shadows come from, as well as your brightest highlights. Typically, you want to set this light just to the left or just to the right of your camera, and you usually want it to be higher than your subject. This placement is to ensure that the shadows fall naturally, and you don't get that creepy flashlight-under-the-chin look that your friends used for telling scary stories around the campfire.

The fill light

After your key light is established, the next light you want to place is the *fill light*. The purpose of the fill light is to brighten up the dark parts of your subject. See, the key light is great for putting shadows on your subject, but without any other light, your shadows end up being very dark (they're actually stark black if you're rendering with BI), obscuring your subject. Unless you're aiming for a dramatic lighting effect, this effect is not what you normally want. The fill light tends to be less powerful than the key, but you want it to have a wider, more diffuse throw. The *throw* is the radius of space that the light reaches. For example, a flashlight has a narrow throw, whereas fluorescent lights like the ones used in office buildings throw light wider. You want this wide throw on your fill because it reduces the amount of highlight generated by this light. Typically, you don't want highlights from your fill to compete with the highlights from your key. As far as placement goes, you normally want to place your fill on the opposite side of the camera from the key and roughly at the same height as your subject, perhaps a little lower than your key light.

TIP

Here's a way to figure out a good place to position your fill light. Draw an imaginary line from your key light to your subject. Now, with your subject as the pivot point, rotate that line 90 degrees. When you do, the line points right where you should place the fill.

The back light

The last light in a three-point lighting configuration is the *back light* or *rim light*. This light shines at the back of your subject, creating a small edge of light around the profile. That sliver of light helps separate your subject from the background and serves as the nice little bit of polish that often separates a mediocre lighting setup from a really good one.

Now, I've sat through many long discussions about the best way to position a back light (yes, my friends are nerds, too). Some people like to place it directly opposite from the key light, which works well, but sometimes the rim effect competes with the key's highlights. Other people prefer placing it opposite to the camera, which, too, is a good way to go, but if the subject moves, you risk the possibility of blinding the audience. And yet another group of people recommend placing the back light opposite to the fill. This approach can create a nice rim of light that complements the key, but it also has the possibility of looking a bit unnatural. As you can see, everything is a trade-off when it comes to lighting. In fact, the only really consistent thing that people agree on is that the light should generally point toward the subject. The bottom line is that the best course of action is to play around with your back light and see for yourself where you get the best results.

As for the power and throw, you typically want to use a back light that is less powerful than your key so things appear natural. The throw can vary because the highlights are all on the opposite side of your subject. I personally like to keep it narrow, but a wide throw can work nicely for large scenes.

That's basic three-point lighting for you. It works well in computer graphics as well as the "real world" and it's the starting point for most other lighting configurations. Lower the angle of your key to make your subject creepy. Remove or reduce the power of your fill and back lights to get more dramatic shadows. Place your key behind your subject to get a mysterious or romantic silhouette. And that's just the tip of the iceberg!

Knowing when to use which type of lamp

After you're familiar with the basic principles of three-point lighting, you can use that knowledge to light your scenes in Blender. To add a new light, use Shift+A ⇨ Lamp and you see the menu shown in Figure 9-3.

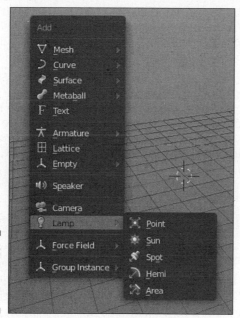

Figure 9-3:
Adding a
lamp in the
3D View.

Although the lamps listed in this section are available in both Cycles and Blender, it's more common to use *mesh lamps* (that is, using meshes as lights in your scene) than lamp objects in Cycles. See the section later in this chapter titled "Using mesh lights in Cycles" for more on setting up and using mesh lights. Of course, some lamps, like the Spot and Sun lamps are still very useful in Cycles as well as BI, so it's still worth reading through this section if you've chosen Cycles as your renderer.

The Lamp menu (Shift+A⇨Lamp) offers you the following types of lights to choose from:

- ✔ **Point:** This type of light is sometimes also referred to as an *omni light,* meaning that the lamp is located at a single point in space and light emanates in all directions from that point. The default Blender scene has a single light of this type. The Point lamp is a good general-purpose light, but I prefer to use it as secondary illumination or as a fill light.

- ✔ **Sun:** The Sun lamp represents a single universal light that comes from a single direction. Because of this single source, the location of the Sun lamp in your scene doesn't really matter; only its orientation is relevant. This type of light is the only one that affects the look of the sky and is well suited as a key light for scenes set outdoors.

- ✔ **Spot:** In many ways, the Spot is the workhorse of CG lighting. It works quite a bit like a flashlight or a theater spotlight, and of all the light types, it gives you the most control over the nature of the shadows and where light lands. Because of this control, Spots are fantastic key lights.

- ✔ **Hemi:** A Hemi lamp is very similar to the Sun lamp in that it doesn't matter where you place the lamp in your scene. Its orientation is its most important aspect. However, because it's treated as a full hemisphere of light around the scene, lighting from a Hemi tends to be softer and flatter than the sun. Hemis are also the only Blender lights that cannot cast shadows when rendering with BI. Technically, Hemi lights are not supported in Cycles. They're treated exactly the same as Sun lamps. In BI I like using Hemis for fills and back lights. They're also handy for outdoor lighting.

- ✔ **Area:** Area lights are powerful lights that behave similar to Spots; however, the shadows tend to be softer and more accurate because they're based on having a grid of lights to work with. As a result, they work well for key lights, but because they tend to take more time to process, you should use them sparingly. Generally, you only use Area lamps when rendering with BI. If you want the effect of an Area lamp in Cycles, it's more common to use a mesh as your light source.

Figure 9-4 shows what each light type looks like in the 3D View.

Universal lamp options

When you've chosen a type of lamp and added it to the scene, the controls to modify these lamps are in Lamp Properties. When you have a lamp selected, the Lamp Properties button in the Properties editor features a lamp icon. With a couple of exceptions, all the lamps share a few of the same controls. Figure 9-5 highlights the options that are universal for nearly all lights.

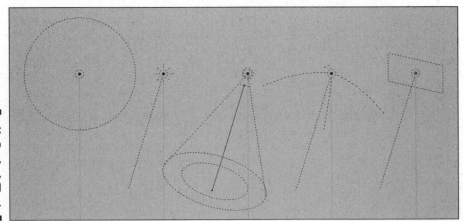

Figure 9-4:
From left to right, Point, Sun, Spot, Hemi, and Area lights.

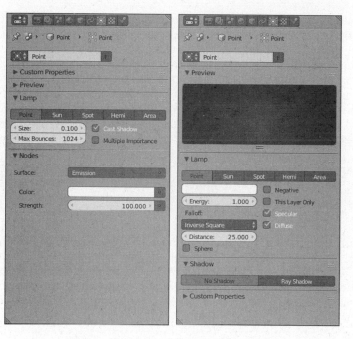

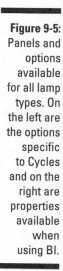

Figure 9-5:
Panels and options available for all lamp types. On the left are the options specific to Cycles and on the right are properties available when using BI.

One cool thing about Blender's lamps is that you can instantly change lamp types whenever you want. Simply select the lamp you want to work with and choose the type of lamp you would like it to be in the Lamp panel. This feature is great for quickly sorting out the type of light you want to use. You can test out different lighting schemes without cluttering the scene by having a bunch of extraneous lights that you have to move to other layers or hide.

Between Cycles and BI, only a few options are available to lamps in both. In Cycles, these properties are in the Nodes panel of Lamp Properties (technically, they're properties of the Emission shader in the Node Editor). In BI, they're the first two options in the Lamp panel of Lamp Properties:

- ✔ **Strength (Cycles)/Energy (BI):** The Strength value (or Energy if you're rendering with BI) controls the strength of light emitted by the lamp. When rendering with BI, I rarely set the Energy to a value greater than 1.000, but when you need it, it's handy to have the option. When rendering with Cycles, the Strength value may often be much higher. It's useful to think of lamp strengths in Cycles similar to how you may think of watts on light bulbs.

- ✔ **Color:** To set the color for your lamp, left-click the color swatch and use Blender's color picker.

Like with materials for objects, you can also apply textures to your lights and apply them to the lamp's color, its shadow's color, or both. This ability is a great way to use lighting to either enhance the environment of your scene or fake certain lighting effects that are typically only achievable with ray tracing. One specific example is caustic effects. If you have some free time, take a glass of water and shine light through it. Due to the refractive nature of the glass and the water, usually you see a strange light pattern on the table near or around the glass. That effect is an example of caustics and (if you don't need 100 percent accuracy) you can fake it with a Clouds texture on a Spot lamp.

On a larger scale, caustics are what make the cool moving patterns you can see on the bottom of a swimming pool. To add a texture to your selected lamp, use Texture Properties and use the same procedures covered for texturing materials as described in Chapter 8.

Technically speaking, you shouldn't have to fake caustics if you're using Cycles, because they're naturally built-in. However, caustic effects tend to take a long time to *converge* or appear cleanly when rendering with Cycles, requiring a lot more samples than you may want to use. For that reason, it still makes sense to occasionally help Cycles along by faking caustics with a texture.

That's pretty much it for the truly universal lamp properties across both render engines. However, after you choose a specific renderer, a few more options are available for all lamps. The next two subsections cover those properties. I encourage you to read both sections so you have a firm understanding of what's available to you in each renderer.

Cycles lamp properties

The amount of properties available to lamps in Cycles is really quite sparse. However, the upside is that those options are very powerful and (for the most part) available to all light types. These options are available to you with all lamps in Cycles:

✔ **Size:** Technically speaking, a lamp isn't much different from an Empty. It's just a point in 3D space. It doesn't really have any geometry, so scaling a lamp in the 3D View is pretty meaningless (in both renderers). However, because Cycles is a ray tracer, it needs a surface to emit light from, even if it's not technically real. The Size property lets you adjust the size of that virtual surface.

The thing to remember is that if you increase the Size of your lamp, but leave its Strength value unchanged, it's still the same amount of light, but it's starting off more dispersed. This gives your shadows softer edges, though with the trade-off of having overall weaker illumination from the lamp.

- **Max Bounces:** Because Cycles is a ray tracer, it's all about rays bouncing around your scene. It's a bit of a simplified description, but imagine one ray coming from your lamp. If Max Bounces is set to 0, that ray hits an object in your scene and stops. All it does is illuminate that object (much like lighting in BI). However, if you increase the maximum number of bounces, you allow that ray to reflect off of objects it strikes.

  This reflecting behavior from bounced rays allows for the realistic color bleeding effect that's the hallmark of global illumination. *Color bleeding* is when light reflected from one surface takes on part of that surface's color. So if you have a bright red object in your scene and Max Bounces is set reasonably high (like the default value of 1024), other objects near your red one will take on a slightly reddish hue from the reflected light.

- **Cast Shadow:** Cycles' lamps have far fewer controls for shadows than their BI counterparts. However, they retain the ability to disable shadow casting with this check box. This option is an attractive feature that you get with lamps that isn't available if you use mesh lamps.

  Why would you want to disable a lamp's ability to cast shadows? In a three-point lighting setup, you often want your fill light to illuminate the scene without contributing unnecessary shadows. In meatspace, lighters go through a lot of efforts and tricks to try doing this; usually by trying to make the shadows from the fill light very soft. In CG it's much easier: you just turn shadows off. Neat, huh?

  With mesh lights (or any meshes, really), you can turn off shadows by disabling the Shadow check box in the Ray Visibility panel of Object Properties.

- **Multiple Importance:** This check box toggles whether the lamp uses multiple importance sampling. Simply put, *multiple importance sampling* is an algorithm that allows Cycles to more intelligently choose which rays to use for lighting your scene. Having this kind of intelligence in sampling becomes important on larger lights and especially on materials with sharp reflections. Generally, you want to leave this check box enabled. You can read up more on sampling in the sidebar in this chapter titled "Adaptive QMC and Multiple Importance Sampling."

BI lamp properties

This section details the wide assortment of properties available to lamps when rendering with BI. On a technical level, Blender Internal tends to use more tricks and fakery in how it handles lights and shadows. As a result, there are more controls for you to fidget with.

The Distance value is only available for the Point, Spot, and Area lamps. The value is in the units defined in the Units panel of Scene Properties and, if an object is farther away from the light than that distance, it receives no light.

For each of the light types, an indicator defines the range of this value. For the Area lamp, it's a line pointing in the direction that the light is facing. For the Spot, it's the length of the cone. For the Point lamp, no indicator is on by default, but if you enable the Sphere check box in the Lamp panel, a dashed circle appears to indicate the distance of the Point lamp's throw. If you don't see this circle immediately, you may have to zoom out in the 3D View so that you can see it.

Be careful when enabling the Sphere check box on the Point lamp. It subtly changes how the light works. With Sphere enabled, light coming from the Point lamp starts to weaken, or *attenuate,* starting at the light's location, so by the time it gets to the Distance value, no light is available. However, if you have Sphere disabled, that attenuation doesn't start until you actually reach that Distance value, so you have a farther throw. Having Sphere enabled makes the light behave more like it would in meatspace, but it's often more convenient to keep it disabled. In either case, you can control how dramatically that attenuation occurs by using the Falloff drop-down menu. The default value of Inverse Square behaves the most like real-world lights.

Lamps in Cycles don't have a Distance value, because all light sources in Cycles share a physically correct falloff rate. Incidentally, all natural light follows the *inverse square law* for falloff. That means that as you get farther from a light source, the strength of its light decreases by the value of $1/distance^2$. So, if the Strength value of your lamp is 100, when you're 1 Blender Unit away, the light's effective strength is 50. At 2 Blender units away, the light's effective strength is 25. And by the time you get just 5 Blender units away from your light source, the effective strength has dropped to just a value of 4. So to make a scene brighter, you need to either make one very strong light source (which may be too bright and overpower the scene) or add multiple smaller lights.

When rendering with BI, each lamp except for the Hemi has the option of using ray tracing to cast shadows. Ray traced shadows are enabled by left-clicking the Ray Shadow button in the Shadow panel, and it's the default behavior for new lights. Know, however, that using ray traced shadows can drastically increase your render times in Blender Internal. The next section goes more deeply into some techniques for optimizing your lighting to try to deal with that. However, if you do want to use ray traced shadows in BI, you should be aware of a few options:

- ✔ **Shadow color:** Left-click this swatch to get a color picker for selecting the color of your cast shadow. Of course, this isn't physically accurate. Real-world shadows are always black unless other lighting is present.

- ✔ **Samples:** This option dictates how many samples the ray traced shadow uses. Increasing this value increases the accuracy of the shadows at the expense of longer render times.

- **Soft Size:** This option controls how blurry the edge of your cast shadows are. The higher the value, the blurrier the shadow. However, with only one sample (the previous option), the shadows won't blur that much. Blurry shadows require more samples.

- **QMC Sampling Types:** You generally have the choice between Adaptive QMC and Constant QMC. QMC stands for Quasi-Monti Carlo and is an algorithm for taking random samples. Generally speaking, the Adaptive QMC setting gives you faster render times and better results.

- **Threshold:** This option is available only when you choose the Adaptive QMC sampling type. It basically helps the renderer decide which samples to use and which ones to ignore. A higher Threshold value shortens your render times, but may decrease accuracy.

Light-specific options

As you can see in Figure 9-5, the Point lamp has options that are available on nearly every other lamp but doesn't have much in the way of unique controls. The same could actually be said of the Hemi lamp. In fact, it has even fewer controls because Hemis can't cast shadows in BI and aren't supported at all in Cycles. However, the remaining three lights have some interesting options that allow you to optimize their usage to meet your needs.

Adaptive QMC and Multiple Importance Sampling

Without getting too deep into all the crazy mathematical details, understanding QMC in BI and multiple importance sampling in Cycles requires knowing a little bit more about how ray tracing works. In Chapter 7, I give a brief description of ray tracing that says it's done by tracing each and every vector from the camera to objects in your scene, including light sources. This description is somewhat oversimplified. Tracing *every single vector* would take an incredibly excessive amount of time. In order to get around that, programmers decided to take a sampling of those vectors and approximate everything between them. To choose which sample vectors to select, they first tried just randomly picking

them. The problem, though, is that raw random selection doesn't give consistent or accurate results. Samples aren't necessarily where they're most useful (like in reflections and highlights). So to accommodate that, it was decided that samples could be random, but evenly dispersed. Evenly dispersed random sampling is basically constant QMC. Of course, the downside to constant QMC is that you still might be taking samples from parts of the scene that don't need very many. If you can stay random, but have more of the samples taken from busier parts of the scene, you might get better performance. This logic is behind adaptive QMC as well as multiple importance sampling.

Options specific to Sun lamps

The Sun lamp is incredibly useful because it has the ability to behave more like the real sun. It's the only type of light in BI that influences the look of the sky and even provides some atmospheric effects. You control this lamp in BI with the Sky & Atmosphere panel that appears when you set your lamp to be a Sun.

The Sky & Atmosphere panel is not available to the Sun lamp in Cycles. In Cycles, those settings are handled with World Properties. I cover that in more detail in this chapter in the section titled "Setting Up the World".

By default, both the Sky and Atmosphere check boxes are disabled, but you can enable them with a left-click. Figure 9-6 shows the options as they pertain to the Sun light type in BI. In Cycles, the Sun lamp has no additional properties beyond the general lamp properties.

When you enable the Sky check box, you can use the controls in its panel to determine how the Sun lamp influences the sky background. At the top of the panel is the Turbidity value. Keep Turbidity low for clear day skies and increase it for hazy, overcast skies. When you see the sky on a clear day — the real sky outside; you know, in the for-really-real world — it's lighter near the horizon and darker as you look farther up. The Brightness and Size values under the Horizon label control this effect in Blender. The Brightness and Size values under the Sun label adjust your sun's visibility.

If you try to render your scene, you may not see the sun in your sky, even if you've placed the Sun lamp within your camera's view. Because the position of the Sun lamp is irrelevant and only its orientation is important, you have to rotate the lamp so that it points in the opposite direction of the camera's orientation.

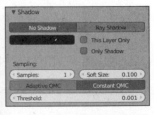

Figure 9-6: Controls for the Sun lamps.

When you enable the Atmosphere check box, you can control the sun's influence on how the air in your scene looks from a distance. These options are best suited where you have a wide outdoor shot of your scene's environment. There's really no good way to preview the effects of these values other than to do test renders or use Rendered viewport shading (Shift+Z) in the 3D View. Here's a quick guideline to help understand what each one does:

- **Sun:** This value adjusts the influence of the Sun's intensity on the atmosphere. Increasing it makes objects in the distance bluer.

- **Distance:** This value controls the distance that the atmosphere has an influence. At low values, you see everything. Increasing this value, the light becomes yellower, and distant objects become more like silhouettes.

- **Inscattering:** Increasing this value makes the light appear to scatter more between the camera and the objects it's pointing at. Set this value to 1.0 for the most physically accurate results.

- **Extinction:** Lower numbers for this option reduce the amount of detail seen in your objects. This setting is similar to Distance, except it doesn't really matter how close objects are to the camera. Like Inscattering, you get the most physically accurate results with a value of 1.0.

Options specific to Spot lamps

When working with Spot lamps in BI, you have the option of two different ways to cast shadows: ray tracing or buffers. The simplest way to know the difference between the two is to know that, generally speaking, ray traced shadows are more accurate whereas buffered shadows render faster. In Cycles, all shadows are ray traced.

Regardless of which type of shadows you cast (if you decide to cast shadows at all with this lamp), a handful of settings are available in the Spot Shape panel:

- **Size:** This setting controls the width of the Spot's throw, measured in degrees. So a value of 180 degrees is completely wide, whereas a value of 30 degrees gives you a narrower cone. Unless I'm doing something special, I like to start with my Spots with a Size value around 60 degrees.

- **Blend:** The Blend value controls the sharpness of the edges at the boundary where the Spot's cone of influence ends. Lower values give you a crisp edge, whereas higher values soften it, making the light appear more diffuse.

- **Halo:** Enabling this check box allows the renderer to show the full cone of light generated by the Spot. This is called *volumetric* light. You see this effect when you use a flashlight in a dusty room or when you want the "sunbeams from the sky" effect. This property is only available if you're rendering with BI. If you're using Cycles, you need to actually have an object with a volumetric material that your lamp shoots light through.

✔ **Intensity:** Specifically speaking, this value controls Halo Intensity. This value has no influence unless you enable the Halo check box. If Halo is enabled, increasing this value brightens the volumetric effect. And, like the Halo value, the Halo Intensity property is only available if you render with BI.

✔ **Square:** Enable this check box if you would prefer the Spot lamp to come from a square source rather than a round one. This option is only available when rendering with BI. To get a square cone in Cycles, you actually need to project the cone of your lamp through a square hole (like in the real world).

✔ **Show Cone:** This feature is incredibly cool and useful. When you enable the Show Cone check box, Blender allows you to more clearly see the volume of the cone, making it much easier to see what objects are within your Spot lamp's influence area.

Using buffered shadows instead of ray traced ones, the options in the Shadow panel change. All the ray traced shadow controls are replaced with a different set of options because buffered shadows use an image-based process instead of ray tracing. You have more ways to control how the shadows look because you're no longer constrained by the limits of reality. Figure 9-7 shows the various settings for a Spot lamp with buffered shadows.

Trying to sort out all these controls can be daunting. However, the following values are the most important ones that you should know about:

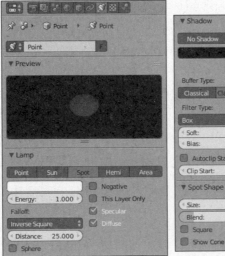

Figure 9-7: Controls for a buffered Spot lamp.

✔ **Sample Buffers:** In essence, Sample Buffers are basically the same as the Samples values discussed elsewhere throughout this chapter, but they're specifically for helping render hair and fur more effectively. Higher values give better results, but at the cost of more system memory when rendering. Unless you're rendering hair or fine detail, keep this set to 1.

✔ **Size:** The technique that buffered shadows uses for generating shadows is image-based. The shadow buffer size is the resolution of the image used to create the shadows. Lower values work faster, but look more jagged.

To avoid jaggies in your buffer shadows, consider the size of your final rendered image. Think about how many pixels the shadow area will take (including any part of that shadow that goes off-camera). The shadow buffer size should be large enough to cover each of those pixels.

✔ **Samples:** Each sample is an offset copy of the shadow buffer. Soft shadow edges come from mixing samples, so a higher value makes them look better. Render time does increase with more samples, but because buffered shadows are typically much faster than ray traced shadows, it's okay to splurge a bit and allow yourself a few extra samples.

✔ **Soft:** Increasing this value makes your shadows softer and blurrier. To use this setting effectively, make sure that you have a Samples value greater than 1. And at the same time, you get the best results by not setting the Soft value higher than double your Samples value. So at the default Samples setting of 3, you should keep your Soft value below 6.

✔ **Bias:** This value offsets the shadow from where it connects to the shadow-casting object. Occasionally, you may get some weird jaggies or *artifacts* in your shadows. Increasing the Bias can help get rid of those artifacts, but you should keep this value as small as possible. If you do have to adjust the Bias, adjust it only as low as it can go before you get artifacts in your renders. Otherwise, your shadows will begin to look very unnatural. A good practice is to do a series of test renders starting with a Bias value of 0.1 and working your way up until you no longer see artifacts.

✔ **Clip Start/Clip End:** Consider these values as a secondary control in addition to the Distance value in the Lamp panel. Objects that appear within these two values, indicated by a line on the Spot lamp in the 3D View, cast shadows, whereas objects outside of this range do not. Keeping the Clip values as close to your shadow-casting objects as possible gives you the most accurate results. If you don't want to adjust these values manually, enable the Autoclip check box to either value. Blender then automatically sets the Clip values to include objects within the Spot's cone.

✔ **Halo Step:** This value is in the Spot Shape panel and has an effect only if you have the Halo check box enabled. Adjusting it controls your *volumetric shadow*, or how much of the volumetric effect your object blocks. Higher values render faster, but are less accurate. Setting it to 1 gives you the best, albeit the slowest, results. However, setting it to 0 means that you have no volumetric shadow, so you have the volumetric cone, but your object won't block it at all.

Options specific to Area lamps

Area lamps are very similar to Spots, except Area lamps can only use ray tracing for creating shadows. The shadows are generally smoother and more accurate; however, they can increase your render time dramatically. Figure 9-8 shows the options and settings for Area lights.

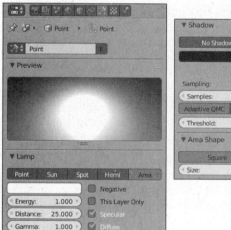

Figure 9-8:
The controls
for Area
lights.

The way an Area light works is pretty simple. Imagine that at the lamp's location, you don't have a single light, but instead you have a grid of lights, and you can control the width and height of this grid as well as the number of lights in it. As a result, you have even more control over your lamp's throw.

To control the dimensions of your Area lamp, use the Size value in the Area Shape panel. This size is measured in units chosen in Scene Properties and, by default, controls both the width and the height of the Area lamp. You control the number of lights in the Area lamp by adjusting the Samples value in the Shadow panel. Because the default shape of the lamp is a square, increasing the number of samples gives you the square of the sample value. So setting Samples to 3 creates 9 lights in the grid, and setting it to 5 creates 25 lights in the grid.

If you'd rather have a rectangular Area lamp, left-click the Rectangle button in the Area Shape panel. If you're rendering with Cycles, there's a Shape drop-down menu in the Lamp panel where you can choose between having a square and rectangular shape for your Area lamp. When you switch the shape to being a rectangle, you can set the width (Size X) and height (Size Y) of your Area lamp. In addition, the Samples value in the Shadow panel changes to Samples X and Samples Y, giving you control over the number of horizontal and vertical lights you have on your Area light's grid. The total of lights you have in the grid is the value of Samples X multiplied by the value of Samples Y. Figure 9-9 shows an illustration of how the lights are arranged in square and rectangular Area lamps.

Figure 9-9:
Light arrangement on a square (left) and rectangular (right) Area light.

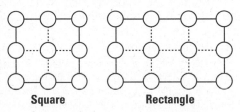

Square   **Rectangle**

When working with Area lights, remember that you actually have multiple lights arranged on the lamp's grid, which can make an Area light with an Energy of 1.0 excessively bright in BI. So if you use an Area lamp, try a much lower Energy value. Depending on the number of samples in your Area lamp, you may want to start as low as 0.050.

Using mesh lights in Cycles

When rendering with Cycles, it's more common to use mesh lights than lamp objects, especially if you want the effect of an Area lamp. Part of this is historical — it used to be that you'd get much shorter render times using meshes as lamps than by using lamp objects. The other reason is more practical: Often, lights take on a specific shape that's more complex than the simple look of lamp objects.

Making any object a light source in Cycles is incredibly easy. You don't even really need to use the Node Editor (at least, not for a simple setup). With your object selected, just follow these steps:

1. **In the Surface panel of Material Properties, change the Surface drop-down menu to Emission.**

2. **Adjust the Color and Strength values to taste.**

That's it! From the perspective of your material's node network, you've connected an Emission shader to the Surface socket of your Material Output node, as shown in Figure 9-10.

One side effect of using a mesh to light your scene is that (unlike lamp objects) meshes are visible objects in your scene, just like they would be in meatspace. The absolute easiest solution is to try to keep your mesh lights off-camera. Sadly, that's not always possible. It would be really nice if you could get the benefits of mesh lights and still keep the mesh object itself invisible from the camera. Fortunately, that's pretty easy to do. Just disable the Camera check box in the Ray Visibility panel of Object Properties.

There's another way to get those results as well. It isn't as simple as a check box and requires a bit of wizardry in the Node Editor (specifically the Light Path node). However, by using the Node Editor, you open the door to the possibilities of much more complex and interesting lighting. Assuming you have a mesh light set up like in Figure 9-10, use the following steps in the Node Editor:

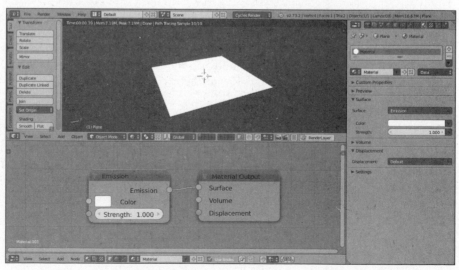

Figure 9-10:
Emitting light from any mesh in Cycles is as easy as wiring an Emission shader to the Surface socket of your Material Output node.

1. **Add a Transparent BSDF shader node (Shift+A ⇨ Shader ⇨ Transparent BSDF).**

   For organization's sake, place the Transparent BSDF node below your Emission node.

2. **Add an Mix Shader node (Shift+A ⇨ Shader ⇨ Mix Shader).**

   For placement, put the Mix Shader node to the right of your Emission and Transparent BSDF nodes, but to the left of your Material Output node. You may need to push your nodes around a bit to give enough space.

3. **Connect the Emission socket of your Emission node to the upper Shader socket of the Mix Shader node.**

4. **Connect the BSDF socket of your Transparent BSDF node to the lower Shader socket of the Mix Shader node.**

   If you preview your scene in the 3D View with Rendered viewport shading (Shift+Z), you should see that your mesh light object emits light, but is semi-transparent. If you adjust the Fac slider in the Mix Shader node, a value of 0, your mesh emits light, but it's completely solid. At a Fac value of 1, your mesh is transparent, but it doesn't emit any light. That's close, but not quite right. The magic happens in the next two steps.

5. **Add a Light Path node (Shift+A ⇨ Input ⇨ Light Path).**

   For organization, place the Light Path node above your Emission node. The Light Path node is an excellent node in Cycles that's useful for all sorts of interesting trickery. The next step will prove the point.

6. **Connect the Is Camera Ray socket of the Light Path node to the Fac socket of your Mix Shader node.**

   Like magic, your mesh object is invisible in the scene, but it's still emitting light.

The technical explanation for what you've done goes something like this: Your mesh object checks each ray that comes in contact with it and determines where that ray came from (the camera, another light source, a shadow, and so on). Then, by wiring the Is Camera Ray socket to the Fac socket on the Mix slider, you're making your material say, "If I'm hit with a camera ray, behave as if I'm transparent, but if I'm hit with any other ray, behave as if I'm a light." And there you go: a mesh light that behaves like a lamp object.

Figure 9-11 shows what your finished node network should look like.

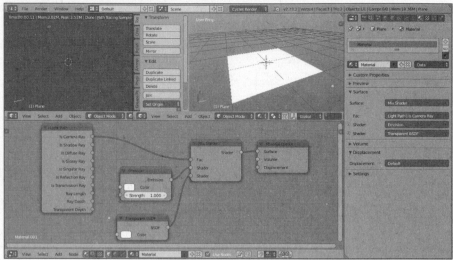

Figure 9-11:
Getting
a mesh
light to be
invisible in
your scene
requires
playing with
the Light
Path node.

Lighting for Speedy Renders

Six additional controls for lamps exist if you're rendering with BI. I like to refer to them as my "cheat buttons" because they're incredibly useful for achieving lighting effects that are difficult or impossible in the real world. The functions that these options control are really what make lighting in 3D computer graphics so powerful. More often than not, if you use these controls effectively, they can speed up your render times without having a negative effect on the overall quality of your image. Figure 9-12 highlights these controls in Lamp Properties.

Here are descriptions of each cheat button in the Lamp panel:

✔ **Negative:** What this check box enables is, in my opinion, one of the coolest capabilities in CG lighting: inverting the light's output. You can basically shine *darkness* on your scene, an impossibility in meatspace that opens the door to all sorts of interesting uses. If part of your scene is too bright or you want to have deeper shadows, don't play with adjusting the Energy of your lights or increasing the Samples for your shadows. Just shine some darkness on the area with a negative light!

You can use negative lights in Cycles, too. It's just a bit hidden. Left-click in the Strength value's field and manually change it to a negative number (like -1 or -10). Boom! Negative lights in Cycles.

✔ **This Layer Only:** Enabling this control makes the light illuminate only the objects that are on the same layer as the light. In real-world lighting, technicians do a lot of work to hide or mask out some lights, so they illuminate only certain parts of the scene. For example, you may want to brighten up the environment without making the lighting on your characters any brighter. Because you're in CG, you don't have to mask anything out: You just enable this check box and make sure that your characters aren't on the same layer as the light. Unfortunately, there's no easy way to get this feature in Cycles yet. For that, you'll need to use some clever organization of your render layers and Blender's node compositor (see Chapter 15).

✔ **Specular:** In three-point lighting, you want to reduce the highlights produced by the fill so that they don't compete with the key's highlights. Meatspace lighting technicians often attempt to reduce the highlights by diffusing or dispersing the fill as much as possible. In BI, you don't have to go through the trouble. You can just turn off the lamp's specular highlights altogether by disabling this check box. Pretty sweet, huh?

In Cycles, you don't have this option. Your choices are to work like a real-world lighting technician: either try disabling multiple importance sampling in your lamp, or disable the Glossy check box in the Ray Visibility panel of Object Properties.

✔ **Diffuse:** Sometimes when you're lighting, you want to have fine control of your highlights, but you don't want to change the basic illumination of the scene. If you turn off shadow casting for the light and disable this check box, you're basically left with a specular highlight that you can move around your subject at will. This feature isn't commonly used, but having it available has certainly made my life easier more than once. In Cycles, you can turn off diffuse lighting by disabling the Diffuse check box in the Ray Visibility panel of Object Properties for your light source.

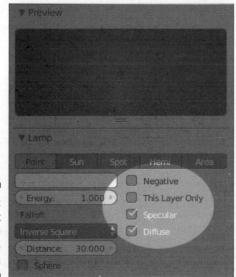

Figure 9-12:
The cheat buttons in the Lamp panel.

The last two cheat buttons are in the Shadow panel, farther down Object Data Properties for lamps. The following describes each one:

- **This Layer Only:** This check box works like the corresponding check box in the Lamp panel, but only relates to shadows. Like the Lamp panel option, this feature isn't available in Cycles.

- **Only Shadow:** Enabling this option allows your lamp to cast shadows without adding more light to the scene. I sometimes use this option to reduce render times by using buffered Spots for shadows while using other lamps without shadows for main illumination. Unfortunately, there's no easy way to achieve this with Cycles materials. All solutions for getting this effect in Cycles involve compositing (see Chapter 15).

Any object — even lamps — can exist on multiple layers. This ability dramatically increases the power of layer-only lamps and shadows. With the lamp selected, press M to reveal the layer selection pop-up. To place your lamp on more than one layer, Shift+left-click the layer buttons you want it on.

I often tell people that when it comes to computer graphics, if you're not cheating or faking something, you're probably doing it wrong. Even though you can get great results by using ray traced shadows everywhere with the highest number of samples, these results all come at the expense of high memory usage and lengthy render times. So your scene may look perfect, but if you're taking 16 hours to render every frame in an animation, you could be rendering for a month and not even have two seconds of it done.

A large part of being a CG artist is doing everything you can to reduce the amount of work that needs to be done by both you *and* the computer, while still creating high-quality images. You don't want to be old and gray by the time your first animation is complete. That's why CG artists worry so much about keeping their render times as short as possible and why they use features like these cheat buttons to cut corners where they can.

Working with three-point lighting in Blender

My preferred lighting rig in Blender usually starts with a three-point lighting setup. Here's what I normally start with:

- **Key:** A buffered Spot works well as the key light in BI. Keep all settings at their default values except for the spot Size, Clip range, and Bias. Set the Spot Size to 60 degrees and activate the Autoclip check boxes for the Clip Start and Clip End values. For Bias, lower it as much as possible until just before you start seeing artifacts in your renders. If you don't feel like fiddling with settings, you can also use ray traced shadows on your Spot lamp, though it will increase your render times. In Cycles, I may use a Spot lamp as my key, but more frequently, I use a mesh light.

✔ **Fill:** In BI, I typically start with a Hemi with an Energy of 0.5 and the Specular check box disabled in the Lamp panel. In Cycles, I may use a large Area lamp or Sun lamp with Cast Shadows and Multiple Importance options disabled. Occasionally, I may also use a large plane as a mesh light with a low Strength value.

✔ **Back:** This is the tricky one. In BI, I also use a Hemi, but the Energy is usually between 0.75 and 1.0 to get a nice rim light. The lamp is behind the subject, so specularity doesn't matter as much, but just to make sure that it doesn't compete with the key's spec, I normally disable the specularity on this light as well. Don't get too picky with the location of the back light just yet. Back lighting in BI is a bit of a mystical art with a lot of trial and error per shot; it's one of the rare situations where real-world lights have an easier time yielding the desired effect. For that reason, you end up tweaking the location of the back light a lot, so it's not critical that you get it right the first time in your initial setup. In Cycles, a Spot lamp usually can work well as a good back light.

This setup is good for studio lighting, and it works really well for scenes set indoors or for lighting isolated objects. I include an example three-point lighting .blend file on the website www.blenderbasics.com.

The only problem with using a Hemi as your back light in BI is that Hemis don't cast shadows at all. This lack of shadows can be an issue, for example, if you're lighting a character who's speaking. If you use a Hemi as your back light, you find that the interior of the character's mouth is unnaturally lit because the Hemi doesn't allow the character's head to cast a shadow on the inside of the mouth. In this situation, you may be better off back lighting with a Point light or a wide-angled Spot.

Creating a fake Area light with buffered Spots

Using a buffered Spot as your key works nicely, but an Area light can usually give you softer shadows. However, in BI, Area lights can only use ray tracing for shadows, and you have somewhat limited control of the Area lamp's shape because it can be only a flat square or rectangle. In Cycles, you can get around that pretty easily by explicitly modeling a mesh light to whatever shape you want. But in BI, to get around these limitations, you need to get a bit creative with buffered Spots and use them to make your own Area light.

To make your own custom Area light out of Spots in BI, start with the three-point rig in the last section and then go through the following steps:

1. **Create a circle mesh (Shift+A ⇨ Mesh ⇨ Circle).**

2. **In the Last Operation panel (F6 or the bottom of the Tool Shelf), set the number of vertices to 8 and the radius to 2.0; also enable the Fill check box.**

3. **Add the Spot to your selection (Shift+right-click), making it the Active object.**

   Adding the circle object makes it selected by default, so all you should have to do is Shift+right-click the buffered Spot you're using as your key.

4. **Copy the location and rotation of the Spot to the circle object.**

   To do so, open the 3D View's Properties region (N), right-click any of the Location values, and choose the Copy to Selected option from the menu that appears. Then do the same sequence on one of the Rotation values. The circle appears in the same place as the Spot with the same orientation.

5. **Make the circle your Active object (Shift+right-click).**

   Both the Spot and the circle are still selected, but now the circle is active.

6. **Parent the Spot lamp to the circle (Ctrl+P ⇨ Make Parent).**

   Now if you just have the circle selected and try to move it around, the Spot follows.

7. **Turn on Dupliverts for the circle (from Object Properties, Duplication ⇨ Verts).**

   Dupliverts are a cool part of Blender. When you have an object parented to a mesh, activating Dupliverts on the mesh object places a copy of the child object at every vertex on the parent.

   You now have an Area light created by buffered Spots arranged on a custom shape.

8. **Select your Spot and adjust its settings to taste.**

   I typically use the following settings as my starting point:

   - **Energy:** 0.200
   - **Blend:** 1.000
   - **Samples:** 8
   - **Soft:** 16.00
   - **Clip Start/Clip End:** These values may need to be manually adjusted to make sure that the shadow appears properly.

Figure 9-13 shows a circular Area light created with buffered spots.

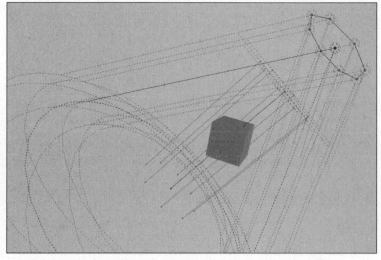

Figure 9-13:
Using
dupliverted
buffered
Spots to
create a
buffered
Area light.

Dealing with outdoor lighting

What if you have a large scene or your scene is set outdoors? The limited lighting cone of a single Spot or Area lamp makes it difficult to illuminate the whole scene in a believable way. In Cycles, the best solution is to use the Sun lamp and then make adjustments to your World Properties (covered later in this chapter). For a large or outdoor scene in BI, I usually bounce between one of two solutions. Both of them also involve the Sun lamp.

The easiest solution to implement is to change the buffered Spot in the earlier three-point lighting setup into a Sun with ray traced shadows. You get shadows for all objects in your scene, and with the sky and atmosphere settings, you can get a really believable result. That said, lighting your scene this way brings two disadvantages. First, it uses ray tracing for your shadows in BI, which can increase your render times if you're not careful. And second, because the Sun illuminates the same everywhere, you don't have as much control over individual shadows. This second point is the bigger issue of the two.

Compared to Cycles, ray tracing in BI is almost painfully slow, but it isn't horrible (and it's a lot faster than it was in earlier versions of Blender). In some cascs, it may be faster to just go ahead and use ray traced shadows instead of fiddling with all the settings involved with Spot lamps. I know of a few projects (my own included) where, in the time I spent trying to get the perfect Spot light settings, I could have rendered my scene with ray tracing and just been done with it.

That said, an alternative solution to using ray traced shadows from a Sun lamp is to keep the Sun for full scene lighting and atmosphere, but leave the shadow creation to the Spot light. To do so, begin with the previous basic three-point lighting rig for BI and proceed with the following steps:

1. **Add a Sun lamp (Shift+A ⇨ Lamp ⇨ Sun).**

   I like to put the Sun at the center of the scene. (Press Shift+S ⇨ Cursor to Center to put the 3D cursor at the center before adding the Sun.)

2. **Add the buffered Spot to your selection (Shift+right-click).**

   The newly added Sun is selected by default. Shift+right-clicking the Spot also selects it and makes the Spot lamp the Active object.

3. **Copy the Spot light's rotation.**

   From the 3D View's Properties region, right-click one of the Rotation values and choose Copy to Selected. Now light from the Sun is coming from the same direction as the Spot. Location for the Sun is irrelevant.

4. **Make the Spot lamp a shadow-only lamp (from Lamp Properties, Shadow ⇨ Only Shadow).**

5. **Disable shadows on the Sun by selecting the Sun (right-click) and then disabling ray traced shadows by left-clicking the Ray Shadow button in the Shadow and Spot panel.**

   Done! If you have other objects in your scene that need shadows, make a linked duplicate (Alt+D) of your shadow-only spot and position the duplicate by grabbing (G) it to the correct location.

Setting Up the World

When you set up your scene for rendering, lighting is really only part of the equation. You must also consider your scene's environment. For example, are you outdoors or indoors? Is it daytime or nighttime? What color is the sky? Are there clouds? What does the background look like? You have to consider these factors when thinking about the final look of your image. Whether you're rendering with Cycles or BI, your starting point for setting up your environment are in World Properties, as shown in Figure 9-14.

Figure 9-14:
On the left
is World
Properties
when
Cycles is the
active ren-
derer and
on the right
is World
Properties
when
using BI.

Changing the sky to something other than dull gray

If you've worked in Blender for a while and gotten a few renders out, you might be pretty tired of that dull gray background color that the renderers use by default. Here's where you change that color:

✔ **In Cycles:** Left-click the color swatch in the Surface panel of World Properties.

✔ **In BI:** Look in the World panel of World Properties. The leftmost color swatch sets the horizon color. You can adjust it by left-clicking the color swatch and using the color picker.

To the right of the horizon color is the *zenith* color. You may notice that trying to change this color doesn't seem to affect the background color at all. By default, Blender is set to use only the horizon color, so you end up with a solid color as the background. To change this default, left-click the Blend Sky check box in the World panel. When you do, the Preview shows a linear gradient that transitions from the horizon color at the bottom to the zenith color at the top. If I'm doing a render where I just want to see a model I've created, I often use this setup with my horizon color around 50 percent gray and my zenith color nearly black.

Of course, the next question you might have is, "Okay, so I'm using BI. What do the other check boxes in the World panel do?" I'm glad you asked. You can actually activate any combination of these check boxes. Here is a description of what each option does when enabled:

- **Paper Sky:** You typically use the Paper Sky setting with both Blend Sky and Real Sky also enabled. This setting keeps the horizon at the center of the camera, no matter where it's pointing. It also adjusts the gradient to make sure that the full zenith and horizon colors are visible.

- **Blend Sky:** Blend Sky enables a gradient going from the horizon to the zenith. When enabled by itself, the horizon is always at the bottom of the camera view and the zenith is at the top.

- **Real Sky:** Enabling Real Sky sets the horizon to the XY ground plane and the gradient to the zenith color along the global Z-axis. A bonus is that, because the horizon is locked to the XY ground plane, the gradient rotates with the camera, giving a much more realistic feeling to the background. I'm very fond of this setting, especially if I'm using a texture in the background.

Figure 9-15 shows a simple scene rendered with the various combinations of the Blend Sky check box enabled with the other two options so that you can get a better idea of what they do.

Figure 9-15:
Ways to control the Blend gradient and the horizon.

Blend | Blend + Real | Blend+Real+Paper

Modifying the World in Cycles

Comparing the options available in World Properties when rendering with BI to those available when using Cycles (look back to Figure 9-14), you may note that World Properties in Cycles seems. . . sparse. This is because, as far as Cycles is concerned, the World is just another kind of material. Therefore, most of your customization happens in the Node Editor.

To see what I'm talking about, split or change an area into a Node Editor (Shift+F3). To the right of the menus in the header are six buttons (two sets of three). The fifth button has an icon that looks like a globe; left-click that button and you can edit the World material for your scene.

If you don't see any nodes in the editor, try pressing Home to make your whole node network visible. If you still don't see any nodes, try enabling the Use Nodes check box in the Node Editor's header. If you still don't see any nodes after all that, double-check that you're actually using Cycles as your render engine. You should see something like what's shown in Figure 9-16. Worst case, you can just manually add the Background and World Output nodes as shown.

Let's say you're using Cycles and you miss having the Sky & Atmosphere panel that BI's Sun lamp has. You just want to quickly make a sky for your scene. Easily done from the Node Editor! Simply add a Sky Texture node (Shift+A ➪ Texture ➪ Sky Texture) and connect its Color output socket to the Color input socket on the Background shader node. And there you have it: a sky. Even better, you don't necessarily need a Sun lamp in your scene like you would if rendering with BI.

Figure 9-16: Cycles treats the World like a material, so most of your modifications take place in the Node Editor. This is a simple node network for a World material.

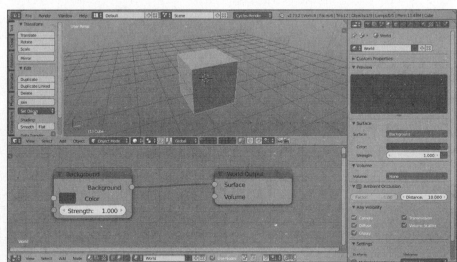

Want to use an image texture for your environment? It's a bit of an advanced topic, but you can download high resolution panoramic images from the Internet (even some digital cameras and smart phones have a built-in ability to create panoramic images) and use those as textures for your environment. You just need to add the Environment Texture node (Shift+A➪Texture➪Environment Texture) and connect its Color socket to the Color socket of your Background shader node. From there, just left-click the Open button for the image datablock in the Environment Texture node and use the File Browser to find your panoramic image. Cycles will even use the colors from your environment texture to illuminate your scene. You may not even need to use lights at all!

"But what if I just want a simple gradient like I can get in BI's World Properties?" Ironically, getting that effect is less straight-forward in Cycles. A viable cheat (that I've used!) would be to use the compositor and put my render over a gradient background (see Chapter 15 for more on compositing). But let's say you're a purist and you want to do it all in your World material. That, too, is still possible. As an example, use the following steps to re-create the effect of enabling the Blend Sky check box in BI's World Properties (these steps assume you're starting with the simple node network in Figure 9-16):

1. **Add a Gradient Texture node (Shift+A➪Texture➪Gradient Texture) and wire its Color socket to your Background shader node's Color input socket.**

   If you're previewing your scene in the 3D View with Rendered viewport shading (Shift+Z), you should see your background become completely black. That's okay. It's supposed to be like that. The problem is that the default texture coordinates don't map in a way that makes your gradient texture easy to see.

2. **Add a Texture Coordinate node (Shift+A➪Input➪Texture Coordinate) and connect its Window socket to the Vector input socket on your Gradient Texture node.**

   Now you should see your gradient, but there's a problem. The gradient goes from left to right, not vertically. You need to tweak your texture coordinates a bit.

3. **Add a Mapping node (Shift+A➪Vector➪Mapping) in-line between your Texture Coordinate node and your Gradient Texture node.**

   At this point, nothing in your background should be changed. You still have a black-to-white gradient going from left to right. The next step fixes that.

4. **In the Mapping node, left-click the Texture button at the top of the node and change the Z rotation value to 90 degrees.**

   Woohoo! You've rotated your texture and it's looking a lot more like the Blend Sky feature of BI. What you're missing now are controls for the colors in your gradient.

5. **Add a ColorRamp node (Shift+A ⇨ Converter ⇨ ColorRamp) in-line between the Gradient Texture node and the Background shader node.**

   On the face of things, it doesn't appear like much has changed. That's because the default gradient in the ColorRamp node is also black-to-white.

6. **Edit the colors on the ColorRamp node to match your desired horizon and zenith colors.**

   That's pretty much it. But really, with this setup you have even more control than you get in BI because with the ColorRamp node you can control the position of the colors and even add more colors to your gradient. It's incredibly powerful. Figure 9-17 shows an example of what your final node network may look like.

Creating sky textures in BI

Flat colors, gradients, and procedural stars are nice, but in some cases, you'd definitely rather have an image as your background. You can apply a texture to the World for your scene, like materials and lights. In the preceding section, I cover how easy it is to add a texture to your World material in Cycles.

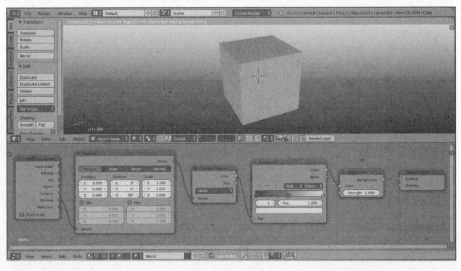

Figure 9-17: A node network for mimicking the Blend Sky feature of BI in the Cycles World material.

In BI, applying a texture is actually a little bit tricky to do. Like with texturing materials and lights in BI, you use Texture Properties. What makes things a little complicated is that, if you want to edit textures for your World, you need to first let Blender know the context in which you want to work. To do so, bring up Texture Properties and left-click the World button in the Context panel. The Texture Properties are the same familiar ones that I describe in Chapter 7. The primary difference is in the Influence panel, visible after you add a new texture.

The Influence panel gives you the ability to map the color of the texture to the blend, horizon color, and the upper and lower zenith colors. To use an image as your Sky texture, follow these steps:

1. **Left-click the New button in the texture datablock.**

   This button is located beneath the list box in Texture Properties.

2. **Change the texture Type to Image or Movie.**

3. **In the Image panel, left-click the Open button and use the File Browser to find the image you want to use.**

   You may want to enable thumbnail view from the File Browser's header.

4. **In the Influence panel, map the texture to the horizon color by enabling the check box next to the Horizon slider.**

5. **Back in World Properties, go to the Preview panel and enable the Real Sky check box.**

   This step ensures that the sky moves properly (or, more accurately, the sky stays still) as you move your camera in the scene.

6. **Switch back to Texture Properties and tweak the mapping and input settings to taste.**

   You may have to adjust the input coordinates as well as the texture size and offset. It's worth it to play around with these settings a bit to land on the look you want. When you're finished, you may have something that looks like Figure 9-18.

Understanding ambient occlusion

Take a look outside. Now, hopefully it's daytime, or this example isn't going to work, but notice how much everything seems to be illuminated. Even on a bright sunny day, the deepest shadows aren't completely black. The reason is that light from the sun is basically bouncing off of every surface many times, exposing nearly all objects to at least *some* amount of light. In computer graphics, this phenomenon is often referred to as *global illumination,* or GI, and it's pretty difficult to re-create efficiently. As you may have guessed, the biggest reason is the "light only bounces once" rule in BI (see Chapter 7).

Another result of GI is that all this bounced light also makes subtle details, creases, cracks, and wrinkles more apparent. At first, this statement may seem like a paradox. After all, if light is bouncing off of everything, intuitively, it would make sense that everything should end up even brighter and seem flatter. However, remember that not only is the light bouncing off of everything, but it's also casting small shadows from all the weird angles that it bounces from. Those small shadows are what bring out those minor details.

The GI effect is most apparent outdoors on overcast days where the light is evenly diffused by cloud cover. However, you can even see it happening in well-lit rooms with a high number of light sources, such as an office building with rows and rows of fluorescent lights lining the ceiling. You can somewhat fake this effect in BI by using a Hemi lamp, but the problem with Hemis is that they don't cast shadows, so you don't get that nice, added detail from GI.

The bad news is that the Blender Internal renderer doesn't have "true" GI capability. Cycles, on the other hand, has that capability. So the quickest way to get GI in your scene is to just render with Cycles. However, there are instances where you need to render with BI, so using Cycles isn't an option. Fortunately, BI does have a great way of approximating GI, thanks to *ambient occlusion* (AO). Often called *dirty GI* or a *dirt shader*, AO finds the small details in your object and makes them more apparent by making the rest of the model brighter or making the details darker.

To enable AO in BI, left-click the check box next to the Ambient Occlusion panel in World Properties. When you enable AO, Blender makes the settings in the Gather panel available. This panel gives you two ways of calculating AO: with ray tracing or as an approximation of the result. Figure 9-19 shows the Gather panel with the options for ray traced AO and approximate AO.

Figure 9-19:
The Gather panel in World Properties with ray traced AO options (left) and approximate AO options (right).

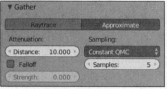 

If you're going to use ray traced AO, make sure that you have the Ray Tracing check box enabled in the Render panel of Render Properties.

Most of the controls in the Ambient Occlusion and Gather panels are the same, regardless of whether you're using ray traced or approximate AO. Here's a description of the options available for both types of AO:

- **Ambient Color:** This color swatch in the World panel controls the source color for the diffuse energy used by AO. The Ambient color adds itself to the overall color of the scene. I don't normally advocate setting the Ambient color to anything other than black because it has a tendency to wash out the shading in the scene. However, when you enable AO and adjust the Ambient color, the shading isn't washed out as much, and you actually end up with a more believable image.

- **Factor:** The Factor value is the strength of the overall AO effect. The effect you choose from the Add/Multiply menu is multiplied by this value. Usually it's a good idea to keep this at 1.0, although I recommend that you play with it a bit to see how it affects your scene.

- **Add/Multiply:** With this drop-down menu in the Ambient Occlusion panel, you can control how AO creates shadows. Choosing Add brightens the rest of the object, making the details apparent by simply staying their own color. Choosing Multiply darkens the detailed areas while keeping the object's original shading. Technically speaking, the Add behavior is more physically correct.

- **Falloff:** This option in the Gather panel controls the size of the extra shadows that AO creates. When you enable the Falloff check box, you can use the Strength value field below it. Setting this value to higher numbers makes the shadows more subtle.

The other values for ray traced and approximate gathering are there for refining and optimizing how they work. If you read about ray traced lights for BI earlier in this chapter in the "Universal lamp options" section, the settings for ray traced gathering are pretty familiar. I recommend using adaptive QMC because it typically yields faster results at good quality. I've even found that in a lot of situations, using ray traced gathering with adaptive QMC sampling is even faster than using approximate gathering. Using the other sampling types usually gives you a *noisier,* or more speckled, result.

When choosing between ray traced and approximate gathering, keep in mind a set of trade-offs. As you might expect, ray traced gathering gives you more accurate results, but it sometimes takes longer to process when you use a higher Samples value to reduce the noisiness of the AO shading. Approximate gathering works fast and doesn't suffer the noise problem that you get with ray traced gathering. Of course, some people actually prefer that noisy grain that ray traced gathering gives, and approximate gathering is a bit more error-prone in creating its shadows, especially where things touch. So it may take some additional time to set things up so that they look believable. You have to weigh out the advantages and disadvantages for yourself and see which method works best for your projects. Figure 9-20 shows the same scene rendered with both types of gathering, as well as without any AO at all.

Figure 9-20:
From left to right, with their render times: no AO, ray traced AO, and approximate AO.

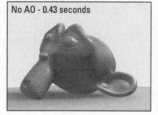
No AO - 0.43 seconds

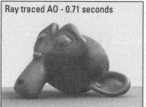
Ray traced AO - 0.71 seconds

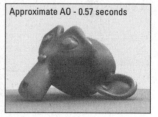
Approximate AO - 0.57 seconds

REMEMBER

You can also enable AO in Cycles from World Properties, but the available options are a lot more limited. When you enable AO in Cycles, the only properties for tweaking are a Factor and a Distance value, corresponding to the Factor and Falloff Strength properties in BI's AO settings. Generally, there isn't much call for using AO if you're rendering with Cycles, because Cycles already has GI.

Adding mist in BI

Another panel in World Properties for BI is the Mist panel. The settings in this panel are somewhat primitive in terms of what they actually do, but they can be pretty handy in a pinch for creating nice atmospheric effects and quick backgrounds.

BI's Mist works by decreasing the opacity of objects as they get farther away from the camera, mixing more with whatever the sky is. To use it, enable the Mist check box and expand its panel. From here, you can adjust the Start and Depth values. Start defines how far away from the camera the mist starts to take effect. Depth is the distance from the Start value that the mist effect is at 100 percent. Anything farther away from the camera doesn't show up in the final render.

These values are in the units you specify in Scene Properties, but it can be difficult to know intuitively where they actually fall in the scene, relative to your camera. Fortunately, you can see mist limits visually. Select the camera and switch to Camera Properties. On the left side of the Display panel are four check boxes. Left-click the Mist check box. When you do, a line appears extending from your camera. If you switch back to World Properties and adjust the Start and Depth values, you can now see exactly where the mist region of influence is. And, of course, if you use Rendered viewport shading (Shift+Z), you can see live updates to your render as you adjust values. Figure 9-21 shows a scene in the 3D View with a camera that has its mist limits visible.

Figure 9-21:
A camera in the 3D View with its mist limits visible. To the right is a render of that scene.

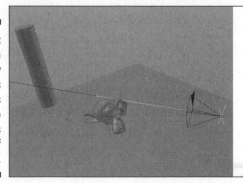

The Falloff drop-down menu controls how the mist gets thicker from start to finish. Quadratic tends to be a more subtle effect, whereas Linear tends to make the mist thicker faster. If you want to limit the mist to a certain height, like when you see an early morning mist in a field, adjust the Height value. Like the other values, Height is set in your specified units and works relative to the XY ground plane. The Intensity value increases the mist's intensity. Be careful with this setting. Putting it too high hides your entire scene from you.

There is no Mist panel when rendering with Cycles, so none of the settings covered in this section are available if you've chosen Cycles as your render engine. However, you can still achieve the mist effect if you render with Cycles. You just need to do it in the compositor. There's more on the compositor in Chapter 15.

Part III
Get Animated

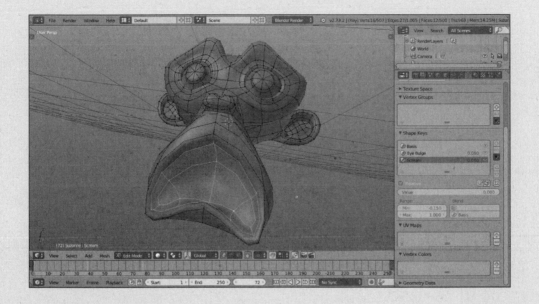

In this part . . .

- ✔ Constraining objects.
- ✔ Using shape keys, hooks, and armatures.
- ✔ Applying the Dope Sheet.
- ✔ Simulating physics.
- ✔ Visit `www.dummies.com/extras/blender` for great Dummies content online.

Chapter 10

Animating Objects

I have to make a small admission: Animation is not easy. It's time consuming, frustrating, tedious work where you often spend days, sometimes even weeks, working on what ends up to be a few seconds of finished animation. An enormous amount of work goes into animation. However, there's something incredible about making an otherwise inanimate object move, tell a story, and communicate to an audience. Getting those moments when you have beautifully believable motion — life, in some ways — is a positively indescribable sensation that is, well, indescribably positive. Animation, and the process of creating animation, truly has my heart more than any other art form. It's simply my favorite thing to do. It's like playing with a sock puppet, except better because you don't have to worry about wondering whether or not it's been washed.

This chapter, as well as the following three chapters, go pretty heavily into the technical details of creating animations using Blender. Blender is a great tool for the job. Beyond what this book can provide you with, though, animation is about seeing, understanding, and re-creating motion. I highly recommend that you make it a point to get out and watch things. And not just animations: Go to a park and study how people move. Try to move like other people move so that you can understand how the weight shifts and how gravity and inertia compete with and accentuate that movement. Watch lots of movies and television and pay close attention to how people's facial expressions can convey what they're trying to say. If you get a chance, go to a theater and watch a play. Understanding how and why stage actors exaggerate their body language is incredibly useful information for an animator.

While you're doing that, think about how you can use the technical information in these chapters to re-create those feelings and that motion with your objects in Blender.

Working with Animation Curves

In Blender, the fundamental way for controlling and creating animation is with animation curves called *f-curves*. F-curve is short for *function curve,* and it describes the change, or *interpolation,* between two key moments in an animated sequence.

To understand interpolation better, flash back to your grade-school math class for a second. Remember when you had to do graphing, or take the equation for some sort of line or curve and draw it out on paper? By drawing that line, you were interpolating between points. Don't worry though; I'm not going to make you do any of that. That's what we have Blender for. In fact, the following example shows the basic process of animating in Blender and should help explain things more clearly:

1. **Start with Blender's default scene (Ctrl+N⇨Reload Start-Up File).**

2. **Select the default cube object and switch to the camera view (right-click, Numpad 0).**

3. **Split the 3D View horizontally and change one of the new areas to the Graph Editor (Shift+F6).**

   I like to make the lower one the Graph Editor, because it's right above the Timeline in the default screen layout.

4. **In the 3D View, make sure that the default cube is selected and press I⇨Location.**

   This step sets an initial location keyframe for the cube. I give a more detailed description of keyframes later in the chapter in the "Inserting keys" section. The important thing to notice is that the left region of the Graph Editor is now updated and shows a short tiered list with the items `Cube`, `CubeAction`, and `Location`.

5. **Press Shift+↑ on your keyboard.**

   You move forward in time by 10 frames.

6. **Grab (G) the cube in the 3D View and move it to another location in the scene.**

7. **Press I⇨Location again in the 3D View.**

   A set of colored lines appears in the Graph Editor. These colored lines are f-curves. Each f-curve represents a single attribute, or *channel*, that's been animated. If you expand the Location block in the Graph Editor by left-clicking the triangle on the left side of its name, you can see the three location channels: X Location, Y Location, and Z Location. To see the actual curves a little bit better, move your mouse to the large graph section of the Graph Editor and press Home. Your Blender screen should look something like the one in Figure 10-1.

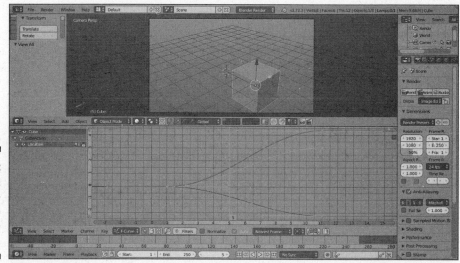

Figure 10-1:
Animating
the loca-
tion of the
default cube
object.

Congratulations! You just created your first animation in Blender. Here's what you did: The largest part of the Graph Editor is a graph (go figure!). Moving from left to right on this graph — its X-axis — is moving forward in time. The vertical axis on this graph represents the value of whatever chan-nel is being animated. So the curves that you created describe and control the change in the cube's location in the X-, Y-, and Z-axes as you move for-ward in time. Blender creates the curves by interpolating between the con-trol points, called *keys*, that you created.

You can see the result for yourself by playing back the animation. Keeping your mouse cursor in the Graph Editor, press Alt+A (alternatively, you can left-click the Play button in the Timeline). A green vertical line, called the *timeline cursor,* moves from left to right in the graph. As the timeline cursor moves, you should see your cube move from the starting point to the ending point you defined in the 3D View. Press Esc to stop the playback. You can watch the animation in a more controlled way by *scrubbing* in the Graph Editor. To scrub, left-click in the graph area of the Graph Editor and drag your mouse cursor left and right. The timeline cursor follows the location of your mouse pointer, and you can watch the change happening in the 3D View.

Customizing your screen layout for animation

There is a screen layout in Blender specifically set up for animation named — conveniently — Animation. You can choose it from the Screen

Layout datablock in the Info editor at the top of the Blender window or by using the Ctrl+←⇨Ctrl+← hotkey combination.

This screen layout isn't too dissimilar from the Default layout, but it does have a few differences. In particular, the Outliner is larger, and on the left side of the screen, there's a Dope Sheet and Graph Editor. A second 3D View is also placed above the Outliner. The Timeline from the Default layout is pretty much unchanged. (For a full reminder of what each editor does, refer to Chapter 1.)

You may be wondering, however, why this layout has three editors (the Timeline, Graph Editor, and Dope Sheet) that allow you to adjust your position in time on your animation. The quick answer is that each editor gives you different kinds of control over your animation. For example, the Timeline gives you a central place to control the playback of your overall animation. This way, you can use the Graph Editor to focus on specific detailed animations and the Dope Sheet for making sense of complex animation with a lot of animated attributes. Like the Graph Editor, you can scrub the Timeline and Dope Sheet by left-clicking in it and dragging your mouse cursor left and right.

One change I usually like to make to this layout is in the secondary 3D View above the Outliner. I like to change the viewport shading in this editor to be Shaded (Z) or Textured (Alt+Z). The reason for this secondary view is so that you can work from any perspective in the main 3D View but still retain an idea of what the camera sees. That way, you don't end up animating something that will never be on camera. The default Wireframe shading in this 3D View is good for fast playback, but it's usually too difficult to tell what's going on. I also like to disable the 3D Manipulator (Ctrl+Spacebar) in that secondary 3D View so it doesn't get in the way of seeing the actual animation.

To that end, I also use Blender's Only Render display. Only Render hides anything that won't be rendered (3D grid, relationship lines, lamps, empties, and so on) from the 3D View, allowing you to get a truer understanding of what your final animation looks like. To activate this feature, reveal the Properties region (N) in this secondary 3D View and enable the Only Render check box in the Display panel.

The last change I make to this screen layout is in the main 3D View. I swap out the Translate manipulator for the Rotate manipulator (if you have the Pie Menus add-on enabled, you can do this quickly by using Ctrl+Spacebar⇨Rotate) and change its coordinate space to Normal (Alt+Spacebar⇨Normal). I do this change because normally I can grab and scale with the G and S hotkeys pretty quickly, but precise rotation when animating is often faster and easier with the Rotate manipulator. Plus, this manipulator doesn't obstruct my view as much as the other ones do. Figure 10-2 shows my modestly modified Animation screen layout.

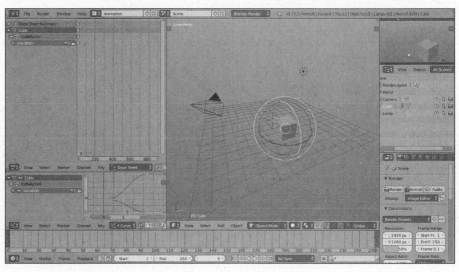

Working in the Graph Editor

Working in the Graph Editor is very similar to working in the 3D View. The following describes the basic controls available in the Graph Editor:

- **Middle-click+drag** moves around your view of the graph.

- **Ctrl+middle-click+drag** allows you to interactively scale your view of the curve horizontally and vertically at the same time.

- **Scroll your mouse wheel** to zoom in and out.

- **Shift+scroll** moves the graph vertically.

- **Ctrl+scroll** moves the graph horizontally.

- **Right-click** selects individual f-curve control points.

- **Press A** to toggle selecting all or no control points.

- **Press B** for Border Select.

- **Press N** to reveal the Graph Editor's Properties region (similar to the Properties region in the 3D View).

- **Left-click** a channel in the left region of the Graph Editor to select it.

  You may need to expand the blocks in this region to drill down to the actual animation channels (such as X Location, Y Location, and Z Location).

- **Ctrl+left-click** allows you to arbitrarily add points to a selected f-curve in the graph. Anywhere you Ctrl+left-click in the graph, a new control point is added to the selected channel.

The Graph Editor also has some handy keyboard shortcuts for hiding and revealing channels. They're particularly useful when you want to manage a complex animation with a lot of keyframes and channels. If you select one or more keyframes, you can use any of these hotkeys:

- ✔ **H** hides the channels that the selected keyframes belong to.
- ✔ **Shift+H** hides all channels *except* for the ones where you've selected a keyframe.
- ✔ **Alt+H** reveals ("unhides") all animation channels in the Graph Editor.

Inserting keys

Instead of Ctrl+left-clicking in the Graph Editor to add control points to a specific f-curve, you have another, more controlled option. Blender also uses a workflow that's a lot more like traditional hand-drawn animation. In traditional animation, a whole animated sequence is planned out ahead of time using a script and *storyboards* (drawings of the major scenes of the animation, kind of like a comic book, with arrows to indicate camera direction). Then an animator goes through and draws the primary poses of the character. These drawings are referred to as *keyframes* or *keys*. They're the poses that the character must make in order to most effectively convey the intended motion to the viewer. With the keys drawn, they're handed off to a second set of animators called the *inbetweeners*. These animators are responsible for drawing all the frames between each of the keys in order to get the appearance of smooth motion.

Creating the illusion of motion with static images

In order to effectively do animation, you really need a firm grasp on how moving pictures work. This is the fundamental basis of animation, and film, television, and even video games. Without getting into the complex details of psychology and neuroscience, the basics are this: humans perceive movement as the apparent difference in what we see at two relatively close moments in time.

If you have two images of the same object in different positions, you can create the illusion that the object moves between positions by swapping between those images very quickly. Now chain a series of those images together and show them in quick succession. Each image is only visible for a fraction of a second before the next one appears. This rapid swapping of images tricks our minds into seeing movement on the screen.

Who said science isn't fun?

Translating the workflow of traditional animation to how you do work in Blender, you should consider yourself the keyframe artist and Blender the inbetweener (at least to start). On a fully polished animation, it isn't uncommon to have some kind of key on every frame of animation. In the quick animating example at the beginning of this section, you create a keyframe after you move the cube. By interpolating the curve between those keys, Blender creates the in-between frames. Some animation programs refer to creating these in-between frames as *tweening*.

To have a workflow that's even more similar to traditional animation, it's preferable to define your keyframes in the 3D View. Then you can use the Graph Editor to tweak the change from one keyframe to the next. And this workflow is exactly the way Blender is designed to animate. Start in the 3D View by pressing I to bring up the Insert Keyframe menu. Through this menu, you can create keyframes for the main animatable channels for an object. I describe the channels here in more detail:

- **Location:** Insert a key for the object's X, Y, and Z location.
- **Rotation:** Insert a key for the object's rotation in the X, Y, and Z axes.
- **Scaling:** Insert a key for the object's scale in the X, Y, and Z axes.
- **LocRot/LocScale/LocRotScale/RotScale:** Insert keyframes for various combinations of the previous three values.
- **Visual Location/Rotation/LocRot:** Insert keyframes for location, rotation, or both, but based on where the object is visually located in the scene. These options are explicitly made for use with constraints, which I cover later in this chapter in "Using Constraints Effectively."
- **Available:** If you already inserted keys for some of your object's channels, choosing this option adds a key for each of those preexisting curves in the Graph Editor. If no curves are already created, no keyframes are inserted.
- **Delta Location/Rotation/Scale:** With the exception of Available, all of the preceding keying options use absolute coordinates for keying animations. *Delta* keys, however, use coordinates relative to your object's current location, rotation, and scale. Delta keys can be useful if you want to have many objects with the same animation, but starting from different origin points.

When Blender sets keyframes for location, rotation, and scale, bear in mind which coordinate system the Graph Editor is using. Location is stored in global coordinates, whereas rotation and scale are stored in the object's local coordinate system.

Here's the basic workflow for animating in Blender:

1. **Insert an initial keyframe (I).**

   A keyframe appears at frame 1 in your animation. Assuming that you enter a Location keyframe, if you look at the Graph Editor, notice that Location channel is added and enabled.

2. **Move forward 10 frames (Shift+↑).**

   This puts you at frame 11. (Of course, when doing a real animation, your keys aren't always going to be 10 frames apart.) The Shift+↑ and Shift+↓ hotkeys move you 10 frames forward or backward in time, regardless of the editor your mouse cursor is in.

   This is a good way to rough in your keys. You can go back later and adjust your timing from the Dope Sheet or Graph Editor. To move forward or back one frame at a time, use the ← and → keys. Of course, you can also use the Timeline, Graph Editor, or Dope Sheet to change what frame you are in.

3. **Grab your cube and move it to a different location in 3D space (G).**

4. **Insert a new keyframe (I).**

   Now you should have curves in the Graph Editor that describe the motion of the cube.

You can insert keys in an easier way using a feature called Autokey. Like its name indicates, Autokey automatically creates keys when you make changes in your scene. To enable the Autokey feature, look in the Timeline. Next to the playback controls in the Timeline's header is a button with a red circle on it, like the Record button on a DVR. Left-click it to activate Autokey. Now you can simply use tools in the 3D View like grab (G), rotate (R), and scale (S) as you move forward in time and keyframes are automatically inserted for you. Pretty sweet, huh?

By default, Blender uses the LocRotScale keying set (there's more on keying sets later in this chapter) for inserting keyframes when Autokey is enabled. This is worth noting because, if you're not careful, Autokey can insert keyframes that are unnecessary or (worse) not wanted. It's for this reason that when I use Autokey, I like to insert my initial keyframes manually and then use the Available keying set for autokeying.

A really cool feature in Blender is the concept of "[almost] everything animatable." You can animate nearly every setting or attribute within Blender. Want to animate the skin material of your character so that she turns red with anger? You can! Want to animate the Count attribute in an Array modifier to dynamically add links to a chain? You can! Want to animate whether your object appears in wireframe or solid shading in the 3D View? Ridiculous as it sounds, that, too, is possible!

So how do you do this miraculous act of animating any attribute? It's amazingly simple. Nearly every text field, value field, color swatch, drop-down menu, check box, and radio button is considered a property and represents a channel that you can animate. Insert a keyframe for that channel by right-clicking one of those properties and choosing Insert Keyframes from the menu that appears. Figure 10-3 shows what this menu looks like.

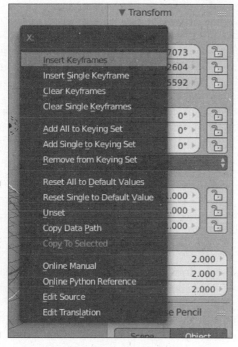

Figure 10-3: Right-click any property in the Properties editor, and you can insert a keyframe for it.

After you insert a new keyframe for that property, its color changes to yellow, and a channel for that property is added in the Graph Editor. When you move forward or backward in time, the color of the control changes from yellow to green. This green color indicates that the property is animated, but you're not currently on one of its keys. Insert another keyframe for that property, and BAM! The field's color turns to yellow and you have two keyframes for your animated property.

For an even faster way to insert keyframes on properties, hover your mouse over the control and just press I. This trick even works on the show/hide/selectable icons (known as the *restrict columns*) in the Outliner. How's that for awesome?

If you want to insert keyframes on multiple properties at the same time (such as the aforementioned restricted columns in the Outliner), keep holding the I hotkey as you run your mouse cursor over those properties. There you go. One key press, many keyframes.

Working with keying sets

When working on an animation, you can easily find yourself inserting keyframes for a bunch of different channels and properties at the same time. The troublesome thing is that, on a complex scene, these properties can be located all over Blender's interface. Sure, you can insert keys for an object's location, rotation, and scale by pressing I in the 3D View, but you may also need to key that object's visibility from the Outliner, the influence of a constraint in Constraint Properties, and the object's material color from Material Properties. They're all over the place! It wouldn't be difficult at all to overlook one while you work, resulting in an animation that doesn't quite behave the way you want it to.

This load can be lightened by using more advanced rigging features (see Chapter 11), but even that doesn't really solve it. A complex character rig can have hundreds of bones and controls to animate. Manually keeping track of all of them for multiple characters in a scene can be a nightmare. (I know. I've tried.)

You know what would be really nice? It would be great if you could make a custom group of a bunch of properties so you can insert a keyframe for all of them at the same time, kind of like the LocRotScale option when you press I in the 3D View. Well, guess what? That exact feature exists in Blender. It's called a *keying set*.

Actually, the LocRotScale option *is* a keying set. It's one of a handful of preconfigured keying sets that ship with Blender. In fact, all of the options in the Insert Keyframe Menu (I) are keying sets.

Using keying sets

To use keying sets, start with a look at the last set of fields and buttons of the Timeline's header, just to the right of the Autokey button, as shown in Figure 10-4.

There are three widgets in the Timeline for working with keying sets:

> ✔ **Active keying set:** This field for this drop-down menu is empty by default. Left-click on it to choose one of the available keying sets to be your active one.

If you have an active keying set, you can make this field empty again by left-clicking the X to the right of your keying set's name.

✔ **Insert keyframes:** Left-click this button to insert a keyframe at the current frame on the Timeline for every property in the current active keying set. If you don't have an active keying set, a little error pops up to let you know.

✔ **Remove keyframes:** Left-click this button to remove any keyframes from the current frame that belong to any properties in the active keying set.

If you don't have any keys on the current frame, this button doesn't do anything.

Figure 10-4:
The Timeline's header has controls for choosing your active keying set and inserting keyframes within that keying set.

To quickly choose an active keying set from the 3D View, use the Ctrl+Shift+Alt+I hotkey combination.

When you choose a keying set, Blender gives preference to the properties in that keying set when you insert keyframes. This means that with an active keying set chosen, you don't get the Insert Keyframe menu if you press I in the 3D View. Blender just quietly inserts keyframes for all of the properties in your chosen keying set. This lack of immediate feedback may be disorienting at first, but it makes for a very fast, distraction-free workflow for animating. Also, as mentioned earlier in this chapter, if you have Autokey enabled, it uses the active keying set. If you don't have an active keying set chosen, Autokey defaults to using the LocRotScale keying set.

Creating custom keying sets

The pre-configured keying sets that come with Blender are handy, but it's much more useful to define your own keying sets (especially as your animations become more complex). Keying sets aren't character or object-specific, so they apply to your whole scene. This means you can use a keying set to insert keyframes for a whole group of characters all at the same time if you like.

Because keying sets are relevant to your whole scene, you can create your custom keying sets from Scene Properties, in the Keying Sets panel. Follow these steps to create a new keying set and populate it with properties to keyframe:

1. **In the Keying Sets panel, left-click the Plus (+) button to the right of the keying set list box.**

2. **Adjust your new keying set's settings.**

   Double-click its name in the listbox to rename it to something other than the generic Keying Set that you get by default. You can use the Description text field to write a few words that explain the purpose of your custom keying set.

   On the bottom right of the panel, there are three toggleable settings that you can choose to enable or disable:

   • **Only Needed:** Enable this option, and Blender only adds keyframes to the properties that changed since the last inserted keyframe. If the property didn't change, no keyframe is inserted, regardless of whether you've pressed I in the 3D View.

   • **Visual Keying:** As covered earlier in this chapter, *visual transforms* the location, rotation, and scale of your object as they appear on-screen, including changes made by constraints. Enable this option and all inserted keyframes in this keying set will use visual transforms for keying.

   • **XYZ=RGB Colors:** This option is enabled by default. It dictates that any new f-curves use red, green, and blue for X-, Y-, and Z-axis channels.

The buttons for the Keyframing Settings are configured in the Blender interface as radio buttons (if you left-click one to enable it, the others are automatically disabled). You can enable two or more of these settings by Shift+left-clicking them.

Figure 10-5 shows the Keying Sets panel with a few custom keying sets added in the list box.

Figure 10-5:
The Keying
Sets panel
is where
you add
new custom
keying sets.

Left-clicking a keying set in the list box of the Keying Sets panel automatically makes that keying set the active one.

At this point, you've created your custom keying set, but it starts as an empty container. You haven't assigned any properties to it. To add, edit, and remove properties from your active keying set, you need to use the Active Keying Set panel in Scene Properties. It appears below the Keying Sets panel when you have a custom keying set selected in the list box.

To add a new property to your custom keying set, you need to tell Blender where to find that property. You need to give Blender that property's *path*, or the way to navigate through your .blend file's internal structure to your property. It's certainly possible (and sometimes necessary for more obscure properties) to manually add new paths from the Active Keying Set panel by left-clicking the Plus (+) button next to the Paths list box and get more specific from there. However, that can be an excruciatingly tedious process, even if you have a strong working knowledge of .blend file innards.

There's a better, easier way to populate your keying set. Rather than go about the painful, manual way, follow these steps:

1. **In Blender's interface, find the property you want to add to your keying set.**

   This could be the material color of your object, just its Y-axis rotation, or its renderability in the Outliner. It can be any property that's capable of being keyframed.

2. **Right-click the field or button or check box for that property.**

   Among all of the various options that are available in the menu that appears, there should be either two or three menu items that are specific to keying sets:

   - **Add All to Keying Set:** If your chosen property is one of a block of properties (such as X, Y, and Z scale), this option can add all of the properties in that block to your custom keying set. If the property isn't part of such a block, this option doesn't appear in the menu.

- **Add Single to Keying Set:** Choose this option to add just the property that you've right-clicked to your keying set.

   If the property isn't part of a block of properties, then this menu item reads as Add to Keying Set.

- **Remove from Keying Set:** If the property in question already is in your active keying set, you can choose this option to quickly remove it.

3. **Add the property to your active keying set by left-clicking one of the Add to Keying Set menu items.**

   Your chosen property is now a member of the active keying set. You can verify that it's there by looking at the Paths list box in the Active Keying Set panel of Scene Properties. Figure 10-6 shows the Active Keying Set panel with a few paths added.

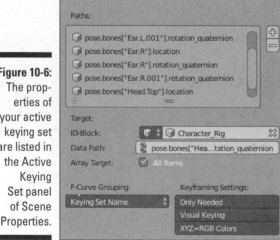

Figure 10-6:
The properties of your active keying set are listed in the Active Keying Set panel of Scene Properties.

You may notice in Figure 10-6 that, like the Keying Sets panel, the Active Keying Set panel features the same three buttons for Keyframing Settings. By adjusting these settings in the Active Keying Set panel, you override the global Keyframing Settings as defined in the Keying Sets panel, but just for that property.

The override behavior in the Active Keying Set panel only works in an additive way. That is, if you have Only Needed disabled in the Keying Sets panel, enabling it for a specific property in the Active Keying Set panel will override as expected. However, if that same option is enabled in the Keying Sets panel, currently there isn't a clean way to do an override that disables it for individual properties in the keying set.

To the left of the Keyframing Settings is a drop-down menu labeled F-Curve Grouping. This drop-down menu dictates how animation channels are grouped in the Dope Sheet and Graph Editor. You have three choices:

- ✔ **Keying Set Name:** This is the default setting. Animation channels in the Dope Sheet and Graph Editor are grouped according to the name of your keying set.

    It generally works well, but if you have a lot of properties in your keying set, this can make that grouping seem a bit like a grab bag of animated properties.

- ✔ **None:** You have the option of not grouping the properties in your keying set at all. This can lead to pretty messy animation editors, so it isn't an option you'll choose often, but it's nice to know it's available.

- ✔ **Named Group:** This is a very powerful option for organizing a large keying set. If you choose Named Group as your method for f-curve grouping, a text field labeled Group appears below the drop-down menu. Type the name of a group in that field. Now, if you choose another property in your keying set and type the exact same group name, both properties are collected together in the Dope Sheet and Graph Editor. As covered in Chapter 11, this is extremely useful for complex character rigs.

Editing motion curves

After you know how to add keyframes to your scene, the next logical step is to tweak, edit, and modify those keyframes, as well as the interpolation between them, in the Graph Editor. The Graph Editor is similar to the 3D View, and you can select individual control points on f-curves by right-clicking or by pressing B for Border Select or even by pressing C for circle selection. Well, the similarities with the 3D View goes farther than that. Not only can you select those control points in the Graph Editor, but you can edit them like a 2D Bézier curve object in the 3D View. The only constraint is that f-curves can't cross themselves. Having a curve that describes motion in time do a loopty-loop doesn't make any sense.

For more detailed descriptions of the hotkeys and controls for editing Bézier curves in Blender, see Chapter 6. Selecting and moving control point handles, as well as the V hotkey for changing handle types all work as expected. However, because these curves are specially purposed for animation, you have a few additional controls over them. For example, you can control the type of interpolation between control points on a selected curve by pressing T or going to Key⇨Interpolation Mode in the Graph Editor's header. You get the following options:

- ✔ **Interpolation:** These three options control the general interpolation between two keyframes.

  - **Constant:** This option is sometimes called a *step function* because a series of them look like stair steps. Basically, this interpolation type keeps the value of one control point until it gets to the next one, where it instantly changes. Many animators like to use this interpolation mode when blocking out their animations. This way, they can focus on getting their poses and timing right without the distraction of in-between frames.

  - **Linear:** The interpolation from one control point to the next is an absolutely straight line. This option is similar to changing two control points to have Vector handles.

  - **Bézier:** The default interpolation type, Bézier interpolation smoothly transitions from one control point to the next. In traditional animation, this smooth transition is referred to as *easing in* and *easing out* of a keyframe.

- ✔ **Easing (by strength):** The interpolation options in this column are preset, "mathematically correct" interpolation methods. You can get the same curve profile by manually editing the handles of a curve with Bézier interpolation, but these easing presets are a faster way of getting the same result.

- ✔ **Dynamic Effects:** When things move in meatspace, there isn't always a smooth transition from one pose to the next. When you drop a ball to the ground, it bounces. When you slam on the brakes while driving, the car over-extends, lurching forward before settling back to rest. In many cases, you can (and should) animate this behavior by hand. However, in a pinch, these three Dynamic Effects interpolation can give you a great starting point:

  - **Back:** In this interpolation type, the curve "overshoots the mark" set by the keyframe before settling back where you want it. To see what this effect is like, try slapping the surface of a table, but stopping just before your hand makes contact. If you watch carefully, you should notice that your hand goes a bit farther than you want it to before it finishes moving.

  - **Bounce:** The Bounce interpolation is a fun one. It makes your object appear to bounce before coming to a rest.

• **Elastic:** Have you ever seen an over-extended rubber band break in half? The loose ends flop all over the place before they stop moving. The Elastic interpolation mode gives your object this kind of effect, like it's stuck to the floppy end of one of those broken rubber bands.

Figure 10-7 shows the Keyframe Interpolation menu.

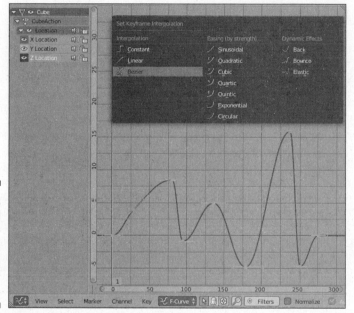

Figure 10-7:
Changing the interpolation type on selected f-curve control points.

The interpolation mode options work only on the selected control points in the Graph Editor, so if you want to select all the control points in a single f-curve, select one of those control points and press L. Then you can apply your interpolation mode to the entire curve.

You can also change what a selected f-curve does before and after its first and last keyframes by changing the curve's *extrapolation mode*. You can change a curve's extrapolation mode by selecting an f-curve channel in the left region of the Graph Editor and then pressing Shift+E or navigating to Key⇨Extrapolation Mode in the Graph Editor's header. When you do, notice four possible choices:

✓ **Constant Extrapolation:** This setting is the default. The first and last control point values are maintained into infinity beyond those points.

✔ **Linear Extrapolation:** Instead of maintaining the same value in perpetuity before and after the first and last control points, this extrapolation mode takes the directions of the curve as it reaches those control points and continues to extend the curve in those directions.

✔ **Make Cyclic (F-Modifier):** This option adds an f-curve modifier (covered in the next section of this chapter) that takes all of the keyframes in your animation and repeats them before and after your first and last keyframes.

If you have a looping animation, like a character who never stops waving at you, this option is an easy way to make that happen.

✔ **Clear Cyclic (F-Modifier):** If your f-curve has a Cycles modifier, it's possible to remove that modifier from the Graph Editor's Properties region (N), but this menu option is faster.

Figure 10-8 shows the menu for the different type of extrapolation modes, as well as what each one looks like with a simple f-curve.

If you have lots of animated objects in your scene, or just one object with a high number of animated properties, it may be helpful to hide extraneous curves from view so that you can focus on the ones you truly want to edit. To toggle a curve's visibility (or that of an entire keying set), left-click the eye icon next to its name in the channel region along the left side of the Graph Editor. If you want f-curves to be visible, but not editable, select a channel from the channel region and either left-click the lock icon or press Tab. You can also disable the influence of a specific f-curve or keying set by left-clicking the speaker icon. (If you're familiar with audio editing, you can think of this as "muting" those f-curves.)

As mentioned previously in this chapter, you can quickly mute/hide animation channels in the Graph Editor by using the H, Shift+H, and Alt+H hotkeys with one or more selected keyframes.

If you need explicit control over the placement of a curve or a control point, the Graph Editor has a Properties region like the 3D View. You bring it up the same way, too: Either press N or choose View➪Properties. Within the Active Keyframe panel of this region, you can enter the exact value that you'd like to set your selected control point or that control point's handles, as well as modify that control point's interpolation type. Figure 10-9 shows the Properties region in the Graph Editor.

Often, you run into the occasion where you need to edit all the control points in a single frame so that you can change the overall timing of your animation. You may be tempted to use Border Select (B) to select the strip of control points you want to move around. However, a cleaner and easier way is to select one of the control points on the frame you want to adjust and press K in the Graph Editor or choose Select⇨Columns on Selected Keys. All the other control points that are on the same frame as your initial selection are selected.

Table 10-1 covers the most common hotkeys and mouse actions used to control animation in the Graph Editor.

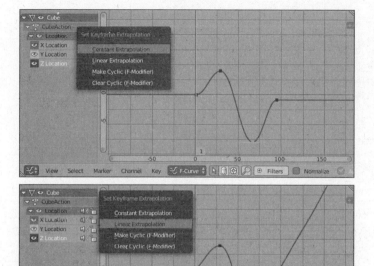

Figure 10-9:
The
Properties
region (N)
in the Graph
Editor.

Table 10-1	Commonly Used Hotkeys and Mouse Actions for the Graph Editor		
Mouse Action	*Description*	*Hotkey*	*Description*
Left-click graph	Move time cursor	Alt+A	Playback animation
Left-click channel eye icon	Hide/Reveal channel	Shift+E	Extrapolation Mode
Left-click channel	Select channel	K	Select columns of selected control points
Right-click	Select control point	L	Select linked control points
Middle-click	Pan graph	O	Clean keyframes
Ctrl+middle-click	Scale graph	N	Properties region
Scroll	Zoom graph	Shift+S	Snap Menu
Shift+scroll	Pan graph vertically	T	Interpolation Type
Ctrl+scroll	Pan graph horizontally	Home	Fit curves to graph

Using F-curve modifiers

One of the biggest appeals of computer graphics in general — and computer animation specifically — is the prospect of letting the computer do all the hard work for you. Or at least you want the computer to handle a big chunk of the boring parts. If Blender's Graph Editor gives you the ability to procedurally manipulate f-curves with modifiers much in the same way that you can with meshes, that's something worth knowing about.

The preceding section addresses modifiers when covering the cyclic curve extrapolation mode (Shift E). The Cycles modifier described there is one of a handful of f-curve modifiers that you can add. The following is a brief rundown of each of the f-curve modifier's that Blender offers:

✔ **Generator:** This modifier generates a new curve based on basic mathematical formulas for lines, parabolic lines, and some more advanced curve shapes. Unless you use additive mode, it completely disregards any existing keyframes on your f-curve.

✔ **Built-In Function:** This modifier generates a curve based on a different set of mathematical formulas than the Generator f-curve modifier. The formulas in this modifier are more naturally cyclic, like sine waves and tangent curves. Like the Generator f-curve modifier, this modifier also completely disregards any existing keyframes on your f-curve unless you use additive mode.

✔ **Envelope:** Though it can be a bit difficult to control, the Envelope f-curve modifier is extremely powerful. It's like the envelopes in audio processing software. You can add control points to define upper and lower thresholds for your f-curve. Any values in the f-curve beyond those thresholds (outside of the envelope) are *attenuated* (reduced so they fit within the envelope's bounds).

✔ **Cycles:** As covered previously in this chapter, this f-curve modifier duplicates your existing keyframes, repeating them over time.

✔ **Noise:** With the Noise f-curve modifier, you can add random variation to your f-curve.

Used judiciously, this modifier can bring a lot of life to an animation. For example, you could animate a car rolling along a bumpy road without actually creating those bumps at all.

✔ **Python:** With a little bit of programming knowledge, you can use Python to have nearly unlimited control over the behavior of an f-curve. Python coding, however, is an advanced topic and out of the scope of this book.

✔ **Limits:** This f-curve modifier is similar to the Envelope f-curve modifier, except you can't set arbitrary control points. You just have minimum and maximum X- and Y-axis control values for your f-curve. Also, rather than attenuating your f-curve when it exceeds those controls, the Limits f-curve modifier simply *clips*, or cuts off the overshoot segments of the f-curve.

✔ **Stepped Interpolation:** Using the Stepped Interpolation f-curve modifier, you can give your f-curve a stepped appearance as it goes from one keyframe to the next. It would be like using constant interpolation on your f-curve and inserting a keyframe on every frame of your animation. This can be useful if you want to give your animation a strobed or stop-motion look.

Figure 10-10 shows the panel for each of the f-curve modifiers.

Like the modifiers that affect your 3D objects (see Chapter 5), you can stack f-curve modifiers so each one contributes to the one before it. For example, you could start with the Built-In Function f-curve modifier on your object's Z location to have your object move up and down sinusoidally. Then you could add a Noise f-curve modifier so it stutters a bit as it moves up and down.

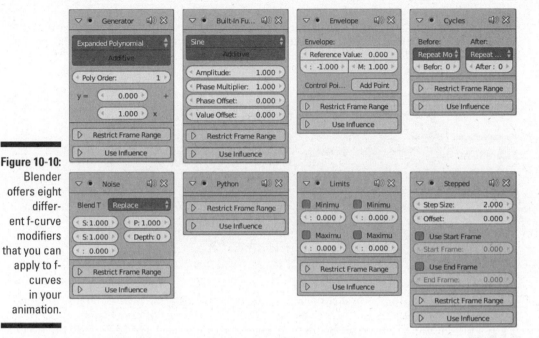

Figure 10-10:
Blender offers eight different f-curve modifiers that you can apply to f-curves in your animation.

Using Constraints Effectively

Occasionally, I get into conversations with people who assume that because there's a computer involved, good CG animation takes less time to make than traditional animation. In most cases, this assumption isn't true. High-quality work takes roughly the same amount of time, regardless of the tool. The time is just spent in different places. Whereas in traditional animation, a very large portion of the time is spent drawing the in-between frames, CG animation lets the computer handle that detail. However, traditional animators don't have to worry as much about optimizing for render times, tweaking and re-tweaking simulated effects, or modeling, texturing, and rigging characters.

That said, computer animation does give you the opportunity to cut corners in places and make your life as an animator much simpler. Constraints are one feature that fit this description perfectly. Literally speaking, a *constraint* is a limitation put on one object by another, allowing the unconstrained object to control the behavior of the constrained one.

With constraints, you can do quite a lot without doing much at all. Animation is hard work; it's worth it to be lazy whenever you can.

To see the actual constraints that you have available, go to Constraint Properties and left-click the Add Constraint button. Alternatively, you can press Shift+Ctrl+C in the 3D View. Either way, you see a menu similar to the one in Figure 10-11.

Figure 10-11: The types of constraints available by default within Blender.

In Chapter 4, I present a mnemonic for remembering how the parenting operation relates to the active object (children first!). For constraints, the mnemonic is a little bit backward because the active object is actually the object you're constraining. Because a constraint, by definition, restricts an object in some way, that object basically becomes a kind of prisoner. So for constraints, I think, "Prisoners last." And there you have it, a handy mnemonic device for remembering selection order when parenting or constraining: children first (parenting) and prisoners last (constraining).

Because of limitations to this book's page count, I can't cover the function of each and every constraint in full detail. However, the remaining sections in this chapter cover features found in most constraints and some usage examples for more frequently used constraints.

The all-powerful Empty!

Of all the different types of objects available to you in Blender, none of them are as useful or versatile in animation as the humble Empty. An Empty isn't much — just a little set of axes that indicate a position, orientation, and size in 3D space. Empties don't even show up when you render. However, Empties are an ideal choice for use as control objects, and they're a phenomenal way to take advantage of constraints.

Empties can be displayed in the 3D View in a number of ways. Because an Empty can be used as a control for constraints and animations, sometimes it's useful to have it displayed with a particular shape. The following display types are available for Empties:

- ✔ **Plain Axes:** Think of this as the default display type. It's just a set of 3D crosshairs.

- ✔ **Arrows:** Occasionally, it's worthwhile to know specifically which axis is facing which direction on your Empty. This display type labels each axis in its positive direction.

- ✔ **Single Arrow:** This display type works great for a minimalist control. The arrow points along the Empty's local Z-axis.

- ✔ **Circle:** If you want an unobtrusive animation control, the Circle display type is a good choice. It allows your Empty to be located inside a volume (like an arm or leg), but still remain selectable because the circle is outside of it.

- ✔ **Cube:** Choose this display type and your Empty appears like a wireframe cube.

- ✔ **Sphere:** Like the Cube display type, this makes your Empty appear as a wireframe sphere.

- ✔ **Cone:** The Cube and Sphere display types can be handy, but they don't naturally give any indication of direction; you don't know which axis is up. The Cone display type draws your Empty like a wireframe cone with the point going along its local Z-axis.

- ✔ **Image:** With this display type, your Empty appears in the 3D View as a plane with any image you choose mapped to it. This display type isn't particularly useful as a controller for a constraint, but it's pretty useful in modeling. You can have a reference image visible in your 3D View from any direction.

As a practical example of how useful Empties can be, consider that 3D modelers like to have a *turnaround* render of the model they create. Basically, a turnaround render is like taking the model, placing it on a turntable, and spinning it in front of the camera. It's a great way to show off all sides of the model. Now, for simple models, you can just select the model, rotate it in the global Z-axis, and you're done. However, what if the model consists of many objects, or for some reason everything is at a strange angle that looks odd when spun around the Z-axis? Selecting and rotating all those little objects can get time consuming and annoying. A better way of setting up a turnaround is with the following rig:

1. **Add an Empty (Shift+A⇨Empty⇨Plain Axes).**

2. **Grab the Empty to somewhere at the center of the model (G).**

3. **Select the camera and position it so that the model is in the center of view (right-click, G).**

4. **Add the Empty to your selection (Shift+right-click).**

5. **Make the Empty the camera's parent (Ctrl+P⇨Object).**

6. **Select the Empty and insert a rotation keyframe (right-click, I⇨Rotation).**

7. **Move forward in time 50 frames.**

8. **Rotate the Empty 90 degrees in the Z-axis and insert a new rotation keyframe (R⇨Z⇨90, I⇨Rotation).**

   The camera obediently matches the Empty's rotation.

9. **Bring up the Graph Editor and set the extrapolation mode for the Z Rotation channel to linear extrapolation (Shift+F6, left-click, Shift+E⇨Linear Extrapolation).**

10. **Switch back to the 3D View and set it to use the camera view. Then playback the animation (Shift+F5, Numpad 0, Alt+A).**

   In the 3D View, you see your model spinning in front of your camera.

In this setup, the Empty behaves as the control for the camera. Imagine that a beam extends from the Empty's center to the camera's center and that rotating the Empty is the way to move that beam.

Adjusting the influence of a constraint

One of the most useful settings that's available to all constraints is at the bottom of each constraint block: the Influence slider. This slider works on a scale from 0 to 1, with 0 being the least amount of influence and 1 being the largest amount. With this slider, you have the capability of just partially being influenced by the target object's attributes. There's more to it, though.

You can animate any attribute in the Properties editor by right-clicking it and choosing Insert Keyframe (or pressing I with your mouse cursor hovered over that property), which means you can easily animate the influence of the constraint. If you key the Influence value of a constraint, a curve for that influence becomes visible in the Graph Editor.

Say that you're working on an animation that involves a character with telekinetic powers using his ability to make a ball fly to his hand. You can do that by animating the influence of a Copy Location constraint (see the "Copying the movement of another object" section) on the ball. The character's hand is the target, and you start with 0 influence. Then, when you want the ball to fly to his hand, you increase the influence to 1 and set a new keyframe. KERPLOW! Telekinetic character!

Using vertex groups in constraints

Many constraints have a Vertex Group field that appears after choosing a valid mesh object in the Target field. In the Vertex Group field, you can type or choose the name of a vertex group in the parent mesh. When you do, the constrained object is bound only to those specific vertices. (See Chapter 11 for details on how to create a vertex group.) After you choose a vertex group from the Vertex Group field of your constraint, the relationship line from the constrained object changes to point to the vertices in that group. Figure 10-12 shows a Suzanne head with a Child Of constraint bound to a vertex group consisting of a single vertex on a circle mesh.

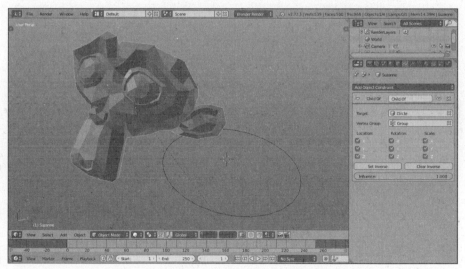

Figure 10-12: Parenting an object to a vertex group.

Copying the movement of another object

Using simple parenting is helpful in quite a few instances, but it's often not as flexible as you need it to be. You can't control or animate the parenting influence or use only the parent object's rotation without inheriting the location and scale as well. And you can't have movement of the parent object in the global X-axis influence the child's local X-axis location. More often than not, you need these sorts of refined controls rather than the somewhat ham-fisted Ctrl+P parenting approach.

To this end, a set of constraints provide you with just this sort of control: Copy Location, Copy Rotation, and Copy Scale. Figure 10-13 shows what each constraint looks like when added in Constraint Properties.

You can mix and match multiple constraints on a single object in a way that's very similar to the way you can add multiple modifiers to an object. So if you need both a Copy Location and a Copy Rotation constraint, just add both. After you add them, you can change which order they come in the stack to make sure that they suit your needs.

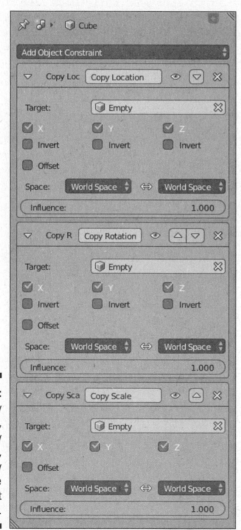

Figure 10-13: The Copy Location, Copy Rotation, and Copy Scale constraint controls.

Words and picture aren't always the best way of explaining how constraints work. It's often more to your benefit to see them in action. To that end, the website that accompanies this book has a few example files that illustrate how these constraints work. It's worth it to load them up in Blender and play with them to really get a good sense for how these very powerful tools work.

Probably the most apparent thing about these Copy constraints is how similar their options are to one another. The most critical setting, however, is the object that you choose in the Target field. If you're using an Empty as your control object, this is where you choose that Empty or type its name (as mentioned in other chapters, you can also hover your mouse over the Target field and press E to enable Blender's eyedropper feature to let you click on the target object). Until you do so, the Constraint Name field at the top of the constraint block remains bright red and the constraint simply won't work.

Below the Target field are a series of six check boxes. The X, Y, and Z check boxes are enabled by default, and beneath them are corresponding disabled check boxes, each labeled Invert. These six check boxes control which axis or axes the target object influences. If the axis check box is enabled and the Invert check box below it is also enabled, the target object has an inverted influence on the constrained object in that axis. Using the preceding Copy Location example, if you disable the X check box and then grab the Empty and move it in the X-axis (G⇨X), the cube remains perfectly still. However, enabling the X check box as well as the Invert check box beneath it causes the cube to translate in an opposite X direction when you move the target Empty.

Next up is the Offset check box, which is useful if you've already adjusted your object's location, rotation, or scale prior to adding the constraint. By default, this feature is off, so the constrained object replicates the target object's behavior completely and exactly. With it enabled, though, the object adds the target object's transformation to the constrained object's already set location, rotation, or scale values. The best way to see this is to create a Copy Location constraint with the following steps:

1. **Start with the default scene (Ctrl+N).**

2. **Grab the default cube to a different location (G).**

3. **Add an Empty (Shift+A⇨Empty⇨Plain Axes).**

4. **Add the cube to your current selection and put a Copy Location constraint on it (Shift+right-click, Shift+Ctrl+C⇨Copy Location).**

   The cube automatically snaps directly to the Empty's location.

5. **Left-click the Offset check box in the Copy Location constraint within Constraint Properties.**

   The cube goes back to its original position. Grab (G) the Empty and its location influences the cube's location from there.

Putting limits on an object

Often when you animate objects, it's helpful to prevent objects from being moved, rotated, or scaled beyond a certain extent. Say that you're animating a character trapped inside a glass dome. As an animator, it can be helpful if Blender forces you to keep that character within that space. Sure, you *could* just pay attention to where your character is and visually make sure that he doesn't accidentally go farther than he should be allowed, but why do the extra work if you can have Blender do it for you? Figure 10-14 shows the constraint options for most of the limiting constraints Blender offers you.

Figure 10-14: The options for the limiting constraints that Blender offers you.

Here are descriptions of what each constraint does:

- **Limit Location/Rotation/Scale:** Unlike most of the other constraints, these three don't have a target object to constrain them. Instead, they're limitations on what the object can do within its own space. For any of them, you can define minimum and maximum limits in the X, Y, and Z axes. You enable limits by left-clicking their corresponding check boxes and define those limits in the value fields below each one.

  The For Transform check box that's in each of these constraints can be pretty helpful when animating. To better understand what it does, go to the Properties region in the 3D View (N). If you have limits and For Transform is not enabled, the values in the Properties region change even after you reach the limits defined by the constraint. However, if you enable For Transform, the values in the Properties region are clipped to the limitations you defined with the constraint.

✔ **Limit Distance:** This constraint is similar to the previous ones except it relates to the distance from the origin of a target object. The Clamp Region menu gives you three ways to use this distance:

- **Inside:** The constrained object can only move within the sphere of space defined by the Distance value.

- **Outside:** The constrained object can never enter the sphere of space defined by the Distance value.

- **On Surface:** The constrained object is always the same distance from the target object, no more and no less.

  The On Surface name is a bit misleading. Your object isn't limited to the surface of the target object; it's limited to the surface of an imaginary sphere with a radius equal to the Distance value.

✔ **Floor:** Technically, the Floor constraint is listed as a Relationship constraint, but I tend to think of it more as a limiting constraint. It uses the origin of a target object to define a plane that the origin of the constrained object can't move beyond. So, technically, you can use this constraint to define more than a floor; you can also use it to define walls and a ceiling as well. Remember, though, that this constraint defines a plane. If your target object is an uneven surface, it doesn't use that object's geometry to define the limit of the constrained object, just its origin. Despite this limitation, this constraint is actually quite useful, especially if you enable the Use Rotation check box. This option allows the constrained object to recognize the rotation of the target object so that you can have an inclined floor, if you like.

When animating while using constraints, particularly limiting constraints, it's in your best interest to insert keyframes using Visual Location and Visual Rotation, as opposed to plain Location and Rotation. Using the visual keying types sets the keyframe to where the object is located visually, within the limits of the constraint, rather than how you actually transformed the object. For example, assume that you have a Floor constraint on an object that you're animating to fall from some height and land on a floor plane that's even with the XY grid. For the landing, you grab (G) the object and move your mouse cursor 4 units below the XY grid. Of course, because of the constraint, your object stops following the mouse when it hits the floor. Now, if you insert a regular Location keyframe here, the Z-axis location of the object is set to –4.0 even though the object can't go below 0. However, if you insert a Visual Location key, the object's Z-axis location is set to what you see it as: 0. If you enable the For Transform check box on all of your constraints, you can get similar behavior and just use regular (non-visual) location and rotation keyframing.

Tracking the motion of another object

Tracking constraints are another set of helpful constraints for animation. Their basic purpose is to make the constrained object point either directly at or in the general direction of the target object. Tracking constraints are useful for controlling the eye movement of characters or building mechanical rigs like pistons. Figure 10-15 shows the options for three of Blender's tracking constraints.

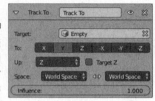
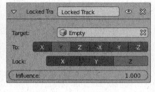

Following are descriptions of each tracking constraint:

- **Track To:** Of these constraints, this one is the most straightforward. In other programs, this constraint may be referred to as the Look At constraint, and that's what it does. It forces the constrained object to point at the target object. The best way to see how this constraint works is to go through the following steps:

    • **Load the default scene (Ctrl+N).**

    • **Add a Track To constraint to the camera with the target object being the cube (right-click the cube, Shift+right-click the camera, Shift+Ctrl+C⇨Track To).**

    • **In the buttons next to the To label, left-click -Z.**

    • **In the Up drop-down menu, choose the Y-axis.**

    Now, no matter where you move the camera, it always points at the cube's origin. By left-clicking the X, Y, and Z buttons next to the To label and choosing an axes from the Up drop-down menu, you can control how the constrained object points relative to the target.

✔ **Locked Track:** The Locked Track constraint is similar to the Track To constraint, with one large exception: It only allows the constrained object to rotate on a single axis, so the constrained object points in the general direction of the target, but not necessarily directly at it. A good way to think about the Locked Track constraint is to imagine that you're wearing a neck brace. With the brace on, you can't look up or down; you can rotate your head only left and right. So if a bird flies overhead, you can't look up to see it pass. All you can do is turn around and hope to see the bird flying away.

✔ **Stretch To:** This constraint isn't exactly a tracking constraint like Track To and Locked Track, but its behavior is similar. The Stretch To constraint makes the constrained object point toward the target object like the Track To constraint. However, this constraint also changes the constrained object's scale relative to its distance to the target, stretching that object toward the target. And the Stretch To constraint can even preserve the volume of the constrained object to make it seem like it's really stretching. This constraint is great for cartoony effects, as well as for controlling organic deformations, such as rubber balls and the human tongue. On a complex character rig, you can use the Stretch To constraint to help simulate muscle bulging.

Chapter 11

Discovering the Tools Used in Rigging

In This Chapter

▶ Making shape keys

▶ Taking advantage of hooks

▶ Working with armatures to control characters

*W*hen it comes to character animation, a character is often a single seamless mesh. As a single seamless mesh, it's virtually impossible to animate that character with any detailed movement using the object animation techniques in Chapter 10. I mean, you can move the whole character mesh at once from one location to another, but you can't make the character smile or wiggle her toes or even bend her arms. You can break the mesh apart and use a complex set of parenting and constraints, but then you lose its nice seamlessness.

What you really want to do is find ways to animate specific parts of the mesh in a controlled manner without tearing the mesh apart. To do so, you need to create a rig for your character. A *rig* is an underlying structure for your mesh that allows you to control how it moves. Rigs are an integral part of modern computer animation, and if done well, they make the life of an animator monumentally easier. Think about it like turning your 3D mesh into a remote-control puppet. This chapter explains the various tools and techniques used to create more complex rigs. Then you can create a rig for nearly any object in Blender and have a blast animating it. The website www.blenderbasics.com has an example tutorial that takes you from beginning to end on rigging a simple character.

Creating Shape Keys

Whether you have to animate a character or a tree or a basketball with any detail, it has to deform from its original shape to a new one. If you know what this new shape looks like, you can model it ahead of time.

As an example, say that you have a cartoony character — maybe the head of a certain Blender monkey. You know that you're going to need her eyes to bulge out because, that happens to all cartoon characters' eyes. One way to create this effect in Blender is by creating a *shape key,* sometimes called a morph target or a blend shape in other programs. A rough outline of the process goes something like this (the next section in this chapter goes into more detail):

1. **Start with your original mesh.**

2. **Edit the vertices of the original mesh *without creating new geometry* to the new pose you want to use.**

   In the cartoony character example, you'd model the character's eyes all bulgy. (Yes, *bulgy* is a real word. I think.)

3. **Record this new arrangement of your vertices as a shape key to be used later when you animate.**

Creating new shapes

Assuming that you selected an object that supports shape keys (meshes, curves, surfaces, and lattices), you can start adding shape keys in the Shape Keys panel of Object Data Properties (Object Data Properties is the generic name for Mesh Properties, and Curve Properties).

Figure 11-1 shows three different states for the Shape Keys panel. By default, this panel looks pretty innocent and empty with just a list box and a few buttons to the right of it. However, when you left-click the Plus (+) button, a *basis shape,* or the original shape that other shape keys relate to, is added to the list. Left-clicking the Plus (+) button a second time gives you an additional set of options that control the change from the basis shape to a new one, named `Key 1`.

The best way to see how to create new shapes is to go through a practical example. Staying with the bug-eyed monkey theme, use Suzanne as your test subject, and follow these steps:

1. **Start with the default scene and delete the cube (Ctrl+N, right-click the cube, X).**

2. **Add Suzanne, give her a Subdivision Surface modifier, and set her smooth (Shift+A⇨Mesh⇨Monkey, Ctrl+1, Tool Shelf⇨Shading⇨Smooth).**

3. **Change to the front view (Numpad 1).**

4. **Add a shape key (Mesh Properties⇨Shape Keys⇨Plus [+]).**

   Your basis shape is created. The other shapes that you create will be relative to this one.

5. **Add a second shape key (Mesh Properties⇨Shape Keys⇨Plus [+]) and rename it, if you want.**

   The Shape Keys panel looks like the last one in Figure 11-1. You've created Key 1. If you want, you can rename it by double-clicking its name field. I named mine Eye Bulge.

6. **In the 3D View, Tab into Edit mode and change the mesh to have bulged eyes**.

   Make sure that your Eye Bulge shape key is active in the Shape Keys panel before making adjustments. As you modify the mode, be sure that you *do not add or remove any geometry* in the mesh. You should define the shape by moving around the vertices, edges, and faces you already have. A quick way to make Suzanne's eyes bulge is to move your mouse cursor over each eye and press L to select just the vertices there. Then with proportional editing (O) turned on, scale (S) the eyes.

7. **Tab back to Object mode.**

Figure 11-2 illustrates this process.

This process creates two shape keys: Basis and Eye Bulge. With the Eye Bulge shape key selected in the Shape Keys panel, you can use the Value slider to smoothly transition from the Basis shape to the Eye Bulge shape. A value of 0 means that Eye Bulge has no influence and you just have the Basis, whereas a value of 1 means that you're fully at the Eye Bulge shape.

Figure 11-1: The three different sets of options that the Shape Keys panel can provide you.

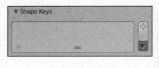

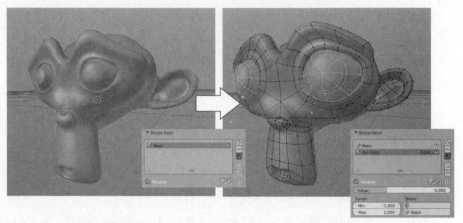

Figure 11-2:
Creating a
bug-eyed
shape key
for Suzanne.

But here's where things get really cool. Notice the Min and Max values at the bottom of the panel, labeled Range. The Min is set to 0.000, and the Max is set to 1.000. Just for kicks, change the Max value to 2.000 and pull the slider all the way to the right. Your bulged eyes grow larger than your actual shape key made them. Now change the Min value to –1.000 and pull the slider to the left. Now Suzanne's eyes pinch in to a point smaller than the Basis pose. Figure 11-3 shows the results of these changes. Adjusting the Min and Max Range values is a great way to provide even more extreme shapes for your characters without having to do any additional shape key modeling. How's that for cool?

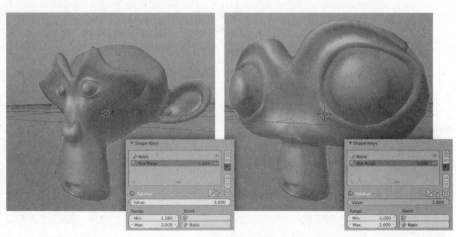

Figure 11-3:
Suzanne
with exces-
sively
bulged and
pinched
eyes, just
by changing
the minimum
and maxi-
mum values
for a single
shape key.

Mixing shapes

From this point, you can create additional shape keys for the mesh. Say that you want to have a shape key of Suzanne's mouth getting bigger, like she's screaming because her eyes have gotten so huge. The process is about the same as when creating your initial shapes:

1. **Add a new shape key (Mesh Properties⇨Shape Keys⇨Plus [+]).**

   Feel free to name this key whatever you want. I called mine `Scream`.

2. **Tab into Edit mode and model the mouth open with the existing vertices.**

   Make sure that you're not touching Suzanne's eyes. You're just editing the mouth to get bigger.

3. **Tab back into Object mode.**

Figure 11-4 shows the results of this process.

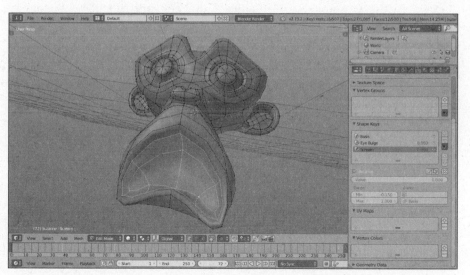

Figure 11-4: Creating a scream shape key.

After you have the `Scream` shape key created, you can freely mix it with the `Eye Bulge` shape key, or you can have Suzanne screaming with her regular, bulge-free eyes. The choice is yours. You have the flexibility here to mix and match your shape keys as it pleases you. And animating the mesh to use these keys is really easy.

In Blender, "(almost) everything is animatable," so animating shape keys is as easy as inserting keyframes on the Value slider in the Shape Keys panel. (Right-click the Value field⇨Insert Keyframe or hover your mouse over that field and press I.) Now you can scrub the timeline cursor forward in time and watch Suzanne bulge and scream to your complete delight.

To see another nice little bonus, split off a Graph Editor from your 3D View. If you enable the Show Sliders feature in the Graph Editor (View⇨Show Sliders), you can see the numeric values for your shape keys' influences and even key them right there.

Knowing where shape keys are helpful

Now, you *could* do an entire animation using shape keys. But do I recommend it? No. You can control your meshes in other ways that may give you more natural movement for things like animating arms and legs.

That said, shape keys are the perfect choice for things that you can't do with these other means (or, at least, that are very difficult). A big one is facial animation. The way parts of the face wrinkle up and move around is pretty difficult to re-create without modeling those deformations. Furrowed brows, squinty eyes, natural-looking smiles, and *phonemes*, or mouth shapes for lip-syncing, are where shape keys shine. You can also team them with other controls discussed throughout this chapter to achieve cool effects like cartoon stretchiness, muscle bulges, and morphing objects from one shape to another.

Adding Hooks

Shape keys work well for getting specific predefined deformations, but they can be pretty limiting if you want to have a little bit looser control over your mesh or if you're animating things that move in arcs. For these sorts of situations, you have another control mechanism: hooks. *Hooks* are a special kind of modifier that takes a set of vertices or control points and binds them to be controlled by another object, usually an Empty.

Creating new hooks

The workflow for adding a hook is pretty straightforward. You tab into Edit mode and select at least one vertex or control point. Then you press Ctrl+H⇨Hook to New Object. An Empty is created at a location that's the median point of all your selected vertices or control points. You also get a new modifier added to in Modifier Properties, as shown in Figure 11-5.

Figure 11-5:
Control
options for
the Hook
modifier.

Tab back into Object mode and transform the hook. All the vertices or control points that you assigned to the hook move with it. And using the options in the Hook modifier, you can control how much influence the hook has over these vertices or control points. The following example gives you a clearer understanding of adding and modifying the influence of hooks:

1. **Start with the default scene in Blender (Ctrl+N).**

2. **Select the cube and tab into Edit mode.**

   All the cube's vertices are selected by default. If not, press A until the vertices are selected.

3. **Do a multi-subdivide with four cuts (W⇨Subdivide, F6⇨Number of Cuts: 4).**

4. **Select one of the cube's corner vertices (right-click).**

5. **Press Ctrl+Numpad Plus (+) a few times to increase the vertex selection.**

6. **Add a new hook (Ctrl+H⇨Hook to New Empty).**

7. **Tab back into Object mode.**

   At this point, behavior is as expected. If you select and move the Empty, all the vertices that hooked to it move as if they're parented to it.

8. **With the cube selected, increase the Falloff value in the Hook modifier to 1.00 (Modifier Properties⇨Hook-Empty⇨Falloff: 1.00).**

   Now when you select and transform the Empty, the way the vertices follow it is much smoother, kind of like when you're modeling with proportional editing (O). For additional kicks, do the next step.

9. **Add a Subdivision Surface modifier to the cube and have it drawn smooth (Ctrl+1, Tool Shelf⇨Shading⇨Smooth).**

Now the transition is even smoother, as shown in Figure 11-6.

Vertices aren't just bound to their hook's location. They're also controlled by the hook's scale and rotation. You can really get some wild and complex deformations using this deceptively simple feature.

Knowing where hooks are helpful

The best use for hooks is for large organic deformations. Like shape keys, hooks are nice for creating muscle bulges and cartoony stretching. You can even use them along with shape keys. Because shape keys always use the same shape as the basis for deformation, adding a hook can bring a bit more variety. For example, in the bug-eyed Suzanne example from the "Creating Shape Keys" section, you can add a hook for one of the eyes to make it bulge asymmetrically. These touches give more *character* to your 3D characters.

Another great use for hooks is in animating curves in the 3D View. All the steps in the previous examples of this section work for curves and surfaces as well as meshes. If you have a curve that you're using as a character's tail, you can add a hook at each control point. Then you can animate that tail moving around.

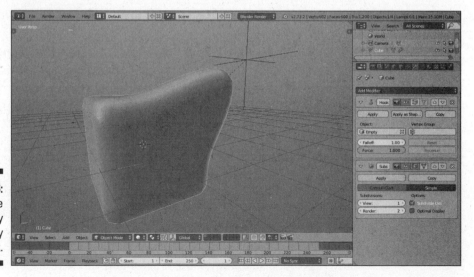

Figure 11-6:
A cube smoothly deformed by a hook.

Using Armatures: Skeletons in the Mesh

Shape keys and hooks are great ways to deform a mesh, but the problem with them is that both are lacking a good underlying structure. They're great for big, cartoony stretching and deformation, but for a more structured deformation, like an arm bending at the elbow joint, the motion that they produce is pretty unnatural looking. To solve this problem, 3D computer animation took a page from one of its meatspace contemporaries, stop-motion animation. *Stop-motion animation* involves small sculptures that typically feature a metal skeleton underneath them, referred to as an *armature*. The armature gives the model both structure and a mechanism for making and holding poses. Blender has an object that provides a similar structure for CG characters. It, too, is called an armature. Armatures form the basis of nearly all Blender rigs.

To add an armature to your scene, go to the 3D View and press Shift+A⟹ Armature⟹Single Bone. As Figure 11-7 shows, adding an armature creates a single object with a weird shape called an octahedron. Continuing to use the skeleton analogy, that octahedron is referred to as a bone in the armature. The wide end of the bone is referred to as the bone's head or root, and its narrow end is referred to as the bone's tail or tip. Typically, a bone pivots at the head.

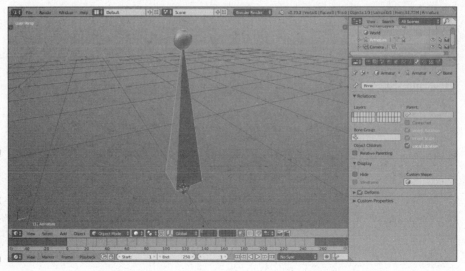

Figure 11-7:
An armature object with a single bone. Woohoo!

Editing armatures

You can take a rather inauspicious single bone armature and do something more interesting with it. Like nearly every other object in Blender, you can edit the armature in more detail by selecting it (right-click) and tabbing into Edit mode. In Edit mode, you can select the sphere at the bone's head, the sphere at the bone's tail, as well as the bone itself. (Selecting the bone body actually selects both the head and tail spheres as well.) You can add a new bone to your armature in five ways:

- ✔ **Extrude:** Select either the head or tail of the bone and press E to extrude a new bone from that point. This method is the most common way to add new bones to an armature. If you add a bone by extruding from the tail, you get the additional benefit of having an instant parent-child relationship. The new bone is the child of the one you extruded it from. These bones are linked together, tail to head, and referred to as a bone *chain*. The Ctrl+left-click extrude shortcut for meshes and curves also works for bones.

- ✔ **Duplicate:** Select the body of the bone you want and press Shift+D to duplicate it and create a new bone with the same dimensions, parent relationships, and constraints.

- ✔ **Subdivide:** Select the body of the bone you want and press W⇨Subdivide. You see two bones in the space that the one you selected used to occupy. The cool thing about this option is that it keeps the new bone in the correct parent-child relationship of the bone chain. Also, you can use the Last Operations panel (F6) and do multiple subdivisions.

- ✔ **Adding:** Press Shift+A while still in Edit mode. A new bone is created with its head at the location of the 3D cursor.

- ✔ **Skeleton sketching:** This somewhat advanced feature is incredibly useful for some of the more complex rigging tasks. If you want to try out skeleton sketching, pop open the 3D View's Properties region (N), enable the Skeleton Sketching check box, and expand its panel at the bottom of the region. The fastest way to see what skeleton sketching does is to enable the Quick Sketching check box. Now, when you left-click and drag your mouse cursor in the 3D View, a red line appears in the view. By simply clicking in the screen, you can draw single straight lines. After you're done drawing, right-click, and Blender generates bones along the line you drew.

Armatures can get very complex very quickly, so you should name your bones as you add them. Let me say that again: *Name your bones as you add them.*

The fastest way to name your bones is from the Item panel in the 3D View's Properties region (N). From there, you edit the names of your bones the same way you edit names of other Blender objects. Left-click the name in the Bone field and type the name of a bone that makes sense. Alternatively, you can go to Bone Properties and change the name of your bone from the text field at the top. As an example, if you have a two-bone chain to control a character's arm, you may name one bone `arm_upper` and the other `arm_lower`.

Unfortunately, both these techniques can be really slow if you're trying to name a lot of bones at once (because maybe, ahem, you forgot to name your bones as you were adding them). For this hopefully rare case, the Outliner is the best tool for the job. Expand the Armature object to reveal the hierarchy of bones within it. Double-click the name of any bone (or any object, for that matter), and you can rename it right there. Figure 11-8 shows the three places where you can name your bones.

Blender has a pretty cool way of understanding *symmetric rigs,* or rigs that have a left side that's identical to the right. For these cases, use a `.L` and `.R` suffix on your bone names. So in the previous example, if you're rigging a character with two arms, the bones in the left arm would be named `arm_upper.L` and `arm_lower.L`. The right arm bones would be named `arm_upper.R` and `arm_lower.R`. This naming convention gives you a couple of advantages, but the one that's most apparent when modeling your rig is the X-Axis Mirror feature.

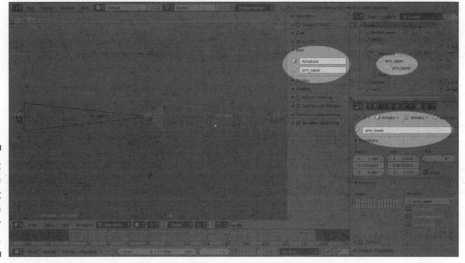

Figure 11-8:
Three
different
ways to
name your
bones.

To understand how symmetric rigs and X-axis mirroring work better, create a new armature at the origin (Shift+S⇨Cursor to Center, Shift+A⇨Armature⇨Single Bone) and follow these steps:

1. **Tab into Edit mode on your armature and change to front view (Numpad 1).**

2. **Rename the single bone to `root`.**

   It's common convention in rigging to use this name for the main parent bone in the rig.

3. **Select the tail of your root bone and extrude a bone to the right (E).**

4. **Name this newly extruded bone `Bone.R`.**

5. **Select the tail of your root bone again and extrude another new bone, but this time to the left (E).**

6. **Name this bone `Bone.L`.**

7. **In the Options tab of the Tool Shelf (T), enable the X-Axis Mirror check box.**

8. **Select the tail of `Bone.R` and grab it to move it around (G).**

   Now, wherever you move the tail of this bone, the tail of `Bone.L` matches that movement on the other side of the X-axis. You can even extrude (E) a new bone, and a new bone is extruded on both sides of the axis. In this way, X-axis mirroring can speed up the rigging process immensely.

 When editing bones, it's a good idea to make visible the mesh for which your rig is intended. This way, you get your proportions correct. A good general rule for placing bones is to think about where the character's real anatomical bones would be located and then use that as a guideline.

Parenting bones

One important thing that makes armatures helpful is the notion of how its bones relate to one another. The most important of these relationships is the parent-child relationships between bones. The same hotkeys for parenting and unparenting objects also work with bones, but with a couple additional features. To illustrate the additional features when parenting bones, start a new scene (Ctrl+N), delete the default cube (X), add a new armature object (Shift+A⇨Armature⇨Single Bone), and then tab into Edit mode. Then follow these steps:

1. **Select the single bone created, duplicate it, and place it somewhere in space (right-click, Shift+D).**

2. **Add the original bone to your selection (Shift+right-click).**

3. Press Ctrl+P to make the original bone the parent of the duplicate.

You're given two options:

- **Connected:** This option moves the entire child bone so its head is in the same location as the tail of the parent, creating a bone chain as if you'd created the second bone by extruding it up from the first.

- **Keep Offset:** Choosing this option leaves the child bone in place and draws a dashed relationship line between the two bones. They're not connected, but one still has an influence on the other, kind of like regular parenting between objects.

4. After you create the parent relationship, select the child bone.

5. Clear the parent relationship by pressing Alt+P.

You have another pair of options:

- **Clear Parent:** This option removes any sort of parent-child relationship this bone has. If the bone was connected to the parent bone, it's now disconnected, and you can move it around freely. Note that this *does not* reposition the child bone back to where you first placed it

- **Disconnect Bone:** This option doesn't actually clear the parent relationship. Instead, if your bones are connected, choosing this option maintains the parent-child relationship, but the child bone can move independently of the parent's tip. The bone behaves as if you made the parent by using the Keep Offset option.

Figure 11-9 shows how two bones in an armature can be related.

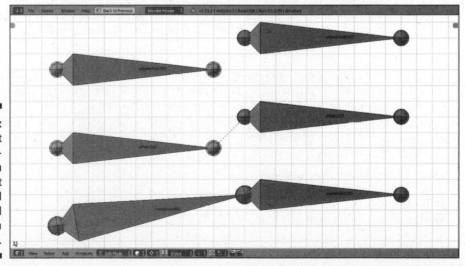

Figure 11-9: Bones that are unparented, with an offset parent, and parented with a connection.

Even with bones parented — connected or otherwise — if you rotate the parent bone, the child doesn't rotate with it as you might expect in a typical parent-child relationship. That's because you're still in Edit mode, which is designed mostly for building and modifying the armature's structure. The parent-child relationship actually works in a special mode for armatures called Pose mode. You access this mode by either pressing Ctrl+Tab or choosing Pose Mode from the Mode menu in the 3D View's header. (If you have the Pie Menus add-on enabled, Pose mode is an option from the pie that appears when you press Tab.)

When you're in Pose mode, if you select individual bones and rotate them, their children rotate with them, as you might expect. From there, you can swap back out to Object mode by pressing Ctrl+Tab again, or you can jump back into Edit mode by just pressing Tab. Chapter 12 has more on working in Pose mode.

Armature properties

When working with armatures, the Properties editor has some sections specific to armatures with options and controls that are incredibly helpful. Select your armature (right-click) and have a look at the Properties editor. In particular, note that in addition to Armature Properties, there are two more sets of properties: Bone Properties and Bone Constraints Properties. Figure 11-10 shows the contents of these panels.

As you may have guessed, Armature Properties provide options for the armature overall, while Bone Properties provide options for the currently selected bone. Looking first at Bone Properties, some options and controls are immediately helpful. The text field at the top lets you rename your bone. The Transform panel gives you precise numeric control over the location of the head and tail of the selected bone, as well as its *roll angle,* or the orientation of the octahedron between the head and the tail, while in Edit mode. These controls are exactly the same as the transform controls in the 3D View's Properties region (N).

In the Relations panel, you can define how the selected bone relates to other bones in the armature. In particular, the Parent field displays the selected bone's current parent, if it has one, and allows you to choose another existing bone as its parent. If you have a parent defined here, the Connected check box beneath it allows you to tell Blender whether it's connected to its parent.

If you enable the Connected check box, the selected bone's head snaps to the location of its parent's tail. However, your selected bone's tail *won't* move. This is a key difference between setting up a parent-child relationship in Bone Properties and using Ctrl+P in the 3D View.

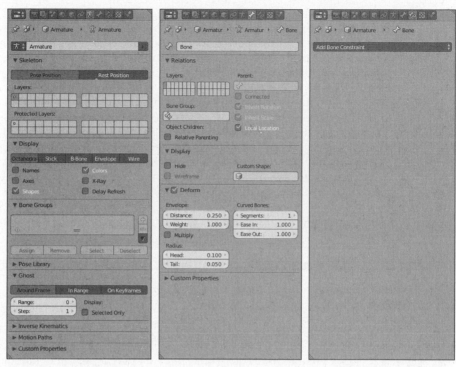

Figure 11-10:
Armature
properties.

On the left side of the Relations panel are a series of buttons, known as *bone layers,* which look like the layers buttons in the 3D View's header. Just as you can place objects on layers in Object mode, Blender's armatures have a special set of layers to themselves. The reason is that character rigs can get pretty involved. Using bone layers is a good way to keep the rig logical and organized. Left-click a layer button to assign the bone to it. If you'd like the bone to live on more than one layer, you can Shift+left-click the buttons for those layers. To add your bone to a lot of layers all at once, Shift+left-click and drag your mouse cursor over the bone layers.

The options in the various armature-related sections of the Properties editor change a bit between Edit mode (Tab), Object mode, and Pose mode (Ctrl+Tab). What I cover is available in Edit mode and Pose mode.

Two other important sets of controls are in Bone Properties. The first is the Deform panel. Simply put, the check box for this panel is a toggle that tells Blender whether the selected bone can be mapped to the geometry of your mesh. If the mesh's geometry is mapped, or *weighted,* to the bone, then that bone is considered a *deformer.* Deformers should have the Deform check box in Bone Properties enabled.

Besides deformers, you can also have bones whose purpose is to control the behavior of the deformer bones. These bones are often referred to as *control* bones. To prevent the control bones from inadvertently influencing your mesh's geometry, you want to make sure that the Deform check box is disabled in Bone Properties.

Back in Armature Properties, there are two sets of layer buttons in the Skeleton panel. These buttons correspond to the bone layers in Bone Properties. The layer buttons under the Layers label control which layers the armature is actually displaying in the 3D View. The layer buttons under the Protected Layers label have an effect only if you're linking your rig into a separate scene file. That topic is a bit more advanced than what this book covers, so I leave it at that for now.

The Display panel contains a set of buttons for controlling how bones in the armature are displayed:

✔ **Bone display types:** You can enable only one of these four buttons at any point in time. Note, however, that even though the bone display type may not be drawn in the 3D View, its influences are still valid. That is, even if you're displaying Stick bones, they still control the same vertices within the range of the Envelope bones. Figure 11-11 shows examples of each of these bone display types:

   • **Octahedral:** The default bone display type, the octahedral shape is great for building a rig because it shows which way a bone points as well as its roll angle.

   • **Stick:** This display type draws the bones as a thin stick. I like to animate with my bones in this type so that they stay out of my way.

   • **B-Bone:** B-bones are drawn as boxes. The interesting thing, though, is that b-bones can be dynamically subdivided and treated as simple Bézier curves. To increase a bone's subdivisions, select the bone and switch to the Deform panel in Bone Properties. In this panel, increase the Segments value, which makes the deformation from one bone to the next much smoother. Even if you don't display the b-bone type, Blender still pays attention to the Segments value. So if your character deforms in an unexpected way, you may want to check the Segments value in Bone Properties.

   • **Envelope:** This display type draws the bones with a scalable sphere at each end and a tube for the bone body. Vertices on your mesh that are within the influence area of these bones will have their locations influenced by them. Use Alt+S to adjust the size of selected spheres and tubes in this display type. Ctrl+Alt+S increases the bone's range.

- **Wire:** The wire display type is very similar to stick, but it's thinner and even less obtrusive with a thickness of only one pixel. As an additional bonus, this display type also shoes b-bone bending, so it's especially useful and a "working" display type that animators can use.

✔ **Extra display options:** You can enable all, one, or none of these options in any combination you desire.

- **Names:** This check box controls the display of each bone's name in the 3D View. Names can make selecting bones and defining constraints much easier.

- **Axes:** This option toggles the display of the center axis of the bones. The Axes check box is helpful for understanding the bones' true roll angle.

- **Shapes:** To help communicate a bone's purpose to the animator, you can display any bone in Blender as any object in your scene. While in Pose mode, select a bone and go to the Display panel in Bone Properties. There, you can define the object you want as your bone shape by choosing it from the Custom Shape field. With the Shapes check box enabled in Armature Properties, the bone is displayed as your chosen object while in Pose mode.

- **Colors:** To help organize bones in an armature for an animator, you can actually define custom colors for bones by using bone groups (see the website, www.blenderbasics.com). Set all facial controls to blue, or the left side of the armature in red. Enable this check box so that you can make use of those colors.

- **X-Ray:** The X-Ray check box in this panel does the same thing that the X-Ray check box in Object Properties does. It allows you to see the bone in the 3D View, even if it's technically inside or behind another object. Enabling this feature makes your bones easier to see and select when rigging or animating.

- **Delay Refresh:** Rigs by themselves can be very complex. After they have a mesh assigned to them, the system becomes even more complex — sometimes to the point that slower computers can't keep up and perform with any reasonable response. In this type of scenario, enabling this check box may be beneficial because it prevents Blender from trying to calculate how your mesh deforms while you modify a pose on your rig, delaying that calculation until after you finish grabbing, scaling, or rotating a bone.

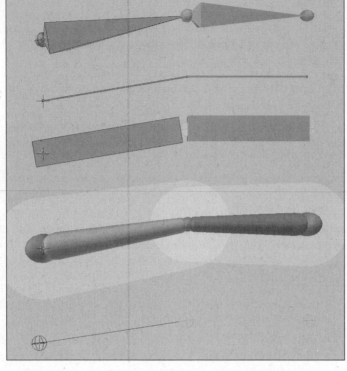

Figure 11-11:
The different display types for bones in Blender from top to bottom: octahedral, stick, b-bone, envelope, and wire.

Putting skin on your skeleton

Armatures and bones are pretty interesting, but they do you no good if they don't actually deform your mesh. When you create your own rig, and Ctrl+Tab to Pose mode, you can grab, rotate, and scale bones, but the moving bones have no influence whatsoever on your mesh. What you need to do is bind the vertices of the mesh to specific bones in your armature. This binding process is commonly referred to as *skinning*. Blender has two primary ways of skinning: envelopes and vertex groups.

Quick-and-dirty skinning with envelopes

Envelopes are the quickest way to get a mesh's vertices to be controlled by the armature. You don't have to create anything extra: It's just a simple parenting operation that seals the deal. To use envelopes to control your mesh, use the following steps:

1. **In Object mode or Pose mode, select the mesh (right-click) and then add the armature to your selection (Shift+right-click).**

2. **Make the armature the parent of the mesh (Ctrl+P).**

   Choose Armature Deform from the menu that appears. Upon completion, your mesh is a child of the armature object, and it also now has an
   Armature modifier applied. The modifier is what allows the armature to
   deform your mesh. Without the modifier, it's just a simple parenting.

   When you Ctrl+Tab into Pose mode on your armature, you may notice
   that the mesh still doesn't appear to be influenced by your armature.
   You need to make a small change in the Armature modifier. Select your
   mesh again and proceed to the next step.

3. **With your mesh selected, enable the Bone Envelopes check box in the
   Armature modifier (Modifier Properties⇨Armature Modifier⇨Bone
   Envelopes).**

   You can also disable the Vertex Groups check box, if you'd like.

4. **Select your armature and go to Armature Properties to enable the
   Envelope bone type.**

   This step reveals exactly where the influence of your envelopes lies.

5. **If some part of your mesh isn't under the influence of an envelope, tab
   into Edit mode and edit its size (Alt+S) and influence (Ctrl+Alt+S).**

   (Actually, if you just want to edit the influence, you can do so directly
   with the Ctrl+Alt+S hotkey combination.)

Figure 11-12 illustrates envelopes in action.

Envelopes are great for quickly roughing out a rig and testing it on your
mesh, but for detailed deformations, they aren't ideal. Where the influence
of multiple envelopes overlap can be particularly problematic, and there's a
good tendency for envelope-based rigs to have characters pinch a bit at their
joints. For these cases, a more detailed approach is necessary.

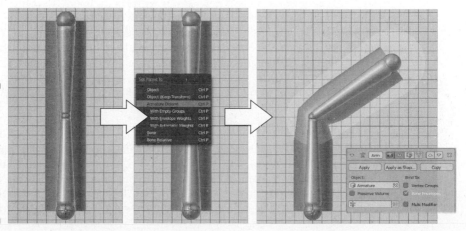

Figure 11-12:
Using enve-
lopes to
control your
armature's
influence
over the
mesh.

That said, using envelopes in your armature does give you one distinct control that you can't have with armatures otherwise. You can actually use an armature with envelopes to control the deformation of curves and surfaces. So long as a control point is within the influence space of a bone's envelope, you can modify it and therefore animate it with the armature.

Assigning weights to vertices

So if envelopes are the imprecise way of controlling your mesh, what's the precise way? The answer is vertex groups. A *vertex group* is basically what it sounds like — a set of vertices that have been assigned to a named group.

In many ways, a vertex group is a lot like a material slot (see Chapter 7). Besides the fact that vertex groups don't deal with materials, vertex groups have a couple of distinctions that set them apart from material slots. First of all, vertex groups aren't mutually exclusive. Any vertex may belong to any number of vertex groups that you define.

A side effect of being able to be a member of multiple groups is another distinction: You can give a vertex a *weight*, or a numerical value that indicates how much that particular vertex is influenced or dedicated to a specific vertex group. A weight of 1.0 means that the vertex is fully dedicated to that group, whereas a weight of 0 means that although the vertex is technically part of the group, it may as well not be.

One thing to note: Vertex groups need to have the exact name of the bones that control them. So if you have a bone called `pelvis`, you need a corresponding vertex group with the same name. The vertices assigned to that group then have their position influenced by the location, rotation, and scale of the pelvis bone, tempered by the vertices' individual weights.

To adjust the assignments and weights of vertices in their respective vertex groups, you can use the Vertex Groups panel in Mesh Properties for your selected mesh. You create a new group with the Plus (+) button to the right of the list box. To select the vertices that you want to assign to the group, you need to tab into Edit mode. With the vertices selected in Edit mode, you can adjust the value in the Weight slider and then assign them to the vertex group by left-clicking the Assign button.

If you don't see the Assign button or Weight slider in the Vertex Groups panel, then you're not in Edit mode. Tab into Edit mode and those controls should appear for you.

Something to note about vertex weights is that, when used for armatures, they are *normalized* to 1.000. That is, a vertex can be a member of two vertex groups and have a weight of 1.000 for both. In these cases, Blender adjusts the weights internally so that they add up to 1.000. So in my example, that double-grouped vertex behaves like it has a weight of 0.500 on both groups.

Of course, on a complex armature, this process of creating vertex groups and painstakingly assigning weights to each vertex can get excessively tedious. Fortunately, Blender has a couple tools to make things less painful. First of all, you don't have to create all the vertex groups by yourself. Refer to the preceding section on the process of skinning with envelopes. By parenting the mesh to the armature there, you're presented with a few options. For using envelopes only, you choose Ctrl+P⇨Armature Deform. However, the other options give you a lot of power when you use vertex groups:

- ✔ **Object:** This option is just a simple parenting operation. Your whole mesh becomes a child of the armature object, just as if you'd parented it to another mesh or an Empty. No modifier is applied to your mesh at all.

- ✔ **Armature Deform:** As in the envelope skinning example of the preceding section, this option doesn't create any vertex groups, thereby ensuring that the mesh is only influenced by the bone envelopes.

  - • **With Empty Groups:** This option creates vertex groups for you using the names of all the bones with the Deform check box enabled in Bone Properties. However, it doesn't automatically assign any vertices to any of those groups. Use this option if you want to manually assign weights. Without assigning any weights, the default behavior is to be controlled only by bone envelopes.

  - • **With Envelope Weights:** This option is a bit of a compromise. It first creates the vertex groups based on the bones with their Deform option turned on. Then it looks at the influence area of the bone envelope and uses that to assign vertices to each vertex group, with their weights varied accordingly. The advantage of this option is that it gets you weighted vertices. The downside, though, is that if the influence area of your envelopes isn't set up well, the weight assignment can look messy.

  - • **With Automatic Weights:** This is my favorite option to use. It works like the With Envelope Weights option, but instead of using the influence area of the bone envelopes to determine weights, it uses a more complex process that generally results in better vertex assignments and weights.

- ✔ **Bone:** This is a simple parenting operation like the Object option. No Armature modifier is applied to your mesh. The only difference here is that rather than parent your mesh to the whole armature object, this option allows you to parent your object to a single bone.

- ✔ **Bone Relative:** This option works like the Bone option, but it doesn't move the child object if the bone is moved in edit mode. This option is handy for specific uses, but it isn't frequently used.

Tweaking vertex weights in Weight Paint mode

Regardless of which option you choose for generating your vertex weights, you'll probably still have to go in and manually tweak the weights of the vertices in each vertex group (unless the object you're trying to rig is incredibly simple). Trying to do those tweaks just from the Vertex Groups panel can be pretty painful. Fortunately, there is Weight Paint mode. This mode is almost exactly like Vertex Paint mode (see Chapter 7), except that rather than painting color on the mesh, you're painting the weight assignment to a specified vertex group.

To access Weight Paint mode from Object mode, select the mesh (right-click) and press Ctrl+Tab. Alternatively, you can choose Weight Paint mode from the Mode menu in the 3D View's header. If you have the Pie Menus add-on enabled, Weight Paint mode is a pie menu option when you press Tab. Even if you don't intend to paint weights, Weight Paint mode is a great way to see how the weights were assigned by Blender if you used the automatic method.

The way that weights are visualized is kind of like a thermal map, where red is the hottest value and blue is the coldest value. Extending this logic to work with bone weights, vertices that are painted red have a weight of 1.0, whereas vertices painted blue are either not assigned to the vertex group or have a weight of zero. The 50 percent weight color is bright green.

If the thermal map color styling isn't your thing (as can be the case if you're colorblind), you can define your own weight paint color range using the ramp editor in the bottom right of the System section of Blender's User Preferences (Ctrl+Alt+U).

When in Weight Paint mode, you get a bunch of painting panels in the Tool Shelf, as shown in Figure 11-13. With a few minor exceptions, these controls are identical to the ones used in Vertex Paint mode.

When weight painting, it's often useful to enable the Wire check box in the Display panel of Object Properties. Enabling this check box overlays the mesh's wireframe on it. Seeing the wireframe is especially helpful when weight painting because it helps you see where the actual vertices on the mesh are. That way, you're not just painting in empty space where no vertices exist. The only slight hiccup is if you're painting *planar vertices,* or vertices that all share the same plane. In this particular case, Blender tries to simplify the wireframe overlay. While that simplification may be nice in general, it can be problematic when painting. To get around that obstacle, enable the Draw All Edges check box in the same Display panel of Object Properties.

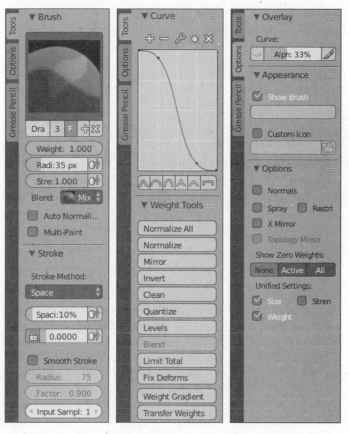

Figure 11-13:
The painting panels in the Tool Shelf when Weight Paint mode is activated.

A handy feature in the Tool Shelf while weight painting is the X-Mirror check box in the Options panel (it's located in the Options tab). X-Mirror can literally cut your weight painting time in half. When you enable this check box, Blender takes advantage of the left/right naming convention discussed earlier in the "Editing armatures" section of this chapter. So if you're tweaking the vertex weights on the left leg, Blender automatically updates the weights for the corresponding bone on the right leg so that they match. If that ain't cool, I don't know what is.

The actual process of weight painting is nearly identical to using vertex paint. However, you need to pay attention to one more thing with weight painting: the need to tell Blender which vertex group you're painting. You can do so in two ways. The slow way, you already know: Select the group from the list box in the Vertex Groups panel in Mesh Properties.

Of course, the kind Blender developers have provided a faster way: you can select (right-click) the bone that you want to paint weights for, even while in Weight Paint mode on your mesh. When you right-click a bone, Blender automatically activates the corresponding vertex group and allows you to paint. As an added bonus, you can test your weights on the fly by grabbing, rotating, or scaling the selected bone while you're still in Weight Paint mode.

To select bones while in Weight Paint mode, be sure that your armature is in Pose mode before selecting your mesh object.

Because weight paint relies so much on color, I highly recommend you look on the Web (perhaps on this book's website) for full-color version meshes in Weight Paint mode.

If you choose to use vertex groups, have a look at the Armature modifier on your mesh. Under the Bind To label are two check boxes: Vertex Groups and Bone Envelopes. By default, only the Vertex Groups check box is enabled. However, both options can be enabled. With both enabled, the mesh is influenced by vertex groups as well as the bone envelopes from your armature. This double influence can be useful in some instances, but most riggers tend to prefer to work with just one or the other. This way, you know that the only reason a vertex is deforming improperly is because its weight isn't assigned properly. You don't have to concern myself with the influence of the bone's envelope.

Chapter 12

Animating Object Deformations

In This Chapter

▶ Becoming familiar with the Dope Sheet

▶ Using armatures for animations

▶ Animating quickly with the Non-Linear Animation Editor

*L*ooking at the title of this chapter, you may find yourself wondering how this chapter is different from Chapter 10. Both chapters cover animation, but this chapter covers the cool things you can do in Blender if you're animating with a fully rigged mesh. Chapter 10 covers what is often referred to as *object animation* — that is, animating the attributes of a single object.

With an animation rig, you have more bits and pieces to manage, keep track of, and control. Managing all that additional complexity can be daunting if you have only the Outliner and the Graph Editor to work with. Fortunately, Blender offers a few more features that help make rigged *character animation* easier to wrap your head around.

Working with the Dope Sheet

So you have a rigged character that you want to animate. Awesome! Change your screen layout to the Animation layout (Ctrl+←⇨Ctrl+←). After that, the first thing that you're probably going to want to do is change the primary 3D View to solid viewport shading (Z), change the Translate manipulator to the Rotate manipulator (Ctrl+Spacebar⇨Rotate if you have the Pie Menus add-on enabled), and set it to Normal orientation (Alt+Spacebar⇨Normal). You should switch to Normal orientation because when you're animating with an armature, most of the time, you're animating bone rotations. By setting the Rotation manipulator to the Normal coordinate space, you can have quick, controlled transformation of bone rotations without having the 3D manipulator get in your way too much. These changes to your work environment in Blender, as well as a few others, are described in more detail in Chapter 10.

The next thing you need to pay attention to is the Dope Sheet. As nice as seeing the Graph Editor may be, seeing all the f-curves for each object and each bone in your scene can quickly get overwhelming. The Timeline shows keys for multiple objects in a simplified way, but you don't have a good way to see which key belongs to which object, and the Timeline provides no tools for actually editing keyframes. You need a different editor — one that gives you a big picture of the keyframes for multiple objects and bones in your animation. And, perhaps more important, this editor allows you to edit the timing of bones, objects, and properties individually. The Dope Sheet (Shift+F12), shown in Figure 12-1, fills those needs.

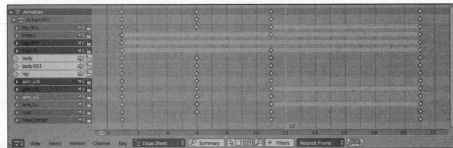

Figure 12-1:
The Dope
Sheet.

In traditional animation, the *dope sheet* was the entire animation planned out, frame by frame on paper, prior to a single pencil line being drawn by the animator. In computer animation, it's taken on a slightly different meaning and purpose, but the core notion of being able to see your entire animation all at once is still there. When you have elements in your scene animated, the Dope Sheet shows a channel for each keyed bone, object, and property.

When it comes to editing the overall timing of a character's performance, the Dope Sheet is really *the* tool for the job.

Like selecting in other parts of Blender, you can select individual keyframes in the Dope Sheet by right-clicking the diamond-shaped keyframe indicator. You can select multiple keyframes in a variety of ways. You can use the familiar Shift+right-click or Border Select (B) functions. However, another way to select keyframes is incredibly helpful. If you have a Dope Sheet open and a few keyframes inserted, right-click any keyframe to select it. Now, with that key selected, press K. This action selects any other key in the armature that's on the same frame as your selected key. This selection method is called a *column key selection,* and it's also available in the Graph Editor. You can get similar functionality with the time cursor. If you place your time cursor on a column of keys and press Ctrl+K, that column of keys is selected, rather than the column with your original selected keys.

Initially, you may not think that column key selection is all that useful. However, if you think about the process used for animating — especially cartoon-style animation — it starts making more sense. The workflow for animation usually goes from one pose to the next. At each pose that you key, multiple bones are all keyed at the same time, forming a column in the Dope Sheet. In fact, unless you're doing some kind of frantic, shaky animations, it's a pretty good practice to make sure that you have nice columns in your Dope Sheet, at least to start. Uneven columns tend to indicate that your timing may be off on a specific part of the rig. Of course, this suggestion is a guideline more than a hard-and-fast rule. As your animation gets closer to being final, your columns will get necessarily messier.

After they're selected, you can manipulate keyframes with grabbing (G) and scaling (S). When performing these actions, there's something you should pay attention to. First of all, when you scale selected keyframes, the scale is relative to the position of the time cursor in the Dope Sheet. So if you want to increase the length of your animation by stretching out the keyframes, put your time cursor at frame 1 before scaling. If you place your time cursor in the middle or at the end, the keys at the beginning of your animation are arranged so that they take place before your animation starts — typically that's something you don't want, so be careful.

By default, the Dope Sheet has Nearest Frame snapping enabled. So when grabbing (G) or scaling (S), your keys snap to the frame to which they are closest. If you disable snapping from the snaps drop-down menu in the Dope Sheet's header by changing it to No Auto-Snap, Blender stops this behavior and allows you to place keys between frames. However, you normally don't want this behavior; usually, it weakens the poses that the audience actually sees.

However, if you do have keys located in-between frames, you can quickly fix that with the Snap Keys feature. Select the keys you want to fix in the Dope Sheet and press Shift+S.

You have four options in this menu:

- ✓ **Current Frame:** This option snaps selected keys to the location of the time cursor in the Dope Sheet.

- ✓ **Nearest Frame:** Choosing this option takes the selected keys and shifts them to the even frame number that's closest to each of them.

- ✓ **Nearest Second:** Like the Nearest Frame operation, but this option snaps the selected keys to the nearest frame that's at the start of a second in time.

✔ **Nearest Marker:** Blender's Dope Sheet allows you to place reminders on the timeline referred to as *markers*. You can add a new marker at the location of the timeline cursor by pressing M in any of Blender's time-based editors (Timeline, Dope Sheet, Graph Editor, NLA Editor, and the Video Sequence Editor). If you have one or more of these markers on your timeline, choosing this option snaps selected keyframes to the marker that's nearest to it.

Generally, though, it's best practice to use Blender's frame-based auto-snap feature that's enabled by default. You can change the auto-snap method by left-clicking the drop-down menu on the far right of the Dope Sheet's header. This menu has almost all the same options as the preceding list. The only difference is the Time Step option, which snap keys to one-frame increments from their initial locations rather than to exact frames.

Animating with Armatures

If you're already used to object animation, using armatures to animate in the Dope Sheet extends naturally from that base. When I animate, I like to use the following process:

1. **Plan the animation.**

   I can't emphasize this point enough: Know what you're going to animate and have an idea about the timing of the motion. *Act out the action.* If you can, record yourself acting it out. Video reference is key for seeing subtle movements. Sketch out a few quick thumbnail drawings of the sequence. Even stick-figure drawings can be really helpful for determining poses and figuring out camera framing.

2. **Set your Timeline at frame 1 and create the starting pose for your character by manipulating its rig.**

3. **Select all visible bones (A) and Insert a LocRot keyframe for *everything* (I⇨LocRot).**

   Granted, there's a good chance that most of the bones can't be grabbed, but only rotated, so setting a location keyframe for them is kind of moot. However, setting a keyframe for all the bones is faster than going through and figuring out which bones can be keyed for just rotation and which bones can be keyed for both rotation and location.

   Alternatively, if you've set up a keying set for your character (see Chapter 10), you can pick that keying set by using Shift+Ctrl+Alt+I and then insert keyframes for every property in that keying set by pressing I.

4. **Move the timeline cursor forward to roughly when you think the next major pose should happen.**

   It doesn't really matter which editor you use to adjust the timeline cursor. It could be the Timeline, the Dope Sheet, or the Graph Editor. In fact, using ←, →, Shift+↑, and Shift+↓, you can even adjust the timeline cursor from the 3D View.

5. **Create your character's second pose.**

   If the next pose is a *hold*, or a pose where the character doesn't change position, you can duplicate the keys of the previous pose by selecting them in the Dope Sheet and pressing Shift+D.

6. **Select all visible bones (A) and Insert an Available keyframe (I⇨Available).**

   Again, if you're using a keying set, you can just press I. If you wanted, you could also switch to the Available keying set (Shift+Ctrl+Alt+I⇨Available) before inserting keyframes.

7. **Continue with Steps 4 through 6 until you complete the last major pose for your character.**

8. **Using the Dope Sheet, play back the animation, paying close attention to timing.**

   At this point, hopefully your poses are acceptably refined, so you should pay even *more* attention to timing than to the accuracy of the poses.

9. **Go through the keys in the Dope Sheet and tweak the timing of the poses so that they look natural.**

10. **Continuing to tweak, go back and start adding additional poses and keyframes for secondary motion between your major poses.**

11. **Continue on this course, refining the timing and detail more and more with each pass.**

One luxury of computer animation is the ability to continually go back and tweak things, make changes, and improve the animation. You can take advantage of this process by training yourself to work in passes. Animate your character's biggest, most pronounced motion first. Make sure that you have the timing down. Then move to the next pass, working on slightly more detailed parts of the performance. For example, animate your character's arm and hand bones before you get into the nitty-gritty details of animating the fingers. The biggest reason to work this way is time. It's much easier to go in and fix the timing on a big action if you do it earlier. Otherwise, you run into situations where you find yourself shuffling around a bunch of detail keys after you find out that your character doesn't get from Point A to Point B in the right amount of time.

Don't be afraid to break out a stopwatch and act out the action to find out exactly how long it takes to perform and what the action feels like. Animation is very much like acting, by proxy. So it helps to know what some actions actually feel like when they're performed. If you're fortunate enough to have friends, have them act out the action for you while you time it or even record it to video. Getting animation to look right is all about having the proper timing.

Principles of animation worth remembering

As you create your animations, try to pull from a variety of sources to really capture the essence of some action, motion, or character expression. My first and most emphatic recommendation is to keep your eyes open. Watch everything around you that moves. Study objects and try to get an idea of how their structure facilitates motion. Then think about how you would re-create that movement.

Of course, merely gawking at everything in the world isn't the only thing you should do (and you should be prepared for the fact that people will probably look at you funny). Studying early animation is also a good idea. Most of the principles that those wonderfully talented pioneers developed for animation are still relevant and applicable to computer animation. In fact, you should remember the classic 12 basic principles of animation that were established by some of the original Disney animators. These principles are a bit of divergence, but if your aim is to create good animation, you should know about them and try to use them in even the most simple of animations:

- **Squash and stretch:** This one is all about deformation. Because of weight, anything that moves gets deformed somehow. A tennis ball squashes to an oval shape when it's hit. Rope under tension gets stretched. Cartoon characters hit all believable and unbelievable ranges of this when they're animated, but it's valuable, albeit toned down, even in realistic animation.

- **Anticipation:** The basic idea here is that before every action in one direction, a buildup in the opposite direction occurs first. A character that's going to jump bends her knees and moves down first to build up the energy to jump upward.

- **Staging:** The idea of staging is to keep the frame simple. The purpose of animation is to communicate an idea or a movement or an emotion with moving images. You want to convey this idea as clearly as possible with the way you arrange your shots and the characters in those shots.

✔ **Straight-ahead action versus pose-to-pose action:** These are the two primary methods of animating. The process that I discuss near the beginning of this chapter is more of a pose-to-pose technique. Pose-to-pose can be clearer, but it may be a bit cartoony. Straight-ahead action is generally more fluid and realistic, but the action may be less clear and may be more difficult to tweak on future passes. Most modern animators use a hybrid approach, blocking in the initial poses and then working straight-ahead between them.

✔ **Follow through and overlapping action:** The idea here is to make sure that your animations adhere (or seem to adhere) to the laws of physics. If you have movement in one direction, the inertia of that motion requires you to animate the follow-through even if you're changing direction.

✔ **Ease in and ease out:** Ease in and ease out, sometimes known as "slow in, slow out," means that natural movement does not stop and start abruptly. It flows smoothly, accelerating and decelerating. By using Bézier curves in the Graph Editor, you actually get this principle for free.

✔ **Arcs:** Along the same lines as the previous two principles, most natural movement happens in arcs. So if your character is changing direction or moving something, you typically want that to happen in some sort of curved, arc motion. Straight lines are generally stiff and robotic (and therefore good for machinery and robots), but they're also very useful for powerful actions like punching.

✔ **Secondary action:** These actions are those additional touches that make characters appear more real to the audience. Clothing that shifts with character movement, jiggling fat or loose skin, and blinking eyes are just a few actions that can breathe life into an otherwise stiff, empty puppet.

✔ **Timing:** Timing is, in my opinion, one of the most important of the 12 principles. Everything happens according to time. If the timing is off, it throws off the effect for the whole animation. I'm not just talking about controlling the timing of actions to appear believable. I also mean *story-based timing* — knowing exactly the right time to make a character give a sad facial expression that impacts the audience the most.

✔ **Exaggeration:** Exaggeration makes animation fun. You can do anything with animation, and you're nearly duty-bound to take advantage of that fact. Otherwise, you may as well just work in video or film with meat-space people.

✔ **Solid drawing:** Solid drawing refers to the actual skill of being able to draw. Computer animators *can* get away with not being experts at drawing, but it's to your benefit to make the effort. Drawing is an extension of seeing. When you draw, you turn on a part of your brain that studies how things look relative to each other. Being able to see the world with these eyes can make all the difference in re-creating believable motion.

✔ **Appeal:** This one is easy. Make things that are awesome. If you're going to animate something that is boring, what's the point? It needs to be interesting for you to make, and it's nice if it's also interesting for other people to watch.

Those are the basic principles of animation, but not a single one of them is carved in stone. You can effectively break every one of them and still pull off some incredible animation. That said, more often than not, it's in the best interest of your work and your sanity that you at least start within these principles and then find ways where you can break them in the best way possible.

Making sense of quaternions (or, "Why are there four rotation curves?!")

Even though the bulk of your time animating with armatures is spent working with the Dope Sheet, you still may frequently need to tweak things in the Graph Editor. If you go to the Graph Editor and view the f-curves for a bone with the intention of tweaking rotation, you may run into a particularly jarring shock. The X Rotation, Y Rotation, and Z Rotation channels that you would expect for rotation aren't there: They've been replaced with *four* channels to control rotation, called *quaternions*. Figure 12-2 shows a set of quaternions in the Graph Editor, describing the rotation of some bone.

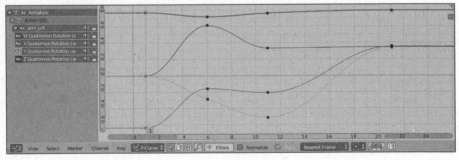

Figure 12-2: Quaternions in action! They're nearly incomprehensible!

Quaternions are a different way of defining rotations in 3D space, and they're quite a bit different from the standard X, Y, and Z rotations, called *Euler* (pronounced "oiler") rotations. Quaternions are used in the rotation of bones because Euler rotations can get into a nasty situation referred to as *gimbal lock*, which involves being mathematically unable to compensate for or adjust a rotation because you only have three axes to define it. Having that happen in an armature is unacceptable. Fortunately, quaternions don't suffer from gimbal lock. However, they do suffer from another affliction: They have virtually no intuitive relationship to rotation that non-mathematicians can understand.

To make a long story short, if you're using quaternion rotations, it may be easier for you to tweak a rotation by adding additional keyframes to the rotation. If you're not fond of mathematics, you may very well go crazy trying to figure out how they relate to your bone's rotation.

You aren't stuck with quaternions if you don't want them, though. You can control the rotation mode of any bone in an armature. To do so, select a bone and bring up its Bone Properties. At the bottom of the Transform panel is a drop-down menu labeled Rotation Mode. By default, its set to Quaternion (WXYZ), and in most cases, you want to use this setting. However, in a couple cases where you're sure that you won't run into gimbal lock problems (like, for example, if you rigged a bone to define the rotation of a wheel), it may be more helpful to use a different rotation mode like XYZ Euler or Axis Angle. The wheel example also is a good one to note, because quaternions don't "spin up" to allow multiple rotations like Euler or Axis Angle rotations can. So unless your wheel only spins once, it's in your best interest to switch.

Copying mirrored poses

One of the beauties of working in computer animation is the ability to take advantage of the computer's ability to calculate and process things so that you don't have to. In the animation world, animators love to find ways that the computer can do more work. Granted, you can (and should) always temper the computer's work with your own artistic eye, but there's nothing wrong with doing half the work and letting the computer do the other, boring, tedious, and repetitive half.

With the auspicious goal of getting the computer to do the work for you, Blender has three incredible little buttons, shown in Figure 12-3, located at the far-right end of the 3D View's header. They are visible only when you have selected an armature and it's in Pose mode. With these buttons, you can copy and paste poses from and back to the armature.

Figure 12-3:
Pose Copy and Paste buttons in the 3D View's header.

From left to right, the buttons are Pose Copy, Pose Paste, and Pose Mirror Paste. Here's how to use them:

1. **Select all bones (A).**

   You can actually get away with just selecting a few bones, but selecting all the bones actually illustrates my point a little better.

2. **Left-click the Copy Pose button.**

   The armature's pose is stored into your computer's memory.

3. **Move to a different location in the timeline where you'd like your character to resume this pose.**

4. **Paste the pose back to the character.**

   In pasting, you have two options:

   - **Paste Pose:** This option takes the coordinates of all the bones you selected when copying the pose and applies those poses back to your character exactly as you copied them.

   - **Mirror Paste:** This option does the same thing as the regular Paste Pose, except it takes advantage of Blender's built-in left/right naming convention (see Chapter 11 for more details) and pastes the mirrored version of the pose to your character. Mirror Paste is really handy if you're doing something like creating a walk cycle. You can create a left-foot-forward pose and then use Mirror Paste to instantly create a right-food-forward pose. Figure 12-4 shows a character posed one way and then mirror pasted to pose the other.

Note that after you paste the pose, you need to insert a keyframe for that pose at that location. Otherwise, the next time you scrub the timeline, the pose won't be there, and you'll have to copy and paste it all over again.

Figure 12-4:
All you have to do is put one foot forward, and Blender handles the other for you.

Seeing the big picture with ghosting

Traditional animation has a process called *onionskinning,* which consists of drawing on relatively thin paper and working on a table with a light in it. With this setup, the animator can stack his drawings on top of each other and get an overall sense of the motion in the animation. Blender has a similar feature for rigs; it's called *ghosting.* The controls for ghosting are in the Ghost panel of Armature Properties.

To get the best sense of what the ghost feature does, increase the Range value in this panel to its maximum value of 30 ghosts. Now, for short animations or simple movement, having ghosting enabled may not be all that useful. However, the ghost feature is great for the more common forms of animation that are a bit longer and more complex. Having Ghost turned on is a great way to get a sense of where your character's coming from and where he's going. Think of ghosting as a way of having three-dimensional onionskinning, and it's certainly useful. Figure 12-5 shows a character jumping up and down, visualized with armature ghosting.

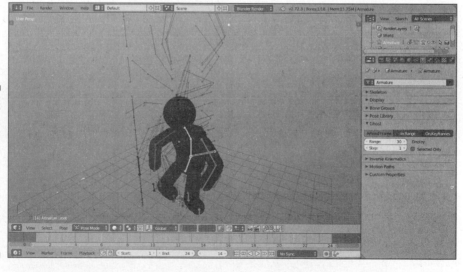

Figure 12-5: Increasing the Range value in the Ghost panel allows you to see a 3D onionskin of your rig's motion.

Visualizing motion with paths

As mentioned earlier in this chapter, one of the fundamental principles of animation is having arcs for movement. Smooth arcs are favorable for believable, natural-looking animated movement. To that end, Blender has a nice feature that makes it easier to analyze your animation and figure out whether you have acceptable arcs in your character's movement. This feature is called Motion Paths and is also available in Armature Properties, within the Motion Paths panel.

This feature isn't like ghosts, where you just increase the range and they display instantly. Motion paths may take a second to generate. In order to generate them, first select the bone or bones that you want to visualize and then left-click the Calculate Paths button on the bottom-right side of the Motion Paths panel. After left-clicking this button, it changes to read as Update Paths and also features a new button with an X on it for clearing your motion paths. An added bonus to this feature is the ability to show the location of the keys along the path as a bright dot by enabling the Keyframes check box. If you want, you can also show the numerical frame numbers along the curves by enabling the Frame Numbers feature in the same panel. Figure 12-6 shows the same jump animation, but this time with motion paths enabled.

One thing to note is that, although it might be nice, you can't currently change or edit the motion path directly. The path can reflect only the motion created by your keyframes. So if you notice that the curve isn't as smooth as you might like, you need to go back and tweak the motion using poses in the 3D View, keyframe timing in the Dope Sheet, or f-curve editing in the Graph Editor. Then when you recalculate the motion paths, hopefully you should have a cleaner result.

Figure 12-6:
Motion paths help visualize the motion of bones in your armature.

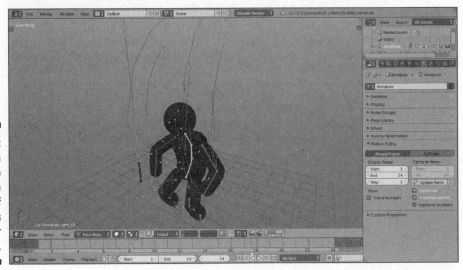

Doing Nonlinear Animation

Animation is hard work, really hard work. So any time you can cut down the amount of work you have to do without detracting from the quality of the final animation, it's a good thing. Computer animation has given you another cool way to effectively and efficiently cut corners: *nonlinear animation*. Nonlinear animation, or NLA, is a way of animating that you can really do only with computers. The process of animating is typically very linear and straightforward (see preceding section). You may animate in passes, but you're still generally working forward in time with the full start-to-finish of your animation already planned out.

What if you didn't have to work this way? What if you could animate little chunks of character motion and then mix and match as you like? Imagine mixing a simple hand-waving motion with a simple jumping animation so that your character is both jumping and waving his arm? This is the basic concept behind nonlinear animation. Nonlinear animation takes many of the same principles used in nonlinear video editing and applies them to 3D computer animation. The idea is that you create a library of simple motions or poses and then combine them any way you like to create much more complex animated sequences. Using a library of motions is useful for background characters in larger productions and is also very handy for video games. Instead of trying to pull a specific set of frames from a single unified timeline, video game developers can now just make a call to one or more of these library animations and let the computer do the rest of the work.

In Blender, the basic building blocks for this library are Actions. *Actions* are collections of f-curves, and they are really cool because they have their own datablock. You can create multiple actions within a single .blend file, share the actions between armatures, and basically build up a library of movements.

To create a new action, first change the Dope Sheet from the default Dope Sheet editing context to the Action Editor context using the Mode drop-down menu in the header. Then you can use the Action datablock, also in the header of the Dope Sheet, to add a new action, as highlighted in Figure 12-7. This datablock widget is just like the one used for materials, textures, and even objects in other parts of Blender's interface. Create a new action by left-clicking the plus (+) icon on the right side of the datablock. After adding a new action, you can (and should) click in the text area of the datablock and give your new action a custom name.

With the new action created, you can create another core animation and start building up your character's action library. Animate waving each arm, a walk cycle, various facial expressions, a standing idle animation, and any other simple action that comes to mind.

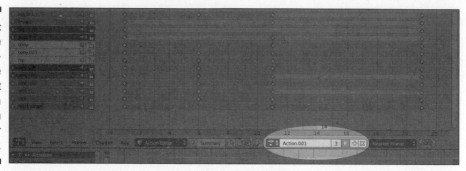

Figure 12-7:
Using the
Action data-
block in the
Dope Sheet
to create a
new action
for your
armature.

Before you create a new action, be sure to left-click the Fake User button in
the datablock widget for your action (it's the button with an F on it). Let me
write that again: *Give your actions a fake user.*

Remember the way that Blender's datablocks work. If a datablock doesn't
have any users, it gets destroyed when you close Blender or open a different .blend file. So if you go through and create a bunch of actions without
giving them users, all of those userless actions will disappear when you close
Blender, regardless of how frequently you saved while working. To ensure
that this doesn't happen, you need to make sure that all of your actions have
users. This is where the Fake User button comes it. When a datablock has
that button enabled, it won't be obliterated when you close your file.

Eventually, your action library will be populated enough that you'll want to
start mixing and matching them together. To do this, you're going to want to
use the NLA Editor. Add the NLA Editor to the Animation screen layout with
the following steps:

1. **In the Animation screen layout, left-click the seam at the top of the
   Timeline and drag it up, making more room for that editor.**

   Because the NLA Editor is covering the entire animation, it makes sense
   to forsake the Timeline and use the NLA Editor exclusively. But if you'd
   still like to use the Timeline, you can split it off of another area.

2. **Change the Timeline to a NLA Editor.**

   Your screen layout may look something like Figure 12-8.

The NLA is a very cool feature of Blender, but don't rely on it too much for
animation. Blender has had the NLA Editor for a long time, but it could still
use some refinement to be a truly effective tool. The good news is that the
NLA is still being developed, and while it's likely to go through design itera-
tions in future releases of Blender, the principles that I explain here should
still apply.

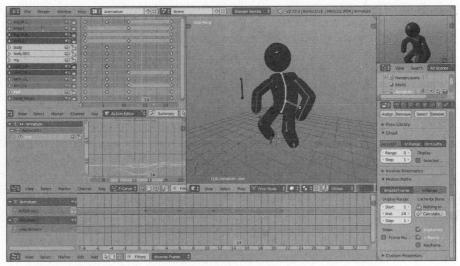

Figure 12-8:
An animation screen layout with the NLA Editor added to it.

Mixing actions to create complex animation

When you have an action loaded in the Dope Sheet's Action Editor, you should notice a bright orange bar in the NLA Editor. This orange bar is the current active action on your armature, and you can push that action on the NLA stack to build your animation.

To add your actions to the NLA Editor:

1. **Push your current action into the stack by left-clicking the button with the double-downward arrow icon in the channel region on the left of the NLA.**

   A new NLA *track* is created, populated with your current action as a bright yellow *strip*. The text on the strip should match the name of your action. The track itself is named NlaTrack, as indicated in the NLA Editor's channel region. Double-click that name to rename it to something more descriptive.

2. **Add a new strip in the graph area of the NLA Editor (Shift+A).**

   You see a menu of all the actions you created.

3. **Choose the action you'd like to add to the NLA Editor.**

   The action is placed in the NLA Editor as a strip in the currently selected track (left-click the track name in the channel region to select a track), and its start position is wherever the time cursor is located.

REMEMBER

If the timeline cursor is in the middle of an existing strip on your selected track, adding a new strip will create a new track. The existing strip doesn't get trimmed or removed.

4. Continue to add actions to the NLA.

Of course, unless you make the last frame of one Action strip match the pose at the head of the next frame, the animation looks pretty erratic.

The way to smooth out the animation is with the Properties region (N) in the NLA Editor. Figure 12-9 shows the Properties region of the NLA Editor. To make the transition from one strip to the next smoother, either make sure that the Auto Blend In/Out check box in the Active Strip panel for each strip is enabled (it should be by default) and let them overlap a bit or manually set the Blend In and Blend Out values in this panel.

Figure 12-9:
Using the Properties region in the NLA Editor.

Taking advantage of looped animation

Another benefit of using the NLA is the ability to easily loop any action strip and rescale its timing. You can loop and rescale the timing in the NLA Editor from within the Properties region. In the Action Clip panel under the Playback Settings label are a pair of values: Scale and Repeat. The very first is

Scale, with a default value of 1.0. However, you can increase or decrease this value as much as you like to adjust the timing on your action, speeding it up or slowing it down as necessary.

Below the Scale value is Repeat. Like Scale, the default value is 1.0, and you can increase or decrease the value to taste. As you do, you should see the strip increase in length proportional to the increase of the Repeat value. Now, to have an effective looping animation, it's definitely in your best interest to make the first and last poses in the action identical. The easiest way to do so would be to go into the Dope Sheet, column select the keys in the first frame (right-click one keyframe, press K), and duplicate (Shift+D) it to the last frame of the action. However, you can also use the copy and paste pose buttons in the 3D View:

1. **In the Dope Sheet, select (right-click) the action strip you want to loop from the Actions datablock.**

2. **While still in the Dope Sheet, move the time cursor to the first pose in the action (left-click and drag).**

3. **In the 3D View, select all bones (A) and left-click the Copy Pose button in the header.**

4. **Back in the Dope Sheet or the Timeline, move the time cursor to some place after the last keyframe.**

5. **In the 3D View, left-click the Paste Pose button in the header.**

6. **Insert a new keyframe (I⇨Available).**

   When you get to this step, all the bones should still be selected, so you don't need to reselect anything.

   When you return to the NLA Editor, the action strip should automatically be longer to account for the additional frame at the end. Furthermore, the action strip should also loop seamlessly upon playback (Alt+A).

Figure 12-10 shows the NLA Editor with a looped strip.

Be careful when changing the scale of Action strips. More often than not, changing the scale results in a keyframe being placed at what's called a *fractional frame* or *intraframe*, a spot on the timeline that isn't a nicely rounded frame number. Fractional frames aren't necessarily a bad thing, but animations do tend to look a little bit better if the keyframes fall on full frames so that the audience has the chance to "read" the pose.

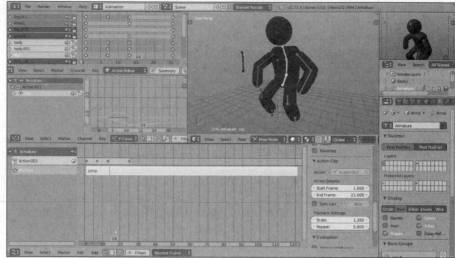

Figure 12-10:
Action
strips in the
NLA Editor,
looped and
rescaled.

Many of these animation concepts, especially ones involving the NLA,
are much easier to grasp if you can see them in motion. After all, this is
animation, the art of motion. The `.blend` files on this book's website
(`www.blenderbasics.com`) provide a stronger notion of how these things
work together.

Chapter 13

Letting Blender Do the Work for You

In This Chapter

▶ Playing with particles

▶ Simulating physics with soft body and rigid body dynamics

▶ Working with cloth simulation

▶ Creating fluid animations with Blender's fluid simulator

*W*hen animating, some actions are difficult or very time consuming to get right, such as explosions, fire, hair, cloth, and physics-related actions like moving fluids and bouncing objects. In order to get these actions to look right, one solution is to let the computer do the work and create a simulation of that action. You use variables like gravity and mass to define the environment, and the computer calculates how the objects in the scene behave based on the values you set. Using the computer is a great way to get nearly accurate motion without the need to key everything by hand.

That said, don't make the mistake of thinking simulations always give you a huge time savings in animation. This assumption isn't necessarily true, as some highly detailed simulations can take hours, or even days, to complete. Instead, think of simulations as a way to more reliably animate detailed, physically accurate motion better than you might be able to do by hand alone. If you look at the process while wearing your "business hat," paying for a computer to crunch through a simulation is cheaper than paying for an artist to create it manually.

This chapter only scratches the surface of what you can do with the simulation tools in Blender, so you should certainly look at additional resources, such as Blender's official online documentation and the wide variety of online tutorials from the community, particularly those on www.blendercookie.com and www.blenderdiplom.com to get a full understanding of how each feature works. But hopefully, this chapter gives you an idea of the possibilities you have at hand.

Using Particles in Blender

Blender has had an integrated particle system from its early beginnings. Over the years, though, it has grown and matured into a much more powerful system for creating particle-based effects like hair, flock/swarm behavior, and explosions. And the particle system gets more and more powerful with every release.

The controls for Blender's particle systems live in Particle Properties, as shown in Figure 13-1. Initially, this section looks pretty barren, with just a single list box. However, if you have a Mesh object selected and click the Plus (+) button to the right of the list box, a whole explosion of additional panels for controlling particle behavior appear. Adding a particle system in Particle Properties also adds a Particle System modifier to your object. Technically, you can create your new particle system from Modifiers Properties as well, but it's better to do it from Particle Properties, because that's where all of the particle controls live.

Figure 13-1:
Left-click the Particle Properties icon to bring up the particle control panels.

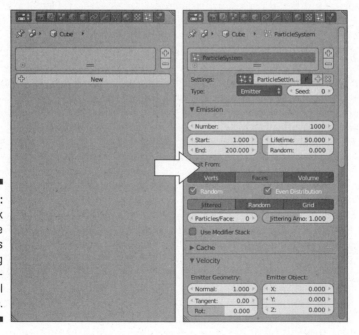

Knowing what particle systems are good for

Particle systems have a handful of good uses. Each use involves large numbers of individual objects that share some general behavior. Consequently, particle systems are ideal for groups of objects that move according to physics, such as fireworks or tennis balls being continuously shot at a wall. Particle systems are also good for simulating hair and fur. If the path along which an individual particle travels was to be considered a strand, you could use groups of these particle strands to make hair. This technique is exactly what Blender does.

There's also one other use for particle systems: simple flocking or crowd simulation. Say that you want to have a swarm of gnats constantly buzzing around your character's head. A particle system is a great way to pull off that effect. In Figure 13-1, a whole mess of configuration panels appear in the Particle Properties. Figure 13-2 boils these panels down and shows the most used and useful panels in this section of the Properties editor.

After you create your first particle system, the context panel at the top of Particle Properties gives you the broadest controls, allowing you to name your particle system or choose a different set of settings from the Particle Settings datablock. Objects in Blender can have more than one particle system and can even share the same particle system settings between objects. Beneath the Settings datablock is a Type drop-down menu that offers you two types of particle system behaviors to work with: Emitter and Hair. In most instances, you'll probably use the Emitter type. Hair particle systems are the way to create manageable hair and fur in Blender (there's more on hair and fur later in this chapter).

Figure 13-2:
The most useful panels in the Particle Properties.

If you choose Emitter, the Emission panel has some of the most important settings for controlling how many particles you have and how long they exist in your scene. Here's a brief explanation for each value:

- **Number:** As the name implies, this value is the total number of particles created by the system. After the particle system generates this number of particles, it stops. You can get additional particles in more than one way, but the most straightforward (though potentially CPU-intensive) way is to increase this value.

- **Start:** This frame is where particles start being emitted from the source object. By default, this value is set to frame 1, but if you don't want to have your particles start until later in your animation, you can increase the value in this field. You can also set this value to be negative, so your animation starts with the particles already in motion.

- **End:** This frame is where Blender stops emitting particles from the source object. By default, it's set to frame 200. With the default values for Amount and Start (1000 and 1.0, respectively), Blender creates five particles in each new frame in the animation up to frame 200 and then stops generating particles.

- **Lifetime:** The Lifetime value controls how long an individual particle exists in your scene. With the default value of 50.0, a particle born on frame 7 disappears from the scene when you reach frame 57. If you find that you need your particles in the scene longer, increase this value.

- **Random:** This value pertains specifically to the Lifetime of the particle. At its default of 0.0, it doesn't change anything; particles live for the exact length of time stipulated by the Lifetime value and disappear, or *die,* at the end of that time. However, if you increase the Random value, it introduces a variation to the Lifetime option, so all the particles born on one frame disappear at different times, giving a more natural effect.

One additional option to pay attention to in the Emission panel is the Use Modifier Stack check box at the bottom. If you're emitting particles from a mesh on which you've used Generate modifiers (such as the Mirror modifier or the Remesh modifier), you may want to enable this check box. Otherwise, only the geometry of your base mesh will emit particles; in some cases, such as hair, that's not likely to be what you want.

You can associate any particle type (Emitter or Hair) with one of five varieties of physics simulation models stipulated in the Physics panel: No physics, Newtonian, Keyed, Boids, and Fluid. Very rarely do you have a need to use the No option, but it's good to have. Typically, the default Newtonian setting is the most useful option because it tends to accurately simulate real-world physical attributes, such as gravity, mass, and velocity. Occasionally, though, you may want to have more explicit control over your particles, such as when you're shaping the hair on a character. This is where Keyed physics come into play. You can use the *emitter object* of one particle system to control the angle and direction of another one. The Boids option tells your particles to have flocking or swarming behavior, and you get a set of settings and panels to control that behavior. The last option, Fluid, is a physics-based choice similar to the Newtonian option, but particles have greater cohesive and adhesive properties that make them behave like part of a fluid system.

To create a basic particle system, use the following steps:

1. **Add a mesh to work as your particle emitter (Shift+A⇨Mesh⇨Grid).**

    In this example, I use a simple grid, but really any mesh works. The key thing to remember is that, by default, particles are emitted from the faces of your mesh and move away from the face in the direction of that face's normal.

2. **Navigate to Particle Properties and add a new particle system.**

    After you click the Plus (+) button next to the particles list box, all the options available to particles become visible. If you try to play back the animation now (Alt+A), you see particles dropping from your grid.

    While your particles play, look at your Timeline. Along the bottom edge of the timeline is a red bar. Some of that bar may be solid, while the rest is semi-transparent. This is your *particle cache*, or the movement in your particle system that Blender has stored in memory. Working with particle caches is a bit of an advanced topic, but the main thing to know is that when your timeline cursor is not in the solid red area, that moment in time for your particle system has not yet been cached. The result is that it may not be accurate to your final results and it may play back slower than the cached part. The cache will be updated with any major changes that you make in Particle Properties.

3. **Decide what type of physics you would like to have controlling your particles.**

    Newtonian physics are usually the most common type of particle system used, but I'm also pretty fond of the Boids behavior for emitter particle systems. It just looks cool, and they're a lot of fun!

4. **Adjust the velocity settings to control particle behavior.**

    You change this setting from the Velocity panel in Particle Properties. For Newtonian physics, you can give your particles an initial velocity. I tend to adjust the Normal velocity first because it gives the most immediate results. Values above 0 go in the direction of each face's normals, whereas values below zero go in the opposite direction. Boid particles don't require an initial velocity, but the settings do adjust how each Boid particle interacts with its neighboring particles.

5. Play back the animation to watch the particles move (Alt+A).

If you followed the tip in Step 2, you could be playing your particle anima-tion already. If not, press Alt+A and see what your settings make the par-ticles do. If your particles start behaving in erratic or unexpected ways, it's a good idea to make sure that your time cursor in the Timeline is at or before the frame you entered for the Start value in the Emission panel when you start the animation playback.

Watch how your particles move and behave. You can now either tweak the particle movement during playback, or if it's more comfortable for you, press Esc to stop the playback and adjust your settings before playing the animation again. I usually use a combination of live adjust-ments and this back-and-forth tweaking to refine my particle system's behavior.

Figure 13-3 shows the preceding process. Bear in mind that these steps show a very basic particle system setup, and you're just barely scratching the surface of what's possible. I definitely recommend that you take some time to play with each of the settings and figure out what they do, as well as read some of the more in-depth documentation on particles in Blender's online documentation.

TIP

If you change a lot of settings, it's a good practice to go back to frame 1 and replay your animation with Alt+A to cache your particle system from the beginning instead of from just the previous frame.

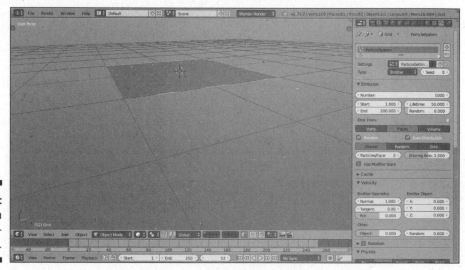

Figure 13-3:
Creating a basic par-ticle system.

Using force fields and collisions

After you create a basic particle system, you can have a little bit of fun with it, controlling the behavior of your particles. You control this behavior by using forces and deflectors. A *force field* is a controlling influence on the overall behavior of the particles, such as wind, vortices, and magnetism. In contrast, you can define collision objects, or *deflectors,* for your particles to collide with and impede their progress. Generally speaking, forces are defined using specialized empties, whereas deflectors are created with meshes.

All the controls for forces and deflectors live in Physics Properties, accessed by left-clicking the last button in the Properties editor's header. Its icon looks a bit like a blue check mark with a white circle at the end of it; it's really a visualization of a bouncing white ball. For particle force fields, left-click the Force Fields button, and a Force Fields panel appears. If you need collision settings, left-click the Collision button, and the Collision panel appears.

You typically use these panels to add force and collision behaviors to objects that are already in your scene. You select an object and then, from Physics Properties, add force field and collision properties to that object. For force fields, however, you can add them in a slightly faster way: from Blender's Add menu in the 3D View. If you press Shift+A➪Force Field, you get a whole list of forces that you can add to your scene. Then you can just adjust the settings for your chosen force from the Force Fields panel in Physics Properties.

Now, I could go through each and every option available for force fields exhaustively, but things usually make more sense if you have an example to work with. That being the case, use the following steps to create a particle system that creates particles influenced by a wind force that causes them to collide with a wall and then bounce off of it:

1. **Create a simple particle system.**

   If you need a refresher, use the steps in the preceding section to create a basic emitter particle system with Newtonian physics.

2. **Add a Wind force field (Shift+A➪Force Field➪Wind).**

   Notice that the Wind force field object looks like an Empty with circles arranged along its local Z-axis. This visual cue lets you know the strength and direction of your wind force. Increasing the Strength value in the Force Fields panel spaces out the four circles to help show how much wind you're creating. Play back the animation (Alt+A) to see how your wind is affecting the movements of the particles. While playing your animation, if you rotate your Wind object or adjust its force field settings, the particles are affected in real time. Neat, huh?

For the remaining steps, you don't have to stop the animation of your particle system. Let it keep playing. This is one of the benefits of Blender's non-blocking philosophy. As you add and change things in your scene, the particle system updates and reacts in real time.

3. **Add a plane (Shift+A⇨Mesh⇨Plane).**

   This plane is your deflector. Grab the plane (G) and move it so that it's in the path of the particles pushed by your wind force. Rotate (R) the plane to make sure that the particles actually run into it head-on.

4. **Make the plane a Collision object.**

   With your plane still selected, add a Collision panel in Physics Properties. Whammo! You made a deflector! If you play back the animation (Alt+A) — or if you've been playing the animation the whole time — your particles should be blown by your wind force into your plane, which they should bounce off of rather than shoot straight through.

Figure 13-4 shows the results of this step-by-step process. And like the section preceding this one, you're just seeing the tip of the iceberg in terms of what's possible with forces and deflectors. You can use all sorts of cool forces and settings to get some very unique behavior out of your particle systems.

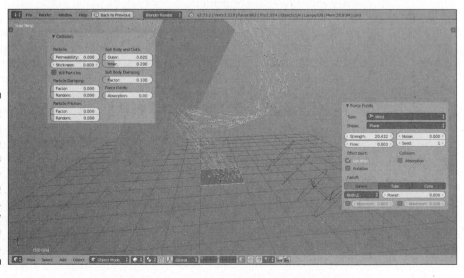

Figure 13-4: Creating a wind force that blows your particles into a plane, which they bounce off of.

Using particles for hair and fur

It would be remiss of me to cover particles and not say anything about Blender's hair and fur system. Blender uses particles to create hair and fur for your characters. As you may have guessed, you choose Hair as the type of particle system you want from the context panel at the top of Particle Properties. From there, the setup is roughly the same as using a regular emitter system with Newtonian physics, but with two notable differences.

The first difference is that Hair particles are, in some ways, easier to edit than emitter particles because you can use Blender's Particle mode to customize and comb your particle hair. When you start combing in Particle mode, Blender freezes the particle settings that you already set, and you can tweak and customize the hair from there. Figure 13-5 shows a screenshot of an object with particle hair being combed in Particle mode.

If you decide that you don't like the results you created in Particle mode, you can always reset your hair particles to their positions defined by the settings in Particle Properties. To reset your hair particles, left-click the Free Edit button in the context panel of Particle Properties. If you haven't edited your hair in Particle mode, this button isn't visible. But after you start combing, the button appears so that you can easily reset everything.

You switch to Particle mode by using the Mode menu in the 3D View's header or (if you have the Pie Menus add-on enabled) by selecting a menu option when you press Tab. With your emitter object selected, switch into Particle Mode. When you're in Particle mode, you have the ability to directly edit particle hair, including combing, cutting, growing, and smoothing it out. To see these controls, look to the Tools tab of the Tool Shelf (T). Particle Mode gives you a circular brush like the one used in Sculpting and Vertex Paint modes. You can adjust the brush's size and strength using the sliders from the Tool Shelf or by pressing F and Shift+F, respectively.

The other thing that differs in the setup of hair particles is the use of *child particles*. Creating and displaying hair particles can take up a lot of computing power. When animating, you don't necessarily want to be waiting on Blender to draw all your character's fur in the 3D View. To deal with this problem, you have two solutions, and the results are best when they're used together. The first thing is to reduce the number of viewable particles in the 3D View using the Display slider in the Display panel of Particle Properties. The Display slider changes the percentage of particles being displayed in the 3D View. When you make this change, fewer particles show up in the 3D View, but all of them appear when you render. You get the best of both worlds.

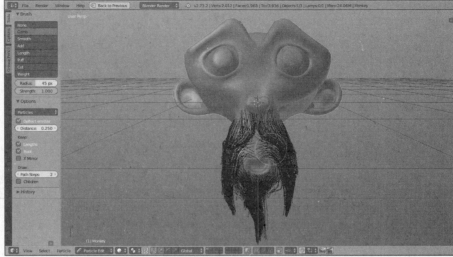

Of course, for characters with a lot of hair, just reducing the displayable particles may not be enough. In this case, child particles are useful. In the Children panel of Particle Properties, left-click the Interpolated button. Additional particle strands grow from the faces of your emitter, with their locations determined by the particles around them. The Children panel has two amount values on the left column: Display and Render. The Display value dictates how many particles are seen in the 3D View. For speed while animating, I often set this value to 0. The Render value controls the number of child particles that each parent particle has at render time.

In both Blender Internal *and* Cycles, Rendered viewport shading (Shift+Z) uses the preview display values for particles. They don't use the render values. This means that, if you're using a display percentage in the Display panel that's less than 100%, Rendered viewport shading isn't showing you an exact depiction of your final render. The same goes for the Display and Render values in the Children panel: Rendered viewport shading uses the Display value, not the Render value.

Rendering hair in Blender Internal

With the particle system properly generating your hairs, the only thing you have to worry about now is controlling how Blender renders this hair. Of course, because Blender ships with two render engines, the process depends on the renderer you're using. Here's a quick-and-dirty rundown of the steps

I go through to get the hair to render nicely using the Blender Internal (BI) renderer:

1. **Enable the Strand render check box in the Render panel of Particle Properties.**

   This step tells Blender's rendering engine to render the particles as strands.

   Another helpful option in this panel is the Emitter check box near the top. Enabling this option makes the emitter visible, a helpful feature if you're using your actual character mesh to generate the hair.

2. **In Material Properties, enable Transparency and verify that Z Transparency is being used; set your Alpha value in the Transparency panel to 0.**

   If you're using the Hair strands preview type in the Preview panel (I recommend doing so), you may notice that your hair is virtually non-existent because of the 0 Alpha value. Don't worry: This setting makes sense in the next couple of steps.

3. **In Texture Properties, add a new Blend texture and use the Ramp editor in the Colors panel to control the color and transparency along the length of the hair.**

   The most important thing here is that the right-hand side of the ramp represents the tip of your hair strand and should therefore be completely transparent. All other color positions in it should be opaque.

4. **In the Mapping panel, choose Strand/Particle from the Coordinates drop-down menu.**

5. **In the Influence panel, enable Color and Alpha.**

   The Preview panel should show hair strands that use your ramp gradient along the length of each strand, feathered out to semitransparent tips.

6. **Back in Material Properties, go to the Strand panel and check the settings.**

   A couple fields are worth mentioning:

   - Make sure that the Tangent Shading check box is enabled. This gives the hair a nice shiny effect.

   - Enable the Blender Units check box. By default, Blender's hair strands are measured in pixels. Using pixels works fine except in situations where you have a hairy object move toward or away from the camera. Enabling this check box makes the hair size relative to your scene's units (set in Scene Properties) rather than the size of your final render.

- Because you're using the Blender Units option for hair size, you need to reduce the sizes for the Root and Tip of the hair strands. I usually use something like 0.02 and 0.01, respectively. You may need a few test renders to get it just right for your object.

- The other sliders control the shape and shading of the strands; you can adjust these to taste with a few test renders.

If you're going to make your emitter visible, you may also want to use a separate material for your hair particles. Otherwise, you may have to do a bunch of extra work to make sure your hair particles are the right color. If you set up a special material for your hair (perhaps using the settings I cover in the preceding steps) and name it something memorable, like `Hair`, you can choose that material for your particle system from the top of the Render panel in Particle Properties. There's a drop-down menu there with a list of all of your object's material slots; you can choose to use any one of those.

If your scene isn't too complex, you can make a lot of these material and texture changes using Rendered viewport shading (Shift+Z). It isn't quite as snappy as in Cycles, but it can be quite fast with a few optimizations (like temporarily disabling ray tracing and hiding any extraneous high-poly meshes). Faster, at least, than doing the tedious back-and-forth of test renders and settings tweaks.

Rendering hair using Cycles

If you're rendering with Cycles, the process is a bit different than with Blender Internal. In many ways, it's actually simpler. For the most part, you don't even need to leave Particles Properties. To render hair particles using Cycles, follow these basic steps:

1. **At the bottom of Particle Properties, make sure that the check box for the Cycles Hair Rendering panel is enabled.**

   That's pretty much all there is to it. Seriously. The rest of the steps here are tweaking to taste.

2. **Change the Primitive Style drop-down to Curve Segments.**

   Curves are a bit more processor intensive, but the results are worth it for smoothly flowing hair.

3. **In the Cycles Hair Settings panel, adjust the Root and Tip values to suit your character.**

   Cycles gives nice scaling to the tips of the hair, so it isn't necessary to use the Ramped transparency trick described in the previous section.

For the last two steps and any adjustments that you make to your hair material (you can specify a separate hair material in Cycles, just like I described for Blender Internal in the previous section), I recommend that you use Rendered viewport shading (Shift+Z). It gives you a very accurate understanding of what your final render will look like.

Figure 13-6 shows the same particle system as Figure 13-5, but rendered in both Blender Internal and in Cycles.

Figure 13-6:
On the left, bearded Suzanne rendered in Blender Internal. On the right, she's rendered with Cycles.

Giving Objects Some Jiggle and Bounce

Have you ever sat and watched what happens when a beach ball gets hit or bounces off of the ground? Or seen what happens when someone places a plate of gelatin on a table? Or observed how a person's hair moves when they shake their head? When these things move and collide with other objects, they have a bit of internal jiggle that can be difficult to reproduce correctly with regular animation tools. This jiggling is the basis for what is referred to as *soft body dynamics*.

You can simulate soft body dynamics in Blender from Physics Properties. Left-click the Soft Body button, and a Soft Body panel appears. In that panel, you can make adjustments and tweak the behavior of your soft body simulation.

Like with particle systems, adding soft body dynamics to an object from Physics Properties also adds a Soft Body modifier to your object. You can verify this addition by looking in Modifier Properties.

What follows is a simple step-by-step process for creating a simple soft body simulation with the default cube object:

1. **Select the default cube with a right-click and grab it up in the Z-axis so that it floats above the 3D grid (G⇨Z).**

   You want to give the cube some height to fall from. It doesn't have to be very high; 3 to 5 units should be enough.

2. **Create a Plane mesh as a ground plane (Shift+A⇨Mesh⇨Plane) and scale it larger so that you have something for the cube to hit (S).**

   This plane is the surface for your jiggly cube to bounce off of. It may be helpful to put your 3D cursor at the origin (Shift+S⇨Cursor to Center) before adding the plane.

3. **With your plane still selected, add a Collision panel in Physics Properties to give your plane collision properties.**

   Doing so makes Blender understand that the plane is an obstacle for your falling cube.

4. **Right-click the cube to select it.**

5. **Make a Soft Body panel in Physics Properties.**

   That's all you really have to do to enable soft body physics on your 3D objects. However, in order to get the cube to properly act according to gravity, there's one more step. Notice that adding soft body properties to your cube reveals a bunch of new panels to Physics Properties.

6. **Disable the Soft Body Goal check box next to its panel.**

   This step disables the default goal behavior of soft bodies. When Soft Body Goal is enabled, you can define a group of vertices in the object to be unaffected by the soft body simulation. A scenario where you may want to have Soft Body Goal enabled would be a character with loose skin, like the jowls of a large dog. You may want the dog's snout to be completely controlled by your armature animation, but have the jowls that hang off to be influenced by soft body simulation. Because in this case with the cube you want the entire object to be affected by the simulation, it's best just to turn it off.

7. **Play back the animation (Alt+A) to watch the cube fall, hit the ground plane, and jiggle as it lands again.**

   Pretty cool, huh? Figure 13-7 shows this process being completed. As with particles, it's a good practice to make sure that you're at the start frame of your animation before playing back your simulation.

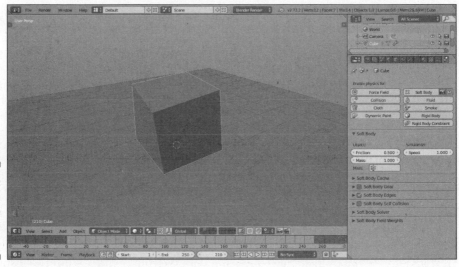

Figure 13-7:
Dropping a
jiggly cube
into the
scene.

Now, I have to admit that I cheated a bit in the preceding example by using a cube. If you were to try those steps with another type of mesh, like a UV Sphere or Suzanne, the mesh would collapse and look like it instantly deflated when it hit the ground plane. In order to get around this issue, you need to adjust one more setting. In the Soft Body Edges panel on the left column of values is a setting labeled Bending with a default value of 0.00. This value sets the bending stiffness of your object. With a setting of zero, you have no stiffness, so the mesh collapses. However, if you change this setting to a higher value, such as 3.0 or 5.0, the falling mesh retains its shape a little bit better when it collides with the ground plane. You can also enable the Stiff Quads check box in this panel to get your mesh to retain its shape even better, but be careful: This setting slows down the soft body calculation substantially.

Similar to particles, if you look in the Timeline when you play your soft body simulation, you should see an orange bar along the bottom. If the orange bar is opaque, Blender has cached that part of the simulation. If it's semi-transparent, that moment in time has not yet been cached. Cached simulation data will play at a rate that's closer to real time. To get a good idea of the timing of your simulation, let it play through all the way once, ensuring that the simulation gets cached. When you play it again, you should get a much more reasonable sense of the simulation's timing.

For any physics-related simulations in Blender, keep interacting objects (such as particle colliders, or obstacles for rigid bodies and fluids) on the same scene layers. That's a hint to Blender that these objects are meant to interact with one another. For example, if you have a soft body object and a plane as its floor on two different scene layers, the soft body will just run right through the floor without stopping.

Dropping Objects in a Scene with Rigid Body Dynamics

Not everything that reacts to physics has the internal jiggle and bounce that soft bodies have. Say, for example, that you have to animate a stack of heavy steel girders falling down at a construction site. For that animation, you don't want to have a soft body simulation. I mean, you could technically get the correct behavior with really stiff settings in the Soft Body Edges panel, but that's a bit of a kludge and potentially very CPU-intensive. You'd be better off with *rigid body dynamics*. As their name implies, *rigid bodies* don't get warped by collisions the way that soft bodies do. They either hold their form when they collide, or they break.

Like the other physical simulation types, the controls for rigid bodies are in Physics Properties. Previously, this wasn't the case. It used to be that you needed to bake rigid body simulations from Blender's internal game engine. That's no longer necessary. You need only left-click the Rigid Body button.

Use the following steps to get a simple rigid body simulation with the default cube:

1. **Select the cube by right-clicking and grab it up in the Z-axis by a few units (G⇨Z).**

   Like the soft body simulation, 3 to 5 units should be fine.

2. **Create a mesh plane to act as the ground (Shift+A⇨Mesh⇨Plane) and scale it larger so that you have something for the cube to hit (S).**

3. **With your plane still selected, add a Rigid Body panel in Physics Properties.**

   Unlike the soft bodies example, your ground plane *should not* get a collision panel. This is unique to how rigid bodies work in Blender.

4. **In your newly-created Rigid Body panel, change the Type drop-down menu from Active to Passive.**

   This tells Blender that the ground plane should be part of the rigid body calculations, but that it isn't going to be a moving object. Setting the type to Passive is basically how you set up a rigid body collier.

5. **Right-click the cube to select it.**

6. **Make a Rigid Body panel in Physics Properties.**

   That's the last step that's really required to have your cube drop into the scene. You may want to give the cube a bit of an arbitrary rotation (R⇨R) so it lands and bounces around on the plane in a more interesting way.

7. Play back the animation (Alt+A) to watch the cube fall, hit the ground plane, and bounce around a bit.

Congratulations! You have a rigid body simulation.

Figure 13-8 shows a breakdown of the preceding steps.

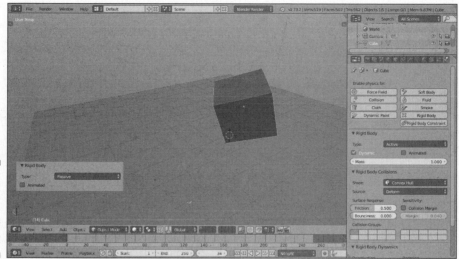

Figure 13-8:
Creating
a simple
rigid body
simulation.

Simulating Cloth

Cloth simulation and soft body simulation are very similar in Blender, despite a few key differences. Both soft bodies and cloth work on open as well as closed meshes — that is, the mesh could be flat like a plane or more of a shell like a cube or sphere. However, soft bodies tend to work better on closed meshes, whereas cloth is better suited for open ones.

Also, the cloth simulator tends to work better with *self collisions*. Think about the fabric of a flowing dress. In the real world, if you bunch up part of a dress, it's technically colliding with itself. In computer simulations, you want to re-create that effect; otherwise, the fold of one part of the dress breaks through the fold of another part, giving you a completely unrealistic result. The cloth simulator handles these situations much better than the soft body simulator.

Revisiting the simple default cube, here's a quick walk-through on getting some cloth to drape across it:

1. **Create a mesh Grid (Shift+A⇨Mesh⇨Grid) and grab it along the Z-axis (G⇨Z) so that it's above the default cube.**

2. **Scale the Grid so it's larger than the Cube (S).**

   It doesn't have to be too high; just a couple of units should be plenty.

3. **Apply smooth shading to the grid (Tool Shelf⇨Shading⇨Smooth).**

   This step is really just to make it look prettier. It has no effect on the actual simulation.

4. **Apply a Subdivision Surfaces modifier to the plane (Ctrl+1).**

   The simulator now has even more vertices to work with. Of course, adding subdivisions causes the simulation to take longer, but this amount should be fine. It's important that you do this before adding cloth properties to your mesh. Like many other simulators, cloth is added in Blender as a modifier, and the order in the modifier stack is important.

5. **In Physics Properties, left-click the Cloth button to enable the cloth simulator.**

   The default preset for the cloth simulator is Cotton. That preset should work fine here, but feel free to play and change to something else.

6. **In the Cloth Collision panel, enable the Self Collision check box.**

   This step ensures that the simulator does everything it can to prevent the cloth from intersecting with itself.

   At this point, your cloth simulation is all set up for the plane. However, if you were to play the animation with Alt+A right now, the plane would drop right through the cube. You want the cube to behave as an obstacle, so follow the next steps.

7. **Select the cube object (right-click) and left-click the Collision button in Physics Properties.**

   Collision properties appear for your cube. Your simulation is set up.

8. **Press Alt+A to watch the cloth simulate.**

   Figure 13-9 shows what the results of this process should look like. It's a good idea to set your time cursor at the start of your animation in the Timeline before playing back the simulation.

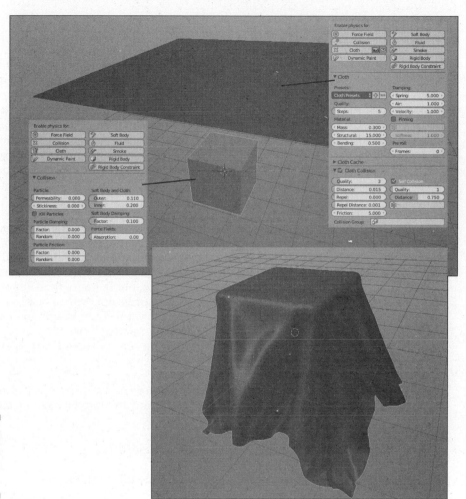

Figure 13-9:
Creating a
simple cloth
simulation.

REMEMBER

As with the other simulation types in Blender, if you look in the Timeline
when you play your soft body simulation, you should notice a bar along
the bottom. In the case of cloth simulation, that bar is blue. If it's opaque,
Blender has cached that part of the simulation. If it's semi-transparent, that
moment in time has not yet been cached. To get a good idea of the timing of
your simulation, let it play through all the way once, ensuring that the simulation gets cached. On the second time playing, you should get a much more
reasonable sense of the simulation's timing.

Splashing Fluids in Your Scene

In my opinion, an especially fun feature in Blender is its integrated fluid simulator. This thing is just really cool and a ton of fun to play with, to boot.

Before running head-long into fluid simulation-land, however, you should know a few things that are different about the fluid simulator. Like most of the other physics simulation controls, the main controls for the fluid simulator are in Physics Properties. However, unlike particle, cloth, and soft body simulations, which can technically work in an infinite amount of space, the fluid simulator requires a *domain*, or world, for the simulation to take place.

Another difference is that the fluid simulator actually creates a separate mesh for each and every frame of animation that it simulates. Because of the detail involved in a fluid, these meshes can get to be quite large and take up a lot of memory. To account for that size, the fluid simulator actually saves these meshes to your hard drive in .bobj.gz files. The other simulation systems can also save data to your hard drive, but because fluid simulation data can take up an enormous amount of hard drive space, you need to explicitly tell Blender where to save these files. The whole fluid simulation can't be cached in RAM. Because these files can get pretty large, it's a good idea to confirm that you have plenty of hard drive space available for storing your simulation.

The fluid simulator has all the other features of the other physics simulators. It recognizes gravity, understands static and animated collisions, and has a wide array of available controls.

Use these steps to create a simple fluid simulation:

1. **Right-click the default cube and scale (S) it larger.**

   This cube serves as your simulation's domain. The domain can actually be any shape or size, but I definitely recommend that you use a cube or box shape as the domain. Other meshes just use their width and height, or *bounding box*, so it's essentially a cube anyway. In this example, I scaled the default cube by 5 units.

2. **In Physics Properties, left-click the Fluid button and choose Domain from the Type drop-down menu.**

   Now the fluid simulator recognizes your cube as the domain for the simulation. Figure 13-10 shows the Fluid panel with the Domain option from the Type drop-down menu.

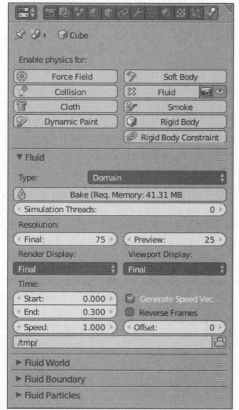

Figure 13-10:
The Fluid panel with options for a domain object.

3. **Set the location where simulation meshes are saved.**

   Use the text field at the bottom of the Fluid panel. By default, Blender sends the `.bobj.gz` files to their own folder the `/tmp` directory. However, I recommend you create your own folder somewhere else on your hard drive, especially if you're using Windows and don't have a `/tmp` directory. Left-click the folder icon to navigate to that location with the File Browser.

4. **Decide at which resolution you would like to bake the simulation.**

   These values are set with the Final and Preview values under the Resolution label. The Final resolution setting is the value that is used when you render. Typically, it's a higher number than the Preview resolution, which is usually used in the 3D View. For the Preview value, you want a smaller number so that you can get your timing correct. The defaults should work fine for this example, although higher values would look better. Be careful, though, depending on the type of machine you're using: very large values may try to use more RAM than your computer has, bringing the simulation time to a crawl.

Conveniently, the Bake button at the top of the Fluid panel gives you an estimation of how much memory it expects to need. As long as that is less than the amount of RAM your computer has available, you should be good to go (though you may still wait quite a while for a simulation to finish. Blender still has to calculate the simulation for all those subdivisions).

Blender's fluid simulator gives you the ability to use multiple *threads*, or processing streams on your computer. If you have a modern computer with multiple cores, you can take advantage of this feature. However — and this is a pretty big however — each thread requires a separate copy of your simulation data. This means that whatever number the fluid simulator is estimating for the amount of RAM it needs, you must multiply it by the number of threads. So if you've set up a simulation with a resolution that uses 1 GB of memory and you set the Simulation Threads value to 4, then you'll actually need 4 GB of memory to do that simulation.

5. Determine the time that you want to simulate the fluid's behavior.

The Start and End values under the Time label in the Fluid panel are the time of the simulation, measured in seconds. By default, the simulator starts at 0.000 and runs until 4.000 seconds. An important thing to realize here is that this time is scaled across the full number of frames in your animation, as noted in the Timeline or the Dimensions panel of Render Properties. If you're using Blender's default frame rate of 24 fps and length of 250 frames, your simulation will be in slow motion, showing 4 seconds of fluid simulation over a span of roughly 10.4 seconds. For this test, I set the End time in the Fluid simulator to 3.000 seconds and the duration of the animation to be 72 frames long.

6. Create a mesh to act as the fluid in your simulation (Shift+A⇨Mesh⇨Icosphere).

I typically like to use an icosphere, but any mesh will work. To give yourself some more room, you may also want to move this mesh up the Z-axis (G⇨Z) to somewhere near the top of the domain cube so that you have some room for the fluid to fall.

7. In Physics Properties, left-click the Fluid button and choose Inflow Type from the drop-down menu.

Your icosphere is set as the source for the fluids entering the domain. Choosing Inflow means that the mesh constantly produces more and more fluid as the simulation goes on. If you prefer to have a single fluid object with a fixed volume, choose Fluid rather than Inflow. Figure 13-11 shows the Fluid panel with the Inflow fluid type chosen.

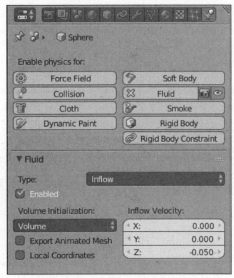

Figure 13-11:
The Fluid panel with options for an inflow object.

8. **(Optional) Give the Inflow object an initial velocity in the negative Z direction.**

   This step is optional because the fluid simulator *does* recognize the Gravity setting in Scene Properties. Adding an initial force in the negative Z direction here just gives it a little extra push. The value doesn't have to be large: –0.10 should work just fine. You want to make this value negative so that it pushes the fluid down. This initial velocity is added to the force already set by gravity. At this point, your simulation is configured.

9. **Select the domain cube (right-click) and bake the simulation.**

   Left-click the large Bake button in the Fluid panel. I know that this sounds odd — "Baking fluids? Really? Won't it boil?" — but that's the terminology used. You're running the simulation for each frame and "baking" that frame's simulation result to a mesh that's saved on your hard drive. If you look at it in that way, it *kind* of makes sense.

10. **Watch the progress of the fluid simulation.**

   Depending on how powerful your computer is, this baking process can be pretty time consuming. I once had a 4-second fluid simulation that took 36 hours to bake. (Granted, it was at a high resolution, and I had a lot of crazy Inflow objects and complex moving obstacles, so it was entirely my own fault.) Just know that the more complexity you add to your simulation and the higher the resolution, the more time it's going to take. As the progress bar at the top of the screen shows your simulation processing, you can interactively follow progress in the 3D View. Remember that Blender has a non-blocking interface, so you can actually scrub the Timeline, use the ←/→ hotkeys, and even play back the animation (Alt+A) while Blender is still baking. How's that for cool?

11. **Play back the finished simulation with Alt+A.**

    One thing to note here is that your mesh looks faceted. You can easily fix this issue by left-clicking the Smooth button beneath the Shading label in the Tools tab of the Tool Shelf.

And, *POW:* You have water pouring into your scene! Using these same basic steps, you can add obstacles to the scene that can move the water around as you see fit.

Knowing when to use the right type of fluids

Blender's particle system also offers a way to do fluid simulation by choosing the Fluid physics type from the Physics panel in Particle Properties. And because that choice is available, you may find yourself wondering why you'd use this mesh-based method when that one is available. The short answer is that it all depends on what you're trying to do. For example, the particle-based fluid technique is useful if you need your fluids to interact with Blender's other simulators (force fields, cloth, and so on) or if you're simulating large-scale

fluids that don't quite fit in the constraints of a 10-meter cube. The particle-based method is not so great, however, for detailed small-scale fluid simulations or if you need to use materials with ray traced transparency or shadows. The particle-based technique doesn't currently generate meshes where you can apply those materials (though that's likely to change in future releases of Blender). For those situations, the fluid simulation technique covered in this section is more useful.

Smoking without Hurting Your Lungs: Smoke Simulation in Blender

In addition to all the other cool physics simulation goodies that come bundled with Blender, you can also do smoke and fire simulations. The process for setting up the smoke simulator is in some ways very similar to the fluid simulator in that it requires that you set up a domain object (under the hood, the algorithms for the two are pretty similar). However, that's where the similarities end. For one, the smoke simulator doesn't generate mesh objects, so you're not compelled to find a clean chunk of hard drive space to store your simulation data. And a much bigger difference becomes apparent when you get down to trying to render the smoke.

First, however, you need to set up your initial smoke simulation. Use the following steps:

1. **From the default scene, scale the cube up.**

   For this example, scaling by a factor of 5 should be fine (S⇨5⇨Enter).

2. **From Physics Properties, left-click the Smoke button to create a Smoke panel.**

3. **In your new Smoke panel, left-click the Domain button.**

   When you click this button, Blender knows to treat your cube as a smoke domain. The cube automatically changes to wireframe display in the 3D View and you get a whole bunch of additional panels in Physics Properties. For now, you can leave all of these settings at their defaults. Figure 13-12 shows the panels for a smoke domain.

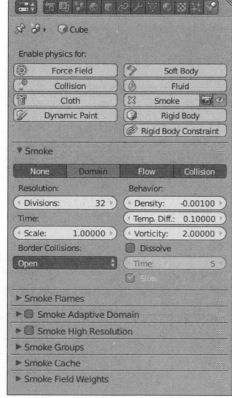

Figure 13-12: A smoke domain object has a lot of options for you to play with.

4. **Back in the 3D View, add a simple mesh and lower it a bit (Shift+A⇨Icosphere, G⇨Z⇨-3⇨Enter).**

   This object will be your smoke source. And your smoke naturally will float up, so it makes sense to lower your object a bit to give the smoke some room to show up.

5. **In Physics Properties, add a Smoke panel.**

6. **In your new Smoke panel, left-click the Flow button.**

   This establishes your smaller object as your smoke source. As Figure 13-13 shows, there are fewer panels and options for a smoke flow object than a smoke domain, but there's still quite a few. Fortunately, you can leave these settings at their defaults for now.

7. **Play back your simulation with Alt+A.**

   Smoke should start billowing up from your flow object and stop when it reaches the faces of your smoke domain.

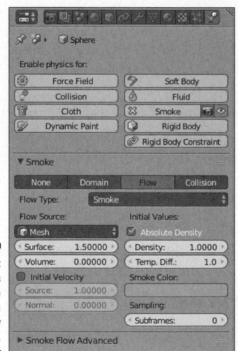

Figure 13-13: The panels showing the options for a smoke flow object.

8. Tweak your smoke settings to taste.

There's a lot of playing that you can do here. Not only does the smoke simulator make smoke, it can simulate fire, and you can add objects to collide with the smoke in all kinds of interesting ways. You really can lose hours — perhaps days — of your life messing around with all the settings in the smoke simulator.

Those are the basics of setting up a simple smoke simulation in Blender. As Figure 13-14 shows, the 3D View gives you a nice preview of your smoke simulation.

Unfortunately, if you try to render your smoke simulation as-is, you'll be disappointed. Regardless of whether you're using Blender Internal or Cycles, all you'll see is the blocky cube shape of your smoke domain. To get your smoke simulation to render, you need to make a few more improvements, as covered in the next two sections.

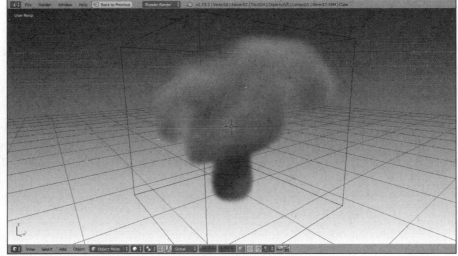

Figure 13-14:
A simple smoke simulation displayed in the 3D View.

Rendering smoke using Blender Internal

In 3D computer graphics, smoke and fire fit into a category of materials referred to as *volumetric effects*. In meatspace, there's no such thing as a smoke object (a *smoking* object, yes, but not a smoke object). It isn't a single object. You see smoke because it's a build up (a *volume*) of millions of small particles floating in the air. They reflect and obstruct light. Unlike solid objects, it just isn't sufficient to render the surface of smoke and fire. The result doesn't look believable. Your renderer must support volumes.

Fortunately, both the Blender Internal and Cycles renderers have support for volumetric materials. They're just a little bit trickier to set up than regular materials. Assuming you already have a smoke simulation created to your satisfaction, follow these steps to get it to render in Blender Internal:

1. **Select your smoke domain object (right-click).**

2. **If your smoke domain doesn't already have a material slot, add one by clicking the Plus (+) icon next to the list box at the top of Material Properties.**

   Your smoke domain should only have one material. If you already have a material slot in use, just use that one.

3. **In the Material datablock, left-click the New button to add a new material.**

   Rename the material to something descriptive, like `Smoke`.

4. **From the row of buttons under the material datablock in Material Properties, left-click the Volume button.**

   Clicking this button tells the Blender Internal renderer that this is a volumetric material.

5. **In the Density panel of Material Properties, set the Density value to 0.**

   If you're watching the material preview at the top of Material Properties, the preview object should disappear, leaving only its shadow. Don't worry. This is supposed to happen.

6. **Switch over to Texture Properties and add a new texture. Change its type to Voxel Data.**

   A *voxel* is a volumetric pixel. This is how Blender stores your smoke simulation. You're telling Blender to use the voxel data from your simulation as a three-dimensional texture. All you need to do is tell Blender where the simulation data is and how it influences the material's appearance. Those are the next steps.

7. **In the Voxel Data panel of Texture Properties, make sure the File Format drop-down menu is set to Smoke and fill in the Domain Object field with the name of your smoke domain.**

   If you gave your smoke domain a descriptive name, it should be easy to find in the Domain Object field. If not, press E with your mouse cursor hovered over the field to enable the eyedropper, then left-click on your smoke domain in the 3D View to pick it.

8. **In the Mapping panel of Texture Properties, change the Coordinates drop-down menu to use Generated coordinates.**

9. **In the Influence panel of Texture Properties, enable the check box next to the Density slider.**

   This maps the voxel data from your smoke simulation to the Density property of your volumetric material.

10. **Render your smoke material (F12) or enable Rendered viewport shading in your 3D View (Shift+Z).**

    There you have it! Your rendered smoke has the same basic smoke effect you see in the 3D View. From here, you can do all kinds of tweaks to your material settings to further customize your smoke material.

Figure 13-15 shows a simple smoke simulation rendered using Blender Internal.

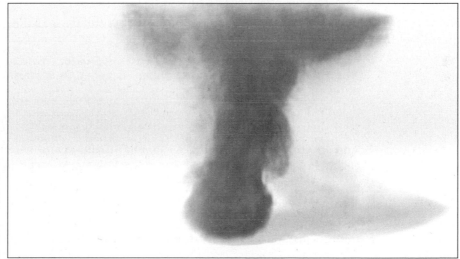

Figure 13-15:
Blender Internal renders smoke!

Rendering smoke using Cycles

Blender's other renderer, Cycles, can also render your smoke simulation. The basic principle is still the same. Your goal is to map the data from your simulation to a volumetric shader. Use the following steps:

1. **Select your smoke domain object (right-click).**

2. **If your smoke domain doesn't already have a material slot, add one by clicking the Plus (+) icon next to the list box at the top of Material Properties.**

   Your smoke domain should only have one material. If you already have a material slot in use, just use that one.

3. **In the Material datablock, left-click the New button to add a new material.**

   Rename the material to something descriptive, like Smoke. From this point, you *could* continue to work in Material Properties, but it's much easier to see what's going on from the Node Editor.

4. **Split the 3D View and change one of the new areas into a Node Editor.**

   Make sure you're using the Shader node tree type. It's the leftmost button of the node tree type button blocks; the one with the same icon as Material Properties in the Properties editor. For more on using the Node Editor for materials, see Chapter 7.

5. **In the Node Editor, select the Diffuse BSDF shader node and delete it (right-click the node, X).**

6. **Add a Volume Absorption shader (Shift+A⇨Shader⇨Volume Absorption) and wire it to the Volume socket of the Material Output node.**

   If you're looking at your 3D View in Rendered viewport shading (Shift+Z), your smoke domain should appear as a kind of smokey cube.

7. **Add an Attribute node (Shift+A⇨Input⇨Attribute) and wire its Fac socket to the Density input socket of the Volume Absorption node.**

   If you're still looking at your 3D View in Rendered viewport shading, your smoke domain should disappear. Not to worry, I told you that there was a tricky part. It's the next step.

8. **In the Name field of the Attribute node, type density.**

   And poof! (Pun intended.) You have smoke in your render. From here, you can tweak colors and other attributes of your material to land on the visual effect that you want. For instance, you may want to try the following steps to incorporate the Volume Scatter node to your material network.

9. **Add a Volume Scatter shader (Shift+A⇨Shader⇨Volume Scatter).**

10. **Wire the Fac socket of your density Attribute node to the Density socket on your new Volume Scatter node.**

11. **Add an Add Shader (Shift+A⇨Shader⇨Add Shader).**

    The plan here is to mix the two volume shaders together.

12. **Wire your Volume Absorption node to one socket of your Add Shader node and wire your Volume Scatter node to the other socket on the Add Shader node.**

13. **Wire the output of your Add Shader node to the Volume socket of the Material Output node.**

    Steps 9-13 make your smoke material disperse light and cast shadows in a more realistic way.

Figure 13-16 shows a screenshot of Blender with a simple smoke material in the Node Editor and shows the results of that material in the 3D View with Rendered viewport shading.

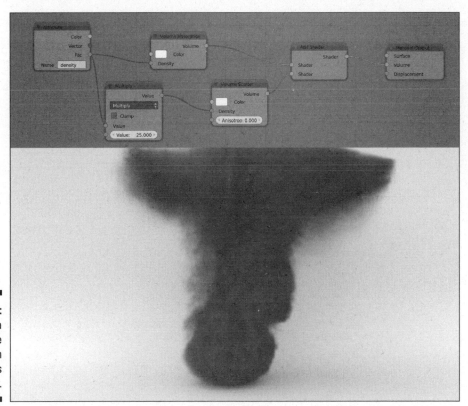

Figure 13-16: Setting up a basic smoke material in Cycles is pretty easy.

Part IV
Sharing Your Work with the World

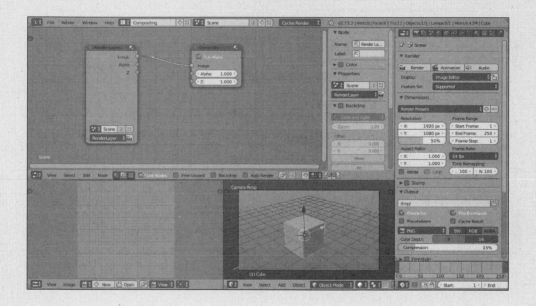

In this part . . .

- ✔ Exporting to external formats.
- ✔ Selecting a renderer.
- ✔ Compositing and editing images and video.
- ✔ Visit www.dummies.com/extras/blender for great Dummies content online.

Chapter 14

Exporting and Rendering Scenes

*W*orking in Blender is great, but eventually, you'll want to make the things you create viewable in places other than Blender's 3D View. You may want to have a printable still image of a scene, or a movie of your character falling down a flight of stairs, or you may want to export the geometry and textures of a model for use in a video game. In these situations, you want to export or render.

Exporting to External Formats

Exporting takes your 3D data from Blender and restructures it so that other 3D programs can understand it. There are two primary reasons why you'd want to export to a 3D file format other than Blender's .blend format. The most common is to do additional editing in another program. For example, if you're working as a modeler on a large project, chances are good that whoever hired you, unfortunately, is not using Blender, so you'll probably need to save it in a format that fits into their pipeline and is understood by their tools.

The other reason for exporting is for video games. Many games have a public specification of the format they use for loading 3D data. Blender can export in many of these formats, allowing you to create custom characters and sets.

With only a few exceptions, all of Blender's exporters are scripts written in the Python programming language. Although all the export scripts that ship with Blender support the basic specifications in their respective formats, they may not support all the features. For example, many of the exporters have difficulty getting armature or animation information out of Blender.

So keep this limitation in mind, do a lot of testing with your exported files, and, as many open source programmers like to say, "Your mileage may vary."

To export to a different format, choose File⇨Export and choose the format that you would like to use. A File Browser then appears so you can tell Blender where to save your new file. The left region of the File Browser contains options that are specific to the exporter you chose. Figure 14-1 shows the Export menu with a list of the available file types.

You may note that the export list appears strangely sparse. Most export-ers in Blender are implemented as add-ons, the bulk of which are disabled by default. If you're looking for a specific exporter and you don't see it in the File⇨Export menu, go to the Add-ons section of User Preferences (Ctrl+Alt+U) and find the add-on that provides the exporter you need. If the add-on is there, enable it, and the exporter should immediately be available in File⇨Export. To make the exporter always available, left-click the Save User Settings button at the bottom of User Preferences.

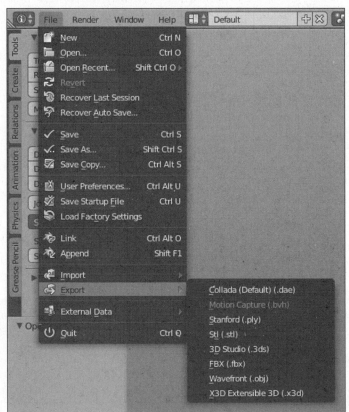

Figure 14-1:
File⇨
Export⇨
Wheee-
eeee!

Blender's Render Engines

Since the last edition of *Blender For Dummies* was released, Blender has gained a whole new renderer, Cycles. Blender includes both Cycles and the classic Blender renderer, now typically referred to as Blender Internal. Cycles and Blender Internal have massive differences, both in how they work internally and how you work with them in Blender. Whatever the technical differences, the important difference boils down to trade-offs between artist time and computer time.

Cycles is a modern renderer. Ironically, the technology is based on ray tracing, an older rendering method that has become more popular as computers have gotten fast enough to use this technique without taking days to output a single frame. A ray tracer works by shooting imaginary lines, called rays, from the camera to the scene. Those rays intersect or bounce off of materials or lights in the scene. Based on where those rays connect, the renderer calculates the correct color and brightness of materials in the scene. Ray tracing can more accurately depict the behavior of light in a scene than the methods used in render engines like Blender Internal (often called scanline renderers, or hybrid renderers if they try to incorporate some ray tracing).

From the user perspective, the trade-off depends on whether artist time or computer time is more expensive:

✔ With a ray tracing renderer, it's often very fast and easy to set up lights and materials on objects, because you basically apply your understanding of the physical, meatspace world. However, that typically comes at the cost of having very long render times.

✔ With a scanline renderer, you can spend a frighteningly long stretch of time tweaking, hacking, and faking lighting and materials, but render times usually are significantly shorter.

Let me throw one more monkey wrench into the mix. One of the key features of Cycles is that it can take advantage of the graphics processing unit (GPU) on certain video cards to accelerate the rendering process (often more than ten times faster than the CPU). This starts to make Cycles a much more well-rounded and compelling choice. But the choice isn't super clear, because Cycles can't take advantage of all GPUs, and many GPUs don't come with sufficient memory for processing large scenes.

If you're just starting out, my recommendation is to forget about trade-offs in speed and focus on the aesthetic. What kind of look are you trying to achieve with your 3D image or animation?

✔ Are you aiming for the kind of realism you see in a photograph? Cycles usually is a better choice for realism. There's much less frustration, because you won't need to be an expert at the nuanced fakery required by Blender Internal.

✔ You don't care about realism, and you're interested in taking more artistic license with the way things look (leaning toward the cartoony or the abstract)? Blender Internal may be a better fit for your project.

Decide case by case. In fact, I've used *both* renderers on a project, then composited the results (using the tools covered in Chapter 15).

Whatever you decide, Chapters 7, 8, and 9 cover how to set up materials, lights, and environments in both Blender Internal and Cycles.

Rendering a Scene

More often than exporting, you probably want to render your scenes. *Rendering* is the process of taking your 3D data and creating one or more 2D pictures from the perspective of a camera. The 2D result can then be seen by nearly anyone using image viewers or movie players.

Rendering is very much like taking a photograph or a movie in meatspace. If you don't have a camera, you can't take a picture. Likewise in Blender, if there's no camera in your scene, Blender doesn't know what to render, so make sure that you have a camera in there. If there is no camera, you can add a camera (Shift+A⇨Camera) and set it as the active camera in the scene (Ctrl+Numpad 0).

If your scene is complex, the Outliner is a fantastic place to find and select your camera object. Assuming you haven't renamed your camera object, you can use the Search field in the Outliner's header. Type in Camera; if that object exists in your .blend file, it appears. (The Search field is case-sensitive; if you don't know whether you've used uppercase for the first letter of your object, you may be better off searching for amera.)

Creating a still image

Rendering single images, or *stills,* in Blender is remarkably easy, regardless of the render engine you choose. Blender actually offers three different ways to do it. The fastest way is to simply press the F12 hotkey. Alternatively, you can left-click the Render button in the Render panel of Render Properties or choose Render⇨Render Image from the Info editor's header menu at the top of each of the screen layouts that ship with Blender. For details on setting up your materials and lighting for each of Blender's renderers, look at Chapters 7, 8, and 9.

Viewing your rendered images in Blender

Any way you decide to do it, Blender uses its integrated UV/Image Editor to display the rendered output. If you don't have a UV/Image Editor already open in your screen layout, Blender takes the largest area in your screen layout and changes it to the UV/Image Editor while rendering. Of course, some people would prefer a different behavior for displaying renders. Fortunately, available options allow you to change that behavior. The control is a drop-down menu in the Render panel of Render Properties, labeled Display. By default, it's set to Image Editor.

Figure 14-2 shows the Render panel and the four different options you have for where to send your renders. I like to use the default Image Editor setting or Full Screen. The following is a quick description of what each option does:

✔ **Full Screen:** This option does the same thing as the Image Editor option, except it also maximizes the UV/Image Editor to the entire Blender window.

✔ **Image Editor:** The default. Blender changes the largest area on your screen to a UV/Image Editor and displays your rendered image there.

✔ **New Window:** Blender creates a completely new window, populated only with a UV/Image Editor that displays your image.

✔ **Keep UI:** Blender doesn't display your render at all if you don't already have a UV/Image Editor available.

This can reduce the resources Blender consumes while rendering, but you don't get to see your render as it progresses.

For any of these render options, you can quickly toggle between your regular Blender screen and the render screen by pressing F11.

Figure 14-2:
To view your renders, choose to use Full Screen, Image Editor, or New Window. If you don't want to view your render, choose Keep UI.

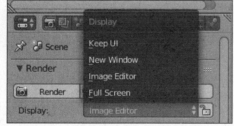

Another cool feature that works regardless of which way you like to see your renders are the render slots (sometimes called *render buffers*). When you have your render output onscreen in the UV/Image Editor, hover your mouse cursor in that editor and press J. Upon doing so, Blender switches to a different image buffer. The first time, it may seem odd because you just see a blank UV/Image Editor. However, bounce back to your scene (F11) and make a small change. Then render again (F12). Now when you press J on your render, it pops back to your previous render. Press J again, and you're back at your current render. The default behavior is to use J to toggle between two slots, but Blender offers you the ability to swap between up to eight render slots.

To use another render slot, left-click the Slot drop-down menu in the UV/Image Editor's header and pick the slot you want to render to. The next time you render (F12), this slot is filled. Using render slots, you can quickly compare the differences between different renders, cycling forward and backward through the non-empty slots by using J and Alt+J, respectively. Render slots are a great way to see whether you like the changes you've made to your scene.

Picking an image format

Now, you have your image rendered, but you still haven't saved it anywhere on your hard drive. It's not quite available for sharing with other people yet. This, too, is easily remedied, but before you save, you may want to change the file type for your image. Go to the Output panel of Render Properties, as shown in Figure 14-3.

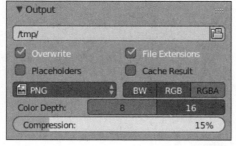

Figure 14-3: Output panel in Render Properties.

When you save with Blender's File Browser, you also can choose the file type for your image from a drop-down menu in the region on the left side.

This works great if you're in a rush or if you forgot to choose your image format ahead of time. In fact, you don't even need to re-render if you change your image format. Internally, Blender stores your renders in the highest possible quality and only compresses when you save to a specific format (see "Saving your still image" in this chapter).

That said, the Output panel in Render Properties is the preferred way because it gives you a few more options for controlling your saved file. The primary control for choosing the format of your file in the Output panel is a file type drop-down menu. By default, Blender saves renders as PNG (pronounced "ping") images. If you want to render to a different image format, such as JPEG, Targa, TIFF, or OpenEXR, left-click this drop-down menu and choose your desired file type. Depending on the file type you choose, the options at the bottom of the Output panel change. For example, with the PNG file type, the Compression slider is available for controlling the level of compression in the image.

The BW/RGB/RGBA buttons below the file type drop-down are always visible, and they're pretty important for both animations and stills. They control whether Blender, after rendering, saves a black and white (grayscale) image, a full color image, or a color image with an alpha channel for transparency. Typically, you use one of the latter two. RGB is the most common and is supported by all formats, creating a full color image. On some occasions, however, you'll want to render with transparency.

As an example, say that you've made a really cool building model, and you want to add your building to a photo of some city skyline using a separate program like GIMP or Photoshop. (You can do it in Blender, too. See Chapter 15.) You need everything that's not your building, including the background of your image, to be rendered as transparent. An alpha channel defines that transparency. The *alpha channel* is basically a grayscale image that defines what is and is not transparent. Totally white pixels are opaque, and totally black pixels are transparent. Gray pixels are semitransparent.

Not all image formats support an alpha channel, such as the JPEG and BMP formats. If you choose one of these file types and have RGBA set, Blender just omits the alpha information when saving. If you want to make sure that your alpha channel is preserved, though, choose one of the following formats: PNG, Targa, TIFF, or OpenEXR.

Setting dimensions for your renders

The Dimensions panel close to the top of Render Properties gives you control over the size of your final render. The X and Y values under the Resolution label set the width and height of your image in pixels. The X and Y values under the Aspect Ratio label are for determining the horizontal and vertical aspect ratio of your image. The ability to adjust aspect ratio is for certain circumstances where you want to render your image with rectangular pixels rather than square ones. Typically, rectangular pixels are necessary only for television formats, so unless you know exactly what you're doing or if you're using a preset, I recommend setting these to the same value. I use 1.000 most of the time.

Speaking of presets, Blender offers a number of rendering presets for you to use. These presets are available from a drop-down menu at the top of the Dimensions panel. Choosing any one of them only affects settings in the Dimensions panel, but they're really handy if you know what your final output should be. Using presets is a great timesaver when you know, for example, that you have to render to high-definition video specifications, but you can't remember the right resolution, aspect ratio, and frame-rate values.

Whenever you change the resolution or aspect ratio values in the Dimensions panel, you need to render your scene again (F12) to get it to appear (and save) in the right size. If you're just changing your output file type, you don't need to re-render.

Saving your still image

After you've adjusted all your settings, rendered, and chosen your output file format, you have just one thing left to do: Save your still. Saving is quick and painless. From the UV/Image Editor, press F3 or choose Image⇨Save As, and Blender brings up a File Browser. Here, you can dictate where on your computer you want to save your render. That's it!

Remember, if you're rendering a still image, it's *not* saved anywhere on your hard drive unless you explicitly save it by pressing F3 or navigating to Image⇨Save As in the UV/Image Editor. I can't tell you how much time I spent re-rendering images that I forgot to save when I first started using Blender. Hopefully, you can learn from my mistake.

For rendering animations, the steps are similar to rendering stills (see preceding section), but you have a few more considerations. The largest consideration deals with the file type you choose. If, for example, you choose a still image format like JPEG, PNG, or OpenEXR, Blender creates an individual image for each frame in your animation. However, if you choose any of the movie options like AVI, QuickTime, or MPEG, Blender creates a single movie file that contains all the frames in the animation, as well as any sound you use for the animation.

Depending on the movie format you choose, an Encoding panel appears in Render Properties in which you have a second set of choices that enables you to pick the *codec,* or compression format, you want to use. Figure 14-4 shows the options in this panel.

The Encoding panel lets you choose which codec you would like to use, and it also offers you the ability to tweak how the actual video gets compressed. More often than not, though, the default settings tend to work pretty well.

Like in the Dimensions panel, a presets drop-down menu appears at the top of the Encoding panel for commonly used configurations. Using this menu automatically enables the proper settings for rendering outputs such as DV, DVD, and web formats (such as h.264).

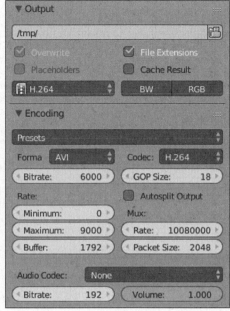

Figure 14-4:
The
Encoding
panel in
Render
Properties.

The Audio Codec drop-down menu lower down the panel gives you similar control over the sound that Blender renders (if the file type supports audio), but arguably the most important thing to remember is to make sure that the Audio Codec drop-down isn't set to None if you want audio to be included with your rendered movie file. The PCM option gives you the best results, but also yields the largest file sizes.

Make sure that you test your files if you want other people to be able to view them. I can't tell you how many times I've rendered a movie file that plays just fine on my Linux machine, but won't even open on a Windows or Macintosh machine. It's ugly and makes everyone look bad. So make sure that you try to view the file on as many machines as possible before sharing it with the world.

The other consideration to make when saving an animation is where on your hard drive you intend to store it. Enter this information on the first field of the Output panel. By default, Blender saves your animations to the /tmp directory on your computer. However, you may not have a /tmp directory, or you explicitly may want to save the animation to a different folder on your hard drive. Left-click the file folder icon to the right of this text field and use the File Browser to navigate where you want to save your animation.

So, to render animation, the steps are pretty similar to rendering a still:

1. **Set up your render resolution from the Dimensions panel and your file type from the Output panel.**

   If you've been working on your animation, hopefully you've set it all up already. Although changing the output resolution (the width and height) of the image after you animate isn't too bad, changing to other frame rates after the fact can ruin the timing of an animation and it gets to be a pain to fix. Set the frame rate from the Frame Rate value in the second block of buttons of the Dimensions panel.

2. **Confirm the start and end frames from the Frame Range values in the Dimensions panel.**

   You probably already made this setting while animating, but double-check these start and end frames to make sure that they're correct. These values also can be set from the Timeline's header.

3. **Verify where you want to save your file in the Output panel.**

4. **Animate by pressing Ctrl+F12.**

   Also, you can press the Animation button in the Render panel or choose Render⇨Render Animation. Your animation immediately starts being created. Now go get a cup of coffee. Rendering an animation can take quite some time.

Unlike rendering a still image, which does not save anything to your hard drive until you press F3, rendering an animation automatically saves your renders wherever you stipulate in the Output panel.

Creating a sequence of still images for editing or compositing

In most situations, rendering out a sequence of still images rather than a single movie file makes a lot of sense. One of the biggest reasons for rendering a sequence of stills is for *compositing*, or combining multiple images together. When you do compositing, you often rely on having an alpha channel that makes everything transparent except for your rendered subject. Most video formats simply don't support an alpha channel, so to accommodate this shortcoming, you render out a sequence of still images in a format that does support alpha, such as PNG.

Another reason that you may want to have a still image sequence rather than a movie file is for *editing,* or sequencing multiple video and animation clips. To get smaller file sizes, many video codecs throw out large chunks of image data from one frame to the next. The result is a small file that plays well, but is pretty difficult to edit because in editing, you may want to cut on a frame that doesn't have very much image data at all. Using a sequence of still images guarantees that all image data for each and every frame is completely there for smooth editing. Chapter 15 covers both compositing and editing in more detail.

The third reason you may want to render a sequence of still images is largely practical. When rendering to a movie format, what happens if you decide to stop the render and change a small part of it? Or what happens if Blender crashes in the middle of rendering? Or if an army of angry squirrels invade your office and shut down your computer mid-render? Well, you have to restart the whole render process from the start frame. Starting over, of course, is painful, especially if you have to wait multiple minutes for each frame in your sequence to render. If you render by using a sequence of still images, those images are saved the second that they're created. If your render process gets stopped for any reason, you don't have to start rendering again from the beginning. You can adjust the Start value in the Dimensions panel of Render Properties (or in the Timeline) to pick up where you left off and resume the render process.

If you choose to save a sequence of still images, you should create a specific folder just for these render files. You're going to create a *lot* of files. If the animation is 250 frames long and you render to still images, you're going to get 250 individual images saved to your hard drive.

Chapter 15

Compositing and Editing

In This Chapter

▶ Taking a look at editing and compositing

▶ Editing video and animations with Blender's Video Sequence Editor

▶ Compositing images and video

*I*n live-action film and video, the term *post-production* usually includes nearly anything associated with animation. Nearly every animator or effects specialist has groaned upon hearing a director or producer say the line, "We'll fix it in post." Fortunately, in animation, post-production is more specific, focusing on editing and compositing.

This chapter is a quick guide to editing and compositing, using Blender's Video Sequence Editor and Node Compositor. Understand that these topics are large enough for a book of their own, so the content of this chapter isn't comprehensive. That said, you can find enough solid information here and in Blender's online documentation (`http://blender.org/manual`) to figure it out. I explain Blender's interface for these tools, as well as some fundamental concepts, including nonlinear editing and node systems. With this understanding, these tools can help turn your work from "Hey, that's cool" to "Whoa!"

Comparing Editing to Compositing

Editing is the process of taking rendered footage — animation, film, or video — and adjusting how various shots appear in sequence. You typically edit using a *nonlinear editor* (NLE). An NLE, like Apple's Final Cut Pro or Adobe Premiere, differs from older *linear* tape-to-tape editing systems that required editors to work sequentially. With an NLE, you can easily edit the beginning of a sequence without worrying too much about it messing up the timing at the end. Blender has basic NLE functionality with its Video Sequence Editor.

Compositing is the process of mixing animations, videos, and still images into a single image or video. It's the way that credits show up over footage at the beginning of a movie, or how an animated character is made to appear like she is interacting with a real-world environment. Blender has an integrated compositor that you can use to do these sorts of effects, as well as simply enhance your scene with effects such as blur, glow, and color correction.

Working with the Video Sequence Editor

The default Video Editing screen layout in Blender is accessible through the Screens datablock in the header or by pressing Ctrl+← four times from the Default screen layout. The large editor across the middle of the layout is a Video Sequence Editor (VSE) in Sequencer view. In this view, you can add and modify sequences, called *strips,* in time. The numbers across the bottom of the Sequencer correspond to time in the VSE in seconds. The numbers to the left are labels for each of the tracks, or *channels,* that the strips live in. The upper left area is a Graph Editor, used in this case for tweaking the influence or timing of individual strips' properties. To the right of the Graph Editor is a VSE in Preview view. When you're editing, the footage under the time cursor appears here. At the bottom is a Timeline, which, at first, may seem odd. However, as when animating, the benefit of having the Timeline around all the time is that you can use the Sequencer to edit a specific portion of your production, while still having the ability to scrub the full piece. The playback controls are also handy to have on-screen.

As with the Animation layout (see Chapter 10), I like to make a few tweaks to the Video Editing layout. When I first start editing in Blender's VSE, I'm usually more concerned with importing image sequences and movie clips than I am with tweaking the timing of edits. So one of the first changes I make is swapping the Graph Editor for a File Browser with files set to display thumbnails. This way, you can easily drag and drop footage from the File Browser directly onto the Sequencer. You may also note that you're missing the Properties editor. While you're in the process of editing, the Properties editor isn't critical to have open, but it's useful when you're doing your initial setup. For that reason, I often split the Sequencer and make a narrow strip on the right a Properties editor (Shift+F7). Figure 15-1 shows my modified Video Editing layout.

The settings in the Dimensions panel amid the Render Properties are important for editing in Blender because that's where you set the frame rate, measured in frames per second (fps), and resolution for the project. If you're editing footage that runs at a different frame rate or resolution than the one that is set here, that footage is adjusted to fit. So if your project is at standard HD settings (24 fps and 1920 x 1080 pixels in size), but you import an animation rendered at 50 fps and at a size of 640 x 480 pixels, the footage appears stretched and in slow motion.

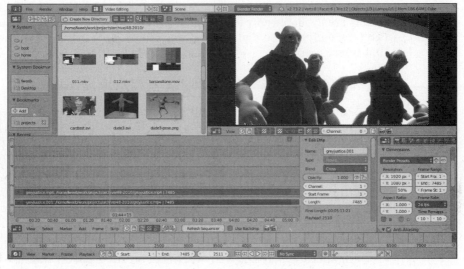

Figure 15-1:
Figure 15-1:
A customized Video Editing layout for when you start a project.

Besides your Render Properties, the Properties region of the Sequencer (press N to toggle its visibility) is relevant to your editing process. Because the default layout doesn't have any strips loaded, this region appears as a blank section on the right side of the Sequencer. However, if you have a strip in the Sequencer and you have it selected, this region is populated and appears like the image in Figure 15-2. (The exact panels in the Properties region change depending on the type of strip you have selected. Figure 15-2 shows panels for a movie strip.)

Figure 15-2:
The Sequencer's Properties region gives you controls on a selected strip.

As you may guess, the Properties region has the most relevant options for working in the VSE. Six panels are available: Edit Strip, Strip Input, Effect Strip, Filter, Proxy/Timecode, and Modifiers. For most strip types, the Edit

Strip, Strip Input, and Filter panels are available. The Effect Strip and Proxy panels are available only for certain types of strips. For example, audio strips can't have proxies, so that panel doesn't show up when you select a strip of that type.

Following are descriptions for the most commonly used panels:

✔ **Edit Strip:** The buttons in this panel pertain to where a selected strip appears in the VSE and how it interacts with other strips. You can name individual strips, control how a strip blends with lower channels, mute or lock a strip, set the strip's start frame, and change the strip's channel.

✔ **Strip Input:** The buttons in this panel allow you to crop and move the strip around the frame, as well as control which portion of the strip shows up in the Sequencer. When you have an audio strip selected, this panel has a few different controls and is labeled Sound.

✔ **Effect Strip:** This panel only appears for certain effect strips that have editable attributes. I give more detail on some effects that use this panel in the section "Adding effects," later in this chapter. The Timeline at the bottom of the screen controls how Blender plays your sequence. However, the most relevant button for the VSE is the Sync drop-down menu. To ensure that your audio plays back in sync with your video while editing, make sure that this drop-down menu is either set to AV-sync or Frame Dropping. Of the two, I tend to get better results when I choose AV-sync. Nothing is worse than doing a ton of work to get something edited only to find out that none of the audio lines up with the visuals after you render. Figure 15-3 shows the options in the Sync drop-down menu of the Timeline.

Figure 15-3: Choose Frame Dropping or AV-sync to ensure that your audio plays back in sync with your video.

Before I get heavily into using the VSE, let me first say that Blender's VSE is *not* a complete replacement for a traditional NLE. Although it is a very powerful tool, the VSE is best suited for animators who want to create a quick edit of their work. Professional video editors may have trouble because VSE is missing a number of expected features, such as a listing of available footage, sometimes called a *clip library* or *bin*. You can use the File Browser in thumbnail view to partially emulate the behavior of a bin, but it's still not quite the same. That said, all of the open movie projects (*Elephants Dream*, *Big Buck Bunny*, *Sintel*, *Tears of Steel*, and the upcoming *Cosmos Laundromat*) were successfully edited using Blender's VSE. I find the VSE more than sufficient for quite a few of my own projects, so you ultimately have to decide for yourself.

Adding and editing strips

If you want to use the VSE to edit footage, you have to bring that footage into Blender. If you're using the modified Video Editing screen layout I describe in the preceding section in this chapter, you can use the File Browser and navigate to where your footage is. Then you can just drag and drop that file from the File Browser directly into the Sequencer. The ability to drag and drop from the File Browser is an extremely handy feature that even many veteran Blender users don't know about. In fact, you can even drop media files from your operating system's file manager, too. Alternatively, you can add a strip by hovering your mouse cursor in the Sequencer and pressing Shift+A (just like adding objects in the 3D View). Figure 15-4 shows the menu of options that appears.

Figure 15-4: The Add Sequence Strip menu.

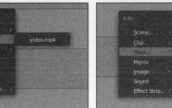

You can import a variety of strips: scenes, clips, masks, movies, still images, audio, and effects. These strips are represented by the following options in the menu:

- ✔ **Scene:** Scene strips are an extremely cool feature unique to Blender. When you select this option, a secondary menu pops up that allows you to select a scene from the .blend file you're working in. If you use a single .blend file with multiple scenes in it, you can edit those scenes together to a final output sequence without ever rendering out those scenes first! This handy feature allows you to create a complete and complex animation entirely within a single file. (This feature also works with scenes linked from external .blend files, but that's an advanced use.) Scene strips are also a great way to use Blender for overlaying graphics, like titles, on video.

- ✔ **Clip:** Clips are newer strips that you can add in Blender. They relate to Blender's built-in motion tracking feature. A Clip is similar to a Movie strip (covered next), except that it's already loaded in Blender in the Movie Clip editor and has its own datablock. In contrast, Movie strips by themselves don't have any associated datablocks; they only exist on the VSE's timeline.

- ✔ **Mask:** To add a Mask strip, you must first create a Mask datablock in the UV/Image Editor. To create a mask, left-click the Editing Context drop-down menu in the UV/Image Editor's header and choose Mask. Masks are pretty heavily used in advanced motion tracking and compositing.

- ✔ **Movie:** When you select this option, the File Browser that comes up allows you to select a video file in one of the many formats Blender supports. On files with both audio and video, Blender loads the audio along with the video file as separate strips in the sequencer.

- ✔ **Image:** Selecting this option brings up a File Browser that allows you to select one or more images in any of the formats that Blender recognizes. If you select just one image, the VSE displays a strip for that one image that you can arbitrarily resize in time. If you select multiple images, the VSE interprets them as a sequence and places them all in the same strip with a fixed length that matches the number of images you selected.

- ✔ **Sound:** This option gives you a File Browser for loading an audio file into the VSE. When importing audio, you definitely want to import sound files in WAV or FLAC (Free Lossless Audio Codec) formats, which give you the best quality sound. Although Blender supports other audio formats like MP3, they're often compressed and sometimes sound bad when played.

- ✔ **Effect Strip:** This option pops out a secondary, somewhat lengthy, menu of options. These strips are used mostly for effects and transitions. I cover them in more depth in the next section.

When you load a strip, it's brought into the VSE under your mouse cursor. Table 15-1 shows helpful mouse actions for working efficiently in the VSE.

Table 15-1	Helpful Mouse Actions in the VSE
Mouse Action	**Description**
Right-click	Select strip to modify. Right-clicking the arrow at either end of the strip selects that end of the strip and allows you to trim or extend the strip from that point.
Shift+right-click	Select multiple strips.
Middle-click	Pan the VSE workspace.
Ctrl+middle-click	Zoom height and width of the VSE workspace.
Scroll wheel	Zoom the width in and out of the VSE workspace.
Left-click	Move the time cursor in the VSE. Left-clicking and dragging scrubs the time cursor, allowing you to view and hear the contents of the Sequencer as fast or slow as you move your mouse.

One thing you may notice is that quite a few of the controls are very similar to those present in other parts of Blender, such as the 3D View and Graph Editor. This similarity is also true when it comes to the hotkeys that the VSE recognizes, although a few differences are worth mentioning. Table 15-2 lists some the most common hotkeys used for editing.

Editing in the VSE is pretty straightforward. If you have two strips stacked in two channels, one above the other, when the timeline cursor gets to them, the strip that's in the higher channel takes priority. By default, that strip simply overrides, or *replaces*, any of the strips below it. You can, however, change this behavior in the Edit Strip panel of the VSE's Properties region. The drop-down menu labeled Blend controls the *blend mode* of the selected strip. You can see that the default setting is Replace, but if you left-click this button, you get a short list of modes similar to the layer blending options you see in a program like Photoshop or GIMP. Besides Replace, the ones I use the most are Alpha Over and Add.

The Graph Editor is useful for animating all kinds of values in Blender, and it's quite useful for strips in the VSE. One of the primary animated values for strips is the Opacity slider in the Edit Strip panel. This slider controls the influence factor that the strip has on the rest of the sequence. For example, on an image strip — say, of a solid black image — you can use the Graph Editor to animate the overall opacity of that strip. Values less than 1.0 make the image more transparent, thereby giving you a nice way to create a controlled fade to black. The same principle works for sound strips, using the Volume slider in the Sound panel of the VSE's Properties region. A value of 1.0 is the sound clip's original loudness and it gradually fades away the lower you get. Values greater than 1.0 amplify the sound to a level greater than the original volume.

Table 15-2	Common Features/Hotkeys in the VSE	
Hotkey	*Menu Access*	*Description*
G	Strip⇨Grab/ Move	Grabs a selection to move elsewhere in the VSE.
E	Strip⇨Grab/ Extend from frame	Grabs a selection and extends one end of it relative to the position of the time cursor.
B		Border select, for selecting multiple strips.
Shift+D	Strip⇨Duplicate Strips	Duplicates the selected strip(s).
X	Strip⇨Erase Strips	Deletes the selected strip(s).
K	Strip⇨Cut (soft) at Current Frame	Splits a strip at the location of the time cursor. Similar to the razor tool in other NLEs.
M	Strip⇨Make Meta Strip	Combines selected strips into a single "meta" strip.
Alt+M	Strip⇨UnMeta Strip	Splits a selected meta strip back to its original individual strips.
Tab		Tabs into a meta strip to allow modification of the strips within it.
H	Strip⇨Mute Strips	Hides a strip from being played.
Alt+H	Strip⇨Un-Mute Strips	Unhides a strip.
Shift+L	Strip⇨Lock Strips	Prevents selected strips from being moved or edited.
Shift+Alt+L	Strip⇨Unlock Strips	Allows editing on selected strips.
Alt+A		Plays the animation starting from the location of the time cursor.

By combining the Graph Editor with Blending modes, you can create some very cool results. Say that you have a logo graphic with an alpha channel defining the background as transparent, and you want to make the logo flicker as if it's being seen through poor television reception. To make the logo flicker, follow these steps:

1. **Add a logo image to the VSE (Shift+A⇨Image).**

2. **Make sure that the logo's strip is selected (right-click) and, in the Edit Strip panel, change the strip's blend mode to Alpha Over.**

3. **Insert a keyframe for the strip's opacity (right-click Opacity in the Edit Strip panel and choose Insert Keyframe or press I with your mouse hovered over the Opacity value field).**

4. **In the Graph Editor, tweak the Opacity f-curve so that it randomly bounces many times between 1.0 and 0.0 (Ctrl+left-click).**

   After tweaking the curve to your taste (see Chapter 10 for more on working in the Graph Editor), you should now have your flickering logo effect.

Adding effects

Pressing Shift+A in the VSE provides you with quite a few options other than importing audio and video elements. A large portion of these options are effects, and many typically require that you select two strips that are stacked on top of each other in the VSE. When necessary, I point out which effects these are.

Pay close attention to the order in which you select your strips because it often has a dramatic influence on how the effect is applied. The second strip you select is the *active strip* and the primary controller of the effect.

Here's a list of the available options:

✒ **Add/Subtract/Multiply:** These effects are the same as the blend mode settings in the Edit Strip panel of the Properties region. Unless you really need some special control, I recommend using those blend modes rather than adding these as effects sequences. It works just as well and keeps your VSE timeline from getting too cluttered. Using these effects requires that you select two strips before pressing Shift+A and adding any of them. The following steps give a quick example of how to use them:

   • *Select the strip you want to start with.*

   • *Shift+right-click the strip you want to transition to.*

   • *Press Shift+A⇨Effect Strip⇨Add.*

     A new red strip is created that's the length of the overlap between your two selected strips. On playback (Alt+A), the bright parts of the upper strip amplify the overlaying bright parts of the lower strip.

✔ **Alpha Over/Alpha Under/Over Drop:** These effect strips control how one strip's alpha channel relates to another. They're also available as Blending modes, and I suggest that you apply these effects that way in most cases. One example of a time where it makes sense to use these as strips is if you need to apply another effect (such as a Gaussian Blur) to a collection of strips that have been alpha'd over one another. Otherwise, stick with the blend mode.

✔ **Cross/Gamma Cross:** These effects are *crossfades* or *dissolves* between overlapping strips. The Cross effect also works in audio to smoothly transition from one sound to another. For images and video, Gamma Cross works the same as Cross, but takes the additional step of correcting the color in the transition for a smoother dissolve.

✔ **Gaussian Blur:** This effect works like a simplified version of the Blur node in the Node Compositor (covered later in this chapter). Using the Size X and Size Y values in the Effect Strip panel of the Properties region, the Gaussian Blur effect gives you the ability to make blurry the images or video in a strip.

✔ **Wipe:** Wipe is a transition effect like Cross and Gamma Cross. It transitions from one strip to another like a sliding door, à la the *Star Wars* movies. This effect also uses the Effect Strip panel in the Properties region to let you choose the type of wipe you want, including single, double, iris, and clock wipe. Also, you can adjust the blurriness of the wiping edge and the direction the wipe moves.

✔ **Glow:** The Glow effect works on a single strip. It takes a given image and makes the bright points in it glow a bit brighter. Ever wonder how some 3D renders get that glowing, almost ethereal quality? Glow is one way to do it. The Effect Strip panel in the Properties region lets you adjust the amount of glow you have and the quality of that glow.

✔ **Transform:** This effect provides very basic controls for the location, scale, and rotation of a strip. The effect works on a single strip, and you can find its controls on the Effect Strip panel of the Properties region. You can use f-curves on this effect strip to animate the transform values.

✔ **Color:** This handy little option creates an infinitely sized color strip. You can use this effect to do fades or set a solid background color for scenes.

✔ **Speed Control:** With the Speed Control effect, you can adjust the playback speed of individual strips. In the Effect Strip panel of the Properties region, you can choose to influence the Global Speed (1.0 is regular speed; setting it to 0.50 makes the strip play half as fast; setting it to 2.0 makes it play twice as fast). You can also have more custom control using the Graph Editor.

✔ **Multicam Selector:** If you're using Scene strips in the Sequencer and you have multiple cameras in your scene, you can use this effect strip to dictate which camera you're using from that scene. As with most things in Blender, you can animate that camera choice, allowing you to easily do camera switching in your scene.

✔ **Adjustment Layer:** Adjustment Layer strips are a bit unique. Like Color strips, you don't need to have any other strips selected when you add an Adjustment Layer strip. The cool thing is that Adjustment Layer strips can make simple modifications (*adjustments*) to the look of all strips below them on the VSE's timeline. If you add an Adjustment Layer strip and look at the mostly empty Properties region, you may wonder exactly how you add those adjustments. This is where you can apply VSE modifiers. In the Modifiers panel of the Properties region, you can left-click the Add Strip Modifier drop-down menu. From here, you can make more modifications, including color correction, brightness and contrast adjustments, and even masks.

Rendering from the Video Sequence Editor

To render your complete edited sequence from the VSE, the steps are largely identical to the ones outlined for creating a finished animation in Chapter 14. Actually, you must do only one additional thing.

In Render Properties, have a look in the Post Processing panel. Make sure that the Sequencer check box is enabled. Activating this check box lets Blender know that you want to use the strips in the VSE for your final output rather than anything that's in front of the 3D camera. If you don't enable this check box, Blender just renders whatever the camera sees, which may be just the default cube that starts with Blender, or whatever else you might place in front of the 3D camera.

Working with the Node-Based Compositor

Compositing is the process of mixing multiple visual assets to create a single image or sequence of images. By this definition, you may notice that *technically* Blender's VSE qualifies as a sort of compositor because you can stack strips over each other in channels and blend them together with effects and transitions. Although this statement is true, the VSE is nowhere near as powerful as the Node Compositor is for mixing videos, images, and other graphics together.

As designed, the VSE is intended for working with multiple shots, scenes, images, or clips of video. It's also meant to play back in real time (or as near to that as possible). In contrast, the Compositor is intended for working with a single shot, and it's most certainly not meant for working in real time. There is a little bit of overlap in the functionality of these two parts of Blender, but depending on the task at hand, one is more suitable than the other.

What makes the Node Compositor so powerful? Well, it's in the name: *nodes*. One of the best ways to understand the power of nodes is to imagine an assembly line. In an assembly line, each step in the process depends on the step immediately preceding it and feeds directly into the following step. This methodology is similar to the layer-based approach used in many image manipulation programs like Photoshop and GIMP. Each layer has exactly one input from the previous layer and one output to the following one. Figure 15-5 illustrates this idea.

Figure 15-5:
An assembly line approach, like the layers in GIMP or Photoshop.

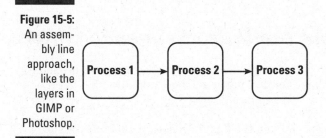

That approach works well, but you can enhance the assembly line a bit. Say that some steps produce parts that can go to more than one subsequent step, and that other steps can take parts from two or more earlier steps and make something new. And take it a bit farther by saying that you can duplicate groups of these steps and integrate them easily to other parts of the line. You then have an assembly *network* like that depicted in Figure 15-6. This network-like approach is what you can do with nodes.

Understanding the benefits of rendering in passes and layers

Before taking full advantages of nodes, it's worthwhile to take a quick moment and understand what it means to render *in layers*. Assume for a moment that you animated a character walking into a room and falling down. The room is pretty detailed, so it takes a fairly long time for your computer to render each frame. However, because the camera doesn't move, you can really render the room just once. So if you render your character with a transparent background, you can superimpose the character on just the still image of the room, effectively cutting your render time in half (or less)!

That's the basics of rendering in layers. The preceding example had two layers, one for the room and one for the character. In addition to rendering in layers, each layer can contain multiple *passes*, or with more detailed content relevant to that layer. For example, if you want to, you can have a render pass that consists of just the shadows in the layer. You can take that pass and adjust it to make all the shadows slightly blue. Or you can isolate a character while she's walking through a gray, blurry scene.

Another thing to understand for compositing 3D scenes is the concept of Z-depth. Basically, *Z-depth* is the representation of the distance that an object is from the camera, along the camera's local Z-axis. The compositor can use this Z-depth to make an object look like it fits in a scene even though it was never rendered with it.

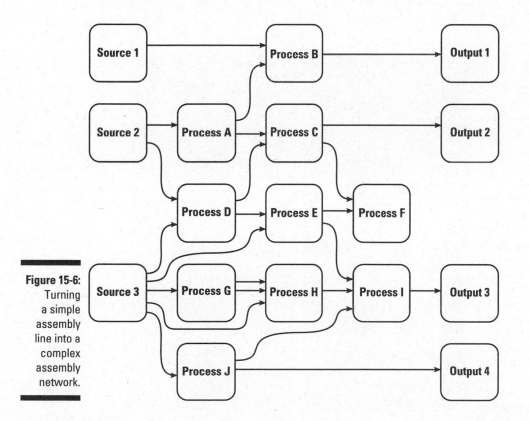

Figure 15-6:
Turning
a simple
assembly
line into a
complex
assembly
network.

In Blender, all of this functionality starts with *render layers*. It's important to make a distinction here between Blender's regular layer system and render layers. Although render layers do use Blender's layer system, they are separate things. Basically, you can decide arbitrarily which Blender layers you'd like to include or exclude from any of the render layers you create. All the controls for render layers are in Render Layers Properties. It's the second context button in the Property Editor's header. Figure 15-7 shows the panels in Render Layers Properties.

At the top of Render Layers Properties is a list box containing all the render layers in your scene. By default, there's only one, named RenderLayer. Double-click items in the list box to change their names. The next section features three blocks of Blender layers. The first block of these layers shows the scene layers; the ones that are going to be sent actively to the renderer.

The next set of Blender layer buttons in the Layer panel determine which Blender layers actually belong in the selected render layer. For example, if you're creating a render layer for background characters and you have all your background characters on layers 3 and 4, you Shift+left-click those layers in this block.

Figure 15-7:
The panels in Render Layers Properties. On the left is what you see if rendering with Cycles, on the right is the BI version.

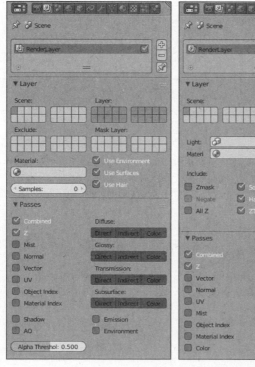

If you press Shift+left-click and keep those buttons held down, you can enable or disable multiple render layers by dragging your mouse cursor over them.

The third set of Blender layer buttons are mask layers. The objects in these layers explicitly block what's rendered in this render layer, effectively masking them out. You typically use these layer buttons for more advanced compositing scenarios.

The series of check boxes that fill the lower half of the Layers panel and in the Passes panel beneath it are where the real magic and power of render layers lie. The first set of check boxes specify which *pipeline products* to deliver, or include (hence the label), to the renderer as input. These pipeline products refer to major renderable elements of the selected render layer that are seen by the render engine. If you disable Halo, for example, no halo materials are sent to the renderer. Basically, they're omitted. You can use these check boxes in complex scenes to turn off pipeline features you don't need in an effort to shorten your render times.

The passes and pipeline products that you have available in your render layers vary a bit, depending on which render engine you're using. For instance, the example from the preceding paragraph is only relevant if you're rendering with BI; Cycles doesn't support halo materials.

Here is a brief description of some of the more useful pipeline features if you're using BI as your renderer (if there's a Cycles equivalent, I mention it in the description):

- ✔ **Solid:** This feature is for solid faces. Basically, if you disable this option, the only things that render are lights, halo materials, and particles. Any solid-surfaced object doesn't appear.

    If you're rendering with Cycles, the equivalent to this pipeline product is the Use Surfaces check box.

- ✔ **ZTransp:** This name is short for *Z-transparency*. If you have an object that has a Z-transparent material, enabling this button ensures that the material gets rendered.

- ✔ **Strand:** *Strands* are static particles rendered in place. They're often used to approximate the look of hair or grass. Keeping this option enabled ensures that your characters aren't bald and that their front lawns aren't lifeless deserts.

    If you're rendering with Cycles, the rough counterpart to this is the Use Hair check box.

- **All Z:** The simplest way to explain this option is with an example. Say that you have a scene with a wall between your character and the camera. The character is on one render layer, and the wall is on another. If you're on the character's render layer and you enable this option, the character is masked from the render layer and doesn't appear. With All Z off, the character shows up on its render layer.

Underneath the Include check boxes is the Passes panel. This panel contains a set of options that control which passes are sent to the selected render layer. These passes are most useful when used in the Node Compositor. They're really what make compositing so interesting and fun. Here are some of the most useful passes:

- **Combined:** The Combined pass is the fully mixed, rendered image as it comes from the renderer before getting any processing.

- **Z:** This pass is a mapping of the Z-depth information for each object in front of the camera. It is useful for masking as well as effects like *depth of field,* where a short range of the viewable range is in focus and everything else is blurry.

- **Mist:** This pass is only available if you render with Cycles. In a way, it's similar to the Z pass because it's based on z-depth information. There are three big differences:

  - Values in the Mist pass already are normalized between 0 and 1.

  - The Mist pass takes the transparency of your materials into account; the Z pass doesn't.

  - Unlike the Z pass, the Mist pass is nicely anti-aliased and doesn't have some of the nasty star-stepped jaggies you may see in the Z pass.

  If you're rendering in Cycles and you want to re-create the effect of the Mist panel in BI, using the Mist pass in the compositor is how you do it.

- **Vector:** This pass includes speed information for objects moving before the camera (meaning that either the objects or the camera is animated). This data is particularly useful for the Vector Blur node, which gives animations a decent motion blur effect.

- **Normal:** The information in this pass relates to the angle that the geometry in the scene has, relative to the camera. You can use the Normal pass for additional bump mapping as well as completely altering the lighting in the scene without re-rendering.

- **UV:** The UV pass is pretty clever because it sends the UV mapping data from the 3D objects to the compositor. Basically, this pass gives you the ability to completely change the textures on an object or character without the need to re-render any part of the scene. Often, you want to use this pass along with the Object Index pass to specify on which object you want to change the texture.

✓ **Object Index:** This pass carries index numbers for individual objects, if you set them. The Object Index pass allows very fine control over which nodes get applied to which objects. This pass is similar to plain masking, but somewhat more powerful because it makes isolating a single object or group of objects so much easier.

✓ **Color:** The color pass delivers the colors from the render, completely shadeless, without highlights or shadows. This pass can be helpful for amplifying or subduing colors in a shot. If you're rendering with Cycles, you can actually have separate Color passes for diffuse, glossy, transmission, and subsurface shaders.

✓ **Specular:** The specularity pass delivers an image with the specular highlights that appear in the render.

Cycles doesn't use specularity, so this pass isn't available when rendering with Cycles.

✓ **Shadow:** This pass contains all the cast shadows in the render, both from ray traced shadows as well as buffered shadows. In my example from earlier in this section about taking the shadows from the render and adjusting them (such as giving them a bluish hue), you'd use this pass.

✓ **AO:** This pass includes any ambient occlusion data generated by the renderer, if you have AO enabled. If you use this pass and you're rendering with BI, it's a good idea to double-check to see whether you're using approximate or ray traced AO in the Ambient Occlusion panel of World Properties. If you're using ray traced AO, verify that ray tracing is enabled in Render Properties.

Working with nodes

After you set up your render layers the way you like, you're ready to work in the Node Compositor. As with the VSE, Blender ships with a default screen layout for compositing, appropriately named Compositing. You can access the Compositing layout from the Screens datablock at the top of the window or by pressing Ctrl+← once from the Default screen layout. By default, Blender puts you in the Node Editor for compositing, which is exactly where you want to be. The other node editors are for materials and textures and are for more advanced work. See Chapters 7, 8, and 9 for other uses of the Node Editor.

By itself, the Node Editor looks pretty stark and boring, like a lame 2D version of the 3D View. However, left-click the Use Nodes check box in the header, and you see a screen layout that looks similar to the one shown in Figure 15-8.

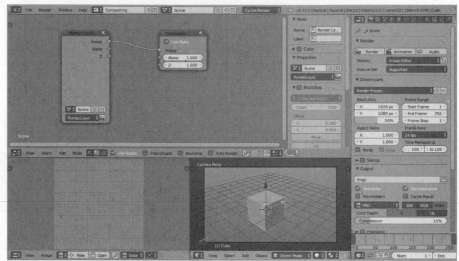

Figure 15-8:
Starting
with nodes
in the
Composite
Node Editor.

Blender starts by presenting you with two nodes, one input and one output. You can quickly tell which is which by looking at the location of the connection points on each node. The left node labeled Render Layers has connection points on the right side of it. The location of these connection points means that it can serve only as an input to other nodes and can't receive any additional data, so it's an input node. It adds information to the node network. In contrast, the node on the right, labeled Composite, is an output node because it has no connection points on its right edge, meaning it can't feed information to other nodes. Essentially, it's the end of the line, the result. In fact, when you render by using the Node Compositor, the Composite node is the final output that gets displayed when Blender renders.

Setting up a backdrop

I personally prefer to see the progress of my node network as I'm working, without having to constantly refer back to another editor for the results of my work. Fortunately, Blender can facilitate this workflow with another sort of output node: the Viewer node.

To add a new node, position your mouse cursor in the Node Editor and press Shift+A. You see a variety of options. For now, navigate to Output⟳Viewer to create a new output node labeled Viewer.

If the Render Layer input node was selected when you added the Viewer node, Blender automatically creates a connection, also called a *noodle,* between the two nodes. Noodles are drawn between the circular connection points, or *sockets,* on each node. If the noodle wasn't created for you, you can add it by left-clicking the yellow Image socket on the Render Layer node and dragging your mouse cursor to the corresponding yellow socket on the Viewer node.

However, making this connection doesn't seem to do much. You need to take three more steps:

1. **Left-click the Use Backdrop check box in the Node Editor's header.**

   A black box loads in the background of the compositor. (Don't worry; it's supposed to happen, I promise.)

2. **Go to the Post Processing panel in Render Properties and ensure that the Compositing check box is enabled.**

3. **Render the scene by left-clicking the Image button in the Render panel or pressing F12.**

   When the render is complete and you return to the Blender interface by pressing F11, the empty black box has been magically replaced with the results of your render. Now anything that feeds into this Viewer node is instantly displayed in the background of the compositor.

This setup is the way I typically like to work when compositing. In fact, I often take it one step farther and press Shift+spacebar to maximize the Node Editor to the full window size. This way, you can take full advantage of your entire screen while compositing.

If you find that the backdrop gets in your way, you can disable it by left-clicking the Backdrop check box in the header, or you can move the backdrop image around in the background by Alt+middle-clicking in the editor and dragging the image around.

The VSE also can show a backdrop. You enable it the same way (enabling the Use Backdrop check box in the VSE timeline's header); you can scale and move the backdrop image around the same way, too. With the backdrop enabled in either case, you can composite or edit your work with a maximized area (Shift+Spacebar) and still see the results of your modifications.

Also, you can get more space by middle-clicking in the compositor and dragging the entire node network around, or by using your scroll wheel to zoom in and out on the nodes. You also have the ability to scale the backdrop image by using the V (zoom out) and Alt+V (zoom in) hotkeys. Table 15-3 shows most of the frequently used mouse actions in the Node Editor.

Table 15-3	Commonly Used Mouse Actions in the Node Editor
Mouse Action	**Description**
Right-click	Select a node.
Shift+right-click	Select multiple nodes.
Middle-click	Pan compositor work area.
Alt+middle-click	Move backdrop image.
Ctrl+middle-click	Zoom compositor work area.
Scroll wheel	Zoom compositor work area.
Left-click (on a node)	Select a node. Click and drag to move the node around.
Left-click (on a socket)	Attach or detach a noodle to/from the socket you click on. Click and drag to the socket you want to connect to.
Left-click+drag the left or right side of a node	Resize the node.
Ctrl+Left-click+drag in the compositor workspace	Knife cut through noodles.
Ctrl+Alt+left-click+drag in the compositor workspace	Lasso select.
Shift+Ctrl+left-click a node	Connect the active Viewer node to the output of the clicked node. If there is no Viewer node, one is automatically created. Continuous Shift+Ctrl+left-clicks iterate through the multiple outputs of the node.

Identifying parts of a node

At the top of each node are a pair of icons: the triangle on the left and a circular icon on the right. Following is a description of what each button (shown in Figure 15-9) does:

- ✔ **Triangle:** Expands and collapses the node, essentially hiding the information in it from view.
- ✔ **Sphere:** View window expand/collapse. This icon is available only on nodes that have an image window, such as a render layer node, any output node, or texture node.

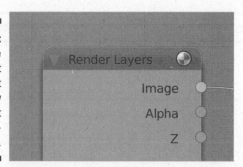

Figure 15-9:
Each node has icons at the top that control how you see it in the compositor.

Navigating the node compositor

For the most part, editing nodes in Blender conforms to the same user interface behavior that's in the rest of the program. You select nodes by right-clicking, you can grab and move nodes by pressing G, and you can border select multiple nodes by pressing B. Of course, a few differences pertain specifically to the Node Editor. Table 15-4 shows the most common hotkeys used in Node Editor.

When connecting nodes, pay attention to the colors of the sockets. The sockets on each node come in one of three different colors, and each one has a specific meaning for the type of information that is either sent or expected from the node. The colors and their meanings are as follows:

✔ **Yellow:** Color information. Specifically, this socket relates to color in the output image, across the entire red/green/blue/alpha (RGBA) scale. Color information is the primary type of data that should go to output nodes.

✔ **Gray:** Numeric values. Whereas the yellow sockets technically get four values for each pixel in the image — one for each red, green, blue, and alpha — this socket gets or receives a single value for each pixel. You can visualize these values as a grayscale image. These sockets are used mostly for masks. For example, the level of transparency in an image, or its alpha channel, can be represented by a grayscale image, with white for opaque and black for transparent (and gray for semitransparent).

✔ **Blue:** Geometry data. These sockets are pretty special. They send and receive information that pertains to the 3D data in the scene, such as speed, UV coordinates, and normals. Visualizing these values in a two-dimensional image is pretty difficult; it usually ends up looking like something seen through the eyes of the alien in *Predator*.

Table 15-4	Commonly Used Hotkeys in the Node Editor	
Hotkey	*Menu Access*	*Description*
Shift+A	Add	Opens toolbox menu.
G	Node⇨Translate	Grabs a node and move it.
B	Select⇨Border Select	Border select.
X	Node⇨Delete	Deletes node(s).
Shift+D	Node⇨Duplicate	Duplicates node(s).
Ctrl+G	Node⇨Make Group	Creates a group out of the selected nodes.
Alt+G	Node⇨Ungroup	Ungroups the selected group.
Tab	Node⇨Edit Group	Expands the node group so you can edit individual nodes within it.
H	Node⇨Hide/Unhide	Toggles the selected nodes between expanded and collapsed views.
V	View⇨Backdrop Zoom Out	Zooms out (scales down) the backdrop image.
Alt+V	View⇨Backdrop Zoom In	Zooms in (scales up) the backdrop image.

Grouping nodes together

As Table 15-4 shows, you can also group nodes together. The ability to make a group of nodes is actually one of the really powerful features of the Node Editor. You can border select a complex section of your node network and press Ctrl+G to quickly make a group out of it. Grouping nodes has a few really nice benefits. First of all, grouping can simplify the look of your node network so that it's not a huge mess of noodles (spaghetti!). More than simplification, though, node groups are a great organizational tool. Because you can name groups like any other node, you can group sections of your network that serve a specific purpose. For example, you can have a blurry background group and a color-corrected character group.

But wait, there's more! (Do I sound like a car salesman yet?) When you create a group, it's added automatically to the Group menu when you go to add a new node (Shift+A⇨Group). To understand the benefit of being able to add groups, imagine that you created a really cool network that gives foreground elements a totally sweet glow effect. If you make a group out of that network, you can now instantly apply that glow to other parts of your scene or scenes in other .blend files. Go ahead: Try it and tell me that's not cool — you can't do it!

When working with nodes, it's a good idea to have the network flow from the left to the right. Wherever possible, you want to avoid creating situations where you feed a node's output back to one of the nodes that gives it input. This feedback loop is called a *cyclic connection*. If you've ever heard the painfully loud feedback noise that happens when you place a microphone too close to a speaker, you have an idea of why a cyclic connection is a bad idea.

Discovering the nodes available to you

Blender has quite an extensive list of nodes that you can add to your network. In fact, it seems like with every release of Blender, more and more incredible node types are added to the compositor. Many nodes have a *Fac,* or factor, value that you can usually either set with a value from another node or explicitly set by typing. Values less than 1 make the node have less influence, while values greater than 1 make the node have more influence than usual over the image.

Input

The input nodes are one of the two most important node types in the Node Compositor. If your node network doesn't have any inputs, you don't have anything to composite. Figure 15-10 shows each of these nodes side by side.

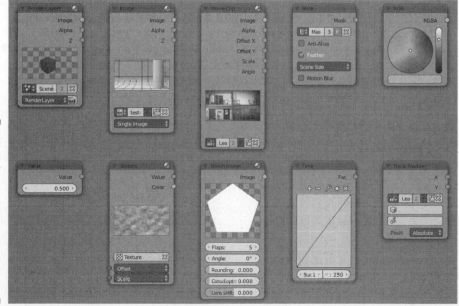

Figure 15-10:
Input nodes:
Render
Layer, Image,
Movie Clip,
Mask, RGB,
Value, Tex-
ture, Bokeh
Image, Time,
and Track
Position.

- **Render Layer:** This node feeds input from a scene into the compositor. The drop-down menu at the bottom of the node allows you to pick any of the render layers you created in any scene. Notice also the button with the camera icon that is to the right of this menu. Left-click this button to render just this layer. This handy feature allows you to update a portion of your node network without needing to re-render all the layers in the network.

- **Image:** The name for this node is a bit over-simplistic because it can actually load more than just a single still image. The Image node allows you to bring any sort of image data into the compositor, including sequences of images and movie files, and allows you to control when the sequence starts, how long it is, and whether to loop it continuously.

- **Movie Clip:** Movie Clips are datablocks that get created in the Movie Clip Editor. They're most frequently used for Blender's motion tracking features. These are the same kinds of Clips that can be loaded in the VSE.

- **Mask:** Masks are created in the UV/Image Editor from the Mask editing context. They're primarily used for hiding and showing parts of images or videos when compositing.

- **RGB:** With the RGB node, you can feed any solid color to any other node in the compositor. This node is a good, quick way to adjust the hue of an image or provide a simple colored background.

- **Value:** This fairly simple input node allows you to feed any scalar (numerical) value to other nodes.

- **Texture:** The Texture node is unique as an input node, because it's the only one that can actually receive input data as well. Through this node, you can take any texture that you built in Blender and add it to your node network. This node is particularly useful with UV data, because it can let you change the textures on objects in your image without re-rendering.

- **Bokeh Image:** The word *bokeh* comes from a Japanese word meaning blur. In photography, bokeh is used to describe the quality of background blur in an image (typically from lenses with a shallow *depth of field*, or focus area). The form of that blur is entirely dependent on how the lens is shaped. Most modern lenses have a circular bokeh, but many photographers and visual artists like the more harsh geometric look (typically hexagons) of older lenses. The Bokeh Image node can procedurally create the bokeh shape. This is particularly useful for the Bokeh Blur node, covered later in this chapter.

- **Time:** This node is probably one of the most powerful, yet misunderstood, nodes in Blender. In the past, the Node Compositor was not tied to the Graph Editor, making it difficult to animate attributes of individual nodes. The Time node was a way around this obstacle. Fortunately, as of

Blender 2.5 and the ability to animate nearly everything, the Time node is less of an absolute necessity in the compositor. You can key node values just like any other value in Blender. However, the Time node is still useful.

✔ **Track Position:** The Track Position node outputs the X and Y coordinates of a marker in a movie clip. It's used by Blender's motion tracking feature. It's a bit on the advanced side, but you can use the Track Position node to make one compositor element follow something moving in tracked footage. For example, if you're tracking the position of a car's license plate in a movie clip, you can use the Track Position node along as part of a noodle network to blur out that license plate.

Output

Input nodes are one of the two most important node types in Blender. As you may have guessed, the Output nodes are the other important node types, for a similar reason. If you don't have an output node, Blender doesn't know what to save when it renders. The following are the two most-used Output nodes:

✔ **Composite:** Blender recognizes the Composite node as the final output from the Node Compositor. When you set up your output files for animation in Render Properties, or when you press F3 to save a render, it's the information from this node that Blender saves out.

✔ **Viewer:** The Viewer node is similar to the Composite node, but it's not necessarily for final output. Viewer nodes are great for spot-checking sections of your node network and making sure that things are going the way you want them to. Also, output from these nodes is seen in the compositor's backdrop, if you enable it.

Color

The Color nodes have an enormous influence over the look of the final output. These nodes directly affect how colors appear, mix, and balance in an image. And because an image is basically just a bunch of colors arranged in a specific pattern, you can understand why these nodes have so much control. Figure 15-11 shows some of the most commonly used Color nodes. Following are descriptions of each node type:

✔ **RGB Curves:** Arguably one of the most powerful color nodes, the RGB Curves node takes image data and allows you to use curves to adjust the combined color, or any of the red, green, or blue channels in the image individually. Left-clicking the C, R, G, and B buttons on the upper left changes between combined, red, green, and blue color channels, respectively. With this node, you can do anything that the Hue Saturation Value, Bright/Contrast, and Invert nodes can do, but with more control.

✔ **Mix:** I personally use this node quite a bit. The Mix node has 18 different blending modes to allow you to control how to combine two input images. If you've used image editing software like GIMP or Photoshop, these blending modes should be pretty familiar to you. One thing to remember in this node — and it's something I used to constantly get backwards — is that the upper image input socket is the background image, whereas the lower image input socket is the foreground image.

✔ **Alpha Over:** This node is very similar to the Mix node, except it deals exclusively with combining images using their alpha channels. The lower socket is the foreground, and the upper socket is the background image. The other thing to note with this node is the Convert Premul check box. Basically, if you see weird white or black edges around parts of your foreground elements, left-clicking this button usually fixes them.

✔ **Z Combine:** Like the Mix and Alpha Over nodes, the Z Combine node mixes two sets of image data together. However, instead of using color information or alpha channels, this node can use Z-depth information.

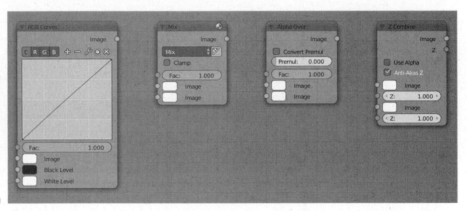

Figure 15-11:
Color nodes: RGB Curves, Mix, Alpha Over, and Z Combine.

Converter

These handy little utility nodes have a variety of purposes, including converting one set of data to another and ripping apart or recombining elements from a rendered image. The ColorRamp and ID Mask nodes in particular get used quite a bit. The ColorRamp node is great for helping visualizing or re-visualizing numerical values on a scale. For example, the only way to get a good sense of what the Z-depth of an image looks like is to map Z values along a manageable scale and then feed that to a white-to-black color ramp, as shown in Figure 15-12.

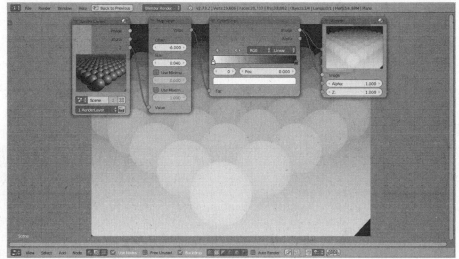

Figure 15-12:
Visualizing
a scene's
Z-depth
using a
ColorRamp.

The ID Mask node is handy because it allows you to isolate an object even more specifically than with layers and render layers. Assume that you want to apply the Glare node to a ball that your character is holding. If the scene is complex enough, it doesn't really make a lot of sense to give that ball a layer all by itself. So you can give the object a Pass Index value in the Relations panel of Object Properties. Then by using the ID Mask node, you can isolate just that ball and make it all shiny.

Filter

Filter nodes can *drastically* change the look of an image and are probably the No. 1 way to fake any effect in an image. These nodes actually process the pixels in an image and can do things like put thick black lines around an object, give the image a variety of customized blurs, or make bright parts of the image glow. Figure 15-13 shows some of the most useful Filter nodes:

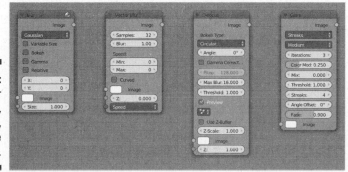

Figure 15-13:
Blur, Vector
Blur,
Defocus,
and Glare
nodes.

✔ **Blur:** As its name implies, this node applies a blur across the entire input image. The first button gives you a drop-down menu to select the type of blur you want to use. I typically like to use Gaussian for most of my effects. When you first apply this node, you may not think that anything is happening. Change the values in the X and Y buttons to adjust the blur size on a scale from 0 to 256, or 0.0 to 1.0, depending on whether you enable the Relative check box. This node is like an advanced version of the Gaussian Blur effect strip in the VSE.

✔ **Vector Blur:** This node is the fastest way to get motion blur out of Blender if you're rendering with BI. The Vector Blur node takes speed information from the Vector pass (enable Vector in the Passes panel of Render Layers Properties) and uses it to fake the motion blur effect. One check box I recommend you enable in this node, especially if you're doing character animation, is the Curved check box. This option gives objects that are moving in an arc a more natural, curved motion blur. This node is specifically for use with 3D data coming from Blender. It can't add motion blur to just any footage. If you're rendering with Cycles, usually you don't need to use the Vector Blur node; you can get more accurate motion blur from the Motion Blur panel in Render Properties.

✔ **Defocus:** Blender's Defocus node is the way to fake the *depth of field,* or DOF, effect you get with a real camera. If you've seen a photo where something in the middle of the picture is in focus, but objects in the foreground and background are blurry, it's called a *shallow DOF,* and it looks pretty sweet. You can get an idea where the camera's focal point is by selecting the camera in your scene and turning on Limits for the camera in Camera Properties. Then when you adjust the DOF Distance value, you can see the focal point as a yellow cross. Generally speaking, you don't need to use the Defocus node if you're rendering with Cycles; depth of field is built into the render engine.

✔ **Glare:** This node is a really quick way to give the bright parts in your render just a little extra bit of kick. The Fog Glow and Streaks options in the first drop-down menu are what I tend to use the most. Of all the values, this node gives you to play with, probably the most influential one is Threshold. Setting the threshold to values between 0.0 and 1.0 tends to work best for me, but results vary from one image to the next.

Vector

Vector nodes use 3D data from your scene to influence the look of your final 2D image. The usage of these nodes tends to be a bit advanced, but they allow you to do things like change the lighting in a scene or even change the speed that objects move through the scene . . . all without re-rendering! If you render to an image format that understands render passes, like the very cool OpenEXR format (more on this topic in the next section), and you include vector and normal passes, these nodes can be a huge time-saver.

Matte

The Matte nodes are specifically tailored for using color information from an image as a way of isolating certain parts of it. Matting is referred to as *keying* because you pick the main color, or *key color,* to represent transparency. Keying is the fundamental basis for those cool *bluescreen* or *greenscreen* effects used in movies. The filmmaker shoots the action over a blue or green screen (blue is used for analog film, whereas green is typically used for digital footage), and a compositor removes the blue or green and replaces it with other footage or something built in 3D.

Distort

The Distort nodes typically do general-purpose image manipulation operations like Translate, Rotate, Scale, Flip, or Crop.

Want to do that spinning newspaper effect you see in old movies? Wire an image of a newspaper and the Time node to the Rotate and Flip nodes, and you've got it! However, three special Distort nodes are worth talking more about: Displace, Map UV, and Lens Distortion. Figure 15-14 shows each of these nodes.

Figure 15-14: Distort nodes: Displace, Map UV, and Lens Distortion.

✔ **Displace:** This node is great for doing quick-and-dirty image distortions, such as generating heat waves in the desert, faking refraction, or making an object appear to push through the image on the screen. The key is the Vector input socket. If you feed a grayscale image to this socket, it uses those values to shift pixels in the image. Connecting a color image, normals, or vectors shifts the image around with a more three-dimensional effect, thereby giving you things like the heat wave effect.

✔ **Map UV:** In this entire chapter, I talk about how one cool thing that the Node Compositor can do is change textures on objects after you've already rendered them. Well, the Map UV node gets you that awesome functionality. To use this node, you need to enable the UV pass on your render layer. Feed that pass to this node, along with the new texture you want to use, and BAM! Your new texture is ready to be mixed back with the image. To make sure that you're changing the texture on the right object, combine the Map UV node with the ID Mask node before mixing.

✔ **Lens Distortion:** Sometimes you want to introduce the effects that some special (or, in some cases, poor) lenses have on the final image. The Lens Distortion node produces those effects for you. You can get everything from a wide fisheye lens look to that strange effect when an old projector isn't calibrated properly and the colors are misaligned.

Group

When you press Ctrl+G to create a node group, that group is placed in this menu. When you group a set of nodes, you instantly have the ability to apply that network to other parts of your compositing node network. Also, grouping gives you the ability to share node networks between `.blend` files. When you append or link a node group from another file, it shows up in this menu. There's more on grouping earlier in this chapter in the section "Grouping nodes together."

Whenever you have the opportunity, name *everything* you create. Unique names are especially important for groups because they're automatically added to the Group menu. Using names that make sense makes choosing the right node group a lot easier. You can always rename node groups from the Properties region of the Node Editor (N) or directly from the datablock selector within the node itself.

Rendering from the Node Compositor

If you're using the Node Compositor, you already know all the basic steps for getting a rendered image out of it. Of course, if you skipped straight to this section, here's the quick version: Make sure that the Compositing check box in the Post Processing panel of Render Properties is enabled.

That said, you need to know one other thing about rendering from the Compositor. Say that you're working on a larger production and want to save your render passes to an external file format so that either you or another compositor can work on it later without re-rendering the whole scene. You'd have to save your renders to a file format that understands render layers and render passes. That format is the venerable OpenEXR file format, developed and gifted to the world by the cool people at Industrial Light & Magic.

Now I know what you're thinking, "Using this format is as easy as setting up my render layers and then choosing OpenEXR from the menu in the Output panel of Render Properties." You're actually two-thirds correct. You do set up your render layers and you do go to the Output panel. *However*, choosing OpenEXR saves only the final composite output (not the layers or passes) in an OpenEXR file (extension `.exr`). In order to get layers and passes, you should instead choose OpenEXR MultiLayer. With this format, you get an OpenEXR file that has all the layer and pass information stored with it.

Pay close attention to your hard drive space when you choose to render to OpenEXR with all your layers and passes embedded. Keeping all your render layers and passes is a great way to tweak and make adjustments after rendering. However, the file size for each individual `.exr` file can be *huge*. Whereas an HD frame in PNG format may be only a couple hundred kilobytes, an OpenEXR file on the same single frame with all the passes enabled may be well over 100 *megabytes* — yes, megabytes. And if your animation has a length in minutes, that 100 megabytes per frame starts taking up space quickly. So make sure that you do test saves to get a good benchmark for the file size and see that you have enough hard drive space to store all those frames.

Motion Tracking

One of the most exciting new additions to Blender in recent years is an integrated motion tracking system. In *motion tracking*, software analyzes video footage and tracks various features in the footage in either two-dimensional or three-dimensional space. With properly tracked footage, an artist can add all kinds of exciting visual effects. Say that you have some video footage of a car driving away from you. With a good motion track (that you can do from right within Blender), you could do almost anything with that footage. It could be as simple as

blurring out that car's license plate or as wild and complex as adding rocket boosters to the car and having it cruise into the sunset through a dystopian wasteland populated by ravenous man-eating cacti. Anything you can do in Blender can be added to that footage!

Blender has a screen layout specifically tailored for motion tracking; conveniently, it's called Motion Tracking. From the Default layout, you can get there by pressing Ctrl+→ twice. The following figures shows this screen layout.

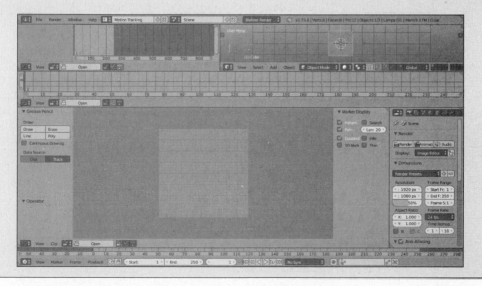

(continued)

(Continued)

The workhorse of Blender's motion tracking system (and the largest editor in the Motion Tracking screen layout) is the Movie Clip Editor. Complete books could be written on the topic of the Movie Clip Editor and motion tracking. there is an incredible video tutorial series produced by Sebastian Koenig called *Track, Match, Blend*. You can find it in the Blender e-shop (`www.blender.org/e-shop`), as well as an updated version on the Blender Cloud (`http://cloud.blender.org`), the Blender Foundation's resource for Blender assets and training. I highly recommend these tutorials from Sebastian; there's really no better place to discover how to take full advantage of Blender's motion tracking features.

Part V
The Part of Tens

In this part . . .

- ✔ Solutions for common problems.
- ✔ Tips for working more effectively.
- ✔ Resources for Blender users.
- ✔ Visit www.dummies.com for great Dummies content online.

Chapter 16

Ten Problems (and Solutions) for Newbies

In This Chapter

▶ Identifying common problems for new users

▶ Finding solutions

The community forums and Web pages for Blender are brimming with questions from new users. Many of them are the same question, or derivatives of the same question. The purpose of this chapter is to identify some of the most common ones and give you solutions to them so that you don't have to dig through these websites (unless you really, really want to).

Blender's Interface Is Weird or Glitchy

Blender uses OpenGL, an accelerated 3D programming library, for its entire interface. Because of the extensive use of OpenGL (and some rather old versions of it), Blender often uses parts of the library that other programs may never touch. Depending what video card you have in your computer, the drivers for that card may not effectively implement these little-used library features that Blender needs.

On some machines, Blender may run very slowly, or you may see weird screen glitches around the mouse pointer or menus. The first thing to check is the drivers for your video card. Go to the website for the manufacturer of your video card to see whether any updates are available.

 You may want to turn off any fancy effects that your operating system adds, such as transparent windows, shadows on the mouse cursor, or 3D desktop effects. Because all these little bits of eye candy tend to be hardware accelerated, they may be conflicting with Blender a bit. At the very least, turning them off usually makes your computer use fewer resources like processor power and memory, thereby making more of those resources available to Blender. If you're using an NVIDIA video card, make sure that the Flipping check box in your OpenGL settings isn't enabled and that full-screen anti-aliasing is disabled.

Within Blender itself, go to the System section in User Preferences (Ctrl+Alt+U) and find the Window Draw Method drop-down menu in the center column. The default setting is Automatic, which normally works pretty well. However, on some Intel-based and ATI-based video cards, you may have better luck manually changing this menu to Overlap or Overlap Flip. Play with the different options here to see which one works best for you. Blender updates immediately when you make the change, so you don't need to restart anything.

A Notorious Black Stripe Appears on Models

Often when modeling, you run into a situation where a strange black crease goes along some edges. The stripe is usually most apparent when modeling with the Subdivision Surface modifier turned on and you're looking at your mesh in Solid viewport shading. What's happening here is that the normals for one of the faces adjoining this edge are pointing the wrong direction.

Usually, the quickest way to fix this problem is to have Blender recalculate the normals for the model and attempt to have them all face outside. To do so, go into Edit mode, select all, and press Ctrl+N. Typically, pressing Ctrl+N alleviates all issues. If it doesn't, however, you may have to go in and manually flip the normals yourself. Manual flipping of normals is easiest to do from Face Select mode with face normals visible. To make face normals visible, enable the Face toggle (its button shows a cube with a highlighted face) under the Normals label in the Mesh Display panel of the Properties region of the 3D View (N). With that set, a cyan line points out from all faces in the direction of their normals. Now you can see which normals are pointing the wrong way. From there, select the offending faces and press W⇨Flip Normals.

If that still doesn't solve your problem, it could mean that you have multiple vertices in the same place, or you have faces inside your mesh. You can fix multiple vertices by pressing W⇨Remove Doubles. Internal faces are harder to auto-detect, but if you view your mesh in Wireframe viewport shading (Z), it may be more apparent. You can also use the Select Non Manifold operator (Shift+Ctrl+Alt+M) to help find internal faces.

Objects Go Missing

Occasionally, you might run into a problem where not everything shows up in your 3D View, even though you're positive you didn't delete anything. The first thing to do is to make sure that nothing is hidden. Pressing H in the 3D View hides whatever you've selected, and it's easy to accidentally hit it when you're actually trying to press G and grab an object. Fortunately, you can unhide all hidden objects pretty quickly by pressing Alt+H. You can also look in the restrict columns on the right side of the Outliner. If your object is hidden, the first icon — the eye icon — appears closed. Left-clicking the eye icon unhides it. The camera icon on the far right controls whether your object is visible when rendering.

If you're sure that nothing is hidden, next try to make all layers visible and check to be sure that you didn't inadvertently move your object to a different layer. You do so by pressing the Tilde (~) key. You may also want to press Home in the 3D View to bring all objects into view.

One last thing to check is whether you're in Local View, the view that isolates all objects except for a few that you select. The hotkey that toggles this view is Numpad Slash (/), and it can be pretty easy to accidentally hit it when using the numeric keypad to change views. One quick way to tell whether you're in Local View is to look at the header for the 3D View. If no layer buttons are where they're supposed to be, you may be in Local View. In the upper left corner of the 3D View, text also tells you how you're viewing your scene. If you're in Local View, (Local) appears as the last part of that text.

If none of these things work, there actually *is* the chance that you deleted your object by accident. Fortunately, if you haven't closed your file, you can recover from this mistake as well. See, when you delete an object in Blender, it doesn't actually get completely deleted until you close the file or open a new file, so it still exists in Blender's internal database for this file.

I'm writing the next few steps under the assumption that your object was a Mesh, but the same technique works for curves, text, and other types of objects. To recover a deleted object, use the following steps:

1. **Create a dummy object that's the same type as the one you're trying to recover.**

   For meshes, use any of the options in Shift+A➪Mesh.

2. **Bring up that object's Mesh Properties and look in the Context panel at the top; in the datablock, left-click the button on the left side.**

   You see a list of all the objects in the scene that share the current selected object's type. Anything you delete has an empty circle to the left of it. Figure 16-1 shows what this screen might look like.

3. **If your deleted object is in this list, select it and the dummy object you added in the first step is instantly replaced with the mesh for your deleted object.**

   Neat, huh?

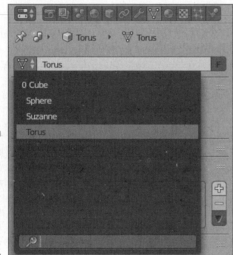

Figure 16-1: Deleted objects in the datablock at the top of Mesh Properties.

Edge Loop Select Doesn't Work

The issue of Edge Loop Select not working happens the most on Linux machines. The Blender hotkey for doing a loop selection in Edit mode is Alt+right-click. Unfortunately, in Gnome 2 and a few other window managers, this key sequence pops up a menu for controlling the window.

You can fix this issue in two ways. The easiest one is to use Shift+Alt+right-click. You typically use this combination to select multiple loops, but if nothing is selected, it works exactly the same as the Alt+right-click combination.

Of course, that's a bit of a kludge. A better solution is to modify the window manager's settings and bind the function that it ties to the Alt key to another key, like the infamous "super" or Windows key that most modern keyboards have. Because the method varies from one window manager to another, you'll need to consult the documentation on your window manager to see the exact steps on how to do this.

A Background Image Disappears

When using a photographic or drawn reference to base your models on, it's a common practice to load the reference image in the background of the 3D View (see Chapter 5). However, when working this way, you may orbit your view to do a spot-check and then when you return to side (or front or top or camera and so on) view, the background image may disappear, even though the Background Images panel in the 3D View's Properties region says it's still there.

The answer here is that you're viewing the scene through Perspective view rather than the Orthographic one. Blender doesn't show the background reference image in Perspective view. Switch back to Orthographic by pressing Numpad 5. It makes sense to use Orthographic for reference images because a Perspective view introduces distortion and scaling to the way the scene is viewed, so it wouldn't be a good idea to model from reference in this type of view even if you could. The Orthographic view is much more effective at getting a model to match a reference image.

Alternatively, you could an Empty with Image set as its display type. This ensures that your reference image is visible at all times and from all angles.

Zooming Has Its Limits

When working in Perspective view, you may notice that occasionally you can't zoom in on your scene as much as you'd like. This limitation is because you're zooming toward a center point, and you're very near it. You can take advantage of four workarounds:

✔ **Place the 3D cursor at the location you'd like to zoom to and press Ctrl+Numpad Dot (.).** This workaround centers the view on the 3D cursor and gives you a clearer target to zoom in on.

✔ **Select the object (or sub-object element, like a vertex or edge in Edit mode) that you want to zoom in on and press Numpad Dot (.).** This workaround centers the view on that selection so that you can now use that as your zoom target.

✔ **Try popping quickly into Orthographic view by pressing Numpad 5.**
Because Orthographic view has no perspective distortion, the way it
zooms is somewhat different, which may give you a better angle.

The only downside to this method is that you can't get a view from inside
your mesh, if that's something you want.

✔ **Enable the Auto Depth check box in the Interface section of User
Preferences (Ctrl+Alt+U).** Enabling this option tells Blender to dynamically change the point you're zooming in and avoid this problem
altogether.

Lost Simulation Data

As mentioned in Chapter 13, Blender saves some simulation data to your
hard drive. Unfortunately, if that simulation data isn't where Blender expects
it to be, your simulation won't show up in your `.blend` file. Generally, lost
simulation data happens for one of three reasons:

✔ **You work on more than one computer.** If you work in Blender on more
than one machine and only copy the `.blend` file between the two, the
simulation data isn't where it needs to be on the second computer. You
need to copy that simulation data to the same place relative to your
`.blend` file on the second computer for it to show up properly.

✔ **You accidentally changed or deleted the path to the simulation data.**
This reason isn't common, but it does happen. Fortunately, the fix is
simple for fluid simulations. Select the domain object for your fluid simulation and go to Physics Properties. In the Fluid panel, the path to your
simulation data is the last field. Enter the proper path here or left-click
the folder icon to the right of the field and find the proper directory with
the File Browser.

✔ **You're using the `/tmp` directory for your simulations.** Initially, using
`/tmp` doesn't seem like that big of a deal. However, on some operating
systems, the `/tmp` directory is periodically purged, deleting everything
in it. If that directory gets purged, your simulation won't show up and
your only option is to rebake it.

Using `/tmp` all the time also has another nasty side effect: Different
`.blend` files overwrite the simulation data that's in there. So you may
run into a situation where you open one `.blend` with a fluid simulation
only to see the simulation results from another file. Again, the only solution in this case is to rebake your simulation. This time, however, set the
path somewhere else so this doesn't happen again.

Objects Don't Appear When Rendering

Sometimes, when you render, you might notice that some objects are perfectly visible in the 3D View, but they don't show up in your render. There are a few reasons that this may happen:

✔ **Camera clipping:** Just like with Spot lamps, as described in Chapter 9, cameras have a *clipping distance* (a range of visible area with a start and an end). The default clipping distance for the 3D View goes from 0.1 to 5000. However, the default camera only has a clipping distance from 0.1 to 100. This means that an object that's 101 Blender units away will show up in the 3D View, but it may not appear when you render.

The fix for this is to either change the position of the object that's too far away or increase the end clipping distance for your camera object (Camera Properties⇨Lens⇨Clipping).

✔ **Restricted rendering:** Blender's Outliner gives you the ability to restrict (disable) rendering for specific objects. While this can be useful for animation purposes, it isn't difficult to forget that you've made that toggle.

Fortunately, the fix is easy. Go to the Outliner, find your object, and re-enable renderability on it by left-clicking the rightmost icon next to it (the icon looks like a camera).

✔ **Non-rendered layers:** Render layers are an incredibly powerful tool for compositing. However, with that power comes the need to be more fastidious in how you manage your scene. It's very possible to disable a scene layer from being used in a render layer. The result is the functional equivalent of enabling restricted rendering on every object in that scene layer.

To fix this issue, go to Render Layers Properties and double-check the scene layers that you have assigned to your render layers. If you know which layers an object is on, you should be able to ensure those layers are enabled.

No GPU Rendering for Cycles

One of the biggest appeals for using Cycles as a renderer is its ability to leverage your video card's GPU to speed up calculations (and, by extension, the overall rendering process). Unfortunately, depending on your computer hardware, you may not be able to take advantage of this speed boost. The first thing to check is whether you're currently using GPU computing at all. If you're using Cycles (by picking Cycles Render from the Engine drop-down menu in the Info editor's header), look at the Render panel in Render

Properties. There should be a drop-down menu there labeled Device and it should be set to GPU Compute. If it's set to CPU or that drop-down menu isn't there, that's the first sign that you aren't using your GPU for rendering with Cycles.

Your next step is to look at the System section of User Preferences (Ctrl+Alt+U). At the bottom of the leftmost column is a little section labeled Compute Device. The first set of radio buttons beneath that should give you the options of None, CUDA, or OpenCL. You want to pick CUDA (currently, that's the only one where Cycles' GPU computing works reliably). CUDA is a GPU computing technology developed by NVIDIA to run on their cards. Cycles uses CUDA for its GPU computing features. This, of course, means that Cycles currently is limited to only working on relatively modern NVIDIA video cards. Once you pick CUDA, you should be able to pick your specific video card from the drop-down menu below those radio buttons.

If you don't have CUDA as an option, you may be in one of small handful of scenarios:

✔ **You don't have an NVIDIA video card.** If this is the case, your only options are to either stick with CPU-only rendering or get a new video card.

✔ **You have an NVIDIA video card, but its CUDA support is too old.** Again, your only options in this case are to stick with CPU rendering or upgrade your video card.

✔ **You have an NVIDIA video card, but you haven't fully installed drivers and CUDA support.** Consult the documentation for your specific operating system on how to properly update your drivers and enable CUDA support. After you do that (and go through the start/restart dances that your operating system requires), you should be able to fire up Blender and enable GPU-accelerated rendering in Cycles using CUDA.

Funky Deformations in Animation Rigs

This isn't necessarily specific to animation rigs, but animation rigs are where you most often see it. The effect is easy to recognize. You'll have a mesh set up to be controlled by an armature, for example; when you grab or rotate any of the bones, the mesh stretches, skews, and scales wildly, like it isn't even really being controlled by the armature at all.

A few different things may cause this behavior, and it may happen any time you add a deforming modifier (such as Armature, Curve, Lattice, or Mesh Deform) or nearly any constraint to an object. If this is happening to you, check for these red flags:

✔ **Non-applied transformations.**

It's possible that you grabbed, rotated, or scaled your mesh (or worse, your armature) in Object mode prior to adding the modifier or constraint. This might not seem like a big deal, but the problem is that modifiers and constraints tend to operate on the original data (the Edit mode data). If you change the location, orientation, or size of that data in Object mode, the modifier or constraint doesn't have a valid frame of reference.

The remedy for this is to apply your transforms (Ctrl+A) or back them — particularly scale and rotation — out to base values (1,1,1 for scale and 0,0,0 for rotation).

✔ **Doubled-up modifiers.**

You can run into this problem with the Armature modifier in particular. It sometimes occurs when you use the parenting shortcut for adding an Armature modifier to a mesh (Ctrl+P➪Armature Deform). If you aren't careful, you could be adding multiple Armature modifiers, each one adding to the influence of the previous one. This results in an effect where you rotate a bone and the mesh ends up moving twice as far as it should.

Fortunately, the fix for this is easy. Check your Modifier Properties and make sure you haven't doubled up.

✔ **Cyclic dependencies.**

This one is probably the most difficult to track down. You may have a situation where a bone in your armature is influencing the location of a hook that, in turn, is the parent of the armature object. Cyclic dependencies like this one can be very difficult to track down, but they're a sure way for a rig to go haywire in all kinds of interesting ways. Blender does its best to advise you of potential cycles by printing warnings to the system console (this is why it's wise to rig with a version of Blender that's launched from the terminal), but it currently can't catch everything.

A good test for cyclic dependencies is to grab (G) a control and move it around, then cancel that operation (right-click). If you have a cyclic dependency, not everything will snap back to its previous position. If you see this happening in a rig of yours, you'll need to sit down and meticulously work your way through the rig to suss out the source of the problem.

Chapter 17

Ten Tips for Working More Effectively in Blender

*W*orking in Blender is a ton of fun, but you can adopt a few good work habits to make the experience even more enjoyable. These good habits let you work faster without sacrificing the quality of your work. In this chapter, I detail ten of my best suggestions for working more efficiently and effectively in Blender.

Use Tooltips and Integrated Search

Blender is a dense program, and users often forget what a button does or discover a new menu. If you don't know what a button in Blender does, hover your mouse pointer over it. More often than not, a helpful tooltip pops up to concisely describe what the button does. And even if the tooltip isn't completely clear, you have a better idea of what to search for to get help.

And speaking of searching, one of the best features of Blender is the fully integrated search functionality. Using the search hotkey (Spacebar) in a particular editor, you can type the name of the feature or tool you're looking for, and Blender shows you a list of operations that may match within the context of the editor that you're working in. Furthermore, if that operator has a hotkey, that hotkey also shows up in the search results.

Look at Models from Different Views

If you work in an environment modeling and animating by using just one 3D View, you should definitely make it a point to periodically orbit around your scene and look at it from a bunch of different angles. Double-checking is particularly important when modeling because it's very easy to get a model that looks perfect from the front, but really distorted and goofy-shaped from one side.

Split off another 3D View if you need it or use the numeric keypad hotkeys to quickly do spot-checks from different angles. If you're coming from a background in 3DStudio Max or CAD applications, you may want to use the Quad View in the 3D window to see multiple views at the same time by going to View⇨Toggle Quad View or using the Ctrl+Alt+Q hotkey. If you have the Pie Menus add-on enabled, the Q hotkey brings up a fantastic menu for changing the view. Used at speed, it feels as if you're flinging the scene in the 3D View around in front of you.

Lock a Camera to an Animated Character

When animating a character, you frequently run into a case where you're trying to animate a secondary detail on the character as he's moving. For these situations, Blender has a handy Lock to Object feature. In the Properties region of the 3D View, look in the View panel. There's an object datablock field there labeled Lock to Object. Type in the name of an object (or hover your mouse over the field and press E to get an object eyedropper) and the 3D View moves wherever that object goes.

For a somewhat more permanent solution, I sometimes like to create a new camera and parent it to the character. This way, the camera goes anywhere the character does. I find this approach helpful for facial animation on a moving character. To lock a camera to your animated character, use the following steps:

1. **Add a new camera (Shift+A⇨Camera) and put it in front of your character's face.**

2. **With the camera still selected, add the head bone of your character to the selection (Shift+right-click).**

3. **Press Ctrl+P⇨Bone to parent the camera to the bone.**

   Now, wherever the head goes and whichever direction it turns, the camera is always looking at your character's face.

4. **Whenever you want to work on the facial animation for your character, select this camera (right-click) and switch to its view by pressing Ctrl+Numpad 0.**

Don't Forget about Add-ons

One of the neat things that's grown in Blender over the years is a thriving ecosystem of *add-ons*. Add-ons are a set of trusted Python scripts written to extend Blender's capabilities. They can be as small as a little script that adds a new menu or as large as a wizard that generates a landscape for you. Although many of these scripts ship with Blender, most are disabled by default because they're meant to serve a specific purpose that not all Blender users need. It's worth your time to go through the Add-ons section of the User Preferences editor (File⇨User Preferences or Ctrl+Alt+U) to see what's available. (Shameless plug: one or two of them might be ones that I wrote and maintain.)

If you find an add-on that you know you frequently use (like pie menus or the Dynamic Spacebar Menu add-on or a specific importer or exporter), enable the add-on and include it on your startup by clicking the Save As Default button at the bottom of the User Preferences editor.

Name Everything

Every time you add something to your scene in Blender, give it a name that makes sense. It's a very disorienting feeling when you open a .blend file that you haven't worked on in a while and you see that your characters are Cube.001, Cube.012, and Sphere.007, and that really cool skin material you made is called Material.015.

On small, one-shot projects, ambiguous names may not be so bad, but properly naming a material makes finding it later that much easier. And on larger projects, good organization is even more valuable. Not only is it smart to name everything in your .blend file, but it's also a good idea to have a good structure for your projects. For most of my projects, I have a separate directory for the project. Within that directory, I create sub-directories for my libraries of models, materials, textures, and finished renders. For animations, my renders directory is broken down even farther into each shot.

Use Scene Layers Effectively

Although only 20 scene layers are available, Blender's layering system is very versatile and can be used for a variety of purposes. Objects can live on more than one scene layer, lights can be made to only illuminate the layers they're on, and you use scene layers define render layers used for compositing. As such, keeping some form of organization in mind is in your best interest.

One thing I like to do is place all my models on the top row of layers (layers 1–10) and all other objects, such as lights, cameras, and armatures, on the bottom row (layers 11–20).

Also keep high-priority objects, such as characters and animated things, on the left-most layers, while keeping static objects like backgrounds on the right-most layers.

Specifically for character animation, when I put my character in one layer, I place his rig in the layer directly below it. I like to stick to this little convention, which is certainly a help for me when I want to quickly make sense of a `.blend` file that I haven't opened in a long time.

Of course, this organizational style may not work for you, but you should definitely make it a point to create *some* conventions that you can remember and reuse.

Do Low-Resolution Test Renders

When you're finalizing the look of a model, you often have to make a quick change to the model and render (F12) it to see what it looks like. If you're not careful, you could spend more time waiting for those little test renders than you do actually working on your model. The progressive render update feature that Cycles uses in the 3D View can help mitigate this, but some projects may require you to use different rendering engines. And even still, on complex scenes even people who use Cycles could benefit from small test renders.

When you're just doing test previews, these tips can reduce the render time:

✔ **Turn off anti-aliasing.** *Aliasing* is that jaggy stair-stepping that happens around some edges in your renders. *Anti-aliasing* is the process of trying to smooth those jaggies out. The way anti-aliasing works in the Blender Internal renderer is by using a technique known as *oversampling,* where it renders the same section multiple times and averages out the results to make those edges smoother. Having anti-aliasing enabled is great for final renders, but can really eat up time when you just want to do a quick test. If you're using Blender Internal, disable anti-aliasing by left-clicking its check box in the Render Properties.

✔ **Render at reduced size.** Most of the time, when you're doing a test, you don't really have to see what the full-size final image will look like. This generalization is especially true if the final render is for print or film, where the final resolution can be greater than 4,000 pixels wide. Of course, you could manually enter a smaller size in the Dimensions section of Render Properties, but Blender offers a faster way. If you look in Render Properties, you see a slider under the X and Y resolution values. Adjust this slider to make Blender render your image at that percentage of the final size, thereby reducing the render time for your test preview. (Bonus tip: If you want to render at *larger* than the render resolution, you can manually enter a percentage that's larger than 100%.)

✔ **Turn off computationally intensive features if you don't need them.** Features like ambient occlusion (AO), ray tracing, and environmental lighting look great in a final render, but if you're just looking at the form of a model, they aren't necessarily needed for a test. In Blender Internal, you can turn off ray tracing in the Shading section of Render Properties. Turning off AO or environmental lighting requires you to go to World Properties and disable it there. If you're using Cycles, you may want to disable the Square Samples check box in the Sampling panel and reduce the sampling values in the Light Paths panel to 0 or 1.

✔ **Render just the layers you need.** If you're working on just one model in a scene and only want to do a test render for that model, disable the layers for other objects in the scene. As long as you have the object and lights in the scene, your test render will be helpful, accurate, and most important, speedy.

✔ **Use the Border Render feature.** If you're only interested in doing a test render on a particular part of your scene, switch to the camera view (Numpad 0) and use Border Render by pressing Shift+B and using your mouse cursor to draw a box around the part of the shot you're interested in. When you finish doing tests, you can take this border off by left-clicking the Border check box in the Dimensions section of Render Properties, or you can press Shift+B and draw a box anywhere outside of the camera's view area.

✔ **If you're animating, use OpenGL previews.** In the header of the 3D View, the last button has an icon of a film clapper. Clicking that icon will render your animation, using the same engine that creates the real-time display in the 3D View. In other software, a render that comes from the 3D View is referred to as a playblast. It allows you to see the action and timing of your animation without waiting for all the fancy render settings to kick in. As an additional bonus, I recommend going into the Display panel in the Properties region of the 3D View (View⇨Properties or press N) and click the Only Render check box before creating your playblast. The Only Render feature hides the extra, non-rendered objects (such as rigs, lights, and the grid plane) in your scene so that you can get a clear playblast without bothersome obstructions.

✔ **If you're rendering with Cycles, lower the number of samples.** Simply put, the more samples that you tell Cycles to use, the longer each render will take. If you keep the sample count low (say, 10), your renders will still be pretty noisy, but they'll be good enough to know whether your lighting and materials are working for you.

Mind Your Mouse

When you're using Blender's hotkeys to transform objects, where you place your mouse cursor before performing the operation can be pretty important. Although the importance of your mouse cursor's location has reduced a bit with the continuous mouse feature, cursor placement can still be an issue, particularly for rotating and scaling.

For rotating, it's a good practice to keep your mouse distant from the object's origin. Doing so gives you more control over how you rotate. If your mouse cursor is too close to the center, you can have your object spinning in all kinds of unpredictable ways.

The same is true for scaling, but it's more dependent on whether you're scaling up or down. If you're scaling up, it makes sense to bring your mouse cursor a bit closer to the selection's origin so that you have more control. If you're scaling down, start with your mouse cursor farther away from the selection's origin and, as with rotation, you have more control of how small your object can get.

For grabbing, it's a bit less important, but I generally like to have my mouse somewhere near my object's origin.

Use Grease Pencil to Plan

Blender's Grease Pencil feature allows you to write or draw simple lines in 3D space. While this feature may seem a bit strange at first, it's actually incredibly useful. As an individual, you can use Grease Pencil to quickly sketch out ideas prior to modeling them in Blender. If you're working with a group of people, Grease Pencil allows you to include notes in the 3D View to facilitate collaboration. You can sketch a pose that a character should go into or draw an arc that the surface of a model should follow and pass those notes back to the original artist. You can even do rough 2D animation with this handy little feature!

To use Grease Pencil, simply hold down D while left-clicking and dragging your mouse cursor around the 3D View. The default color for Grease Pencil strokes is black, but you can adjust it, as well as other attributes from Grease Pencil section of the Properties region (N).

Have Fun, but Take Breaks

Don't be afraid to just play with Blender. If you ever find yourself wondering "What does this button do?" just press it and find out. Now, if you're working on something important, you should probably save first, but definitely make it a point to experiment and try things out. By this kind of playing, not only can you figure out how to use new parts of Blender, but you can also find new ways of using existing features in cool ways that might not have been intended.

Working in 3D can be incredibly serious fun, but it can also be addictive. Too much computer time can ultimately hurt the quality of your work. Try to step away from the computer for a bit to rest your eyes, get some food, stretch your legs, or even talk to another human being.

Chapter 18

Ten Excellent Community Resources

In This Chapter

▶ Discovering websites that are valuable sources of information and help in Blender

▶ Finding a place for real-time communication with other Blenderheads

The true strength of Blender is in its community. It's strong, organized, passionate, and perhaps even a little bit crazy. People use Blender for a variety of reasons, from producing animated films and video games to creating scientific and architectural visualizations to even wackier things (such as controlling unmanned drones and 3D printing interactive art installations). The following community resources give you a good idea of just how diverse and motivated this group is.

Blender.org

The official Blender website, www.blender.org, is *the* place to go for nearly anything Blender related. Most obviously, this website is the one to visit when you want to download the latest stable version of Blender. Not only that, but you can also track new developments in the Blender Foundation and Blender Institute, including new features being coded into Blender.

Another item of interest is the official Blender User Manual online. This "live" manual is located at www.blender.org/manual. Like Blender itself, the manual is constantly being updated as changes are made to Blender.

You can also use this site to find Blender trainers who have been certified by the Blender Foundation or go to the Gallery to sit back and enjoy some of the best artwork created by the many skilled artists in the community.

BlenderArtists.org

If you had any questions about how active the Blender community is, you would only have visit www.blenderartists.org once to quell those doubts. The primary community website for Blender artists, this site is the main place to go for English-speaking Blender users.

BlenderArtists.org (or BA.org, as many affectionately refer to it) is a web forum for Blender users. Here you can see artists of all skill levels sharing their work, learning new features, offering tips, participating in contests, and engaging in idle chitchat. (Disclaimer: I'm a moderator on BA.org. I go by the username Fweeb.)

A particularly cool thing on the BA.org forums is the Weekend Challenge. Late Thursday night (GMT), a theme is posted. Participants have until the same time Monday evening to model and render a scene to fit that theme. At the end of the weekend, the community votes on a winner, and that winner gets to pick the theme for the next Weekend Challenge. This is a great way to find out just how good you really are, and it's a lot of fun, too!

BlenderNation

If any new developments with Blender occur or anything interesting happens within the Blender community, BlenderNation, the main news site for anything Blender-related, reports on it. BlenderNation (www.blendernation.com) covers events, reviews books, and presents tutorials.

In particular, this website is a great way to see what kind of professional work is being done with Blender. (Many working professionals don't always have time to be active on the forums at BA.org.) BlenderNation also reports on topics that, although perhaps not directly related to Blender, may be of interest to Blender users (such as news on open source software or events in the larger computer graphics industry).

BlenderBasics.com

This is the *Blender For Dummies* website that I maintain for this book. Not only can you find all of the sample files available for this book, but I also have additional content video tutorials, additional files, and errata updates. In addition, there are a few sections in this book where I refer to helpful written tutorials. This is the website where I have them posted.

blender.stackexchange.com

The Blender section on StackExchange (`http://blender.stack exchange.com`) is a relatively new Blender site, but it's already one of the best places to go for support. If you have a question about using Blender, chances are good that it's been asked here. And if your question hasn't been asked yet, you can expect to get a very clear, well-researched, and extremely thorough response from the Blender users and developers who populate that site.

BlenderCookie.com

A regularly updated and high-quality site loaded with education material for Blender, BlenderCookie was one of the first sites to provide video tutorials and documentation for Blender's new interface. It's been successfully cranking out great content ever since. BlenderCookie continues to provide high-quality examples and tutorials for anyone interested in advancing their CG skills with Blender. The vast majority of materials on this website are freely available, although some tutorials offer the ability to purchase supplementary files and source files for a small fee.

The fine folks at BlenderCookie also manage the Blender Market, a website designed to facilitate Blender users to sell their useful additions to Blender. These include highly advanced add-ons, pre-modeled asset packs, and refined materials and shaders for Cycles. The site (and the concept) is still young, but some great tools already are being made available there.

Blendswap

At this online repository of a variety of 3D models created in Blender, models are contributed by the community and organized by category. Associated with each model is a license that clearly shows what you have permission to do with it. Blendswap played an instrumental part in some of the weekend modeling sprints for the *Sintel* open movie project from the Blender Institute.

Blenderart Magazine

Focusing on creating artwork with Blender, Blenderart is a very well-designed free online magazine in PDF format that is released on (roughly) a bimonthly schedule. Some of the best artists in the community have written for this magazine, and it's a great place to pick up new tricks.

builder.blender.org

When you really start getting into Blender, it can become highly addictive. One of the huge benefits of Blender being open source is the sheer amount of access you have to developers and, by extension, development versions of Blender.

builder.blender.org is a website set up by the core Blender developers to provide everyone with daily builds from the development source tree. An automated system creates an executable build for each of the major platforms Blender supports, and they're uploaded to the site each evening. This way, regular users can play with new features while they're being developed and, hopefully, contribute to the process by creating bug reports and providing feedback to developers. This level of access is unheard of for regular users of any of the proprietary 3D packages, and it's one of those things that you get with Blender precisely because it's open source.

Blender IRC Channels on freenode.net

The ultimate place to go for instant discussion and feedback from other Blender users is the Blender IRC channels on freenode.net. IRC is Internet Relay Chat, one of the oldest protocols on the Internet. Using a chat program (called a *client*) like mIRC or Chatzilla or even the open source IM program, Pidgin, you can log into the freenode server. If you don't want to install anything, you can use a Web interface at http://webchat.freenode.net/. Simply choose a nickname and join one of the many channels devoted to Blender.

In particular, the following channels may be most interesting to you:

✔ **#blender:** Kind of the obvious de facto official Blender channel. You can often get quick help here, but sometimes the channel is populated with people who only know as much about Blender as you do.

✔ **#blenderchat:** For general discussion, critique, and occasional help in Blender. This is probably the most active Blender channel on freenode and is a great place to interact directly with other Blender users.

✔ **#blenderQA:** As the name suggests, for getting your Blender questions answered. This is usually a pretty good place to go if you're having problems and need help quickly.

✔ **#smc:** Speed Modeling Challenge. Visit this channel to really challenge yourself. Artists here organize challenges where everyone is given an object to model and a time limit (usually 30 minutes to an hour) to create that model and render it.

✔ **#blendercoders:** For people involved with actually writing the code that makes Blender. Although discussions here might be a bit technical for new users (and even some experienced ones!), it's a good place to find out the latest information on Blender's development. Also, if you think you've found a bug or error in Blender, this is a good, quick way to talk with a developer and find out if the error is real or if you're just doing something incorrectly.

Index

About the Author

Jason van Gumster does a lot of things. Mostly he makes stuff up. He writes, animate, and occasionally teaches. With heavy entrepreneurial tendencies that run nearly as deep as his creative ones, he has a constant fascination with producing creative content with as much control and independence as possible. Naturally, that makes him a big proponent of open source software; very nearly everything that he produces is made using Free and open source tools.

Using those open source tools, he ran his own small, independent animation studio for 8 years. And in the course of that, he had the privilege of managing large international production teams on ridiculously tight deadlines (4 to 7 minutes of CG animation in 2 days) . . . for fun. He's transferred some of that experience in writing to two different books, *Blender For Dummies* and *GIMP Bible*. The rest of that experience he continues to blurt out a bit at a time during his (mostly) weekly podcast, the *Open Source Creative Podcast*.

Currently based just outside of Atlanta, Georgia, Jason spends the majority of his time drinking coffee and trying to be awesome. The former he's pretty much gotten down to a science. The latter . . . well, every now and again he succeeds at that one and makes it look like it wasn't an accident.

Dedication

Who gets this? You do!

Authors' Acknowledgments

As with previous editions of this book, my first thanks *must* go to the team of developers behind Blender, including our "benevolent dictator", Ton Roosendaal. Without the regular commitment of these developers, Blender would never exist in the state that it does today. Of course, equally deserving gratitude is the overall Blender community, without which Blender would never have been made open source.

Thanks, also, to everyone at Wiley, particularly Cherie Case, Kyle Looper, and Andy Cummings. They've been exceedingly helpful in getting this edition of the book produced and amazingly tolerant of all the ridiculous questions I've thrown at them. I'd also like to specifically thank Pat O'Brien for his work as the book's project editor, and Bassam Kurdali for sticking with me as this book's technical editor for all three editions. Bassam is still one of the most knowledgeable and talented members of the Blender community. I dread how little sense this book would've made without his input.

Continuing the tradition of the first two editions of this book, I maintain my thanks for the brilliant human that first filtered water through ground coffee beans. But I rescind my thanks of pastries. You're the most delicious kind of horrible and I love you... but I can no longer find it in my heart to thank you.

And finally, I want to thank my wife and children. No, strike that. I *need* to thank you. Because I don't do that nearly enough.

Publisher's Acknowledgments

Project Editor: Pat O'Brien

Technical Editor: Bassam Kurdali

Editorial Assistant: Claire Brock

Sr. Editorial Assistant: Cherie Case

Project Coordinator: Kumar Chellappan

Cover Image: ©iStock.com/Sylverarts

Apple & Mac

iPad For Dummies,
6th Edition
978-1-118-72306-7

iPhone For Dummies,
7th Edition
978-1-118-69083-3

Macs All-in-One
For Dummies, 4th Edition
978-1-118-82210-4

OS X Mavericks
For Dummies
978-1-118-69188-5

Blogging & Social Media

Facebook For Dummies,
5th Edition
978-1-118-63312-0

Social Media Engagement
For Dummies
978-1-118-53019-1

WordPress For Dummies,
6th Edition
978-1-118-79161-5

Business

Stock Investing
For Dummies, 4th Edition
978-1-118-37678-2

Investing For Dummies,
6th Edition
978-0-470-90545-6

Personal Finance
For Dummies, 7th Edition
978-1-118-11785-9

QuickBooks 2014
For Dummies
978-1-118-72005-9

Small Business Marketing
Kit For Dummies,
3rd Edition
978-1-118-31183-7

Careers

Job Interviews
For Dummies, 4th Edition
978-1-118-11290-8

Job Searching with Social
Media For Dummies,
2nd Edition
978-1-118-67856-5

Personal Branding
For Dummies
978-1-118-11792-7

Resumes For Dummies,
6th Edition
978-0-470-87361-8

Starting an Etsy Business
For Dummies, 2nd Edition
978-1-118-59024-9

Diet & Nutrition

Belly Fat Diet For Dummies
978-1-118-34585-6

Mediterranean Diet
For Dummies
978-1-118-71525-3

Nutrition For Dummies,
5th Edition
978-0-470-93231-5

Digital Photography

Digital SLR Photography
All-in-One For Dummies,
2nd Edition
978-1-118-59082-9

Digital SLR Video &
Filmmaking For Dummies
978-1-118-36598-4

Photoshop Elements 12
For Dummies
978-1-118-72714-0

Gardening

Herb Gardening
For Dummies, 2nd Edition
978-0-470-61778-6

Gardening with Free-Range
Chickens For Dummies
978-1-118-54754-0

Health

Boosting Your Immunity
For Dummies
978-1-118-40200-9

Diabetes For Dummies,
4th Edition
978-1-118-29447-5

Living Paleo For Dummies
978-1-118-29405-5

Big Data

Big Data For Dummies
978-1-118-50422-2

Data Visualization
For Dummies
978-1-118-50289-1

Hadoop For Dummies
978-1-118-60755-8

Language &
Foreign Language

500 Spanish Verbs
For Dummies
978-1-118-02382-2

English Grammar
For Dummies, 2nd Edition
978-0-470-54664-2

French All-in-One
For Dummies
978-1-118-22815-9

German Essentials
For Dummies
978-1-118-18422-6

Italian For Dummies,
2nd Edition
978-1-118-00465-4

Available in print and e-book formats.

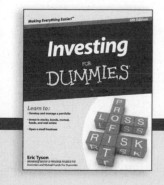

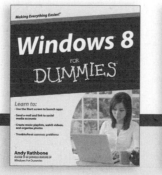

Available wherever books are sold. **For more information or to order direct visit www.dummies.com**

Math & Science

Algebra I For Dummies,
2nd Edition
978-0-470-55964-2

Anatomy and Physiology
For Dummies, 2nd Edition
978-0-470-92326-9

Astronomy For Dummies,
3rd Edition
978-1-118-37697-3

Biology For Dummies,
2nd Edition
978-0-470-59875-7

Chemistry For Dummies,
2nd Edition
978-1-118-00730-3

1001 Algebra II Practice
Problems For Dummies
978-1-118-44662-1

Microsoft Office

Excel 2013 For Dummies
978-1-118-51012-4

Office 2013 All-in-One
For Dummies
978-1-118-51636-2

PowerPoint 2013
For Dummies
978-1-118-50253-2

Word 2013 For Dummies
978-1-118-49123-2

Music

Blues Harmonica
For Dummies
978-1-118-25269-7

Guitar For Dummies,
3rd Edition
978-1-118-11554-1

iPod & iTunes
For Dummies, 10th Edition
978-1-118-50864-0

Programming

Beginning Programming
with C For Dummies
978-1-118-73763-7

Excel VBA Programming
For Dummies, 3rd Edition
978-1-118-49037-2

Java For Dummies,
6th Edition
978-1-118-40780-6

Religion & Inspiration

The Bible For Dummies
978-0-7645-5296-0

Buddhism For Dummies,
2nd Edition
978-1-118-02379-2

Catholicism For Dummies,
2nd Edition
978-1-118-07778-8

Self-Help & Relationships

Beating Sugar Addiction
For Dummies
978-1-118-54645-1

Meditation For Dummies,
3rd Edition
978-1-118-29144-3

Seniors

Laptops For Seniors
For Dummies, 3rd Edition
978-1-118-71105-7

Computers For Seniors
For Dummies, 3rd Edition
978-1-118-11553-4

iPad For Seniors
For Dummies, 6th Edition
978-1-118-72826-0

Social Security
For Dummies
978-1-118-20573-0

Smartphones & Tablets

Android Phones
For Dummies, 2nd Edition
978-1-118-72030-1

Nexus Tablets
For Dummies
978-1-118-77243-0

Samsung Galaxy S 4
For Dummies
978-1-118-64222-1

Samsung Galaxy Tabs

Samsung Galaxy Tabs
For Dummies
978-1-118-77294-2

Test Prep

ACT For Dummies,
5th Edition
978-1-118-01259-8

ASVAB For Dummies,
3rd Edition
978-0-470-63760-9

GRE For Dummies,
7th Edition
978-0-470-88921-3

Officer Candidate Tests
For Dummies
978-0-470-59876-4

Physician's Assistant Exam
For Dummies
978-1-118-11556-5

Series 7 Exam For Dummies
978-0-470-09932-2

Windows 8

Windows 8.1 All-in-One
For Dummies
978-1-118-82087-2

Windows 8.1 For Dummies
978-1-118-82121-3

Windows 8.1 For Dummies
Book + DVD Bundle
978-1-118-82107-7

Available in print and e-book formats.

Available wherever books are sold. **For more information or to order direct visit www.dummies.com**

Take Dummies with you everywhere you go!

Whether you are excited about e-books, want more from the web, must have your mobile apps, or are swept up in social media, Dummies makes everything easier.

Leverage the Power

For Dummies is the global leader in the reference category and one of the most trusted and highly regarded brands in the world. No longer just focused on books, customers now have access to the For Dummies content they need in the format they want. Let us help you develop a solution that will fit your brand and help you connect with your customers.

Advertising & Sponsorships

Connect with an engaged audience on a powerful multimedia site, and position your message alongside expert how-to content.

Targeted ads • Video • Email marketing • Microsites • Sweepstakes sponsorship

21 Million Monthly Page Views & 13 Million Unique Visitors

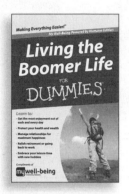

Dummies products make life easier!

- DIY
- Consumer Electronics
- Crafts
- Software
- Cookware
- Hobbies
- Videos
- Music
- Games
- and More!

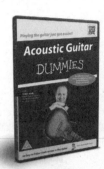

For more information, go to **Dummies.com** and search the store by category.

FOR DUMMIE

A Wiley B